2

THE STATE OF THE ART IN SMALL BUSINESS
AND ENTREPRENEURSHIP

The State of the Art in Small Business and Entrepreneurship

Edited by
PIERRE-ANDRÉ JULIEN
for
GREPME - Research Group in the Economy and
Management of Small and Medium-Sized
Enterprises

Ashgate
Aldershot • Brookfield USA • Singapore • Sydney

Published by
Ashgate Publishing Limited
Gower House
Croft Road
Aldershot
Hants GU11 3HR
England

Ashgate Publishing Company
Old Post Road
Brookfield
Vermont 05036
USA

British Library Cataloguing in Publication Data
Julien, Pierre-André
    The state of the art in small business and entrepreneurship
    1.Small business - Management
    I.Title
    658'.022

Library of Congress Catalog Card Number: 97-071715

ISBN 1 85972 409 4

Printed in Great Britain by The Ipswich Book Company, Suffolk.

Contents

ix

List of diagrams, figures and tables

Chapter 12

The Authors

Robert Beaudoin, Doctorate in Management Science, Université d'Aix Marseille III. Professor of Finance at the Université du Québec à Trois-Rivières. His research interests are concerned with financial management in small businesses. He has considerable experience in the management of university enterprises, having been Head of Department for four years and Vice-President of Administration and Finance for nine years.
Chapter 9

Samir Blili, Ph.D. in Business Administration, HEC (the University of Montreal Business School). Associate Professor at the Université du Québec à Trois-Rivières and Head of Research for the Research Group in the Economy and Management of Small and Medium-Sized Enterprises (known by its French acronym GREPME). He is specialized in organizational competitiveness, strategic management of new technology and international management. He is the author or co-author of a dozen papers published in scientific journals, thirty international conferences and five books on business management. In 1988, he received the award for Best Researcher from the *International Council for Small Business and Entrepreneurship*. He is also a consultant, and works regularly with businesses and organizations on the consolidation of their competitiveness.
Chapter 10

Laurent Deshaies, Ph.D. in Geography and Professor of Geography at the Université du Québec à Trois-Rivières. His research is concerned with industrial location, urban geography and the epistemology of geography. His epistemological reflections and geographical writings have led him to question the value of geographical business distribution models.
Chapter 3

Bruno Fabi, Ph.D. in Industrial and Organizational Psychology from the University of Montreal. Full Professor in the Department of Management Science and Economics at the Université du Québec à Trois-Rivières where he is also an associate member in GREPME. He teaches and coordinates human resource management (HRM) courses at the undergraduate and graduate levels. He has written a number of books, academic papers and professional articles published in North America, Europe and Australia. His research and consulting interests, in both private and public organizations, are concerned mainly with HRM, participatory management and organizational development. He also acts as referee for a number of journals and grant-giving bodies.

Chapter 11

Louis Jacques Filion, Ph.D. in Systems and Entrepreneurship from the University of Lancaster, Great Britain. Maclean Hunter Professor of Entrepreneurship at HEC, the University of Montreal Business School. His academic background includes a B.A. (Classics), an M.A. in International Relations from the University of Ottawa and an M.B.A. from HEC. His broad professional experience in management covers the fields of human resources, operations management and marketing. He was also a management consultant with the firm Ernst & Young. He is the author of more than 100 publications, including papers in refereed and professional journals, working papers and books. His research, essentially applied in nature, is concerned with the activity systems of entrepreneurs and the self-employed, small business strategy, epistemology and research methodologies in administrative science research. He has a special interest in entrepreneurial vision.

Chapter 4

Denis J. Garand, M.Sc., Small Business Management, Université du Québec à Trois-Rivières; doctoral student in management at University of Metz (France). Assistant lecturer and research professional, he has held various positions as project manager, supervisor and personnel manager and is involved in Canada and Europe as consultant in organizations of all sizes and types. GREPME external member, he is co-author of several papers on HRM practices, and innovation in SMEs, and is writing a doctoral thesis on the relations between entrepreneurial vision, formalization, and HRM effectiveness in innovative SMEs.

Chapter 11

Réal Jacob, M.Ps., C.E.A. (Labour Science), Professor in the Department of Management Science and Economics at the Université du Québec à Trois-Rivières since 1983. He is principal researcher with the Bombardier Chair in the Management of Technological Change in Small and Medium-Sized Enterprises, and works on organizational flexibility, the management of technological change, the network enterprise, intelligence subcontracting and technological scanning. He is the co-author of several books in French. Since 1995, he has also been Head of the Research Group in the Economy and Management of Small and Medium-Sized Enterprises (known by its French acronym GREPME). Before joining the academic world, he was a management consultant.

Chapter 7

André Joyal, Doctorate in Economic Science, Université de Dijon. His early publications were concerned with comparative economic systems and decentralization in the socialist economies. His interest then shifted to the social economy, particularly the so-called alternative economy (juxtaposition of social and economic objectives), on which he has published a number of papers, chapters and books. In recent years, he has also examined small business and market globalization, and local development strategies with special emphasis on rural environments. His most recent book is concerned with small business and the challenge of globalization.

Chapter 2

Pierre-André Julien, Doctorate in Economic Science, Université Catholique de Louvain (Belgium). Also a graduate in Management Science from Laval University. Bombardier Professor of the Management of Technological Change in Small and Medium-Sized Enterprises, Université du Québec à Trois-Rivières. He is editor of *La Revue Internationale PME*. He has worked in universities in England, Spain, France and the United States. He took part in the European Economic Community's FAST project and in the industrial district project run by the Social Studies Institute of the International Labour Office in Geneva. He is currently acting as consultant for the Organization for Economic Cooperation and Development (OECD) in Paris. He has published more than 250 reports and scientific papers in French, English, Spanish, German, Finnish and Italian, and is the author or co-author of eighteen books on small business prospectives and economics.

Team Leader
Foreword
Introduction
Chapter 1
Chapter 7
Conclusion

Michel Marchesnay, Doctorate in Theory of the Firm from the Université de Paris, and Professor at the Université de Montpellier I (Management Science). He is Director of the Research Team on Firm and Industry (known by its French acronym ERFI) and co-editor of *La Revue Internationale PME*. He has written a number of books and papers on strategy and small business, and is the author or co-author of eighteen books on general economics, business economics and business strategy, and approximately fifty papers in French and foreign journals.

Chapter 5

Jocelyn D. Perreault, Doctorate in Management Science, Université d'Aix-Marseille. He is Professor of Marketing at the Université du Québec à Trois-Rivières, and has provided consulting and training services to small business owner-managers. His main interest is distribution and he is Director of the Desjardins Marketing Collection for independant workers. (He thanks Jean-Luc Hermann, Professor of Marketing at IUT, Metz, France, for his contribution to this chapter.)

Chapter 6

Louis Raymond, Ph.D. in Administration, École des Hautes Études Commerciales, Montreal. Full Professor of Information Systems at the Université du Québec à Trois-Rivières. He has written a number of books on information systems, and has published papers in journals such as *MIS Quarterly*, *Journal of Management Information Systems*, *Journal of Small Business Management* and *International Small Business Journal*. He is also assistant titular of the Bombardier Chair on the Management of Technological Change in Small and Medium-Sized Enterprises.

Chapter 10

René Rochette, Engineer, Ph.D. in Industrial Engineering/Operational Research, University of Massachusetts is a Full Professor of Production Management in the Department of Industrial Engineering at the Université du Québec à Trois-Rivières. He is co-founder of the CADCAM laboratory, and the author or co-author of a number of research papers and reports on production management. He also offers consulting services for small businesses. (He thanks Philippe Poirier, Jr. Eng., B.Sc.A., research assistant, for his contribution to this chapter.)

Chapter 8

Josée St-Pierre, Ph.D. in Finance from Laval University, Professor of Finance at the Université du Québec à Trois-Rivières. Her research interests cover the field of corporate finance, and more specifically business governance, the financial problems of small business and project financing. She has published a number of papers in journals such as the *Journal of Corporate Finance*, *Canadian Journal of Administrative Sciences*, *Finance*, *Finéco*, *Revue Internationale en gestion et management de projet*, *Revue Internationale PME*, and so on. She is also the co-author of scientific studies published by Industry Canada and the Economic Council of Canada.

Chapter 9

The original French text was translated into English by Christine Gardner and Benjamin Waterhouse.

Preface

"I am so lukewarm towards freedom that if anyone were to prevent me from accessing some corner of the Indias, I would not feel more uncomfortable for it; provided I will find open air or ground elsewhere, I shall not linger in a place where I must hide." Michel de Montaigne, "Essai".

Michel de Montaigne wrote only one book, his "Essays", in the period 1595 to 1597, but it is still read and re-read even now, and his reflections remain as relevant today as those of many contemporary authors. Montaigne was first and foremost a great traveller who, by his own admission, went abroad not to seek out "le Gascon ou le François" (Gascons and Frenchmen), but to enjoy the society of different races. He did not, to use his own terms, consider people to be "barbares, puis qu'elles ne sont françoises" (barbarians because they are not French). Critical of quick judgments and condemnations in all their forms, he believed that human beings should instead cultivate humility towards others. He saw no reason why women should not be managers, and recommended that they practise "la vertu oeconomique" (economic virtue) rather than the art of "se coiffer et atiffer en son cabinet" (combing and preening in the boudoir). He was a staunch defender of the sovereignty of ownership and the importance of the middle classes in the development of trade and credit, and his statement that armies often lost good captains by turning them into bad generals can be seen as a precursor of the Peter principle. In later life, Montaigne said he would rather die on horseback than wait for gradual death at home: "puisqu'il y a des mors bonnes aux fois, bonnes aux sages, trouvons en qui soyent bonnes à ceux d'entre deux" (there are kinds of death that we consider appropriate for madmen, and others we consider appropriate for wise men; why, then, should there not also be other kinds of death that are appropriate for men who are neither one nor the other?). With his Essays, Montaigne tried to leave his contemporaries an account of an art of living and an art of learning.

This book is also the result of experience - the small business experience as developed in extensive research by the Université du Québec à Trois-Rivières' Research Group in Economy and Management of Small and Medium-Sized Enterprises, known by its French acronym GREPME, and the Bombardier Chair in the Management of

Technological Change in Small Businesses, as well as through the growing amount of work on small business theory by international researchers in research centres throughout the world. The book is an anthology of concepts and practices gradually developing into a general theory applicable to the field of small business. Although it makes no claim to attain the standards of Montaigne's "Essays", it does aim to provide a review of the most significant current knowledge in the field and to question the probable future development of the concepts and practices it presents. Each chapter is preceded by a short text from Montaigne, to symbolize the authors' desire to create a link with the reflections and processes of a great thinker who constantly sought the truth, in an era when the first modern economic theories were being developed by de Malestroit and Jean Bodin (followed by the mercantilists), and when the first major work on enterprise management was produced, in the form of Olivier de Serres' *Théâtre d'Agriculture*. The authors of this book have also followed Montaigne's example by remaining humble in the face of what remains to be learnt.

The book is divided into three parts. The first part examines the field of economics and defines the dimensional and spatial aspects of small businesses, first by describing the characteristics that distinguish them from large firms, and then by situating them in the general economic context at regional and local levels. The second part is concerned with organizational management, beginning with the general strategy that combines the organizational functions into a coherent whole, and going on to look at the individual functions of marketing, production, financing, information systems and human resources. The third part contains a conclusion and sketches a general theory of small business.

The authors are all members of GREPME, with four exceptions: our associate member Michel Marchesnay, from the University of Montpellier, France, with whom we have worked for the last ten years; René Rochette, a colleague from the Université du Québec's Engineering Department, who has contributed to some of GREPME's research; Louis Jacques Filion, a colleague and Maclean Hunter Professor of Entrepreneurship at HEC, the University of Montreal Business School; and Denis Garand, a graduate student. Other GREPME members who have not contributed directly to the book have done so indirectly through their criticism and ideas for improving the content and by helping the authors develop their reflections.

The process has been long. Production of the first edition began in 1992, with publication in 1994, and was based mainly on course notes from the Master's program in the management of small business and its environment offered at the Université du Québec à Trois-Rivières. It also included extracts from a number of academic papers written by GREPME members and presented at small business conferences. The text makes reference to several hundred papers and books by researchers throughout the world, to research by colleagues abroad with whom we have worked over long periods, and to the often animated discussions at our weekly "Joseph Chicha Seminars" given by GREPME members and invited speakers. The authors designed the book as a consistent whole, with related chapters covering every aspect of the fascinating world of small business. In the second edition, produced in 1996, much of the information was updated and enriched by new research, papers and conferences.

To illustrate the integrality of the book, each chapter makes reference to the preceding one and announces the following one. Some parts of the text were transferred between chapters to improve the structure of the final product. The authors' names therefore do not appear individually at the beginning of each chapter, but together at the beginning of the book. The whole text was re-read by Pierre-André Julien. The latter, with the help of other colleagues, was also responsible for coordinating the process and encouraging the contributors to respect deadlines.

The book's spiritual father is our colleague and friend, Joseph Chicha, who died on October 23, 1989. When the research team was first created, in 1975-76, it was Joseph Chicha who "sold the idea" of working on small business at a time when few people believed in its importance or recognized its special characteristics. He maintained contact and worked with foreign researchers, in particular the Americans, including Michael Piore, Robert Brockhaus and Neil Churchill. He led a personal crusade to have the concepts and practices inherited from research on large firms replaced with new concepts and practices adapted to the realities of small business. If GREPME has become an internationally-recognized research unit, and if the Bombardier Chair was created at Trois-Rivières, it is thanks mainly to the perseverance and patience of Joseph Chicha. In addition, many of the ideas in this book were verified in the spirit of the particularly critical mind of our departed colleague. The volume is dedicated to him.

We consider this book to be not only a summary of many years of reflections by many different researchers, but also a guide for future research and for the continuing development of a theory of small business and its environment; a theory that will truly apply to small businesses everywhere and that, at the dawn of the twenty-first century, will help them become what they are destined to be.

Pierre-André Julien
Bombardier Sea-Doo/Ski-Doo Professor of the Management of Technological Change in Small Business

Introduction

"I find it difficult to begin, but having been put on my way, I go on for as long as it pleases. I toil as hard for small as for large undertakings..." Michel de Montaigne, "Essai".

1. The importance of small business research in recent years

In the last ten years or so, the importance of small business and entrepreneurship has begun to be recognized not only by researchers, but also by universities. In the research field, many new scientific journals have been created[1]. The universities, for their part, began by offering new courses in entrepreneurship, and later introduced separate programs in small business.

The interest in small business has also led to the creation of specialized conferences and conventions, some of which have become regular fixtures in recent years. These include the Babson Conference in the United States, the small business weeks at St. Gall, Switzerland, and the International Council for Small Business Annual World Conference.

The volume of research in the small business field is relatively new. Forty or fifty years ago, in our universities, a few isolated researchers such as A.H. Cole (1942), J. Steindl (1947), G.H. Evans (1949) and C. Barnard (1949) were beginning to take an interest, albeit a marginal one, in small business. Before then, entrepreneurs had been studied by the disciples of Richard Cantillon, Turgot and Jean-Baptiste Say, and more

---

1   The first scientific publication on the subject was a German journal called "Internationales Gewerbearchiv. Zeitschrift fur Klein und Mittlunternehmen" (St. Gall and Munich), created in 1952. It was followed in 1962 by the *Journal of Small Business Management*, published by the University of West Virginia in the United States, and in 1975 by the University of Baylor's, *American Journal of Small Business*, which later changed its name to *Entrepreneurship: Theory and Practice*. The 1980s saw the creation of the *International Journal of Small Business* (1982, Stirling University, U.K.), the *Journal of Small Business and Entrepreneurship* (1982, Toronto), the *Journal of Entrepreneurship and Regional Development* (1987, Dublin and University of South Carolina), the *Revue Internationale PME* (1988, Universities of Trois-Rivières (Canada), Montpellier (France) and Louvain (Belgium)), *Piccola Impresa* (1988, Milan and Urbino, Italy) and finally, *Small Business Economics* (1989, Berlin (Germany) and Babson (U.S.A.)). More recently, several new small business development, finance and marketing journals have also been created.

recently by Joseph Schumpeter (Laurent, 1989; Pelletier, 1990). However, as Baumol (1968) pointed out, their work was quickly dismissed in discussions of economic theory. Thirty years ago, small business researchers, although more numerous (for example, B.C. Churchill, 1955; H. Gross, 1958; A.C. Cooper, 1964; E.D. Hollander, 1967; G.A. Steiner, 1967), continued to be viewed as slightly eccentric, in some cases as not very serious, or at least as spending their time on something that, for many people, was simply not worth the effort. In the 1970s, small business research became much more prevalent, and sometimes aroused interest among other academics, although it remained on the fringes of so-called "major" research (Kilby, 1971; Waite, 1973; Boswell, 1973; Echène, 1975; Desjardins, 1975). In the last decade, however, the field has exploded, and many specialized research teams now exist.

Nevertheless, this new attention is still not accepted in some circles. Certain people continue to view small businesses as "little big businesses" displaying the same characteristics as their larger counterparts, and to which the same concepts and theories can be applied. Others consider that small businesses deserve attention only because they are in the process of becoming big. And most macroeconomists persist in believing that only big corporations, especially multinationals, are capable of leading or conditioning the economy, in particular because of the theory of economies of scale. Thus, in their view, small businesses are economically irrelevant, in that they simply follow the lead of their larger counterparts. And yet, as we will see in Chapter 2, the vast majority of enterprises now in existence are small, and most of them will stay small all their lives. Moreover, most new jobs are now created by entrepreneurs.

This book aims to show beyond a shadow of a doubt that small business is a separate field and should be studied as such. We are not trying to deny the importance of the corporate sector, or to claim that the small business sector will replace it. Nevertheless, small businesses and entrepreneurs are here to stay, and a better knowledge of their specific characteristics and behaviours can only be of benefit to our economies.

In many regions, small businesses are the only source of jobs and economic renewal. For these companies, large investments are out of reach or demand too many resources.

For developing countries too, local entrepreneurship and small business, whether formal or informal, is often seen as providing an answer to the shortcomings of major export-focused investment and public companies often hampered by cumbersome bureaucracies. The smaller units are in the process of weaving a basic economic fabric likely to help generate trade throughout the territory, and thus to boost the economy.

This is beginning to be recognized by international bodies such as the World Bank and the American Development Fund. It would not be an exaggeration to speak of the internationalization of interest in small business. For example, between 1964 and 1971 the OECD carried out only a few sporadic studies of small business, and yet in the last four years it has created a standing analysis committee and launched several sizeable research projects. It will shortly be creating an International Institute for Small Business Research. Similarly, the International Labour Office's International Institute for Social Studies in Geneva has produced a number of reports on the rise of small business and its impact on job creation and local development (Sengenberger et al., 1990). The OECD has also entered into an agreement with the European Community's statistics office, EUROSTAT, for the gradual creation of a data bank on small business development in the industrialized world, to enable comparison of detailed data between countries. In the French-speaking world, the *Agence de coopération culturelle et technique* (Cultural and Technical Cooperation Agency) has recently defined the training of small business research teams in developing countries as one of its priorities.

2. What does "small business" mean?

Most specialists consider one of the greatest difficulties in small business research to be the extreme heterogeneity of the subjects. What could there possibly be in common between an unemployed miner who opens a grocery store in his local village, a student who, after obtaining her degree, leases photocopying machines to offer a photocopying service near her old university, a specialized worker with several years' experience in a large firm who decides to work for himself, and an engineer who starts a high-tech electronics business in the local incubator? A minimum-level distinction has been drawn between the manufacturing, trade and service sectors, on the basis that they have few similarities. We also know that small businesses operating under franchises or banners have specific characteristics that distinguish them from truly independent companies. Similarly, the "craft" companies, employing two or three people, function according to a completely different logic from companies with 100 or 150 employees. We are also beginning to differentiate medium-sized businesses, which lie closer to corporations than to small or very small businesses in terms of their operational features.

This heterogeneity, together with the greater level of volatility caused by the high rate of new venture creation and the disappearance of many small units in their first years of existence, seems to be one of the reasons why researchers hesitated for so long before entering the small business field. The situation was exacerbated by the difficulty of formulating adequate theories and concepts specific to small businesses. While the rule of numbers applies to the behaviour of corporations, which employ many hundreds of managers and executives with widely differing profiles, thus increasing the probability of identifying "means", this is virtually impossible in the case of small businesses, which employ no or a handful of executives, who are in any event likely to be psychologically very different, or to operate within very different organizations.

Science functions mainly by generalizing and grouping. The scientific approach to small business is no exception, although the process seems particularly difficult. Many researchers have tried to construct operational small business typologies, precisely to identify similarities or "mean" behaviours.

Many of the earlier typologies used divisions based only on the number of employees. However, the limits of this approach led authors to go further, by including the characteristics of the owner-managers, their managerial and organizational behaviour, the firm's development and its relationships with different markets.

2.1   Quantitative typologies

The primary task of all small business typologies is to distinguish enterprises from establishments. When we talk of enterprises or "SMBs" (small and medium-sized businesses), we mean control centres with defined ownership. In the case of very small and small businesses, the distinction, or lack of it, is clear. The establishment and the company are often one and the same, and ownership is usually common knowledge. In the case of medium-sized businesses, however, the situation may be less obvious. One of the main criteria in making the distinction is thus the legal notion of company independence. For example, a small establishment controlled by a corporation is not a small business.

The notion of "independence", however, does not solve all the problems. What about franchises and banners, for example? Some franchisers provide very few central services and can be considered on the same footing as the banners used by groups of independent companies joining forces simply to increase their purchasing and marketing power. In other cases, the unit owners make simple financial decisions while management and strategy are taken care of by the parent company; these businesses would be considered to be a type of subsidiary. The same applies to "capacity" subcontractors (working for a minimum price to the order-giver's specifications) with ties to a single buyer, because their independence is not straightforward. On the other hand, "speciality" subcontractors (who help define the product or component specifications) hold a certain amount of power over the order-givers. Each case must thus be considered on its merits.

Despite the notion of independence, it is still true that the best-known and most frequently-used small business typologies use quantitative employment, asset or turnover data. Table 1 provides an overview of the size, by number of employees, used by the OECD to differentiate companies in the industrial and service sectors.

Table 1
Division of enterprise size by number of employees

	Micro	Very small	Small	Medium
Number of employees	1 to 4	5 to 19	20 to 99	100 to 499

Source: OECD, "Globalization of economic activities and the development of SMEs", *Summary Report*, Paris, 1995.

Size in terms of number of employees differs by country and even within countries, depending on government programs. Thus, in the United States, Japan, Germany, France and Britain, small businesses are defined as having less than 500 employees, but this is not the case in other countries. For example, in Spain and Sweden, businesses are "small" if they have less than 200 or 250 employees. In Greece, Portugal and Ireland, a small business is one with less than 50 employees. Table 2 shows small business sizes by country.

Table 2
Classification of businesses by size in various European countries

Country	Small firms	No. of employees Medium-Sized firms	Large firms
Austria	1 - 9	10 - 100	> 101
Belgium	1 - 50	51 - 200	> 201
Denmark	1 - 50	51 - 200	> 201
Finland	1 - 50	51 - 200	> 201
France	1 - 49	50 - 499	> 500
Germany	1 - 49	50 - 499	> 500
Great Britain	1 - 50	51 - 200	> 201
Japan	1 - 49	50 - 500	> 501
Norway	1 - 20	21 - 100	> 101
	1 - 49	50 - 499	> 500
Switzerland	1 - 20	21 - 100	> 500
United States	1 - 250	250 - 500	> 501

Source: OECD, Ibid.

Such differences are common. Many countries have one standard for some programs and a higher standard for others (computerization and exports, for example). In the United States, the Small Business Administration accepts companies with up to 1000 employees in some of its small business programs. Differentiation by size obviously affects the weight of businesses in fiscal terms as well as from the point of view of program qualification. Table 3 shows small business distribution in certain countries by number of employees.

Table 3
Division of companies by size for certain industrial countries in 1986 (in %)

Country	Micro-enterprises 0 to 9 employees	Small and Medium-Sized firms 10 to 499 employees	Large corporations More than 500 employees
Germany (ex FRG)	86.0	13.8	0.2
Spain	94.8	5.1	0.1
France	93.5	6.4	0.1
Italy	90.6	9.3	0.1
United Kingdom	90.0	9.8	0.2
Europe (12)	91.3	8.6	0.1

Source: Problèmes économiques, No. 2257, January 1992.

On the one hand, quantitative typologies result from the traditional economic approach which leaves aside the "black box" and uses only the most obvious elements. They are, however, the most easily available and, as we said earlier, tend to be used as qualifying criteria for government support programs. On the other hand, these same typologies are often the first step for researchers in identifying samples that will subsequently be studied in more detail.

Clearly, the statistical measure of number of employees also generates its own problems, such as what exactly constitutes an employee: do we mean permanent employees, part-time employees, seasonal employees, semi-executives, and so on? The problem is usually solved fairly easily by the use of particular definitions and calculations. However, this does not settle the issue of sector differences, such as those existing between the manufacturing and industrial sectors. And even within the manufacturing sector, a machine tool shop with 50 employees would be a medium-sized company in its industry, while a clothing company with 100 employees would be considered small.

Such differences are often major between labour-intensive and capital-intensive industries. As a result, assets have been introduced in addition to the number of employees to define what is "small". Here again, however, turnover can vary considerably between growth and non-growth industries and large and small market industries. Moreover, it may be manipulated for tax reasons. Sales may be affected by the economic context, or may vary seasonally. Added value may be difficult to assess. The list goes on. And, while there may be a certain correlation between these two measures of size, they are not completely interchangeable (Nguyen and Belhumeur, 1985).

For this reason, the Bolton Committee and the American government both added the notion of market share to their definition. A small business cannot control a large market share. But here again, do we mean local markets, regional markets or national markets?

In short, the quantitative typologies, although easy to use, are also easy to criticize and should only be taken only as a preliminary approach[2]. Other criteria are needed to distinguish small business types.

---

2   Other problems may be caused by the quality of the statistical data used, especially when it includes very small businesses, or at least those with less than 20 employees. It is rare for two different sources to produce the same results.

2.2 Multicriteria or qualitative typologies

Many researchers have tried to go beyond these basic typologies by delving into the black box and considering the firm's relationship with its environment. In doing so, they have used a much more managerial and organizational approach.

These more complex typologies can be divided into four main groups: those based on the company's origin or ownership, those that use strategies or management objectives, those based on stage of development or organization, and those that consider the sector or type of market in which the company operates. Table 4 shows some typologies based on type of ownership and related elements, drawn from theoretical analysis or tested on small business samples.

The older technologies in this initial group (Deeks, 1973; Gélinier and Gaultier, 1974; Barry, 1978) are based on one very simple criterion. They are not substantially different from entrepreneurial typologies, although the latter are not discussed here (Smith and Miner, 1983; Lorrain and Dusseault, 1988). Origin of ownership might be thought, up to a point, to affect the form of company organization, or at least its long-term development. However, similar typologies also exist for corporations, where it is still possible to see major conglomerates in the hands of a family, or recently created corporations still entirely controlled by the founder. They are therefore not particularly interesting or useful in distinguishing different types of small businesses, and have been more or less abandoned.

Table 4
Typologies by type of ownership

J. Deeks (1973)	Oligarchic (more than one owner)	Patrician (family, managed by a manager)	Monocratic (one shareholder)
O. Gélinier and A. Gaultier (1974) or B. Barry (1978)	Family (passed on to a member of the family)	Personal (still controlled by the founders)	

The second group (Table 5) considers type of ownership or the interests of the owner-manager. The oldest (Liles, 1974; Stanworth and Curran, 1976; Filey and Aldag, 1978) were entrepreneurial typologies drawing parallels with size (very small or craft businesses to larger, better structured or more professionally-managed businesses). The more recent (Cooper and Dunkelberg, 1982; Miller and Friesen, 1982; Carland et al., 1984) have added elements of strategy followed by management, organization and company potential. Finally, Marchesnay (1988) links strategy to the entrepreneur's desire for independence and the market impact of growth or stability. This particular typology has many similarities with Marchini's (1988) work on traditional and "emerging" small businesses.

The third group (Table 6) contains the largest number of typologies including, to our knowledge, the oldest (1969). The first subgroup (Greiner, 1972; Churchill and Lewis, 1984; Vargas, 1984) emerged directly from the idea of company life cycle, already described in detail by Edith Penrose as an analogy to biology[3] or historical philosophy[4], an idea taken up later by Mueler (1972). The approach used by this subgroup is related to positivist philosophy by which, in this particular case, all businesses follow more or less the same development path, being created small and moving through different phases until they become large or very large or perish *en route*.

In this respect, these typologies raise a number of problems, as we have seen. First, most small businesses remain small, even after 50 or 100 years, and some firms are large and well organized from the time they are created. Second, development paths may differ considerably, for example by industry or by market, and depending on the economic context.

In some cases, the authors have examined only company development from micro to small or medium-sized. This group includes Thain (1969) and Webster (1976). The typologies of Steinneetz (1969), Kroeger (1974), Basire (1976), Hosmer et al. (1977) and Susbauer (1979) can also be used to view development either within the concept of small business, or from small to large.

Despite this major limit, the idea of structural development as the business grows is interesting. Although the organizational point of arrival may differ considerably from one small business to the next, Basire's (1976) schema, with its four-part subdivision of the first stage, is particularly useful for assessing the structural development of small businesses. In the table, the last-but-one typology (Ibnabdeljalil, 1980), is shown as an example of a large group of typologies that use financial elements to define the different stages.

---

3 Based on a paper published in 1952 and subsequently taken up in her well-known book published in 1957 (Penrose, 1952, 1957).
4 Especially among historical philosophers such as Spencer, Huxley and Toynbee.

Table 7 shows typologies that use sector-based differences - in other words, the types of markets and market opportunities within which small businesses operate. Here, emphasis is given to the links between the owner-manager's behaviour (conservative, professional, innovative, etc.), the type of industry or market (traditional or mature, modern, new, local, national or international, etc.), the products offered (unique or niche, competitive through price or features, primary or secondary, etc.), the technology used (mature, modern, high-tech) and the links with other companies, especially large corporations (small independent businesses, subcontractors or satellites, niche businesses, etc.). Some of these typologies were obtained from empirical research[5] (Preston, 1977; Candau, 1981; Julien and Chicha, 1982) while others were based on applied research by different authors (Vesper, 1979; Potier, 1986).

Table 5
Typologies by type of management objectives, strategy and firm's potential

P. Liles (1974)	Marginal (traditional)	Interesting (size and growth to come)	High potential (fast growth)
M. Stanworth and J. Curran (1976)	Craft (Intrinsic satisfaction)	Classical entrepreneurial (profit)	Managerial (Recognition by performance)
A. Filey and R. Aldag (1978)	Craft (conventional, low risk, survival strategy)	Promotional (entrepreneurial, innovative technique, growth strategy)	Administrative (professional, structured, higher risks, planned)
A. Cooper and C. Dunkelgerg (1982, E)	Craft type (autonomy)	Seeking independence	Growth-oriented
D. Miller and P.H. Friesen (1982)	Entrepreneurial (seeking different initiatives)	Conservative (traditional)	
J. Carland et al. (1984)	Entrepreneurial (profit, growth, creativity)	Managerial (quest for personal goals)	
M. Marchesnay (1988)	G.A.P. (favouring, in order, growth, autonomy, perpetuation)	P.I.G. (favouring, in order, perpetuation, independence, growth)	
I. Marchini (1988)	Traditional	Emerging	

---

5   See especially B. Harrison (1994) and the discussion of his theory in a special issue of *Small Business Economics*, Vol. 7, No. 5 (1995).

Table 6
Typologies by organization and growth or development

D. Thain (1969)	Stage 1 one unit (a single man)	Stage 2 one unit with specialization	Stage 3 Decentralized by function		
L. Steinneetz (1969)	Stage 1 (direct supervision)	Stage 2 (supervised supervision)	Stage 3 and above (complex management)		
L. Greiner (1972) and G.Vargas (1984)	Stage 1 (leadership crisis: creativity)	Stage 2 (autonomy crisis: management)	Stage 3 (control crisis: delegation)	Stage 4 (bureaucracy crisis: co-ordination)	Stage 5 (crises: in cooperation)
C. Kroeger (1974)	Initiation (generating ideas)	Development (organizing)	Growth (imple-menting)	Maturity (managing)	Decline (reorganizing successor)
F. Webster (1976)	Pre-start up	Stage of cooperation and enthusiasm	Stage of financial threat	Stage of introduc-tion of new products into initial market	Stage of disengagement or renegotiation
M. Basire (1976)	Stage of priority to production	Stage 1b (development of commercial and administrative functions)	Stage 1c (development of planning)	Stage 1d (systematiza-tion of forecasts and development of financial function)	
		Stage 2 (appointment of commercial manager)	Stage 3 (appointment of production manager)	Stage 4 (appoint-ment of manager for forecasting and financial functions)	Stage 5 (appointment of personnel manager)
L. Hosmer (1977)	Stage of operator-founder	Beginning of growth	Management by delegation	Direction and management at multiple levels	

J. Susbauer (1979)	Survival (small market, under capitalized)	Growth (professional and financial management)	Sub-realist (good potential, blocked)	Highly successful (good potential, sought)	
N. Ibnabdeljalil (1980)	"Food or income-producing" (low growth)	"Fragile" (poorly controlled growth)	"High-performance" (sustained growth)		
N. Churchill and Lewiss (1983, E)	Existence (single owner, centralized, limited markets)	Survival (beginning of decentralization, more complex markets)	Success (profits, functional structure)	Growth (delegation, divisions, mature markets)	Large corporation (growth, diversification, etc.)

Table 7
Typologies by sector, type of market or market opportunity

L. Preston (1977, E)	Rare successes (growth, even direct)	Small, optimal size firms	Firms based on innovation	Satellite firms	Firms with regular operations
K. Vesper (1979)	"Self-entrepreneur"	Users of unexploited resources	Product innovators	Users of economies of scale	Franchises and copiers
P. Candau (1981)	Craft (high level of managerial intensity)	Average (administrative substitution)	Highly centralized (strong desire to control by manager)	Typical family (mandated managers)	Transitional (family to average)
R. Huppert (1981)	Small firm protected from international competition		Small firm active in international competition		
P.A. Julien and J. Chicha (1982, T)	Very small traditional (very centralized, urban end consumption market, older technical management)	Small traditional (trad./moderate centralization, local market, intermediate products, educated technical management)	Small modern (participatory, open market, products to order, young uneducated or highly educated management)	Medium-sized (professional, national markets, serial production, professional educated management)	
C. Potier (1986)	Manpower, traditional sectors (tailored products, high turnover)	Specific production (know-how, high quality)	Manual (capacity subcontracting, speciality)	High-tech	

12

A. Rizzoni (1988)	Passive (mature sector, local market, survival)	Traditional (niches or mature sector, regional market, centralized, stability)	Dominated or related (to large corps., average tech., slow growth, centralized)	Imitational (flexibility, higher level of technology, more complex structure)	Technology-based (Schumpeterian entrepreneur, non-radical innovation, growth)	High-tech (techno. firm, more professional, radical innovation)

Many other typologies exist, including those based on financial situation (Mader, 1979; Robitaille and Marchesnay, 1988) and capitalistic intensity (Eymard-Duvernay and Delattre, 1983), but they will not be considered here. We have also left aside the typologies specifically concerned with craft industries (EEC, 1976; Jaeger, 1982; Arena et al., 1985) and small "alternative" businesses (Joyal, 1988). Clearly, we have made no attempt to be exhaustive in our inventory, but have selected the typologies best able to illustrate the complexity of the problem and the broad diversity of small businesses.

Most of the typologies considered here address elements found in small businesses (or at least in those with more than five employees), and especially in small manufacturing businesses. However, very few qualitative typologies applicable to the trade and service sectors have been produced so far.

2.3   Towards a complex overall typology

To summarize these various typologies, their elements can be arranged on a less-to-more continuum, as illustrated in Diagram 1, showing size, sector, branch of activity, type of market, centralization or control, structure or organization, level of independence, type of strategy, type of technology used and the presence of innovation.

However, this vision is still too simplistic. Although continua may exist, they will not necessarily be linear. In some cases, certain stages may be skipped. For example, an organization may not become more complex evenly in all its functions. An owner-manager of a very small business may see the firm's production increasing and hire a supervisor or production manager, and then an accountant. Only later will he create one or two management levels in the marketing function, and even then will continue to maintain personal control of purchasing and human resources. In fact, the organizational continuum is more likely to be divided by function, as shown in Diagram 2.

Depending on the viewpoint taken or the discipline addressed, typologies place emphasis on one single aspect, several aspects at once, or a handful of aspects, and will thus vary in complexity.

On a continuum, small and very small firms would probably lie towards the left, although this may differ on a continuum by sector, by market or by management, while medium-sized firms would lie further to the right, and large or very large corporations on the far right. Again, some differences would arise due to the broad diversity of small businesses.

Diagram 1
Typology on a continuum

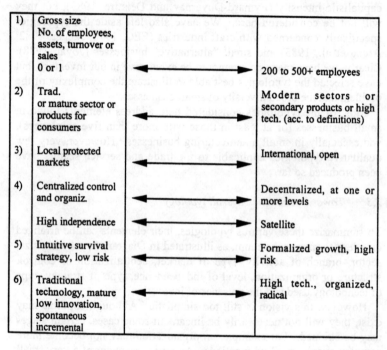

1)	Gross size No. of employees, assets, turnover or sales 0 or 1		200 to 500+ employees
2)	Trad. or mature sector or products for consumers		Modern sectors or secondary products or high tech. (acc. to definitions)
3)	Local protected markets		International, open
4)	Centralized control and organiz.		Decentralized, at one or more levels
	High independence		Satellite
5)	Intuitive survival strategy, low risk		Formalized growth, high risk
6)	Traditional technology, mature low innovation, spontaneous incremental		High tech., organized, radical

14

Diagram 2
Development of management levels

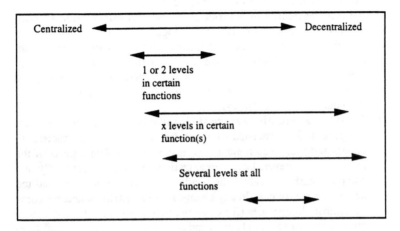

The continua shown here illustrate different small business characteristics. Based on our own research and the work of other authors including those named above, we have established the following six characteristics as those which best define the concept of small business:

1. First, and most obviously, **small size,** based on a number of elements (number of employees, turnover, etc.), and with the nuances discussed earlier.
2. **Management centralization.** In very small firms, management is almost always concentrated in the person of the owner-manager. However, medium-sized firms in traditional sectors sometimes also have highly centralized management, as Candau (1981) and Rizzoni (1988) have shown.
3. **Low level of specialization,** from the point of view of management (which undertakes both management and executive tasks, especially when the company is small), employees and equipment. Specialization emerges as size increases and the company moves from varied production (to order or short run), to serial or repeat production. Thus, as the company grows, it has to create different organizational levels, usually in the accounting and production functions first, then in the marketing function and finally in purchasing, R&D and personnel.
4. **An intuitive or informal strategy.** While large corporations need to prepare fairly specific plans for future action, to provide a point of

reference for the whole organization, in smaller companies the owner-manager has a close enough relationship with key employees to explain changes of direction as they occur.

5. **An uncomplicated or unorganized internal information system**. Small organizations function by dialogue or direct contact. Larger organizations, on the other hand, need a formal (written) mechanism that transfers information while minimizing noise and fostering control. Very large corporations will often produce a company "newsletter" to disseminate general information and prevent rumours from undermining efficiency.

6. **Finally, a simple external information system**. In craft companies, the owner-manager can talk directly with customers, to understand their requirements and tastes and explain aspects of the products. However, larger organizations must carry out costly and complex market research, the results of which are often applied too late, when reality has already changed. Some small businesses come up against oligopsonies (for example, purchasing groups serving as a buffer between small industries and consumers) that cut them off from real markets and direct information sources.

Once again, these characteristics can all be viewed on a less-to-more continuum.

2.4 Conclusion

Given the above analysis, it would be easy to think that enough typologies exist to satisfy most purposes. However, finding a truly general typology is far from easy, even today.

This is especially true since the typologies in question have not yet been properly tested on different markets and in different economic conditions. Moreover, as we said earlier, we still do not have many operational typologies for small trade and service businesses. And not least, current changes in the small business community, such as the growing importance of after-sales service, have generated new types of small businesses that have not yet been studied adequately. Consequently, a vast amount of research remains to be done.

In the last few years, some researchers have concentrated on entrepreneurial behaviour, while others have examined the concept of strategy in small businesses. This latter aspect will be discussed in detail in Chapter 5. Chapters 2 and 3 look at research into the role of small business in local development. However, the difficulties encountered by small businesses in the areas of marketing, finance and human resources management, which we will consider in Chapters 6 and following, have been somewhat neglected. The aim of this book is to sketch the state of current knowledge and highlight recent research trends. The problem it faces is the extreme complexity of the small business field.

3.   The analysis framework

While large corporations can be divided into functions and each function analyzed in depth, the task is rather more difficult when it comes to small businesses. In this book, we have nevertheless approached the subject in this way because of the inherent complexity of considering all the aspects at once. In fact, however, every small business is an undivided whole within which all functions are combined, or at least very closely linked, and where the owner-manager controls most of the elements, directing several functions and, in some cases, participating directly in production as well. Thus, the entrepreneur or owner-manager, as the main player, defines the firm's behaviour and consequently its development. However, entrepreneurs and owner-managers must also consider internal and external company variables - in other words, the firm's internal organization and the type of economy in which it operates. Their decisions are strongly influenced by, or at least should take systematic account of, what is referred to as the internal and external environment. Small businesses can be depicted in three dimensions, as shown in Diagram 3, where the vertical columns represent the enterprise functions (bearing in mind that, in small businesses, the functions are not necessarily separate), the horizontal rows represent the functional elements, and the third dimension represents the three decision-making levels: the player, the organization and the environment.

Diagram 3
Small business analysis framework

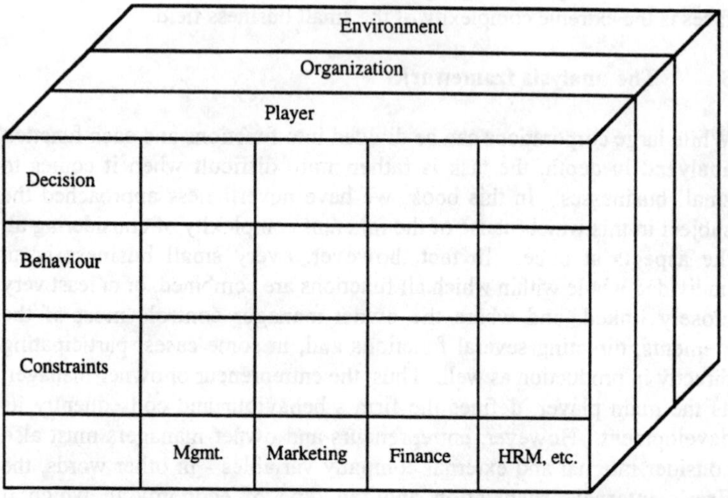

Environment				
Organization				
Player				
Decision				
Behaviour				
Constraints				
	Mgmt.	Marketing	Finance	HRM, etc.

The diagram also shows that, in a small business, management, and thus strategy, covers all functions and co-ordinates them very closely. This is explained by the personality and training of the owner-manager (the player) and is conditioned by the type of organizational system in which the company operates (the organization). The diagram also shows that small businesses exist in symbiosis with their *environment*, in a system of complex interrelations formed by networks of all kinds and all levels that develop within and outside the region, as we will see in the first few chapters. Such businesses are responsible for a large proportion of local and regional development and, in return, profit from that development.

4.   The plan of the book

This configuration explains the plan of the book, which is divided into three main parts.   The first part examines the socio-economic environment of small businesses and the behaviour of the players within this transaction space.   The second part discusses the strategy of the players in their companies and the different company functions. Finally, the third part sketches out a small business theory.

The first part examines the small business boom from the point of view of different economic concepts. The first chapter presents data showing that the boom has been experienced in most industrialized countries and is now tending to extend throughout the world. Different concepts and theories are discussed as explanations for the upsurge in small business power over the last 20 years, and the probability of the trend continuing in the future is examined. The second chapter considers the role of territorial governments in supporting and taking advantage of this boom, together with the networks and other regional structures that foster and feed on short-term and long-term dynamism. The last chapter in this first part discusses regional localization factors as elements likely to develop small business dynamism even further.

The second part is concerned with the mechanisms underlying company behaviour and development. Chapter 5 examines strategic management in small businesses - in other words, objectives and general management. Chapter 6 concentrates on what many people believe to be the motor of the firm: the marketing function, which directs the choice of product and market and subsequently drives production. Chapter 7 examines the technological aspects of production, in terms of technology implementation, management and organization of work. Chapter 8 also considers the question of production, and discusses the various techniques or approaches available to improve business competitiveness. Chapter 9 analyzes the problem of financing for current operations and investments, to enable the company to function properly and renew itself. Chapter 10 examines the importance of control and the mechanisms available for gathering internal and external information within a constantly-changing environment. Finally, Chapter 11 discusses the need for proper management of human resources, a major element in maintaining the company's competitive capacity and thus guaranteeing its development.

Once again, however, we must stress that all these aspects should be viewed together, as a combined whole. They are analyzed separately here partly for practical reasons and partly because of the scientific habit of sifting out the different aspects of a unit in order to understand it properly, on the basis that it is difficult to look at everything at once. However, all these separate analyses are aimed at producing a single, overall theory. This is precisely the purpose of the conclusion, or third part of the book, which outlines a developing global theory of small business. The theory in its present form is not definitive, and much still remains to be done to reach a coherent conclusion. Already, though, through the various elements addressed in this book, it has been possible at least to sketch out the framework. Further work will be needed to perfect, criticize and transform it as the results of new research enable the field to progress.

5.   Who should read this book?

The book is aimed at researchers and students working in the field of small business. It is thus a university publication, although practitioners and others working with small businesses (consultants, banks and civil servants, etc.) will find many elements to help them understand the domain.

As readers will see in the different chapters, the aim of book is to describe the current state of knowledge in each of the areas addressed, to summarize the information into overall diagram form where possible, and then to define some of the elements yet to be studied.

In other words, it is first and foremost a reference book summarizing current knowledge in the field of small business, pointing the way to future research and thus encouraging development. We have tried to avoid closing doors, by seeking to provide a basis that will enable researchers to go even further. So much work still remains that it is vital for specialists to do their share by criticizing and questioning the book. This message is repeated at the end of each chapter, after the description of the limits of current knowledge.

20

1 Economic theory of small business

"As the Stoics say, there is such a close link and relation between the wise that a person who takes his meal in France also feeds his colleague in Egypt; and whoever manages to understand if only his own finger, wherever he may be, all the wise men in all inhabited lands will feel his help." Michel de Montaigne, *"Essai"*.

1. Introduction

The available data show that small business activity began to increase in most industrial countries around 1970, a trend that seems to have been maintained ever since. Compared with large corporations, small businesses have increased their share of job creation, added value and even exports. In fact, it seems that in the last 20 years the trend in big business development has reached a kind of asymptote, followed by a reversal[1], although we do not know if this new trend will continue, and further research is needed to verify the quality of recent data and thus the trend itself.

Many reasons have been put forward to explain this structural change. However, they do not allow us to state categorically that the small business sector will be able to take back the place it lost as the industrial revolution gradually spread its tentacles. Instead, what we may be witnessing is a new balance between big business and small businesses, in which the latter will play a more important role in economic development, especially in outlying regions, while in many cases acting as partners in the development of their larger counterparts.

In the pages that follow, we will first examine some small business development figures drawn from industrialized countries, illustrating this reversal in enterprise concentration. We will then review the various explanations for the re-emergence of small businesses, before going on to discuss the theories underlying the new situation. The chapter will end with a discussion of some elements likely to encourage small business development in the future.

---

1 See, for example, M. Didier's (1982) analysis of statistical data in France from 1906 to 1982.

2. The re-emergence of small business

The re-emergence of small business in industrialized countries has been amply proved. As we said earlier, the number of small businesses continues to grow and the sector now creates most new jobs. In addition, it is often at the root of economic renewal in previously disadvantaged regions or cities.

Yet, we know that the number of small businesses decreased regularly, at least from the end of the last century until about 20 years ago, as Table 1.1 shows for companies in the former Federal Republic of Germany and the United States.

Table 1.1
Share of employment by size of establishment, various years

	1882	1895	1907	1925	1933	1950	1970	
Federal Republic of Germany (1)								
Small (2, 3)	78.0	70.4	62.9	53.3	62.0	56.8	43.6	
Small & medium (2,4)	88.1	84.4	79.7	69.9	76.4	73.0	63.2	
	1909	1919	1929	1933	1939	1947	1967	1977
United States (5)								
Very small (6)	14.4	10.3	9.8	10.0	9.5	7.2	6.6	6.5
Small (7)	37.8	29.2	29.1	30.8	30.0	25.0	23.2	25.3

Notes: 1. Census data, all sectors
       2. Including individual workers
       3. Less than 50 employees
       4. Less than 200 employees
       5. Census data for manufacturing firms
       6. Less than 20 employees
       7. Less than 100 employees

Source: W. Sengenberger, G. Loveman and M. Piore, *The Re-Emergence of Small Enterprises*, Institut international d'études sociales, Genève, 1990, table 9.

However, in the last two decades we have witnessed a reversal of this century-old trend. Table 1.2 illustrates the reversal that occurred in France after 1970. Venture creation was especially active during the two oil crisis periods in the 1970s, and slowed down with the beginning of the severe recession in the early 1980s. It has since picked up again, especially in recent years, with the creation of more than 220,000 businesses in 1989. The recovery was particularly marked in the manufacturing sector, where nearly 20,000 firms were created in 1986, although the number fell to 18,000 in 1989. More recently, in 1993, France's national venture creation agency, known by its French acronym ANCE, estimated venture creation over all sectors at 170,000 mostly very small units.

Similar venture creation trends occurred in other countries too. In the United States, for example, the number of small businesses with less than 250 employees increased by 3.2% during the 1980s, while the number of large corporations (more than 250 employees) remained unchanged. As Table 1.3 shows, the trend was the same in all the countries listed, although actual rates differed.

In the late 1980s, for example, Denmark appears to have created the most businesses, on a relative basis, followed by Belgium, Germany (federal), the United Kingdom, Spain and Portugal. The lowest venture creation rates were observed in the United States, followed by Holland, Italy and France. Care is needed with such comparisons, for several reasons. For example, the data do not always include venture creation by self-employed workers, estimates are not based on the same definitions, and the information was compiled in varying economic contexts (for instance, in 1993 the United States was just emerging from a severe recession).

Nevertheless, overall the figures show an increase both in the number of small businesses and in job creation by small businesses. They include new ventures and expansion of existing businesses, and also closures or disappearances and job cutbacks. Table 1.4 and Figure 1.1 show the development of small business as compared with big business in Canada between 1970 and 1988.

Table 1.2
Business registrations in France between 1978 and 1989

Year	Economy as a whole			Manufacturing sector(1)		
	Total	Creations	Seizures	Total	Creations	Seizures
1978	239 890	176 100	63 790	20 330	-	-
1979	247 040	186 350	60 690	19 800	-	-
1980	255 400	193 460	61 940	20 250	17 274	2 976
1981	241 860	182 280	59 580	19 630	19 742	2 888
1982	229 490	172 910	56 680	19 010	16 340	2 670
1983	209 190	160 830	48 360	17 530	14 934	2 596
1984	217 490	168 750	48 740	18 310	15 841	2 496
1985	244 520	192 200	52 320	21 590	18 720	2 870
1986	266 220	208 730	54 490	22 310	19 419	2 891
1987	274 480	212 590	61 890	20 560	17 423	3 137
1988	279 000	216 580	62 420	20 170	16 840	3 330
1989	278 950	221 520	57 430	21 220	17 870	3 330

Note: 1. Sector, including energy, but excluding agro-food.

Source: Les PMI, Les chiffres clés. *Small Business Delegation, Department of Industry and Foreign Trade and SESSI*, Paris, Dunod, 1991, p.35.

Table 1.3
Number of firms per 1,000 inhabitants (1990), average size of firms (1990) and rate of venture and self employment creation (various years) by population (1990)

Country	No. of firms per 1 000 i.	Average size of firms	No. of creations per 100 000 inhabitants	Rate of creation %	Rate of survival after 5 years %
Belgium (1988)					
without independents	49	6	1304.0	1.3	-
with independents	-	-	1704.6	1.7	50
Denmark (1989)	33	9	2908.0	2.9	52
France (1990)	35	7	461.0	0.4	48
Germany (FRG) (1988)	37	9	522.2	0.5	49
Holland (1990)	28	10	276.0	0.3	67[1]
Italy (1990)	68	4	471.9	0.4	-
Luxemburg (1990)	41	10	793.0	0.8	45
Portugal (1990)	59	5	812.0	0.8	-
Spain (1990)	63	4	513.3	0.5	-
United Kingdom (1990)	46	8	520.0	0.5	40/45[2]
United States (1993)	-	-	200.0	0.2	50

Notes: 1. After three years, R. Van der Horst calculated the rate at 60% after five years ("The Volatility of the Small Business Sector in the Netherlands", paper presented at the Montreal conference of the FDB and OECD, May 1992).

      2. The rate is 49% for firms registered for VAT. After ten years, it is 29%.

Sources: Julien, P.A. and M. Marchesnay, Paris, *Economica*, 1996.

The figures reflect a high level of volatility in most countries, especially for very small businesses. There may even be a link between the large number of new ventures and the large number of bankruptcies. Mostly, however, the net balance is positive, as Table 1.3 shows.

Table 1.4

Job turnover by size class using base-year size class
(average 1970-88)

Size class	Job change rates using base-year size (average 1970-88)		
	Job creation	Job destruction	Net change
0 to 19	28.8	17.5	11.3
20 to 49	18.0	14.2	3.8
50 to 99	12.6	11.9	0.7
100 to 249	9.0	9.7	-0.7
250 to 499	6.8	8.4	-1.6
500 to 999	5.1	7.3	-2.2
1000 to 2499	4.9	6.6	-1.7
2500 to 5000	5.8	6.5	-0.8
5000 +	3.9	5.1	-1.2

Source: Baldwin, J. and G. Picot, "Employment Generation By Small Producers in the Canadian Manufacturing Sector", *Offprint from Small Business Economics*, ISSN 0921-898X, p. 324.

The net balance may vary up to a point according to the context. For example, it will generally be higher in periods of expansion or recovery than in recessions (Contini, 1992). At least, the number of bankruptcies will tend to increase in difficult economic times. There is therefore a certain correlation between venture creation and disappearance rates, or expansion and contraction rates. Nevertheless, the net balance since 1970 has almost always been positive, even though very small businesses find it more difficult than their larger counterparts to survive in the earlier years, as we can see in Table 1.4 for Canada and Figure 1.1 for Canada and the United States.

We know that nearly 50% of new businesses, depending on country, will survive for less than eight years. Bruce Phillips and Bruce Kirchoff (1989) followed the progress of new ventures between 1977-1978 and 1985-1986 in the United States. They found that the failure rate for new ventures was higher in the first few years (27%) than after five or six years (9%). However, they pointed out that enterprise closure did not necessarily mean bankruptcy. Some of the firms that closed down had moved, changed their products or services, or quite simply suspended their activities for a time. Only 20% or 25% of all new ventures failed, and even then the failure often served as a learning experience that enabled the entrepreneurs to start up anew later. In fact, several studies have shown that more than 75% of all new entrepreneurs are still in business four or five years later (Reynolds and Miller, 1989; Cooper et al., 1988).

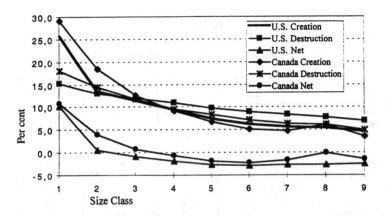

Source: Picot, G., J. Baldwin and R. Dupuy, "Employment Generation By Small Producers in the Canadian Manufacturing Sector", No. 9.

Figure 1
Job creation and job destruction rates in Canada and the United States by base-year plant size: Average 1970-88

Survival rates vary by sector. For example, it has been calculated that in Holland, more than 50% of the firms created in 1985 in the wholesale sector had "disappeared" five years later, compared with just 25% in the manufacturing sector (see Table 1.5)[2].

Thus, while some researchers contest the so-called re-emergence of small businesses, either regionally or nationally, on the basis of difficulties with definitions or statistics, or because the figures include a large percentage of small units that subsequently fail (Storey and Johnson, 1987; Léonard, 1986; Hull, 1986), others have shown that these criticisms are unfounded (for example, Contini and Revelli, 1987; Loveman, 1989). According to C.C. Gallagher and J. Doyle (1986), statistical limits mean that most findings are fairly conservative, and that small business creation (especially craft businesses) in industrialized countries is likely to be even higher. As we have just shown, while more venture creation also means more bankruptcies, illustrating the volatility of the small business sector, the balance is almost always positive

---

2   See also the analysis by Lindmark et al (1992) for Sweden.

(Evans, 1987). For this reason, the share of small businesses is increasing systematically in most, if not all industrialized countries, and probably in developing countries too.

Table 1.5
Survival rate of new ventures created in 1985 by sector of activity, in the Netherlands between 1985 and 1990 (1985=100)

Branches of Activity	4th quarter 1985	June 1987	January 1989	June 1990
Manufacturing sector	100	84	68	64
Construction	100	90	83	75
Wholesale trade	100	78	60	49
Retail trade	100	79	63	58
Hotels and restaurants	100	95	75	68
Garages, repairs	100	98	93	86
Transport	100	85	65	57
Business services	100	81	63	60
Total	100	82	66	60

Source: Van der Horst, R., "The Volatility of the Small Business Sector in the Netherlands", paper presented at the Conference on Small Business and Economic Globalization, Montreal, FDB and OECD, May 24-27, 1992.

The contribution of small business is not limited to creation or employment growth. Many small businesses have done better than their larger counterparts in terms of added value and investments, despite the fact that productivity used to be considered a function of size. In France, for example, recent research has shown that the contribution of small businesses to manufacturing sector turnover rose from 37.8% in 1978 to 41% in 1989 (Crosnier, François and Lehoucq, 1991). Similarly, the export and investment share of small manufacturing businesses increased by between two and four points in the period 1986-1989[3].

2.1 Industrial restructuring and small business

Despite the above figures, it is true that small business dynamism may cover the fact that the sector lags behind the corporate sector, exacerbating what some economists have referred to as the development of a dual economy, with large modern corporations employing fewer people or withdrawing from less interesting sectors on the one hand, and

---

3 See also Bucaille and Costa de Beauregard (1987) or Devillers (1986).

more traditional smaller businesses on the other (Boyer, 1986). In fact, there are many different kinds of small businesses, mostly in the tertiary sector, but in the manufacturing and construction sectors too. As we saw in the preceding chapter, some manufacturing sector firms export or have the potential to export, while others operate within very small or local markets. Some small businesses address traditional or mature markets, while others operate in modern or fast-changing markets. Some offer unique products in specific niches, some compete with other firms on price or quality, and some use very specific technology. There are also "capacity" subcontractors, trading with a single order-giver, and "speciality" or "intelligence" subcontractors that develop a symmetry in their relations with the order-giver(s) to achieve a truly cooperative relationship. A final distinction can be drawn between small businesses operating in isolated or peripheral regions and those operating in city centre or highly urbanized areas.

The dynamism to which we refer here is generated mainly by modern small businesses, as we will see in Chapter 7, and is not restricted either to the service sector, where it is easier to start a business (because much less capital is needed), or to the traditional labour-intensive sectors, better sheltered or protected from the recession. In France, for instance, the reversal of the trend in the 1970s was particularly evident in the food sector, but also in the office machinery and armaments sectors (Guesnier, 1986). In Quebec, the most dynamic sectors between the two major recessions of 1975 and 1982 were printing, machinery and metal products, and not the more traditional industries (Thibodeau and Julien, 1986). The same situation has been observed recently in other countries (Loveman, Sengenberger, and Piore, 1990).

In Italy, in the region known as "third Italy"[4], several "industrial districts", such as Prato and Modena, have specialized in traditional sectors such as textiles, clothing and shoes. Even here, though, the firms have managed to compete with their counterparts in developing countries by opting for high quality production and modern machinery (Sforzi, 1989; Berlandi, 1989).

Another indicator of industrial structure modernization by small businesses lies in the development of exports, especially towards the so-called more dynamic markets, as we saw earlier for France. In Quebec, it has been shown (Julien and Morin, 1996) that, for the period 1984-1992, (1) Quebec's exports outside Canada increased nearly ten times faster than its exports to other Canadian provinces, and (2) exports to the southern, central and western American states (i.e. those furthest away

---

4   Between the highly industrialized north and the developing south.

from Quebec's borders) of new high value-added products (communications and other electronic equipment, transportation equipment, scientific equipment, etc.) grew the fastest.

2.2 Small businesses and the regions

The statistics also show that small business dynamism has been particularly evident in non-traditional regions where the economy has not been monopolized by big business - in other words, regions that are not too urbanized and not too rural either. In France, Geneviève Duché and Suzanne Savey (1986) had already shown that the regions with the highest rates of GNP and job creation development were those where the contribution of small manufacturing businesses (especially those with 100 employees or less) to regional added-value was highest, i.e. in the West, Southwest and Languedoc-Roussillon - economies with little or no industrial history. In Quebec, much has been said about the "economic miracles" of the Beauce and Bois-Francs regions, which are geographically distant from the larger, traditionally industrialized region of Montreal. England seems to be an exception to this rule, since small business seems to be more dynamic in already prosperous regions (Hirst and Zeitlin, 1989).

These regional analyses confirm findings in other countries, especially in England (Cross, 1987) and Italy (Sforzi, 1989), either to the effect that some situations discourage regional venture creation or, on the contrary, that certain conditions are needed to support it. In particular, the presence of large primary sector corporations often constitutes an obstacle to entrepreneurship since they offer very little in the way of subcontracting and yet attract the best regional resources[5]. On the other hand, a major market fairly close by and a minimum amount of cluster economies are required to support the structuring information network needed to create the synergy that will encourage local development by small businesses (Julien and Parellada, 1995). An exception would be the existence of a specific impetus generated, for example, by the presence of a large corporation producing complex goods and offering subcontracting and local spin-offs on a major scale.

---

5   Large investments are already very expensive for the number of jobs created (for example, every job created in a new aluminium plant requires investments of more than $3 million). But by employing potential entrepreneurs in executive positions, attracting the best-qualified workers, draining financial resources and directing the industrial network for their own benefit, they probably cost even more in terms of lost opportunities for small business.

3. The causes of the re-emergence of small business

Many researchers have examined the re-emergence of small business to try to identify its causes. In some cases, the reasons for the trend were found to be identical across the industrialized world, and in others they were specific to certain types of economy.

The former category includes reasons based on the new national and international economic environment resulting from the transformation of economies in the last two decades, together with those based on the limits of big business, especially the multinationals. In fact, the economic transformation seems to facilitate the use of the capabilities and flexibility of smaller organizations.

3.1 The general reasons related to economic transformation

The first such reason is the trend towards segmentation in an increasing number of markets. Segmentation is a product of higher individual incomes that allow growing numbers of consumers to satisfy their "need for variety" and thus for "differentiation", as explained by Thorstein Veblen at the end of the last century[6], or more recently by Igor Scitovsky (1978). This leads to multiplication of fashions or various small consumer groups. As a phenomenon it is well-known to marketing specialists, as Chapter 6 will show, although it is contested by some economists[7].

Market segmentation clearly favours job lot production. In addition, the demand for short runs seems to be accentuated by a new distribution behaviour that is forcing merchants to minimize the time between orders and sales. Thus, an economy based on thousands of small businesses would be much more likely to adapt to the growing "personalization" of markets and faster change.

A second cause is related to what has been referred to as the labour crisis. As we will see in Chapter 11, the special relationship that often

---

6   In particular by studying the consumer behaviour of rich families from the New England coast (Veblen, 1899). See also the work of French sociologist J. Baudrillard, especially "La société de consommation" (1976).
7   The critics of the phenomenon are, however, not very convincing. In fact, the proponents of increasing market segmentation do not claim that it signals the end of mass consumption, but rather that it is a parallel, very different development. To support the concept of market segmentation, we might add that most new small businesses are created in end-product sectors, i.e. where these markets are developing.

31

exists between management and employees gives small businesses an advantage, despite the fact that they usually offer inferior conditions of employment. Smaller firms, with their less formal organization and lower levels of labour and production specialization, seem to be much better prepared to respond to new worker demands (Loveman, Sengenberger and Piore, 1990, p.42).

A third reason, that we will consider in more detail in Chapter 7, is the development of new computer technologies that are much better suited than before to the requirements of small firms and job lot production. In fact, some researchers have found that the smaller new technologies are optimized much more quickly, and in some cases actually lead to developments in larger versions (Acs and Audrestch, 1988; Carlsson, 1984).

3.2   Criticism of economies of scale

Another reason for the re-emergence of the small business sector is the fact that small firms are much more efficient (Amar, 1987[8]) than might be thought, even in comparison with large corporations. This, of course, contradicts the theory of economies of scale[9]. In fact, new research has identified certain limits of economies of scale, pointing out that they are often accompanied by diseconomies of scale, at both the management and production levels, especially in the medium-term. To understand this, we need only think of the cluster economies that are cancelled out by traffic problems and the poor quality of life in big cities[10].

As far as management scale costs are concerned, we need simply measure the effects of "slack" mentioned by Ijiri and Simon (1977) and management organization or information costs[11] (Aoki, 1986), not to

---

8   Clearly, it is not easy to compare enterprise performance, partly because of balance sheet manipulation. However, large firms, in the long term, do not seem to hold any particular advantage in terms of profits.

9   F. Leroux (1982), in an analysis of the efficiency of Canadian firms by size, based on various criteria, showed that for most branches and sub-branches of industrial activity, optimal size is between 5 and 500 employees or more - in other words, any size above a minimum threshold.

10   For example, while large cities provide plenty of cultural activity, they are also home to illegal "gang" activities often on an equivalent scale - to a point that one does not seem to be able to exist without the other.

11   These administrative costs were analyzed by G. Stigler as early as 1939, and the results enabled him to demonstrate the limits of the production line.

mention the effects of bureaucracy[12]. Production scale costs include control costs, capacity costs, exit costs or switching costs (Marchesnay, 1969), or adjustment costs (Gould, 1969) - in other words the major inertia costs - to which we can add the social costs that the government requires or will be requiring from companies under the "polluter pays" policy (Julien and Lafrance, 1983).

For this reason, large corporations are making increasing use of small businesses to take advantage of their special flexibility and reduce "size costs", as we will see later.

3.3   Specific reasons

D. Audrestch (1990) identified two other reasons that he claimed were more specific to particular economies like the United States. The first of these was the major change in the labour market, including the massive influx of young people following the baby boom in the 1950s, leading many to create their own jobs when they were unable to find what they wanted in the big business sector. The high current unemployment rates throughout the industrialized world and the significant proportion of formerly unemployed people who go on to become entrepreneurs seem to support this hypothesis. The second reason was the increase in the number of women on the labour market. In many cases, small businesses, especially in the service sector, are better able to provide women with the flexible schedules they need to coordinate their work and their role as mothers (Evans and Leighton, 1989).

A third reason also put forward is the deregulatory policy applied by governments to many markets, removing barriers that prevented entry of new firms. It is true that in some cases, for example in the road transportation sector, this movement actually produced an increase in enterprise concentration (Bigras and Pettigrew, 1991). However, to serve smaller centres, firms also had to use small trucking or transportation firms (the same thing happened in the air transportation market: Philips, 1985).

Also worth mentioning is the impact in many countries of government decentralization towards regional and territorial authorities. This has led, for example, to the division of previously centralized contracts too big

---

12 For example, the different organizational limits described by Arrow and related to "Parkinson's Law" or the Peter Principle. For an in-depth study of the theory of economies of scale, see especially the work of Bela Gold (for example, Gold 1981). We have summarized some of this work in Julien and Marchesnay (1990).

for any but the biggest firms, and thus to diversification of contracts according to the needs of the regions and their environment.

A final reason for the re-emergence of the small business sector is, of course, government support to small businesses at various levels, when just a few years ago state aid went exclusively to large corporations. Current support takes many different forms, including the creation of technological information development or transfer centres, funding through direct subsidies or tax exemptions, advice, export aid, etc. State intervention in the small business sector will be discussed in more detail later.

4.   The theories that explain small business dynamism

All these reasons for the small business boom, even when taken together, do not fully explain the new distribution of small and big business in the economy. Additional theoretical analysis is needed, to go beyond the contingency produced by the major recessions in the period since 1970. Some causes, such as the crisis of the traditional work ethic with new reforms in large corporations, or deregulation, which generates unexpected disadvantages, may in fact disappear. It should be remembered that a similar reversal of the trend in business concentration also occurred in the early 1930s, but lasted only a few years.

It is therefore important to go beyond contingency reasoning, and back to more fundamental theories. The literature offers at least four theories that might support the notion that the current small business boom will remain constant in the future. These theories are concerned with the role of entrepreneurs in economic renewal, the presence of niches suited to small businesses, increased uncertainty that wipes out the traditional aversion of business leaders to risk, and the new need for flexibility in production. Some economists would add a fifth, the stochastic division of enterprises on the basis of entrepreneurial skills. We will take a critical look at this later in the chapter.

4.1   The role of the entrepreneur in economic dynamism

One of the oldest explanations for the specific role of small business dynamism in the development of capitalism was put forward by Joseph Schumpeter, mainly in his earlier work[13]. He explained changes in the

---

13. See especially chapter 7, "The Process of Creative Destruction", in his book "Capitalism, Socialism and Democracy", published in 1942. The

34

capitalist economies by the systematic renewal of entrepreneurship, and anticipated that this system would gradually disappear, since the number of new entrepreneurs would decline in an economy dominated increasingly by huge conglomerates. For Schumpeter, the bureaucratic effects of big business concentration were killing off the entrepreneurial spirit that guaranteed systematic renewal of industrial structures.

It seems that Schumpeter was wrong, and the acceleration of change in our economies is in fact due to the emergence of entrepreneurship as the driving force of economic development, as Wallerstein (1985) showed in his history of capitalism. It is therefore no accident that entrepreneurs, after being set aside for so long in the "black box" described by Machlup in 1967, have once again become a fashionable subject in economic research. The emergence of entrepreneurship is evident through the creation of many small ventures[14]; and their renewal can only be parallel to small business research.

However, some small business research has perpetuated the error of judgment that most traditional economists continue to make, by viewing small business as a preliminary phase of big business. Whatever the proponents of the enterprise life cycle theory (discussed in the previous chapter) may think, the vast majority of small businesses not only remain small, but their owner-managers seek and actively encourage this state of affairs.

4.2   The theory of niches

To explain the permanent smallness of many small businesses, Edith Penrose, in 1959, suggested that the economy generates different types of market spaces, some of which are not suited to large-scale production. These small markets may be created by local customs (for example, religious practices), luxury requirements (Rolls Royce), highly specific uses (racing yachts), or geographical considerations (isolated populations, etc.). Such markets are inaccessible to corporations, or demand a type of production that is too specialized or not profitable enough for a large undertaking.

---

importance that Schumpeter attaches to the entrepreneur is also evident in his earlier work, including his "Theory of Economic Development", published in German in 1926, and his "Business Cycles", published in the United States in 1939.

14 For the big business context, a special term had to be invented - intrapreneur - although the concept is not yet crystal clear.

The current multiplication of niches within the economy is due in part to market segmentation and the desire for variety or change that we mentioned earlier. In particular, change systematically creates new needs that are taken up first by small groups before being extended to larger markets.

4.3 Change, uncertainty and "economies of risk"

The multiplication of niches within the economy is associated wity the increasing speed of economic change and the growing difficulty firms face in reducing uncertainty, especially through industrial concentration.

Niches also exist in sectors where economies of scale are slight or non-existent. Elsewhere, as we said earlier, many economies of scale are cancelled out by diseconomies of scale that develop at approximately the same rate.

In fact, the belief in the inherent benefits of large size is usually based on the notion that large corporations tend to become even larger (which is equivalent to explaining the causes by the consequences!). It is, however, possible to offer a non-economic explanation of this phenomenon, based on the concept, well-known among management specialists, of "aversion to risk" among business leaders. This will be discussed in more detail in Chapter 5[15].

Risk can be minimized by reducing market uncertainty, for example uncertainty related to competition, government intervention in the economy, innovations by competitors, and so on. Large corporations do this directly, by increasing their size, or indirectly, by forming cartels and taking up oligopolistic or monopolistic positions on national and international markets[16]. An investigation by R. Petrella (1989) showed that many multinationals use the support of their national governments to reduce national competition, and then develop multiple agreements with their international competitors to do the same on the international

---

15 The idea that business leaders are more prone to take risks than the rest of the population seems to have taken root among economists. Although it may be true in the case of real entrepreneurs, it is not true of managers. And even among the former, research has not yet been able to provide proof. See the critiques by Brockhaus (1983) and Kirzner (1980).

16 W. Ouchi (1980) talks of "economies of power" as explaining much big business behaviour, especially during periods of rapid change, when uncertainty increases.

market. Adam Smith himself observed that businessmen rarely meet without plotting to deceive the public[17].

On the other hand, the growing difficulty of facing up to economic uncertainty may force firms, large and small, to operate in business groups or constellations, for example in vertical quasi-integration (Enrietti, 1990) or other types, such as purchasing groups in the trade sector), or in systems that are much more flexible than traditional conglomerates. By grouping together, they can take advantage of information and innovations by members to reduce uncertainty, while at the same time encouraging change.

In 1919, Alfred Marshall had already described this type of grouping, where economies of scale can be shared between large numbers of firms in local industrial areas, for example the industrial districts mentioned earlier (Beccatini, 1987). The idea of the industrial areas is to minimize transaction costs, for example by creating a "transaction space" managed by small business leaders and based on systematic relationships of trust between the partners, thus reducing the effects of Williamson's three factors (uncertainty, complexity and the number of partners) (Marchesnay and Julien, 1990)[18]. On the other hand, internalization of transactions also generates costs, such as those mentioned in section 3.2.

4.4   The new need for flexibility

The need for a transaction space to reduce uncertainty and foster change is expressed through what has been referred to as the pursuit of flexibility. Flexibility means internal management and technology able to provoke or adapt quickly to external change. It demands business

---

17 See p. 137 of C.J. Bullock's 1909 edition of "The Inquiry into the Nature and Causes of the Wealth of Nations". The theory of aversion to risk as an explanation of the trend towards enterprise concentration goes much further than the idea of Coarse/Williamson, taken from Marshall, to internalize transaction costs when it is profitable to do so (i.e. when market use costs are higher). This calculation does not consider the need for "peace" in the face of uncertainty. Frank Knight, in his quasi-rent theory, had already understood this as early as 1920. The result of this trend is the formation of multiple coalitions or "clans, cliques and clubs", to use Ouchi's (1980) terms.

18 The notion of "transaction space", which gives small firms access to resources without completely binding them, largely solves Dosi and Metcalf's problem of irreversibility, referred to by Foray (1990). Richardson (1977) has also shown that the competitive market is the exception rather than the rule; most markets seem to function on the basis of different forms of cooperation.

compatibility with change, divisibility and reversibility of production (Reix, 1979; Kickert, 1989). In practice, it is achieved by a trade-off between time management and the cost of adaptation.

Small businesses, which as Mintzberg (1990) explained, have a more "organic" as opposed to mechanistic or hierarchical style of organization, are generally much more flexible than large corporations. Their flexibility is due, among other things, to greater labour adaptability and a much lower level of specialization in the various production factors (Scott, 1988), as well as to technical changes that enable the firms to produce job lots at lower cost (see above).

Carlsson (1989), based on work by Mills and Schumann (1985), showed that small businesses compensate for the absence of economies of scale by greater flexibility, especially in periods of rapid change.

One of the ways in which big businesses can obtain more flexibility is by using small firms to compensate for their inertia effects in a rapidly changing economy. This can be done through subcontracting or "outsourcing", mainly for services but also for different segments of production previously performed within the firm, in various types of partnership agreements. In economies such as France, outsourcing is responsible for the creation of more than a quarter of small manufacturing ventures (Hanaut and Torre, 1985).

The characteristic flexibility of small firms is also responsible for the creation of services and small manufacturing business networks, and thus for new local development, as discussed in the next chapter.

4.5   The distribution of managerial capacities

The systematic arrival of new firms in the economy, despite the traditional trend towards business concentration, has also been discussed by neo-classical economists like Lucas (1978) and, more recently, Oi (1983). As an explanation for this contradictory phenomenon, they suggested that the economy generated all kinds of entrepreneurs and managers, only a few of whom were capable of managing large corporations. The others had to make do with small or medium-sized firms.

Despite all the econometric calculations, this vision remains tautological. These authors have simply concluded that big businesses are managed by managers who are capable of managing big businesses, and small businesses by managers who are capable of managing small businesses. This may be a statement of fact, but it explains nothing. In taking this approach, these economists have made the same mistake as their colleagues who tried to explain the problem of income dispersal by suggesting that rich people were rich because they had the capacity to be or to become rich, when in fact we know that wealth is more often a product of luck - being born into a rich family, and thus being sent to the best schools, starting work in daddy's factory and having a flock of specialists at hand to provide advice.

The proponents of this view have not understood that entrepreneurs may have other objectives than the pursuit of profit and growth at all costs, and that management capability does not depend on exceptional characteristics or talents, as entrepreneurship specialists have shown. They attribute only two functions to entrepreneurs: the ability to coordinate production and the capacity to manage production factors. Yet, entrepreneurs have other socioeconomic functions and are guided by very different goals (Julien, 1989). For example, some choose to stay small rather than losing control of their firms. In other cases, managers have chosen to leave large corporations, and the possibility of becoming top dog one day, to create their own jobs on a more human scale or to coordinate production resources in their home towns.

If the theory of the stochastic distribution of management skills were true, dispersal would follow a normal curve, based on the economic size of the country, with the largest firms in all sectors operating in the largest countries. However, what we in fact have is a wide variety of industrial structures, with a low concentration of some activities in some large countries and a high concentration in others, regardless of their size.

5.   Towards a new small business/big business equilibrium

All this should not be taken to mean that big business is on the road to extinction. In fact, as we have said, what we are probably witnessing is the development of a new balance between small and very large firms that will stabilize in the 21st century, provided small businesses are able to maintain or improve their competitiveness in an increasingly competitive market.

In today's rapidly-changing context, small business competitiveness clearly requires a better control of information and regular if not systematic innovation, as well as the creation of networks. It also presupposes renewed training for small business managers and key employees, together with effective government support in these areas.

5.1 Controlling information

In fact, competitiveness depends not only on the new management and production technologies described in Chapter 7, which fall under the heading of material investment, but also on new, complex forms of management and organization, or immaterial investment in R&D and extensive technological scanning. Immaterial investment should, in the longer term, lead to systematic renewal of products and production organization, and it thus presupposes innovation at all levels.

Researchers in different countries have shown that between 50% and 60% of all small businesses innovate, at least spontaneously and incrementally. Of these, only 5% to 10% innovate more radically (Archibuggi and Cesaretto, 1989; MRFT, 1989; Bernard and Torre, 1994). Small business innovation is thus mostly gradual. Although very few small businesses perform systematic R&D, they seem to do it more efficiently, given the money involved, than large firms (Rothwell, 1989).

Innovation exists at many different levels. For example, some small businesses, unable to buy modern or high-tech equipment, take other innovative steps to obtain competitive unit costs, ranging from seasonal use of manpower (creating manpower loyalty by adjusting to unemployment insurance rules), flexible work organization, high employee involvement to compensate for out-of-date equipment by increased productivity, spontaneous innovation to improve the performance of old equipment, recycling and identification of new applications for second-hand equipment bought from large firms, and special agreements or relationships with buyers or order-givers.

However, if firms are to avoid being overtaken by progress, all these measures or strategies must be updated regularly in response to change. In other words, innovation means listening to the environment and thus requires implicit or fairly well-organized technological, competitive and commercial scanning.

Technological and commercial information is expensive, and changes quickly. It is essential to the long-term vision, and is taken into account by large firms through their research centres and other specialized departments. Small businesses are particularly vulnerable in this area because of the limited resources they are able to devote to creating, obtaining and assessing information.

5.2 The importance of networks

For this reason, small businesses must join or construct networks that allow them to obtain the information they need at a lower cost. The networks may include research centres or other public or private information transfer organizations, business associations, consulting firms, suppliers, and so on.

Our study of the information needs of different industrial sectors revealed that the plastics sector tends to use technological information provided mainly by raw materials suppliers, while machine tool firms obtain their information from order-givers and sawmills from equipment suppliers. Firms in all these sectors also make extensive use of industrial exhibitions and sometimes approach specialized public or parapublic research centres (Julien, Carrière and Hébert, 1988). They obtain commercial information mainly from their "personal networks".

The resources of small businesses are limited, and networks enable them to reduce the transaction costs involved in obtaining commercial and technical information. Small business networks are usually informal (friends, social or professional acquaintances, and so on), and become more structured or formal (support programs, consulting firms, research centres, etc.) as the business develops and perfects its technological scanning activity (Julien et al., 1995). They allow the more dynamic small firms to *arrange* their environment in order to reduce uncertainty and manage better in the long-term (Marchesnay and Julien, 1990).

Specifically, the networks are vital for small business exports. Export-related costs are too high for small businesses to function like their larger counterparts in starting or maintaining activities abroad. This element will be considered in more detail in the next chapter.

5.3   Training

To use information properly and take full advantage of networks, business leaders must be trained appropriately or have competent staff, and the training or competence must be kept up-to-date.

Training is another key element in immaterial or intellectual investment. It may even be more important than the use of new process technologies. At the very least, it is a condition for taking full advantage of technology spin-offs and thus making the most of their performance capabilities.

The quality of management training has been identified as one of the main variables separating firms making systematic use of modern technologies from their more traditional counterparts.

This aspect has been somewhat neglected by researchers in the past. Yet, we do not really know how small businesses offer training. We do know, however, that those that offer it tend to favour internal rather than external training (see Chapter 11).

5.4   State intervention

In view of the limited resources of small businesses, direct or indirect government assistance is often required, especially at start-up and to improve competitiveness, and in the longer term to help firms make any structural changes required.

Certain theorists believe that the market is deficient in some ways, or that it is inadequate when it comes to giving small firms the same opportunities as big firms. For example, small businesses face many different entry barriers set up by oligopolies or monopolies; some technological and economic information is controlled by big business, as William Ouchi (1980) pointed out; resources are often badly distributed; etc. And whatever neo-classical economic theory might say, useful information, as opposed to general information offering little or no benefit and therefore of little or no interest, is often protected by patents or biased following manipulation. Or it is too uncertain and requires research and analysis resources beyond the reach of most small businesses.

In the creation and initial competitiveness phase, small businesses are vulnerable, especially in the area of financing. In the structural change phase, they need support in the form of advice and expertise, to encourage them to use new management and production technologies or to export. As far as the other elements are concerned, they usually have to be able to defend themselves on the free market with nothing but their own resources, even if this means paying the price for their weaknesses and inefficiencies.

One of the major problems of government programs is that they are often poorly adapted not to the general needs of small businesses, but to their management philosophy and behaviour. The programs are often unsuited to the type of decision-making employed by owner-managers, who have very little time available for deciphering civil service jargon and program philosophies. Some require excessive input in return for minimal benefits, and are not widely used (OECD, 1993).

Such programs may be offered by several levels of government. Territorial and local authorities seem to be to small business what central government is to big business. In other words, they are closer to small businesses and may thus have a better understanding of the sector's needs. In recent years, they have begun to intervene more systematically to support small business creation and development. As a result, the number of players in the small business market is increasing steadily, and it has become vital for all these different interventions to be coordinated.

There would even be a case for a division of tasks between the different levels of government.

At the central government level: development of international, technological and commercial information. Technological and international information is not held back by national boundaries.

At the regional authority level: additional resources: risk financing, continuing education (especially through the education network), synergy between distribution and production.

At the local level: the creation of some economic complicity networks, bringing about synergy between local players and fostering complementarity and new information.

In other words, the central government should pay more attention to the problems faced by small businesses in adapting to new technology and managing technological resources, especially at the meso-economic and micro-economic levels:

At the meso-economic level:
a) by fostering research and information transfer, in particular by creating more systematic links between research, development and application of technologies (the role of innovative environments and networks, etc.). Support should thus allow *effective* transfer of technological information, its subsequent *assimilation* and then its management.
b) by supporting training and efforts to provide small businesses with additional resources so that they can obtain and use technologies (seed or risk financing, consulting and technology management services, etc.). The absence, poor quality or high cost of these resources may act as a major brake on production development.
c) by joining forces with local authorities to enable them to act as catalysts or stimulators in the development of entrepreneurial synergy and local or regional resources.

At the micro-economic level: The measures that foster the implementation of small business development and competitive strategies. In particular, measures aimed at improving small business capability in three areas: identifying, processing, assessing and applying technological information, introducing and managing new technology, and procuring additional resources.

In other words, central government support should be designed first and foremost to help small businesses to develop their competitiveness, by intervening:

1. on the sources and quality of international, technological and commercial information;
2. at the level of opportunities or the suitability of the technologies available to firms, and
3. in cooperation with other government levels, to support or develop favourable micro- and macro-economic conditions for technology appropriation.

6.   Conclusion

We live in an ever-changing structural environment that makes every kind of forecast possible, since we are both players and observers in the transformation. In addition to the transformation itself, the arrival of new industrial countries continues to disrupt an international market that is not expanding quickly enough, for reasons including the demographic slump and the very high debt levels of developing countries, and the substantial problems to be overcome by the former socialist countries before they can play an effective role in the consumer economy.

The response of industrialized countries to this upheaval must lie to a large extent in "more intelligent" production, whether through design, pure innovation or new technology. Mass production, with its corollary, the scientific organization of work (Taylorism), will continue to move towards the new industrial and developing countries, where the poorly-educated workforce, giving priority to its income requirements, will accept the socioeconomic conditions of this type of production. The industrialized countries must therefore turn towards top-of-the-range production, complex products or products with high added-value, niches that change regularly and related services (especially what has been called the propulsive service industry: R&D, consulting, high-tech information, etc.). The central element of this new production is and will continue to be technical and organizational creativity and innovation (product and process), which is particularly present in small businesses. This means an economy that will be increasingly unstable or in constant renewal.

Clearly, an economy based on thousands of small businesses is much better able to adapt to market segmentation and rapid change. Small firms, firmly rooted in a country, region or city, are in a position to seize all the aspects of rapid change. An economy with large numbers of such firms may well constitute a highly "self-adaptive" system where experiments can be multiplied and competition encouraged on the basis of needs. This type of economy would permit the "creative destruction" described by Schumpeter. On the other hand, the hyper-centralized systems such as those that still exist in the former socialist countries and oligopolistic sectors, are more difficult to shift and much less flexible.

In short, these economies would benefit from greater decentralization to encourage what Lawrence and Lorsch (1973) called "contingency". This also means more entrepreneurship, and thus more small businesses, operating in networks or in association with big firms, on standard markets or to support or complete mass production and allow it to develop. We will come back to these aspects in the conclusion to the book.

Control of the competition-related issues of firms in industrialized countries should lead to what we have just called "intelligence management", as opposed to management based on low cost and just-in-time or job lot production, which still exists in traditional systems, although it is tending to be transferred to low wage countries. Intelligence management involves better control of information, through training, the use of new management and process technologies, and systematic innovation. However, this will not happen on its own. Small businesses, with their low resource levels, must learn to operate in synergy with their environment.

It is through symbiosis between the interests of society and the interests of small business that the small business sector will be able to pursue its development and maintain its dynamism into the next century.

2 Small businesses and local development

"I know friendship is strong enough to hold and to join from one corner of the world to the other; and particularly in this part where there is continual communication between different functions, which awakens friendship's obligation and remembrance." Michel de Montaigne, "Essai".

1. Introduction

1.1 The emergence of local initiative

During the 1960s and 1970s, an entire category of economists, land planners, sociologists and geographers began to specialize in regional development. In industrialized economies everywhere, the reduction of regional disparities through the combined actions of government and big business had become a priority. The turnaround in the economic situation, however, fuelled by two oil crises and characterized by an epidemic of business closures and layoffs, put the whole question of economic strategy in a new light. Now that the relevance of the mega-projects was being challenged, a new approach based on small businesses and local entrepreneurship began to attract attention. Throughout western nations, in city neighbourhoods, small towns and outlying regions, the signs of a new dynamism could be observed as the human, physical and financial resources of local communities were developed. Reports on the initial results of experimental work flowed in from all quarters: from working-class neighbourhoods in Chicago and Montreal, from former mining areas in the Appalachian mountains of Pennsylvania, from a satellite city in the Paris basin, from the far north of Lapland, from the islands of Cyprus and Cape Breton. Everywhere, whether in urban, semi-urban or rural areas, joint efforts by various social players to stimulate employment through the creation of small businesses provided evidence of a healthy reaction to the devastating economic crisis which struck in the mid-1970s.

Despite the misgivings expressed about local development programs too exclusively centred on job creation and income enhancement (Shapero, 1984), we have retained E.J. Blakely's definition of "local initiative" (Blakely, 1994) as the action undertaken by various levels of government, business, unions and the cooperative movement in order to increase employment and income in a circumscribed area. This view is close to that developed in the OECD Program on Local Initiatives for Employment Creation (ILE)[1], in which initiatives are equated with activities designed to create viable employment that (1) are developed in response to local needs, problems, potential and resources; (2) are initiated and controlled by individuals, groups or institutional players from within the local community; and (3) result from the creation or development of production (or sales-related) activities for marketable goods and services, and that ensure a return in financial, economic and social terms (1990).

The interest generated in Canada and in Quebec by these attempts by local communities to break away from their dependence on the two main levels of government and on big business attracted the interest of the Economic Council of Canada. Some twenty case studies were published in 1989 and 1990 as part of a research project to examine the diversity of experiments in local development and isolate their worthwhile aspects[2]. In Quebec, the 55 Community Development Councils (formerly known as Community Futures Committees)[3], located in small-scale territories in which the unemployment rate is above the Canadian average, reflect the importance placed by government authorities on the development of local potential. Working in similar spatial surroundings, the efforts deployed by a number of Quebec's 96 regional county municipalities (RCMs) as part of their economic revival plan, provide further evidence of the desire of individuals in specific areas to take charge of their own future.

Montreal is no exception to this new approach to economic development. Seriously affected by the closure of several petrochemical plants and many other businesses in different sectors of activity, the east end of the city has established a body to draw up the framework of an economic revival and conversion program. The Committee to Revive Employment And The Economy in the east of Montreal (known by its

---

1   This program, authorized in July 1992, has three objectives: the exchange of experiences and information regarding employment development at the local level, the design and application of assessment methods for each initiative, and the provision of assistance to the twenty-one participating countries in implementing and assessing their national programs.
2   See *infra* for a description of one such case study.
3   The program was under the responsibility of the former federal Department of Employment and Immigration, known since 1994 as the Department of Human Resources Development.

French acronym CREEM) was set up in 1987, and was superseded by Pro-Est whose main task was to consolidate existing employment and to stimulate new employment through the creation of small businesses. It was able, among other things, to call upon the services of an intermediary organization, the Corporation for Economic And Community Development in the East (known as CDEST), which was established in 1985 after two similar organizations had been set up in the south central and southwest districts of Montreal, both of which had been affected by the economic slowdown. In the southwest, a committee to revive employment and the economy had produced a report in early 1990 that made recommendations in four main areas: assistance for the unemployed and to improve the socioeconomic situation of the population; protection of economic activity and job creation; consolidation of the territory and improvement in living conditions; and collective responsibility for development through the Southwest Economic And Social Revival Group (RESO). The assistance provided for the creation and consolidation of small businesses was, obviously, only one element among the many included in this development strategy, but the program nevertheless provides a further example of the importance of support for small businesses in creating a local dynamic (Joyal, 1994a).

In France, the passage of decentralization legislation in 1982 reflected the interest shown in entrepreneurship as a means of dealing with the problems of a country that was all too aware that the prosperous post-war years, the so-called "thirty glorious years", were a thing of the past. Throughout France, much activity has been generated by support organizations which, despite their differing structures, all share the same objective: venture creation (Joyal, 1994b). To ensure the operation of these organizations, master's-level university programs have been set up in various universities around France to train economic development agents to work in the new organizations.

The negative connotations until recently associated with local development, seen as an attempt to move away from the dominant economy to a kind of rural idyll (the "return to the land") characterized by projects revolving around flock, field and forest (Lacour, 1986), are thus tending to disappear. This observation is also made in an OECD publication (1989a), which recognizes that local development has changed its "fringe" image to one stressing its role as a complement or counterweight to regional and industrial policy. The approach has changed from an ideology associated with fringe culture to a more pragmatic, rational approach based on strategic planning.

Although concrete illustrations of the consequences of this outburst of energy are not hard to come by, theorists and practitioners are still not speaking the same language. What exactly is meant by "local development"? Do we really need to add the word "economic"? And what does "local" mean? If different strategies exist, are there any traits that are common to all local development strategies? Who are the main players in local development and how do they interact? What are their limits, and what obstacles tend to reduce their effectiveness? Given the destructive effects of free trade on the agricultural sector, how is the problem of rural development to be situated? Lastly, what steps must be taken to counter the still-prevalent scepticism towards the whole question of local development? The following discussion is obviously not intended to provide answers to all these questions, but rather to clarify certain issues with the help, in some cases, of real-life examples that tend to support the position of economic decentralization and small business development.

2.   The local scale, or zone of action

"Localism" has often been criticized by the supporters of labour force mobility, in other words all those who believe that the victims of unemployment should move towards job-rich areas, as for example when thousands of workers flowed across the US border from Quebec to work in the New England cotton mills. Besides the obvious social upheaval, M.E. Chassagne (OECD, 1988) points out two other consequences. The first, negative, consequence relates to the lack of a sufficient number of jobs, even in regions in better economic health, to meet the needs of a population uprooted from its familiar environment. The second, positive, consequence relates to the creation of small businesses in outlying regions, resulting in a clear reduction in induced costs for infrastructures, communal facilities, housing, etc., while promoting the property base and identity of the communities concerned.

For these reasons, the question of identity is at the very centre of research into local economies, which has evolved from being the science of activity location to become the study of phenomena relating to local systems growth. This point of view is shared by R. Boure and J. Menville (1990), who consider that the decentralization encouraged by government policy, and the presence of a pool of expertise around "its" projects has progressively led each "locality" to become a "subject" in itself. "Localities" are thus, for researchers, both a field of study and a field of intervention.

2.1 *"Localities" as a field of intervention for the creation and consolidation of small businesses*

The increasingly frequent use of the word "locality" raises a number of questions. What is meant by "local" and "locality"? P. Derycke (1993) discusses the confusion created in French by the use of the same word ("local") as both an adjective and a noun, and examines the concerns of economists who see "localities" as being both an object for analysis and a field for observation and intervention.

Given that even the word "region" never fails to create unlimited confusion and endless debate between economists and geographers, the ambiguity created by references to a spatial framework that can range in size from an urban neighbourhood, a small or medium-sized town, to a group of villages encircling a small town, is not hard to imagine. To help clarify the issue, the Economic Council of Canada (1990a) defined a "local community" as an entity - made up of small and medium-sized towns and villages - whose inhabitants share interdependent economic, social and political activities and institutions, and also share a range of public and private services.

This concept of a geographical area made up of a number of local administrations that share a common economic base explains why the terms "local" and "regional" are used interchangeably by some writers. E.J. Blakeley (1994) tends to confuse the two notions in an examination of how easy it is for the population of a given region to travel to the site of their work, shopping and leisure activities, an approach reminiscent of France's employment pools. The OECD (1987), in a document associated with its ILE program, defines a "locality" as an area with its own identity and dynamics, and with specific characteristics that interrelate with the broader zones (regional, national and global) of which it forms a part. This view is similar to that held by the coordinator of a research project on local development led by the Economic Council of Canada (1990b), who links the word "locality" to the geographical areas formed by municipalities or groups of municipalities whose inhabitants share the same group of institutions and common infrastructures. This corresponds, in Quebec, to the notion of Regional County Municipality, in France, to that of around 300 "pays", and in the US to the areas under the jurisdiction of a "local government", the third level of government administration. We shall therefore rely here on this sub-regional definition, even though in many cases administrative demarcations take no account of the elements that lead to a feeling of common purpose within a given territory.

The word "locality" also contains shades of "community" (Maillat, 1992): a community to which people belong, that provides them with characteristic traits and social links, and that exerts a degree of influence over socioeconomic change by intervening with the means placed at its disposal by government and cooperative institutions. In other words, it is a community that corresponds to a spatially contiguous environment offering various players sufficient information and facilities to ensure stability and links between the various networks (Perrin, 1990). This concept of "community", on the basis of the work carried out by the European Research Group on Innovative Communities, has been examined using three different approaches to reveal its main components:

a) a micro-analytical approach essentially based on an articulation of the concepts of uncertainty, information and transaction costs;

b) a cognitive approach, articulated mainly around the notions of knowledge, skills and technical culture;

c) a organizational approach that reveals the systems of players and structures as observed during reciprocal interaction (Maillat, 1994).

Especially with regard to the existence of networks, which we shall examine later, the "community" includes local and regional environments, social structures, family links, linguistic links, training and research activities, inter-business mobility for researchers and administrators, links between training and research establishments and business, synergy and collaboration between the private sector and the municipalities in the region, and collaboration between the municipalities themselves (Proulx, 1990). The concept can thus be seen to refer to a medium-sized town, or to a group of smaller municipalities situated sufficiently near one another to allow a high level of interaction between the different player categories: public officials, business leaders, the representatives of financial institutions, representatives from the cooperative movement and unions, etc.

This sub-regional space, with the emergence of small businesses, presents both economists and entrepreneurial specialists with a field of investigation situated somewhere between the micro-economic and macro-economic levels. This so-called meso-economic level allows priority to be given to the examination of inter-business relationships within certain sectors of activity and industrial clusters (Mifsud, 1990).

2.2   The meso-economic approach

In a recent study centred on the meso-economic approach, Marc-Urbain Proulx (1995) underlines the fact that the term "meso" refers to a mid-way point. In biology, mesology is defined as the study of the effects of a given environment on the humans, animals and plants living in it. Mesoeconomy, therefore, can be defined as the study, within a particular environment, of the factors that influence its economic evolution. The goal of the analysis is no longer to integrate the community under examination with micro- or macro-economic realities, but rather to reveal the specific rules governing the community through recognition of the primacy of the ecological variable. The community becomes a substrate whose elements (micro-organizations) undergo interconnection and interdependency in order to promote the dynamic of the community as a whole. Each micro-organization positions itself as both an emitter and receiver of communications and information (see *infra* on the subject of the network concept). Meso-analysis in spatial economics, seen in this light, reveals an openness towards appearances providing promises for the future.

Although the information gathered cannot dispel all the ambiguities concerning the nature of the field of observation, it can nevertheless allow the framework governing the various interventions to be better situated. Certain interventions, in fact, justify a reference to a type of development involving the promotion of employment by means of small businesses on the basis of an appropriate use of the market mechanism (Cochrane, 1987). Where new ventures result from the joint efforts of various players, they in fact belong to a local development oriented approach.

3. The concept of local development as it relates to small businesses

There can be no doubt about the importance of the direct and indirect jobs created when new businesses emerge thanks to the vision and dynamism of entrepreneurs acting individually. However, this phenomenon cannot be related to local development as the term is generally understood in Quebec and France, given that nothing links these initiatives to a structured strategy devised by a group of partners acting together. The specific nature of local development, as it is understood in Quebec and France, derives from the joint actions undertaken by a group of partners in order to develop the human, financial and material resources of their community and create jobs (Joyal, 1987). It must therefore be differentiated from the expression "local development" as it is generally used in the US which, more often than not[4], has a merely

---

4   The interesting book by E.J. Blakely (op. cit.) is an isolated exception.

spatial connotation and relates mainly to initiatives undertaken to satisfy individual interests. In the US, development strategies based on mutual assistance, solidarity, respect for the environment and a switch to a more humane type of development, implemented in the form of small businesses, are generally referred to as "neighbourhood development" or "community-based economic development" (*Le local en action*, 1989), and no clear distinction seems to be made between the two approaches.

As several people working in the field of local development have pointed out, some of this ambiguity can be traced to the lack of a well-defined theoretical corpus (Arocena, 1986). "Local" development suffers from a lack of reference points and its practice is not theory-driven (Sorbets, 1990). The concept, deprived of a solid theoretical basis, can be seen, almost essentially in some cases, as a line of action with an ideological slant (Greffe, 1988). In other words, it is considered to be a movement rather than as a well-defined model, although it nevertheless offers a certain unity of conception that cannot be found in the dominant economic theory (Newman et al., 1986).

A refusal to allow the fate of urban neighbourhoods or economically weak regions to be dependent on market forces tends to lead to the adoption of a voluntarist strategy marked by a level of state intervention. Although intervention by the "welfare state" is clearly becoming a thing of the past, recognition of that fact is not necessarily synonymous with a call for the withdrawal of the State, as urged by the neoliberalists. On the contrary, the State must intervene, as one among a number of players required to collaborate in a partnership-oriented approach, as part of a local development strategy. However, before examining how such a process operates in more detail, we must further clarify both the concepts and the elements that characterize this approach to economic development.

3.1 Trigger elements

Considering the weakness of the theoretical basis for the question of local development, François Plassard (1988) suggests the image of a makeshift solution that gives meaning to situations where development problems are being experienced. His observation is judiciously based on the fact that no two situations and no two testimonies are the same, given the differing human and economic context involved. Nevertheless, certain constant factors unfailingly appear, that are neither individuals, events or institutions, but rather functions that are performed by various players, sometimes unconsciously. One such function, the so-called "catalyst function", reflects the feeling expressed as "things can't go on like this".

Persistently high unemployment, unfulfilled expectations of change, disappointment with government action, and declining public services, all have a negative impact on a given community. The combination of some or all of these factors encourage socioeconomic leaders to come together to, at least, carry out an assessment of the situation. An opening up to the outside world is one of the components of this function[5], stimulated by a new awareness of how the same problems are being tackled elsewhere. Positive results obtained in another community encourage a belief in "new possibilities". "Why not do the same in our community?" is a typical response. Lastly, an observation of the facts shows that a third component joins the first two in playing a determining role, what F. Plassard calls a "micro-rupture event": the last straw. It is easy to imagine this micro-rupture event being the disappearance of the last major business in a sub-region, the closing of a factory in a one-industry town, the imposition of new quotas in the fisheries, the closing of institutions in the educational or health sectors following administrative reforms, and so on. The community can only take so much; no choice remains but action. The community decides to face its problems by taking charge of its own future.

3.2 Local development and community development: similarities and significant differences

In the early 1970s, the threat of closure hanging over a number of parishes in the Gaspé and Lower Saint Lawrence regions of Quebec, following a negative government assessment of their viability, resulted in a mobilization of the population that provides a good example of the "catalyst function" described above. The reaction of the local population, gathered behind parish priests and other leaders, led to a radical alteration of the scenario prepared by the government bureaucracy for the area. The main inspiration was the American phenomenon known as *community-based economic development* that had been promoted, in particular in urban areas, during the late 1960s to help ethnic minorities through *Community Development Corporations* (see *intra*), thus providing an example of the new awareness of outside experiences mentioned above. The movement marked the beginning of the first experiments in

---

5   Montreal's economic and community development corporations would never have seen the light of day had it not been for the success of similar organizations elsewhere in Quebec and especially in the U.S.

community development in Quebec[6], and indeed not until the mid-1980s did the expression "community development" give way to that of "local development".

Is there a distinction to be made between "local" and "community" development, or are they merely terminological variants used to describe one and the same reality? In the years when the population of the Lower Saint Lawrence and Gaspé regions of Quebec were mobilizing to take responsibility for their own economic future, the expression "community-based economic development", as used in the US, had strong social connotations. The types of action promoted by the various agents of social change who contributed towards improving the living conditions of the most deprived segments of the population by providing various services, were all based on a desire to promote greater social justice. Over time, the entrepreneurial dimension became more important but never replaced the social dimension. For these reasons, D. Douglas (1994) defines *community-based economic development* as a set of collective actions designed to satisfy local, socioeconomically-oriented interests. In contrast to traditional economic development initiatives, the community was both the subject and the object of the strategy implemented. The local population defined its problems, established its priorities and selected appropriate solutions (MacFarlane, 1990). The community, in such cases, was formed by a combination of the local population and its immediate surroundings, delimited by an imaginary boundary that brought together a stable and relatively well-defined population with an unambiguous common destiny. The community became involved in its economic future through its organizational network which included both private businesses and non-profit organizations. The social dimension is still in evidence, since community development works in several different directions and integrates social and economic objectives (Perry, 1987, 1989; Tremblay and Fontan, 1994).

In Eastern Quebec, the "community" aspect is reflected in the wish of each community to find alternatives to an "untenable" situation. The social dimension was obviously a consideration, since the type of change envisaged was based not only the population's desire to remain in familiar surroundings, and not to strive for monetary gain at any cost, but also to find "new ways to work". A network of support cooperatives and work cooperatives was set up, targeting the involvement of as many

---

6   Much has been written on the subject. In the words of one person involved, "we have lost track of how many Master's theses have been written about us".

people as possible in various capacities. Community development was thus synonymous with the pooling of the resources of as many people as possible affected, whether directly or indirectly, by the projects proposed in the action plan. The first community businesses closely resembled their counterparts in Scotland, which had grown out of similar circumstances, and were characterized by:
- the identification of resources and needs by the population;
- the growth of local entrepreneurship;
- the reinvestment of profits at the local level;
- the combination of economic and social projects;
- local input into the various possible strategies (Watt, 1988).

Over the years Quebec, like other areas, has seen its strategies develop in ways that are sometimes hotly disputed.

3.2.1   Over-emphasis on economic aspects

The current tendency of governments to intervene in local development by encouraging an entrepreneurial approach that ignores the social dimension and local input has been a cause of concern for some observers. A clear distinction exists between the kind of local community development centred on a geographical area, the home of a specific population whose cultural identity is to be strengthened, and local development as practised by government authorities throughout the western world. The latter approach is distinguished from the former by its strictly **economic** logic, on the basis of which local territories must be rationalized, parcelled up and placed in a hierarchy according to their capacity for production. In the words of H. Dionne (1989): "Community- and territory-based local development relies on an established economy and remains attentive to the social and communal effects of its evolution, in harmony with the vision for social development that it supports (...). Local development can only be global, integrated, relational and identity-driven; it cannot be imposed, it must result from social momentum." The so-called economist approach reflects the promotion of entrepreneurship and individual initiative that characterizes the US *local development* approach in which entrepreneurs, with the exception of conventional services provided by municipalities, act individually and are essentially motivated by the economic consequences of their actions. In contrast with this approach, the partisans of community-based local development prefer to promote a type of integrated development "... that supports local pride, community spirit and quality of life" (GRIR, 1990).

Placed in this context, the conception of local development presented here, targeting, as it does, the creation of jobs in areas in which they are often cruelly lacking, necessarily involves an interrelation between social and economic objectives. It therefore falls somewhere between the two approaches outlined above. It is clear that the community development approach, as experienced in Eastern Quebec in the 1970s, now represents a historical example rather than an avenue for future exploration. The fact that most of the cooperatives that emerged as a result of the movement had been privatized by the early 1980s shows the importance of a certain amount of pragmatism, whatever the supporters of social change may think.

3.2.2 Pragmatism

"Community development", as it refers to the involvement of as many people as possible, from a given community, in a collective decision-making process, is well-known for its tendency to deflate rapidly. Positive spin-off from the energy invested is not always proportionate to the expectations generated, and even the most enthusiastic and hard-working proponents of a scheme eventually succumb to a form of psychological weariness. Given this fact, it should come as no surprise that certain socioeconomic leaders in the Pabok Regional County Municipality, at the tip of Quebec's Gaspé peninsula, are now in favour of a less public input-oriented approach than the one implemented in the same region over fifteen years ago. Based on the approach defined by B. Vachon (1993), among others, and targeting the joint action of various support organizations[7], the community is taking action through its organizational network to encourage local entrepreneurship, in order to respond to the difficult problem of under-employment and dependence on government handouts. This approach corresponds almost exactly to the vision of R. MacFarlane (1990), in whose view only a small segment of the local population is involved in the development and management of the small businesses created by a community-based approach, since most projects depend on the action taken by community leaders acting in the interests of their community. In Scotland, for example, this role is played by elected local officials, whereas in the rest of the British Isles it is played mainly by representatives from various organizations selected on the basis of their experience or skills.

---

7   Such as economic development corporations and community development assistance boards.

The idea that development projects are drawn up during meetings of the local population held in schools or church halls corresponds only to a naive vision of decentralization. Economic development does not result from a show of hands. The local population prefers to delegate responsibilities to its representatives, duly mandated to take advantage of the resources of the community. In recent years, in Quebec, several support organizations have adopted a strategy similar to that implemented in France by that country's *Boutiques de gestion* (management groups), *Plate-formes d'initiatives* (forums for initiative), *Comités de bassin d'emplois* (workforce pool committees), various economic development associations, and municipal economy departments. The main characteristic of this approach is thus in no sense the promotion of the selfish interests of the resourceful few. In fact, as we shall see in the following section, local development, even when it no longer seeks to involve "everybody and their dog", involves far more than the mere provision of subsidies to the creators of new businesses.

4. The local development process and small business creation

References to local development often include the word "strategies", used in the plural to emphasize the fact that several variants, corresponding to various contexts, may exist within a common process. In an OECD (1989) document, a "strategy" was defined by several specialists as being a realistic vision of the future state of a given community, together with an accurate assessment of the starting point for the process and of the factors that will have an influence during its implementation. For these specialists, strategic planning is ideally suited to local development, given that a local development project involves:

- a *commitment* made by people with access to the resources of the community and with responsibility for its future;
- an *organization* under the responsibility of a planning group provided with all the required resources and skills, and mandated to lead the community;
- a *long-term view*, characterized by objectives fixed in a long enough time-frame for factors specific to the community, considered to be unchangeable in the short term, to be transformed during the implementation of the development plan;
- *research and analysis* into the situation of the community and its various sectors as compared to the competition, based on an identification of strong and weak points;
- the setting of clear, realistic and measurable *objectives*;

- the *participation* of the people who hold most of the information needed for analysis, and whose interest and commitment are essential if the plan is to be implemented;
- the *implementation* of small business creation projects supervised, monitored and adjusted as necessary.

A similar view is found in P. Prévost (1993), who describes six inter-related elements:
- the production of an overall development *project*;
- *decrystallization*, in other words the raising of awareness in the local community;
- the development of the necessary *credibility* by local community leaders;
- the definition of the *framework* for the overall development project;
- the setting up of *support structures*;
- the implementation of *research and development* activities.

Diagram 2.1
The transformation process: local community to entrepreneurship incubator

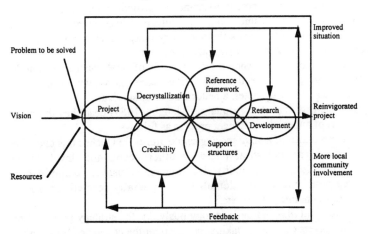

Source: P. Prévost (1993), *Entrepreneurship et développement local*, Les éditions Transcontinentales inc., Montréal, p. 36.

The process transforming a local community into an incubator for entrepreneurship is shown as a whole containing six overlapping elements each of which, although dealing with a single subject, reacts with the other elements in the system to various degrees.

All these steps, or phases, can be grouped together into three main stages, the first of which is the **information stage**. Development agents must ensure that their target clientele is properly identified, and that their objectives are well understood. The information flow between these agents and the population is bi-directional, which allows the major obstacle encountered at this stage, that of scepticism and a lack of confidence, to be neutralized. This is also the stage at which the means used to ensure the collaboration of the main partners in the project should be identified.

The next stage is the **design stage**. Specific objectives and the means of achieving them, especially through technical and vocational training, must be identified, and overall coordination must be assured by a support organization such as an economic and community development corporation or any other similar organization.

The last stage is the **implementation stage**. Recourse must be had to local savings or government assistance to provide some of the start-up capital for the first business creation projects. Close supervision by the support organization allows the necessary readjustments to be made as part of its on-going monitoring and assessment.

This type of process should give the 60% of small businesses that do not manage to survive their first five years, as shown by the data discussed in the last chapter, a better chance of survival.

As one last example, Jacqueline Mengin (1989) describes the main elements of a local development process as follows:

1 - the existence of a *body seeking applications*: in Quebec this takes the form of an industrial board or other economic development corporation, a community development assistance committee, a regional county municipality, a specially-formed group of socioeconomic players, etc.;

2 - a clear-cut *area*: as defined, obviously, by the strategy proposed by the players concerned, taking into account the coherence between the activities and the links of dependency they create;

3 - *group strategies*: decisions reflecting the wishes of various players, following the creation of alliances and exclusions. Consensus is reached following the inevitable clashes, once the necessity of reaching a decision has been accepted;

4 - *structuring*: depending on the organization of the body seeking applications, the creation of a support organization, with a varying

degree of autonomy, is indispensable, since it is responsible for the implementation of the following point;

5 - *drawing on local resources*: training-related aspects, the channelling of local savings to create or consolidate existing small businesses by calling on traditional skills, improvements in marketing procedures, and the promotion of specific advantages such as tourist attractions, etc.

This process obviously relies on the involvement of a number of players who will have various roles to play in its implementation. The following section describes the main players and the positions they occupy within the more or less structured organizational framework that guides their actions.

5.   Key players

Community development, as we have seen, involves everybody in the community, from housewives to pensioners, from parish priest to local grocer. In contrast, local development often involves, besides elected officials and representatives from business and industry, only representatives from well-established socioeconomic organizations. The latter organizations, in conjunction with business and industry, provide a given environment with the coherence required to prepare it for outside intervention. They include:

- the cooperative sector: chambers of commerce, economic development associations, employers' and business leaders' associations, cooperatives, professional organizations, citizens' committees;
- the financial sector: banks, local savings depositaries and venture capital providers;
- educational institutions, which provides special training programs for those responsible for business creation projects, or for the workers concerned;
- the print and electronic media, which disseminate information and raise awareness concerning action undertaken and priorities;
- local administration: representatives from various levels of government, and local officials.

Depending on circumstances and existing potential, other players can emerge: union organizations, research centres, big business and any other organization willing to get involved in the economic promotion of the community. Once the process has been triggered by a specific player who assumes the role of leader (often the local chamber of commerce or,

61

in Quebec, the research and development council, which has responsibility for regional-level economic dialogue and action), a partnership-based approach is set in motion. The information needed for the promotion of the various development projects filters through the various elements of a decision-making web that is increasingly referred to as the "partnership network".

5.1 The network concept

As mentioned in the previous chapter, the network concept constitutes the major innovation in the field of inter-organizational relations in recent years (Szarka, 1990). A number of recent publications underline the importance of inter-player networks, especially in connection with the circulation of information via the non-structured networks (family members, friends, personal and business contacts) on which entrepreneurs rely as they build and consolidate their business (Aldrich and Zimmer, 1986; Birley, 1985). Other writers, such as D. Maillat, O. Crevoisier and J.Y. Vasserot (1992) use the network concept as an example of the interdependence created among small businesses by their membership of a territorial production network. The territorial integration of such businesses in fact constitutes one of their shared characteristics. As a result, they can be seen as a system of interlocking networks that override local animosities thanks to the creation of integrated programs in collaboration with the territorial and national levels of government (Julien and Marchesnay, 1990).

The existence of various types of networks, bringing together the main players involved in business creation and consolidation, was highlighted at the international symposium organized jointly by the *Équipe de Recherche sur la Firme et l'Industrie* (business and industry research team) at the Université de Montpellier I and the GREPME[8]. Networks of business leaders, consumers and government and financial institutions were described, together with the almost always non-structured links existing between the various players. Given this context, the opportunities opened up by periodic meetings, such as lecture-lunches, are evident. A government representative can bring a support organization director up to date with the new possibilities offered by a subsidy program, while another civil servant can discuss a new training program with a business leader and two more business people exchange views on the relative performance of different facilities. Often such

---

8   *Petite entreprise et développement local*, under the direction of C. Fourcade, Éditions Eska, Paris, 1991.

62

meetings are the source of solutions to problems concerning suppliers, the hiring of qualified staff, new sources of capital, access to new markets, government regulations and investment assistance programs, and so on. In addition, at a more formal level, the drawing up of a development plan brings various players together in an organizational structure that tends to encourage dialogue.

In general, however, as shown in Figure 2.1 from a publication by B. Pecqueur (1989a), the network of a small business is composed of the players with which it deals on a regular basis. Clearly, this first type of network, known as a *production-based network*, involves more than the links created by buying and selling and by the search for capital, since it is part of a process of partnership-based action that can affect the economic development of its immediate environment.

Pecqueur also identifies a second category of networks, called *informal networks*, which includes family, professional and institutional networks. The family network provides what is known in the US as friendly financing, whereas the professional network generates advice and information through the experience gained in certain sectors of activity. B. Lecoq (1989) places *institutional* networks in a separate category, containing all the organizations responsible for consolidating small businesses and supporting project leaders as they go through the various stages leading up to the launching of a business.

On the other hand, B. Pecqueur, in a study of medium-sized European towns (1989b), warns against the trend of citing the network concept as a cure-all for the problems facing entrepreneurs, pointing out, rightly, that a network cannot be manufactured. In the phrase coined by C. Neuschwander (1991), a network cannot be decreed, only observed. The most that can be done is to bring various players together using existing structures. In contrast, some observers consider that the importance of networks in small business performance is minimal (Carsrud, Gaglio and Olhm, 1986; Filion, 1991). A wide variety of conceptions and convictions prevails in this area.

Despite (or perhaps because of) the abundance of references to the network, as a concept it tends to have a somewhat hazy, even unclear, outline, which goes some way to explaining the divergence of opinions. M.U. Proulx (1995), based on an extensive analysis of existing literature on the subject, attempts to clarify the discussion by making an initial distinction between the concept of *network* and that of *networking*, thus removing the confusion between the structure and its activation. In other works, the existence of the constituting elements of a network is no guarantee that the network will actually function effectively. The components needed to encourage dialogue, once set in place, can, for whatever reason, be ignored by the players concerned.

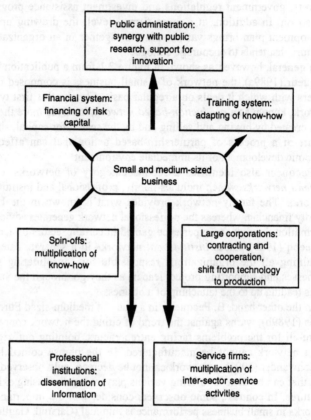

Source: B. Pecqueur, 1989, *Le développement local*, Paris Syros, p. 53.

Figure 2.1
Local or regional networking

One problem raised by references to the network concept arises from the fact that several authors use it restrictively, in relation to a specific context, while others use it so broadly that it loses much of its meaning. The lack of a theoretical framework has prevented recognition of its scientific value. Each author in turn defines categories of networks that all tend to resemble those described above. M.U. Proulx identifies three main categories, the first of which includes the *natural* networks that form the underlying structure of society. Often called social or personal networks (Johanisson, 1987), they facilitate the personal fulfillment of human resources according to social, cultural and, to a lesser degree, economic requirements. Next come the *functional* networks that include the operational framework provided by a wide range of organizations in a given environment. All players, whether private or public, are part of these networks, and in fact constitute their centres (as in networks of clients, natural resource providers, beneficiaries, and so on). The final category is that of the *utilitarian* networks, sometimes called horizontal or tactical networks, which are by their very nature highly diversified and designed to improve the action of the functional networks.

The functional networks are the basis for M.U. Proulx's research into the organization and development of regional territories. They include the intermediary structures which in recent years, in Quebec and elsewhere, have come to take the place of the omnipresent industrial parks (or zones) following the realization that infrastructures, however useful, are an essential, but not a unique, ingredient in the success of local entrepreneurship.

5.2 Small business support organizations

Industrial motel, incubator and nursery are some of the words increasingly used to describe support structures for small business creation. The first two essentially concern the provision of premises for new entrepreneurs, together with certain shared services such as telecommunications, photocopying, security, etc. A nursery provides, in addition, services to help prospective entrepreneurs design and implement their projects, through feasibility studies, help in drawing up business plans and seeking financial assistance, training in basic management, the provision of contacts with possible partners and various actions undertaken during on-going supervision of newly created businesses. Similar organizations are increasingly to be found in certain city neighbourhoods, and in semi-urban or outlying regions. However, in most industrialized nations, the most commonly-encountered structures are lightweight, strongly decentralized teams with relatively small staffs. Their characteristics have been described as follows by Michel Quévit (1986):

- they take the overall needs of each entrepreneur into consideration;
- they rely on teams of professionals that supervise businesses according to their sector of activity;

-   they select projects, entrepreneurs and action and supervise each entrepreneur's current operations;
-   they organize interface structures and set up interactive networks with other entrepreneurs in the region.

In Canada, the business development centres that formed part of the community futures committees provide an example of this approach[9]. Their role consists in supplying advisory services, loans, and loan or capital stock guarantees to prospective or existing small businesses. By positioning these committees within the "production-based network", as a *third party player* (MIS Report, 1985), their directors seek to take advantage of the various resources of the community in order to ensure that businesses get started in the best possible conditions.

Although recognizing the usefulness of these support structures, G. Macleod (1989), the founder of the *New Dawns* community development corporation in the Cape Breton town of Sydney (Nova Scotia), nevertheless expresses certain concerns. Thus, each centre, although founded as the result of a local initiative, is ultimately under the authority of the Government, and a simple change of government or cabinet shuffle can bring about its disappearance. The situation is different where the support organization results from a local initiative taken following a groundswell of community opinion, in which case the organization can count on a minimum of financial assistance and volunteer work, and thus on a minimal level of independence from government authorities.

Examples of - support organizations such as these are generally - described as being a group of local residents, under the guidance of a small number of directors who in many cases have no official title and are unknown outside the community. The dynamic they create helps to trigger the launching of a community renewal program focusing on the creation of businesses by local entrepreneurs. This approach sometimes leads to the setting up of a community development corporation with responsibility for the various stages connected with the strategic planning described above. Monetary gain, for this type of structure, constitutes a means rather than an end, for the pursuit of both social and economic objectives. A minimal reliance on outside financial assistance (after the start-up stage), as compared to contributions from within the community, tends to suggest that the approach is likely to be viable.

---

9   As explained above, they are under the authority of the former federal Department of Employment and Immigration.

The apparently successful results achieved by the *Great Northern Peninsula Development Corporation*, set up in 1987 on the model of the *New Dawn* community development corporation, are an illustration of the role played by organizations designed to assist small businesses. The Great Northern Peninsula on the island of Newfoundland extends towards the Labrador coast and has a scattered population of some 26,000 inhabitants. As in the Gaspé region of Quebec, fishing, forestry and mining have always been the principal job providers, with similar consequences: seasonal employment, an uncertain future, dependence on government handouts, an exodus of young people, etc. The realization that the breaking point had been reached occurred in 1985 for representatives from various associations, the provincial government and Memorial University, and the idea of creating a community development corporation began to take shape, achieving its final form two years later thanks to financial support from federal authorities. Placing the emphasis squarely on local resources, the corporation created one business and acquired another in 1988, involving several hundred jobs in all. The first project was, in cooperation with small forest operators, to set up a wood chip plant to meet the needs of Newfoundland Hydro. The second involved taking over a bankrupt fish packing plant that had laid off over two hundred workers[10]. In brief, the corporation's action is based on a three-fold development strategy: (1) providing services, paid for by the user, to facilitate the implementation of local projects; (2) associating with private businesses through joint investments; and (3), initiating projects using a proactive approach (MacLeod, 1989; Sinclair, 1989).

This example of economic rehabilitation, in a region handicapped both by its isolation and by its excessive dependence on primary sector activities, provides an idea of what can be achieved in rural regions when an adequate strategy is implemented. This will be discussed in the last section.

6. Small business development in rural communities

It is still common to equate rural areas with agriculture. Although during the early twentieth century agricultural activities dominated the rural landscape, nowadays the situation must be viewed from a completely

---

10 This initiative was, unfortunately, compromised by a drastic drop in fish stocks, followed by a moratorium on fishing.

different angle. A drastic reduction in the number of farms has not necessarily resulted in a similar reduction in the population in areas which have benefited from a recent wave of industrialization created by a proliferation of small businesses. The meaning of the word "rural" now extends to cover areas in which a scattered population inhabits a number of villages or small towns. In line with this view, F.W. Dykeman (1989) considers a rural area to be an area in which a certain number of small urban centres are coordinated by the same local administration. In Quebec, rural development can thus occur within the regions considered to be central regions by Quebec's planning and development office, excluding, obviously, the areas covered by medium-sized towns or cities. The exclusion also applies, in outlying regions, to the setting up or consolidation of a large-scale industrial operation, such as the pulp and paper plants found in several Quebec single-industry towns. In the latter case the municipalities concerned, through their regional county municipalities, are increasingly taking responsibility for promoting the development of their surrounding regions by encouraging the emergence of local entrepreneurship. Rural industrialization is dependent on such initiative.

6.1   Rural industrialization

Obviously, the first type of industrialization in a rural setting to capture our attention is the processing of natural resources. For some regions of Quebec, such as the Gaspé peninsula before the collapse of the fisheries, it had been suggested that a secondary, and even a tertiary, processing of fish products be introduced, beyond the traditional filleting of fish. The processing of forestry or mining products is also an avenue that can be explored, since the availability of natural resources has always supported such scenarios. However, with the advent of new technologies, proximity to resources and markets is of lesser importance in deciding where to locate an industry. Information becomes the key variable. A good illustration of this development is the twenty-employee business located in a rural area of central France. Free to set up where it chose, the company manufactures optical encoders for the arms industry (Chassagne, 1988). It is easy to imagine a similar business becoming established on a hillside in the Eastern Townships region of Quebec or alongside the Yellowstone National Park in Montana.

Rural industrialization, according to M. Quévit (1986), whose experience covers several countries, involves various processes. In some cases, a process of *scattered industrialization* occurs, characterized by traditional activities that rely on local resources and skills. The local skills pool is tapped into by means of a network of small businesses that, from the outset, avoid any kind of government assistance. This type of process has allowed the modernization of the Marshallian concept of "industrial district", discussed in the previous chapter.

Another type of process observed is the *spontaneous industrialization* process, often set in motion by young unemployed workers who refuse to accept migration as the only solution to their problems. Their collective efforts centre mainly on safeguarding jobs, an objective which can be linked to social economy and thus to the Quebec approach associated with community development (see above). Lastly, a process closer to our conception of local development is the *deliberate development* process. This involves certain key players in the socioeconomic field becoming aware of the fact that an emergency situation has developed that requires immediate action. The interaction of these community leaders (who use the cooperative sector as a catalyst for local aspirations) with government authorities is determinant, and almost inevitably results in the creation of a central structure (support organization). This organization becomes responsible for the first step of drawing up a diagnosis of the situation, followed by its first concrete actions involving the creation of small businesses. This, as we have seen, was the approach followed in Newfoundland's Great Northern Peninsula, and is based on the following elements:

- optimum use of the human resources available;
- innovative use of the resources of local institutions;
- reliance on local income and savings to reinforce production and develop local markets;
- investment in local resources, rather than mere exploitation;
- recognition of the key role played by training in the development process;
- production of a specific entrepreneurial strategy (OECD, 1988).

However, several major obstacles stand in the way of a successful conclusion to any of the above processes or the strategy described in detail. These include:

- *economic obstacles*: dependence on a traditional activity associated with the primary sector, difficulties in gaining access to sources of financing or a lack of local savings, the lack of the critical mass needed to form an integrated economic fabric;
- *social obstacles*: turf wars between a number of small communities or two small towns, suspicion of new ideas; insufficient academic or

vocational training of the workforce; mimicry of successful projects undertaken by innovative business leaders leading to saturation of the market niche;

- *geographical obstacles*: location at too great a distance from sources of information on innovative ideas and possible outlets, or from supplies, certain national markets, or training centres;
- *physical obstacles*: insufficiency of transportation infrastructures, or of adequate premises for introducing innovative projects.

The task in not an easy one, but success is possible for those who believe in their own capabilities and dare to implement a development strategy rather than wait for a miraculous (outside) investment that will solve the under-employment problem of the local community at a stroke. The following section gives an example of a micro-region that, following the contribution made by certain key players, decided to build on the basis of its own strengths.

6.2   Case study: CADC Mékinac-Des Chenaux Inc.

The Mékinac-Des Chenaux region is situated on the north shore of the Saint Lawrence River between Montreal and Quebec City, to the east of Trois-Rivières. It has a population of 26,000 divided between twenty municipalities, and covers an area of 6,338 km2, 55% percent of which consists of unorganized Crown lands. The region is composed of the Mékinac regional county municipality (the tenth poorest in Quebec) and part of the neighbouring county municipality, which were merged to meet the "critical mass" requirements under the Community Development program of the then federal Department of Employment and Immigration. The amalgamation of two different micro-regions necessarily reduces the sense of belonging of the local population, which tends to relate its history and activities to a given environment; this is a factor to be taken into consideration by local development agents.

As in most rural regions, there had been a perceptible decline and aging of the population. Agriculture, forestry and mining (the local gold mine employed around one hundred workers), together with the clothing and metal products plants, could no longer provide reasonable living conditions. An unemployment rate of over 30% and an average annual income well below the Quebec average also produced an exodus of young people, and the precarious situation led some of the more dynamic elements of the community to seek ways of reducing the socioeconomic decline that had been observed over a number of years. The setting up of a Community Futures committee was quickly seen to be an important first step.

The composition of the committee reflected the willingness of many different players (elected officials, representatives from various sectors of activity and social groups) to work together in a partnership-oriented approach. Having set the objective of reducing the unemployment rate to around 13%, the region's economic development promoters decided, in 1989, to consolidate existing activities and to identify possible job creation opportunities. First, though, the various stages of a strategic planning process had to be implemented.

An examination of the region's socioeconomic characteristics revealed that, in 1986, existing jobs were divided between the primary, secondary and tertiary sectors in the proportion of 16%, 32% and 51%. In 1993, manufacturing was mainly concentrated in the areas of timber processing (35.1%), clothing (12.2%), leather working (11.9%), food and drink manufacturing (11.7%) and furniture making (9.7%). These five sectors accounted for over 80% of the manufacturing jobs (SADC de la Vallée de la Batiscan, 1994). The region's strengths and weaknesses were also assessed through a series of interviews with industry leaders, farmers, forestry operators, representatives from public and parapublic organizations and financial institutions.

The main strengths of the secondary sector were found to be:
-   the existence of several well-established small businesses;
-   a good spread of small businesses among the various sectors of activity;
-   the availability of a qualified workforce in the leather, timber and clothing sectors;
-   a non-confrontational employment situation;
-   access to local investment capital;
-   a large population base in neighbouring regions;
-   transportation facilities.

Its weaknesses were identified as follows:
-   the vulnerability of the industrial structure, based on traditional sectors of activity;
-   a lack of infrastructures for new businesses (few industrial buildings);
-   a non-specialized, ageing workforce;
-   little commitment from the manufacturing sector in economic development organizations;
-   deficient support structures for small business creation;
-   a lack of secondary timber processing businesses;
-   no prospecting of outside investment (CADC Mékinac-Des Chenaux, 1989).

The strategy selected was based on a two-step approach. The first step involved carrying out business opportunity studies in certain specified sectors: the rearing of bullocks and exotic animals, forest farms, and horticulture. The second stage, which was never implemented, was to have involved a search for promoters willing to invest in the sectors selected. The strategy was clearly oriented towards a type of economic development in which private entrepreneurs were expected to be the main players. Despite the gulf between expectations and actual results, the new strategic plan centres on the prospecting of promoters, mainly in the food, agriculture and forest farm sectors.

The 1994-99 plan contains recommendations for each of the two communities, including suggestions concerning:
- the stimulation of local entrepreneurship through information sessions, training and business opportunity prospecting;
- the creation of a structure to assist in the financing of local initiatives;
- emphasis on the development of activities and facilities for recreational and tourist use;
- better marketing for local food and farm products (SADC de la Vallée de la Batiscan, 1994).

As we said earlier, the plan exists on paper but has yet to be put into practice. It is an example of a three-stage strategic planning process: study, design and implementation. After five years of effort and the preparation of a second plan, the process is still in its first stage. The SADC authorities are aware that the strategic planning process must be continued, that the "designers" must design and the "implementers" implement. The extended "study" phase has provided many players with opportunities to learn and clarify certain issues, and there is consensus on the fact that everything needed to "trigger" action is now in place and should shortly produce results.

7. Conclusion

Although it is generally accepted that action in the area of local development can make a significant contribution to the development of small businesses, local development is not a cure-all for all the problems encountered in the aging urban neighbourhoods and rural areas of the industrialized world. Although the victims of the on-going economic mutation must be encouraged to rely more on their own resources, indiscriminate use of the slogan "take charge of your own future" can create false hopes and lead to bitter disappointment. The road to hell is paved with good intentions, and experience has shown that, in many cases, the strenuous efforts of committed players have led to nothing except, perhaps, an opportunity to learn from their mistakes. The phrase "we'll know better next time" is sometimes heard, and in fact new players in the economic development field could have been spared some of this learning process if they had received the requisite warnings beforehand. According to the overview of the studies carried out on local development by the Economic Development Council of Canada (1989a), a lack of the information that constitutes the foundation of modern economic development is the major handicap facing communities located far from the major urban centres. To counter the relative scarcity of financial, educational and research institutions, and the absence of what J.C. Perrin (1990) calls territorial synergy, it is important to set up support organizations designed, among other things, to provide the information that is otherwise unavailable to players at the local level.

Information, though, for all its importance, cannot be effective unless the financial support needed for the emergence of new approaches is also made available, as shown in an OECD (1989b) study devoted to US examples. In connection with a type of urban development marked by the interrelation between social and economic goals, the *Illinois Neighborhood Development Corporation* (INDC) is given as an example of the involvement of various community players to respond to the needs of the population of underprivileged neighbourhoods. This alternative bank holding company controls a bank (the *South Shore Bank*), a construction company and a non-profit organization providing remedial classes. Over a 14-year period INDC programs have led to the renovation of some 6,900 rental housing units with or without the provision of financial assistance. The South Shore Bank, in addition to granting high-risk loans to large families for the renovation of their dwellings, lends money to people planning to launch a small business and helps raise the commercial profile of the area. The same OECD study contains examples of alternative businesses in the neighbourhood services field, in other words activities involving daycare, home care, remedial and support classes, protection services and other types of services generally neglected by traditional businesses with a profit-oriented approach. The South Bronx area of New York can thus boast the largest home care cooperative in the US, known as *Cooperative Home Care Associates*. The cooperative's objective is to provide home care for handicapped or elderly patients, while giving poor, mainly female, black or Hispanic workers an opportunity to work in favourable conditions. In keeping with the alternative approach, the cooperative intends to provide its employees with a place to learn and to build their self-esteem and confidence. Similarly, an official at the Washington DC organization

73

Corporation for Enterprise Development has taken the initiative of promoting the creation of small businesses by welfare recipients, an idea borrowed from various European "unemployed entrepreneur" programs and applied in the neighbourhood services field with especially encouraging results.

However, our research into the factors influencing the success or failure of alternative businesses (Joyal, 1991) support the findings of other researchers in the definition of a list of failings that cannot be ignored: a poor definition of objectives (often connected with the interrelation between social and economic goals), a lack of managerial capacity, an excessive dependence on government assistance and sector-based policy, inadequate training of managers and workers, insufficient financial resources, a poor assessment of the market and competition, a lack of medium-term forecasts, an unwieldy decision-making process based on participatory management, and so on. Most of these problems are, obviously, not confined to alternative businesses. Problems with financing, marketing and the skills of both managers and workers, in particular, are encountered by most recently-created small businesses, leading to the judgmental attitudes of the supporters of big business and old-fashioned laissez-faire.

In the view of these critics, local development (whether involving the creation of traditional or alternative businesses), costs more to implement than it can hope to generate as profit, or, at best, breaks even. S. Perry (1989) is quick to challenge this assertion, stressing the fact that the cost of local development bears no relation to the enormous amounts invested to establish businesses based elsewhere. This reasoning is based, among other things, on the three main conclusions of studies conducted by the National Center for Economic Alternatives in Washington: (1) a financial assistance program aimed at businesses in underprivileged regions can lead to positive results; (2) resources need not be concentrated only in centres of strong economic growth; and (3), people do not have to be encouraged to leave underprivileged areas to find employment.

Despite the soundness of these arguments, until a theoretical basis is established to support them, the on-going dispute between the opponents and proponents of local development is likely to continue. Although some progress has been made in this direction, much remains to be accomplished and the challenges are great, not least because of the difficulty of defining the spatial characteristics of the object under examination. In addition, the diversity and complexity of the web of links between the players in a given community make generalizations founded on the measuring instruments currently available to researchers difficult. F. Lamontagne (1989) rightly considers it impossible, given the current state of knowledge, to reach any conclusions at all regarding the superiority of present-day local development approaches as compared to those implemented in the past. In Quebec and Canada, too few examples of local initiatives, and too few analyses of their results, exist to be able to draw irrefutable conclusions. The weakness of the attempts made to assess local development constitutes a barrier to systematic assessment, especially as regards the public sector. As a result, it is important that the strengths and limits of the approach be identified, in order to better assess its potential. This will involve, first, a systematic evaluation of the local development strategies proposed; second, a distinction drawn between action taken in urban environments and action taken in rural regions; and, third, the creation of a typology to separate the various experiments and facilitate comparison and contrast, justified, in the view of Lamontagne, by the range of activities concerned.

Luckily, practice seldom lags behind theory (in fact, as we have seen, the reverse is true), and the spotlight on local development has caused M.P. Rousseau (1989), for example, to evoke the possible emergence of a new economic and territorial profession. Similarly, D.S. Douglas (1989) underlines the necessity of a multidisciplinary approach in training future local development agents. This is also the view taken by J. Lotz (1990) who, after a study mission to Scotland, comments unfavourably on the lack of programs to train these new economic players in Canadian universities[11]. Canada is certainly a fertile ground for the emergence of new businesses which, while protecting local populations against the less beneficial aspects of market mechanisms, offer researchers the materials they need to broaden the scope of their investigations.

---

11 The observation requires some qualification in Quebec, since various Master's-level programs, following the introduction of the economics and small business management program at the Université du Quebec in Trois-Rivières, provide training that should meet the requirements of local development support organizations. In France, more than a dozen university programs relate directly or indirectly to local development.

3 Small business distribution and location

"My father liked to build in Montaigne, where he was born; and in this whole policing of domestic affairs, I like to avail myself of his example, and will attach my successors to it as much as I shall be able. If I could do better for him, I would do so." Michel de Montaigne, "Essai".

1. Introduction

In the manufacturing sector, as we saw in Chapter 1, small businesses in industrialized countries went through a period of relative decline until the 1970s (Nelson, 1990, pp. 11-12). The phenomenon was generalized, even if the situation differed from one country to another. For example, in the United Kingdom, the number of businesses with less than 200 employees declined by 50% between 1935 and 1968, with a less marked decline in Japan. Since this time, however, the decline has been halted and in many countries the number of small businesses is now growing. In developing countries, where the small business concept must be viewed in a different light, small businesses have always constituted the main source of employment. The distribution of businesses by size in these countries often reflects their dual economic structure: large businesses operating in a strongly capitalized market sector, and small businesses operating in the traditional economy in local markets. The number of small businesses has, however, declined in countries that are in the process of becoming industrialized, such as South Korea, Malaysia, Singapore, etc. Thus, the continuing existence of small businesses in under-developed countries is accompanied, on the one hand, by their decline in rapidly industrializing countries, and on the other by their renewed growth in industrialized countries. In both cases, small businesses constitute an inescapable economic reality of increasing importance in terms of job creation.

Given this context, the geographical distribution and location of small businesses has become an interesting point of departure for a review of the existing literature. Few authors examine the distribution and location of businesses according to size, and although it seems reasonable to suppose that most would admit that the size of a business is an independent variable in any distribution and location model, few actually take it into account. Most rely on general location factors such as the cost of transportation, energy and raw materials, the cost and availability of labour, and the cost of transporting finished products, together with the availability of funding, government policies, and entrepreneurial spirit (Thomas, 1962). Few authors, however, in their analyses of geographical distribution, assess the weight of these factors in light of business size. Several new questions need to be asked. Do small businesses, with regard to distribution and location, behave like large or very large businesses? What is known about the spatial behaviour of small businesses? Do the distribution and location factors carry the same weight for small businesses in the decision-making process? Should a different spatial model be developed for each size of business? These are the questions that underlie this review of the literature, and our thoughts on the subject.

There is no simple answer pertaining to a list of the elements to be taken into account in business distribution and location analyses. First, the existing literature is abundant, but deficient in the area of small business. The diversity of locations is in itself a handicap, although some common points can be detected (Claval, 1976) such as the unequal geographical distribution of business inputs (relating to transportation and distance) and spatial transparency (relating to fluidity). The diversity of the businesses studied also adds to the complexity, since ideally it should be possible to distinguish between the industrial, commercial and service sectors, and to introduce other sub-categories. As stated in the introduction, small businesses cover a wide spectrum. In the manufacturing sector, it is clear that the location of a printing plant is not based on the same factors as that of a cement works. In addition, the quality and quantity of existing studies varies widely according to the types of activity covered. Lastly, analysis is further complicated by the fact that an allowance must be made for different scales of geographical analysis, since the results obviously depend on whether an international, regional or local scale is used, and on whether an entire firm on an individual establishment is being examined.

Despite these difficulties, and the variations to be taken into account according to the different small business types, we will attempt to summarize the main points of the current state of knowledge regarding the geographical distribution and location of small businesses, for various spatial scales. The chapter is divided into sections dealing with the commercial, service, and manufacturing sectors. The primary sector, including agriculture and mining, is excluded, as are construction, transportation, storage and finance (except banks). Each section is further subdivided to distinguish between geographical distribution and business location.

It is important to mark the distinction between these two fundamental concepts. In geography, the expression "geographical distribution" is passive rather than active in meaning, since, with the exception of certain new services provided by the State (such as regional environmental services), no active, deliberate distribution of commercial, service-related or industrial activities in a given territory is actually carried out. Rather, the distribution results from a series of micro-decisions made by individual entrepreneurs, and the expression takes on a passive, static meaning that describes the arrangement or distribution of a given number of objects (in this case small businesses) in space. The expression "location" refers to the identification of a place or space in which to install a given object. Thus, location studies are carried out before a commercial or industrial activity begins, whereas geographical distribution studies take place at some point after activities have begun. The term "location" is thus dynamic, whereas the term "distribution" is essentially descriptive.

After presenting a brief summary of existing distribution and location studies for commercial activities (including services for which a uniform demand exists throughout a given territory), for specific services (public and private) and for small manufacturing operations, we will underline the differences and similarities observed as regards location, especially for the purposes of analysis.

2. Geographical distribution and localization of small businesses in the tertiary sector

In this section, we will examine the main elements influencing the geographical distribution of businesses, and then the stages of a business location study. A large amount of material exists in this field, and the discussion here will be limited to a description of the essential characteristics of each model, with emphasis on small businesses. It is not our intention here to discuss the operational definition of a tertiary-sector small business (c.f. introduction) given the numerous theoretical and methodological difficulties presented by such a diversified sector of activities. The central place theory will be described first, followed by a discussion of location studies and of specific examples of certain public and private services.

2.1   A well-known distribution model: central place "theory"

The geographical distribution of businesses is a well-researched area. During the 1960s and 1970s, a number of geographers, in particular, produced empirical studies for a large number of countries in different continents, and other studies have appeared since the 1980s, giving emphasis to the perceptual and behavioural dimensions. Nevertheless, the central place model is still included in recent economic geography and marketing textbooks.

Briefly, the central place model is a conceptual corpus articulated around a number of fundamental concepts: central place, commercial area, central function, establishment, appearance threshold of a function, and geographical scope of a product or service. According to this theory, or model, a crossroads, hamlet, village or town constitutes a *central place* bringing together a certain number of functions performed by *establishments* (one or more per function). The number of functions, and thus establishments, of each central place varies according to the size of its *commercial area* (measured in terms of volume and density) and its position in the urban hierarchy. A small village has fewer functions and establishments than a large urban centre, which supplies specialized products and services for smaller centres and the surrounding agricultural zones. Each urban centre must, in order to support its specialized products and services, possess a fairly large, fairly well-populated zone of influence. In order for an urban centre to obtain the distribution of a product or service, the zone of influence must provide a *minimum customer base* that allows each business or service to generate sufficient income for its owner. This threshold is a prerequisite for the appearance of a function or establishment in a given site, and once exceeded by a certain margin, can lead to the creation of a second establishment. Through a dual process of competition and complementarity, a national space is entirely covered by a series of different-sized central places, each with its own zone of influence (Graph 3.1).

Graph 3.1
Schematic hierarchy of central places

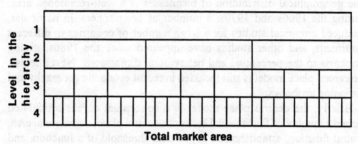

Total market area

N.B.:   Each rectangle represents one urban place

Source: Shaffer, R. (1989), *Community economics, Economic structure and change in small communities*, Ames, Iowa State University Press, 321 p.

Graph 3.1 shows the coverage of commercial areas. The higher-level centres offer the same products and services as all the lower-level centres, whereas lower-level centres offer only a restricted number of functions. The hierarchy can be symbolized by a series of overlapping hexagons (Graph 3.2), each covering the zone of influence of a village or town.

Central place theory applies not only at the regional level, but also at the urban level. Several authors (Bailly, 1984) have underlined the model's weaknesses, such as the fact that it fails to account for cost variance, consumer perception, variations in transportation modes and networks, parking availability and business hours, and distortions in commercial areas (roads, rivers, etc.). Its drawback, in short, is its static, reductionist nature. In our opinion, these points are relevant, but do not amount to actual criticism. What has been called a "theory" is in fact a "model" which has been aptly described by Peter Hagget (1973) as a representation of reality that has been idealized in order to make it clearer and more easily understood. Despite all the shortcomings defined by various authors, the model's empirical power is still as strong as when Christaller Lösch and Reilly defined its fundamental concepts. Since the model applies to an existing geographical distribution of businesses and services, it cannot be used for location analysis, but it can be used at a preliminary stage to identify possible commercial gaps in a specific urban fabric using the lists of functions established for the central places of other similar geographical and economic zones.

The central place model does not provide an explicit description of the specific characteristics of small and medium-sized businesses. It can be safely assumed that the businesses that emerge once the minimum function threshold has been attained, or that are located outside or at the limit of highly-populated areas, have smaller work forces or turnovers. For example, it is likely that businesses and services situated in low-population peripheral regions are of a small size. Because of the *geographical scope of a product*, in other words the distance that consumers are willing to travel to obtain a product or service, businesses or services providers sometimes become established even when the minimum demand threshold has not been reached. This is sometimes achieved by a business that couples two functions, such as groceries and hardware. In short, despite all the plausible hypotheses that can be put forward to explain size phenomena, the factors affecting geographical distribution do not apparently change according to business size. Nor does it appear that the size of businesses is a particularly relevant variable in their distribution, especially since in major central places big commercial enterprises exist side-by-side with tiny businesses such as convenience stores, small shops, and bakeries, particularly in Europe, sometimes in 2 or 3 square metre premises.

In addition to distribution, other elements must be taken into consideration in location studies. Ron Shaffer (1989) refers to central place theory to explain change and economic structure in small communities, even though,

"It does not provide all the details needed to determine the feasibility of a particular investment in a particular market, but it does help to collect the details necessary for community analysis." (p.125)

Graph 3.2
Overlapping market areas in a central place system

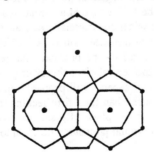

Source: Schaffer, ibidem.

2.2   Business location studies: a well-defined field

It is not our intention here to review all the studies on business location that have been published; the reader is referred to the basic works by Nelson (1958), Kane (1966), Applebaum (1968, 1974), Fenwich (1978), Davis and Rogers (1984), and Pettigrew (1989), among others. The abundance of literature in this field can be explained by the fact that location factors are clearly identified and easily weighted, especially those involving the concepts of agglomeration, function appearance threshold, accessibility, product usefulness, and satisfaction (Fielding, 1974). In addition, location analyses (see section 2.1) can be used effectively to describe the geographical distribution of businesses not only in national and regional areas, but also in urban areas (Berry, 1971). Lastly, business location is an item of major importance in feasibility studies, since it constitutes the central portion of such studies (Colbert and Côté, 1990). In agreement with the latter authors, it must be emphasized that a business location study is "more than a question of site", since it must include an examination of financial and marketing aspects. In their words,

"A location analysis is one of the components in a firm's marketing strategy, and its importance is directly linked to the financial life of the business. A location analysis can be defined as follows: an analysis of a group of geographical, economic, sociological and cultural variables, designed to assess an existing location or to select the best possible location for meeting a retail business's sales and profit objectives." (p. 8, our translation)

Locating a business involves answering, first, the following question: in which locality should the business or service be established? If the projected business will sell consumer goods, the range of possible sites is broader that it would be in the case of a specialized business or service. A bookstore requires a wider commercial area than a small grocery store. If the decision involves the selection of a locality (rather than of a specific site within a locality), the promoter can refer to the empirical results obtained using the central place theory or gravitation models. The financial and commercial aspects will probably, in such a case, be less important for an individual than for a firm seeking to establish affiliates. Personal factors, such as the place of residence, will probably play an important role in an individual promoter's decision to establish a business in a given community.

The real importance of location analysis has to do with the selection of the best site or the most advantageous location within a given locality, especially in an urban context. The first step in the analysis is an assessment of demand based on a study of demographic data, consumer spending habits and recent trends, market location and area, residential development poles, natural and physical barriers within the territory, road networks, complementary services, and so on. The next step is to estimate the theoretical and actual supply, taking into account the fact that some trade inevitably gravitates to the major urban centres. The data on supply and demand allows them to be compared and a decision to be made, either to "close a shop, maintain the *status quo*, expand, or open another sales point" (Colbert and Côté, 1990). A decision to expand requires a further analysis of the balance between supply and demand, including relatively simple calculations to determine market shares, attraction rates and the additional floor space that will be necessary or useful. A decision to open a new shop requires a projection of future sales. In short, a location analysis must allow a business's potential success to be estimated, depending on a choice of sites for each of which market potential and competitiveness have been assessed. A business location study thus contains a number of aspects, that can be resumed in a simple graph (Graph 3.3). Readers should consult Colbert and Côté for a discussion of an actual case in which the various technical studies used to analyze the feasibility of a commercial or service-oriented business are combined.

Graph 3.3
Stages in a business feasibility study

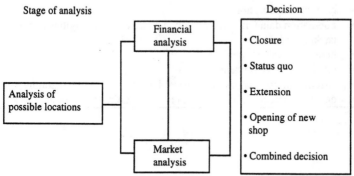

Source: Adapted from Colbert, F. and R. Côté, *Localisation commerciale*, Boucherville, Gaëtan Morin Éditeur, 152 p.

It is clear from Table 3.1 that a location study, whatever the size of the business, involves the same series of elements to be taken into consideration (listed in all the basic handbooks). Does this mean that the weighting of the various factors is the same for both small and medium-sized business projects and for large-scale projects? The head of a small business has less information, and uses it less in making a decision, than a large firm which bases its decision on a highly complex analysis. The small business owner thus faces greater uncertainty, and the chances of failure are indirectly proportional to cognitive mastery of the facts. On the other hand, the small business owner, who often lives in the region concerned, can "feel" things that go unnoticed in scientific studies. If this small business owner decides to become part of a chain, he or she can benefit from both the visibility of the chain name and from the experience of a system that has been tested elsewhere. The experience of the franchiser provides greater certainty in decisions on where to locate. According to the US Department of Commerce, survival rates for franchise outlets are 92% after 5 years, compared with 23% for independent dealers. After ten years, the respective rates are 90% and 18%. It is true, however, that franchise awarding is in itself a selective process and that results differ from country to country and depend on the type of franchise.

Table 3.1
Elements in a business location study

1. General data
• geographical location
• population data (size, occupation, age, education, religious and ethnic background, etc.)
• household characteristics
• residential development
• spatial features (natural or physical barriers, road access, zoning)
• demand characteristics (income levels, spending by category, etc.)

2. Business data
• overall demand • overall supply in terms of quality and quantity (types of products and services offered, after-sales service, etc.) • comparison of supply and demand • assessment of competition: business area, productivity, site analysis, penetration rate, attraction rate, market share, etc.
3. Customer mobility
• travel type data • time and cost of travel • parking availability • distance and accessibility

2.3 Specific nature of certain public and private services

Location studies for businesses and services have many points in common, despite the range of activities covered, because the customer pool is spread throughout the territory and is highly diversified. Since most businesses and services are designed to meet the general needs of the population, the market is characterized by a large number of buyers and sellers and the territory is divided up to allow each business to function at the lowest possible cost. Certain services, however, can be distinguished from this homogeneous group, and form a heterogeneous group of their own.

Services differ from businesses in that the role of the State is more in evidence. Since this study focuses on small businesses, the question of whether or not to include public organizations supplying services, and sometimes products, must be addressed. If they are taken into account, the location of certain small and medium-sized organizations in local communities requires examination, since they provide services such as street lighting, water treatment, public transit, land and urban planning, primary education, health care, and so on. Several trends can be observed in their location patterns.

A summary examination reveals that the location of certain services reflects the population spread within the territory. Since the population must be provided with these services, they are established where warranted by population size and density. They include health care, primary education, public housing (welfare recipients and the elderly, mobile and non-mobile), public parks, post offices, public transit and related infrastructures, police, telephone and construction permit services, garbage collection, water, sewage and electricity lines, sports facilities, and cemeteries, among others. For these services, the division of the territory is of major importance for ensuring a sufficiently large customer pool and coverage of all populated areas.

In this connection, the remarks made previously with respect to regular demand for businesses apply also to the services listed above, with an added political dimension (such as public pressure or the presence of a government MP in the territory). Service accessibility and coverage, demand density and distribution, fairness (for isolated centres), transportation costs, etc., are the major factors taken into consideration in locating the services. For example, the "optimum location" for a post office is defined by five series of factors:

-   the intensity of the demand;
-   the distance from the post office to the mail boxes where letters are collected;
-   the distance travelled by users to reach the post office;
-   the distance travelled by users to the nearest mail box;
-   political and social considerations.

This analysis for post offices reveals a number of similarities with analyses for other services (Thomas, 1982 and 1984; Eilon, 1971). The Christaller approach is a good starting point for finding the optimum location of a service for which there is a regular, sizable demand dispersed throughout the territory (Dreycke and Gilbert, 1988).

In contrast to commercial enterprises, which are generally privately-owned (except for liquor stores in Quebec and Ontario, for example, or PTT (post office) and EDF (electricity) outlets in France), the public sector provides services to relatively stable population pools that are essentially public in nature (municipalities, school boards, churches, various organizations). Whereas competition affects the private sector in that unprofitable businesses and services are often eliminated because they cannot benefit from economies of scale or for other reasons, despite their usefulness, it has less effect in the public sector where social considerations and long-term economic planning take precedence. This is illustrated by the difficulties experienced in merging municipalities in North America and *communes* in France, in closing primary schools in North American inner cities, and in the costs arising from some economies of scale, from direct or indirect subsidies to local communities, and so on.

A second group of services, which are not designed to meet a regular, large-scale demand, are characterized by a specific or emergency need, and therefore by a specific and temporary location. Examples include national defence, action taken in response to certain natural disasters (fires, tornadoes, floods, drought, pollution, infectious diseases, etc.), the preservation and safeguarding of natural and historic sites or sites of major importance, radio and television relay sites, ambulance services, and so on. In the case of the latter service, for instance, response time is obviously a major factor. The location of national museums is also based on considerations that do not depend on regular, widespread demand.

A third group of services is offered to businesses. Given their relative scarcity and the size of the geographical area served, they are mainly found in the centres of medium-sized and large cities (Beauregard, 1987; Morvan and Marchand, 1994). The study of industry-to-industry links must be extended to cover service-to-industry links. In 1982, Normand Brouillette, in a study of the Mauricie/Bois-Francs region of Quebec, demonstrated that small and medium-sized manufacturing businesses, as compared to large-scale businesses, had more links with their region for both purchases and sales, and relied more on wholesalers for their supplies. An examination of the non-material links, in other words the service links, for the same region has shown that small and medium-sized businesses are more likely to use services offered in their own region (Brouillette, 1986).

In the Greater Montreal area, Ludger Beauregard (1987) has observed a change in the location of services provided to businesses in downtown Montreal between 1970 and 1983:

"Besides the up-market filter, which tends to reserve the downtown core for the most powerful and prestigious organizations, in other words the financial institutions, a new filter has appeared in addition to "prestige": that of business size. The heart of the downtown area has become the natural habitat of large firms, measured in terms of number of employees rather than turnover, although the two are normally closely correlated. The pivotal city centre attracts large offices, relatively speaking, as well as large institutions. Big accounting, engineering, law and stockbroker firms become the neighbours of banks, trusts, insurers and financiers, ... often under the same roof." (p. 26, our translation)

In conclusion, an analysis of the service location literature, especially in connection with the services provided by local communities, underlines the need for more extensive, and more specific, research into some service sub-categories. A broad range of services exists, and several aspects must be considered.

"The "public facilities" to be located are highly diversified; they include schools, post offices, hospitals, administrative buildings, fire stations, emergency response centres, emergency services, etc. The service can be stationary or mobile (library v. mobile library), demand can be steady (primary schools), intermittent (town hall information services), or random (forest fire-fighting). There can be a need for the installation of stationary facilities, or for mobile services using fixed infrastructures. This range of possibilities explains the existence of a number of location models." (Derycke and Gilbert, p. 112)

We can therefore conclude that an examination of the distribution and location of businesses and services demonstrates that the factors of distribution and location are similar for both small businesses and large-scale operations, although market size, in some geographical zones, probably influences the size of some businesses and services. Where the market is spread out and density is low, businesses tend to be smaller than their counterparts in other zones. In this context, size is the dependent variable and the market is the independent variable. In location studies, which by their very nature place the emphasis on profit expectations for each possible site, location becomes a major independent variable, both for small businesses and big businesses. A better location corresponds to better sales, and better sales to larger premises, and vice versa. These observations cannot, however, be extended to the tertiary sector as a whole, especially in the case of the services provided by governments.

3.   Geographical distribution and location of small manufacturing businesses

Geographical distribution and location studies for small manufacturing businesses present particular difficulties for researchers and practitioners. The tertiary and manufacturing sectors differ from each other by their very nature. Whereas retail businesses and services must cater to the market as a whole, and therefore cover a given territory with a series of establishments, manufacturers are mainly concerned with processing raw materials or assembling objects, and can work from sites that are not necessarily central or median in terms of customer access. There is sometimes an advantage to be gained from proximity to sources of supply. For retail businesses, location is an essential element in being able to meet consumer demand for a product throughout the territory, while for manufacturers, the market is only one in a complex series of factors including the availability of capital and access to suppliers, raw materials, power, labour, and other businesses. Despite this distinction, certain industrial concerns have a spatial behaviour that resembles that of retail and service outlets. Cement plants and cemeteries, among others, are examples of businesses that respond to market needs and consumer location. Some services, especially those that cater to the needs of manufacturers, can have a spatial strategy that resembles that of industry.

Despite these distinctions, the spatial behaviour of small manufacturing businesses must also be analyzed in terms of geographical distribution and location. In the latter case, the analytical approach for a new business will differ from that used for the projected purchase or acquisition of an existing business.

3.1 The theory of manufacturing places: a basic model

G.B. Norcliffe (1975) was the first to propose a "theory of manufacturing places", named after the theory of central places discussed earlier. The idea was promising but difficult to develop, as we will see later. Norcliffe's work stems from the weakness of the models developed in the wake of the work of Weber (1909). The explanatory factors presented by Weber were no longer as relevant in the 1970s as they had been at the beginning of the century, and the reduction in transportation costs, the relative decline of heavy industry in the secondary sector, technological innovation, the substitution of raw materials and energy sources, and the importance of added value, among other factors, had rendered Weber's model obsolete. The new industrial context stimulated Norcliffe's interest in correcting the deficiencies of the old model to obtain a "better explanation". He first identified three factors that he saw as being important for industrial location, both then and in the future: the availability of infrastructures, internal and external economies of scale, and industry-to-industry exchanges. In the first category, he stressed the importance of electricity, water, wastewater sewers, environmental services, and transportation infrastructures, and concluded that major urban centres had a clear advantage, even before economies of scale were taken into account. As for internal and external economies, they were most readily available in major urban centres which could provide complex technology and modern marketing services, and where business decisions are based more on considerations of minimized risk rather than of cost. Lastly, the third element underlined the necessity and importance of personal contacts between upper-level managers, facilitated by the networks existing in large cities and by the necessary distinction drawn between production units and administrative units where important decisions are made in industrial concerns.

The various factors observed by Norcliffe in the literature and in the field are most apparent in big cities and in the industrial heartland. Their combined effects result in a reinforcement of the industrial areas of existing manufacturing-based cities. The relationship between industry and cities needed to be articulated, and Norcliffe's analysis contains the following ideas:

- the existence of a differentiated and delimited territorial economy;
- the existence of one or more industrial zones or "manufacturing belts";
- the existence of a network of towns and cities within the manufacturing belt.

In order to define the relation between the spatial structure and the distribution of industrial concerns, Norcliffe used a classification based on the work of Wallace (1972) and Törnqwist (1968), that classified industrial functions into four categories:

a) processing, characterized by the input of raw materials (agricultural products, mineral products, timber, etc.). The manufacturing firms in this sector of activities are located both in the industrial heartland and in the hinterland, and also formed the basis for Weber's industrial location theory (see infra);

b) fabrication, characterized by the input of processed materials that require additional transformation. Output is mostly in the form of intermediate or semi-finished products. These manufacturing firms tend to be located in the heartland;

c) integrative manufacturing, in which the input undergoes little transformation before being assembled into a finished consumer product. This type of manufacturing is mainly located in the central manufacturing zone;

d) administrative activities, with neither input nor output, unless involving research and development. These activities require an advantageous site in the central zone.

As Norcliffe mentions, these different industrial activities can be located in the same building, and administrative activities in particular often share premises with one of the other three categories. After presenting this classification, Norcliffe describes the relation between

90

cities and specific industrial characteristics. Four variables and their interrelations are examined:

- factory size;
- factory function (processing, fabricating, integrative activities or administration);
- the industrial type or sector involved;
- the size of the city, which becomes an independent or explanatory variable.

Norcliffe presents a summary of the relationship existing between city size, on the one hand, and the function, size and sector of activity of a factory, on the other (Graph 3.4). With respect, first, to the relationship between factory size and city size, he concludes as follows:

"The anticipated relationship between plant size and size of town is summarized thus: a minimum threshold size of town exists for plants of any given size, and towns below the threshold size are not likely to be selected as locations, so that large plants tend to be confined to large towns. This does not imply that the plants located in large towns are exclusively large ones; small plants may be located in towns both large and small because their minimum threshold is commensurately small. The relationship will be violated in cases where plants have grown over a long period and have come to dominate a town." (Norcliffe, 1975, p.42)

If we follow Norcliffe's line of reasoning, it would appear that big corporations become established in or close to big cities because they thereby gain access to economies of scale, specialized services in the fields of technology, marketing, transportation, and sophisticated advice. On the other hand, small and medium-sized cities are unable to attract big businesses because the geographical, social and economic disturbances would be too great, given the lack of high-level or large-scale infrastructures.

The relationship between manufacturing function and city size tends to show that administrative and assembly functions are concentrated in big cities, although not exclusively, and also in the biggest businesses. Processing activities, on the other hand, tend to be typical of the hinterland and of smaller cities. Lastly, medium-sized cities tend to be characterized by the processing of raw materials and the production of semi-finished products.

The relationship between city size and manufacturing sector has received little attention, but has been studied by Norcliffe. Certain

91

businesses, in order to gain access to specialized services, tend to locate in big cities, as do other industries such as car factories, shipyards, steelworks, aircraft factories and breweries. Small jewellery businesses also tend to concentrate in big cities. Norcliffe points out that more research is needed in this area.

Graph 3.4

A summary of the proposed relationship between city size and the function, size and activity of a plant

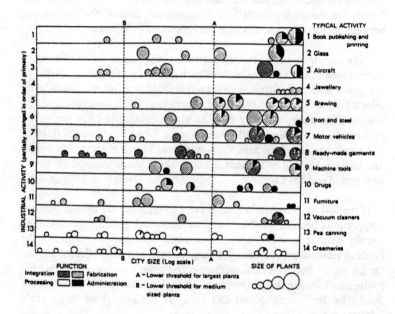

Source: Norcliffe, G.B. (1975), *A theory of manufacturing places* in L. Collins and D.B. Walker (eds.), Locational dynamics of manufacturing activity, London, John Wiley and Sons, p. 19-57.

After setting out the theoretical aspects of the problem, Norcliffe describes several empirical elements that support his view. We will examine only the relationship between factory size and the size of the city in which it is established. Norcliffe states that for 69 towns in the south-west of England in 1964, there was a strong positive correlation between the size of the largest factory in the town and the size of the town (see Graph 3.5). In the same region, an analysis of new factories with over 99 employees established between 1956 and 1964 gave similar results, since towns with less than 50,000 inhabitants, which accounted for 37% of total manufacturing jobs, were selected as the location for only 16% of the jobs created by new *large* factories. It is therefore possible to deduce that new, small factories tended to become established in urban centres with less than 50,000 inhabitants.

Graph 3.5
The relationship between the population of the largest town and the employment in the largest plant for 69 functional urban areas in South-West England in 1964

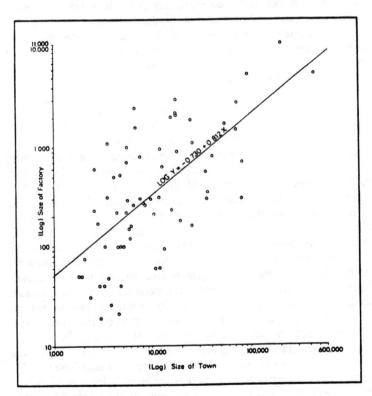

Source: Norcliffe, 1975, p.49.

93

In conclusion, Norcliffe attempts to define a theory for factory distribution using the same model as Christaller's central place theory. The new theory draws on the availability of infrastructures, internal and external economies, and person-to-person links in the technological context of developed western countries. Whereas in Christaller's theory space is divided into market zones, in manufacturing place theory it is subdivided into two zones, the central zone (the heartland) and the peripheral zone (the hinterland), on which the urban network is superimposed. The notion of hierarchy in Christaller's theory is replaced by an ordinal classification of factories and towns by size, with small and medium-sized businesses gravitating to small and medium-sized towns and large and very large businesses gravitating to large towns. The difference between the two theories lies in the level of importance assigned to the market. Although manufacturing businesses designed according to market needs do exist, this factor is increasingly being replaced by factors relating to input (industrial links, infrastructures, internal and external economies, social and cultural services, etc.). For small and medium-sized businesses, Norcliffe's theory underlines the correlation between business size and town size, and characterizes businesses on the basis of their industrial function, whether processing or assembly.

The results of Norcliffe's theory appear somewhat limited, since, to begin with, the town/factory relationship based on size is either redundant, leading to a chicken-and-egg situation (do small businesses beget small towns or vice versa?) or, at best, random, since large numbers of small businesses are in fact situated in large towns and, in addition, their activities are not limited to processing and assembly. More empirical elements are needed to support Norcliffe's hypotheses. The model contains an interesting spatial perspective, but neglects the historical side to industrial development, especially since it applies mainly to recently-populated and industrialized countries such as the USA and Australia. In addition, since Norcliffe does not examine the internal factors influencing management decisions, his model is basically deterministic, relying on environmental criteria and limited data for each factory (size, function, and type of activity). Lastly, he fails to take into account the negative economies of scale (in urban centres) discussed in Chapter 1, that encourage many firms to leave the city. In short, the manufacturing places theory is closer to a factory distribution model than to a theory of business location. His criticism of Weber-based models loses some of its pertinence, since they are actually location models. In this connection, Norcliffe fails to dispel entirely the ambiguity existing between distribution studies and location analysis, and his remarks on the dynamic or non-dynamic nature of his manufacturing places theory could be reformulated and corrected accordingly. Another approach than Norcliffe's is needed in order to evaluate the location theories developed on the basis of the work carried out by Weber.

3.2   Classic Weber-based location models

The early twentieth century saw the creation of numerous general models addressing the location of production activities. Von Thünen formulated a well-known description of concentric agricultural zones surrounding towns, with variables based on the market prices for certain products, transportation costs, production costs, product perishability, market size, and so on. The interest of Von Thünen's model lies in its simple, coherent, descriptive and comprehensive formulation of the distribution of agricultural zones. In 1909, the now famous work of Alfred Weber introduced a similar model to describe the location of manufacturing businesses. This is the model to which all the nuances and distinctions introduced later apply, and in any analysis of the location of manufacturing industry, a comparison with Weber's model constitutes a compulsory first stage.

In contrast to primary-sector activities such as agriculture and mining, land is not a basic element in manufacturing. Other elements determine the location of a factory, especially transportation costs for energy, raw materials, a low-cost workforce and the cost of delivering finished products to various markets. Transportation costs, in turn, depend on the availability of various forms of transport and on technological progress. An advantageous location can, in the space of a few years, lose its attraction following the introduction of a technological innovation in the field of transport.

Alfred Weber produced a schematic representation of the links between the various factors influencing location. Since processing activities rely on both raw materials and market outlets for finished products, three locations are possible: close to the raw materials, close to the market outlet, or a combination of the two. Finding the most advantageous location depends on two variables: the transport costs in terms of the distances to be travelled (Table 3.2), broken down into transport costs for supply, and transport costs for distribution. The technical solution involves calculating the total transport costs, both for raw materials and for deliveries (Graph 3.6).

95

Table 3.2
Transport cost variables

- distance from market outlet
- distance from raw materials
- degree of dispersal of raw materials and market outlets
- type of product; transportability, unit cost, perishability, hazard level, handling, size, etc.
- quantity or volume to be transported
- means of transport: average cost per unit of distance, competition from other means of transport, complementarity and integration of means of transport, return trip cost, etc.

Graph 3.6
Industrial location on the basis of transport costs
(2-site case)

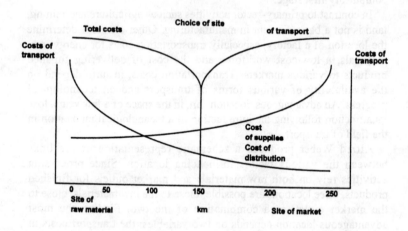

If the number of raw materials sites increases, the technical solution becomes more difficult (Graph 3.7). For example, if the energy source and the raw materials are situated in different locations, the calculation of transport costs must be shown, not on a graph, but on a map including the geographical coordinates and value "Z", "transport costs". In this situation, the most advantageous location for a factory is the centre of gravity of the triangle ABC, determined by calculating transport costs and specifying the site where they are at a minimum. For example, in Graph 3.7, for each point in the space, the transport costs associated with a given production can be calculated. Lines of equal transport costs, called isolines, can be drawn and used to specify the point at which the attraction of the market outlet, raw materials and energy source balance.

Graph 3.7
Weber's industrial location triangle

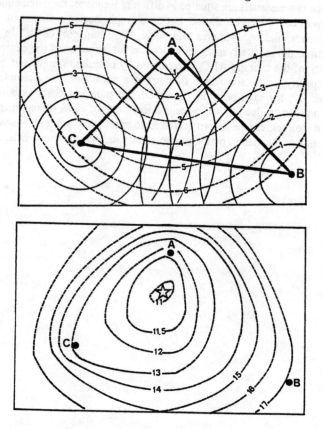

Key:
A   raw material source
B   energy source
C   market
∩   lines 1 2 3: transport cost isolines from A, B and C
☆   most advantageous location

Source: Claval (1976). As stated by Paul Claval (1976), *Éléments de géographie économique*, Paris, Éditions M. Th. Génin, 361 p.

"..the calculation is particularly simple for an iron and steel works, which needs one ton of coal and one ton of ore to obtain one ton of iron; the location point is at the junction of the lines bisecting each side of the triangle. If more energy is needed, the point will be closer to the source of energy. If the finished product is heavier than the raw materials and energy used to produce it, the factory will be drawn towards the market." (p. 82-89, our translation)

Weber's work has been refined by subsequent researchers, but has also been subjected to a barrage of criticism. It remains useful for the updating of transport costs in location studies. The schematic, simplistic nature of Weber's model has attracted the most criticism, but Weber, in the words of Claude Manzagol (1974a):

"... has received the treatment reserved for pioneers, and his work has been attacked from all sides. It has aged, however, mainly because of the progress made by the industrial system. The emphasis formerly placed on transport costs has disappeared, first because of the technological improvements that have reduced those costs, and second because of the extension of the product chain. The first characteristic of the neo-technical phase is the use of light, high-value materials, and high-value-added processing. The proportion of *tied industries* has thus decreased greatly, whereas industries that are free (by which we mean not a complete absence of constraints but a break with old-fashioned determinism) multiply. Location decisions today include a multitude of other elements that do not invalidate Weber's approach, once it has been reformulated and equipped with new mechanisms, as can be seen in some linear programming studies carried out recently." (p. 294, our translation)

Other factors also intervene in the location decision-making process, such as the wish to maximize profits (and not minimize costs as in Weber's model), market potential, agglomerating forces, and social, cultural and political factors.

The excellent work of Manzagol (1974a, 1974b and 1980) cannot make up for the lack of theoretical and empirical studies of small manufacturing businesses, and especially very small businesses launched by dynamic entrepreneurs. The non-existence of any serious investigation into small business location can be traced, in our opinion, to a lack of interest (at least until recently) in the less visible elements of the industrial landscape, and probably also to the low demand for industrial location studies from small business entrepreneurs. The last section of this chapter will therefore deal with research into small business location in more detail.

4. A more realistic approach to small business location

The above discussion of models describing the distribution and location of tertiary-sector and industrial activities is by no means exhaustive; the models presented were selected on the basis of their overall value and their reliance on fundamental variables. We can now turn to a more in-depth examination of these models, and suggest directions for future research, with emphasis on the specific field of small businesses, particularly small manufacturing businesses. We will first recapitulate the discussion so far.

4.1 Overview of previous discussion

After examining the models presented, their failure or inability to deal with the specific location problems of small businesses can be linked to:

- a *deterministic approach* to geographical distribution analysis and location studies, as revealed by the emphasis placed on "spatial geometry" and structural factors. The large numbers of small businesses makes an overly mechanistic, deterministic approach unreliable;
- the ambiguity surrounding the notions of *site* and *location* in analysis of location factors;
- the lack of a clear distinction between *distribution* models and *location* models, especially in the work of Norcliffe, who situates his distribution model with classic location models;
- the low priority assigned to the *temporal dimension*, since the dynamics of a small business can lead to relocation decisions spaced out over time;
- a *neglect of the personal factors* influencing a small business location decision, such as proximity to, and availability of premises at, home;
- a failure to assess the *influence of industrial mutations* on the growth, decline and closing of small businesses;
- an emphasis on *big business* rather than on small business, in conjunction with a clear emphasis on economies of scale and agglomeration, and economic considerations;
- a reliance on *classic location factors* for small manufacturing businesses, such as market forces, raw materials, and energy sources,

whereas structural changes in the industrial world have upset the order of priority (technology has become a major element) and introduced new factors (contracting out);

- discussion of the *location* aspect as *one element among many* in the decision-making process, as can be seen in a number of the business plans examined.

These more or less dynamic deficiencies are not corrected by the models described, mainly because of their dynamic nature, and the deterministic nature of the geographical distribution models. Another lesson that can be drawn from the preceding analysis concerns the fundamental distinction between manufacturing activities and tertiary-sector activities (Table 3.3), which can be more easily analyzed in terms of location. Location factors tend to lead to the major concept of centrality, whereas for manufacturing businesses, the large number of location factors makes the formulation of general principles difficult. In addition, business opportunities are harder to assess in the industrial sector as compared to the tertiary sector, especially if the entrepreneur intends to create a new product or invent a new process. In the tertiary sector, innovation carries less weight, since it generally concerns a new way of presenting a product or service (Table 3.3).

Table 3.3
Fundamental distinctions, as regards location, between tertiary sector activities and manufacturing

	Manufacturing activities	Tertiary-sector activities
At the pre-startup stage	• Idea for a new product ("heavy" innovation)	• Idea for a new way to present a product or service to the consumer ("light" innovation)
	• Idea for a new industrial process	• Infrequent "heavy" innovation (such as computer software)
	• Emphasis often placed on the innovative idea rather than on the business opportunity	• Emphasis placed on business opportunity
At the location stage	• Factors relating to a multitude of aspects including input and supplies	• Mainly market-related factors (centrality, accessibility, visibility, customer base)
	• Factors generally related to a specific market (relatively few purchasers)	• Generally "scattered" market (high dispersion)

In addition, the distinction between geographical distribution and location is fundamental (see Table 3.4). The models associated with each type are complementary, although each category has its own goals. A clear distinction must be made to dispel any ambiguity in a review of the literature and research work. Norcliffe, in particular, fails to dispel the ambiguity and is thus vulnerable to criticism of his manufacturing place theory.

Among the other lessons to be gained from the models examined is the advantage of a location analysis based on specific geographical scales (Graph 3.8). A large firm makes a decision to locate first in a given region, then in a given locality. It must then select a site for its business. An entrepreneur launching a small manufacturing business, especially at the start-up stage, does not normally make the decision in the same order. These considerations bring us to an examination of the variety of decision-making processes for business location, going beyond the rigid framework of geographical scales illustrated in Graph 3.8.

Table 3.4
Comparison between geographical distribution studies and location studies for small businesses

Characteristics	Location studies	Distribution studies
Type of analysis	Study carried out at the pre-startup stage, at the beginning of the business creation stage and before establishment	Study carried out after the creation of several businesses
Origin of models	• Demonstration of the player/entrepreneur relationship in a partially defined environment (*a priori* model) • Dynamic decision-making process	• Description of a geographical distribution (*a posteriori* model) • Emphasis on static model
Examples of analytical tools	• List of factors • Assessment and weighting of location factors • Maps, tools for research and decision-making • Impact studies for the business and the environment	• Various distribution "coefficients" • Map as a tool of representation • Correlation techniques to explain geographical distribution

Graph 3.8
Geographical scales in the business location decision-making process

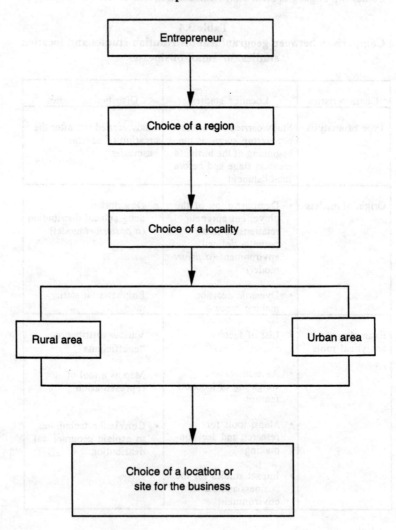

4.2 Business location and a multiple decision-making process over time

Business location studies are essential because location has long-term effects and influences direct and indirect costs. The degree of vulnerability of a small business in the marketplace can depend on the suitability of its location, especially in the tertiary sector. The low survival rates of small and medium-sized businesses, particularly small businesses, create problems for researchers attempting to generalize location factors and propose plans of action. 80% of small businesses close down during their first ten years of existence, although the percentage, as we saw in Chapter 1, must be treated with caution since the survival rate of entrepreneurs is a lot higher, and closure does not always mean bankruptcy. It is difficult to reconcile the need for practical models with the lack of data on the factors influencing the survival of small businesses, and the role played by their location. Despite these drawbacks, however, the usefulness of location studies cannot be questioned.

To explain this contradiction, the *first step* is to examine the characteristics of the decision-making process for the location of a small business and to compare them with the process used by a large company. Table 3.5 summarizes these differences. In the case of a small business, the location decision is often made by a single person using less, and less fully analyzed, information, whereas in the case of a large company, the decision is made by a team and involves the deployment of extensive financial and human resources before the decision is made.

The *second step* is to circumvent certain difficulties by analyzing small business location on the basis of the various stages of a business's development, from production start-up to maturity or closure (Julien and Marchesnay, 1995). A given entrepreneur, or small business owner, is not necessarily involved in each of these stages, since he or she may have bought or inherited an existing business, purchased or opened a franchise, obtained a dealership, etc., thereby avoiding the pre-startup and startup phases. Another entrepreneur may not experience the later stages of development, having sold or merged the business. A third will look for a more advantageous location following an expansion to meet increased demand. Should the existing premises be extended, or should be business be relocated in the same, or a different, locality? The question of location will never affect some other entrepreneurs, if the small plant to be established (as a production or retail unit) is a branch of a larger business that has already made a location decision.

Table 3.5
Decision-making process for location according to size of business

Small business	Big business
• Large number of entrepreneurs/decision-makers because large number of businesses	• Few decision-makers because few businesses
• Decision often made:	• Decision often made:
- By a single person	- By a team
- With restricted financial resources	- With extensive human and financial resources
- Using intuitive, often insufficient and even deficient information	- Using better-quality information (although sometimes received too late)
- On the basis of unrefined information, except when obtained through a network	- Using more structured information
- On the basis of reasons unconnected with the business	
• Location based on decisions that are harder for researchers to discover	• Location based on a more rational choice of criteria providing better accessibility for researchers

The difficulties encountered in analyzing small business location decisions at the pre-startup stage are different from those encountered at other stages in the business's development. The pre-startup phase can be subdivided into four stages, corresponding to four distinct series of actions:

- from the exploratory studies of a business idea or opportunity, up to the definitive acceptance of the idea or opportunity;
- from the preparation of a business plan, up to community support for the entrepreneur;
- the search for a business site;

106

- the establishment of a workshop or the outfitting of a shop or service (Graph 3.9).

As shown in Graph 3.9, observation is difficult at the pre-startup stage. Information must be collected *a posteriori* through interviews with entrepreneurs. At this stage, location is often a secondary aspect when compared to other more important elements such as product or process design, opportunity analysis, the outfitting of a workshop, etc. Little attention is paid to the choice of a location, since the entrepreneur usually selects a site near to, or in, his or her home.

If the business is established and grows normally with an expanding market, the entrepreneur may consider extending the premises or looking for larger premises. At this point, relocation in an industrial zone or a more spacious building may be considered. Given the costs involved in such a move, the entrepreneur will normally make a more careful decision than at the pre-startup stage, based on a comparative analysis of several possible sites and/or consultation with various resource people (such as a bank manager). Table 3.6 shows a schematic representation of reasons for the location/relocation of a small manufacturing business, according to the stage of development reached.

Graph 3.9
Location decision during the four stages of the pre-startup phase

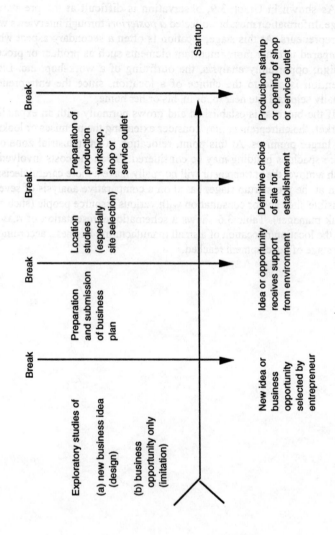

Table 3.6
Location of a small manufacturing business: A decision process in several stages

Characteristics	1. Pre-start-up and start-up	2. Growth	3. Maturity
Study and decision about location by the entrepreneur	• Little or no study • Location, a secondary aspect • Focus on product and production • Decision often individual	• Problem of growth: expansion or relocation? • Consideration of various sites • More accurate analysis of factors • External consultation or team decision	• Problem of adapting to increased competition: location as a factor for minimizing cost • More detailed analysis of the advantages of different sites • Better knowledge of factors • Analysis shared by several players (team)
Site	• Usually close to residence • Nurseries in some cases • Indifferent to location (rural or urban)	• Possible migration to industrial zone • More visible location	• Migration to best industrial zone (according to product cycle) • Difference of interest in rural and urban environments
Reasons and factors for location	• New idea (product, process, etc.) • Existence of a business opportunity (new distribution network, new market, etc.) • Availability of premises nearby, at low cost • Minimization of risks and costs (proximity to residence)	• Enterprise development becomes a factor requiring a change of location which becomes a dependent variable	• Location: factor for minimizing costs or maximizing profits (location becomes an independent variable)

As can be seen in the schematic summary shown in Table 3.6, each new phase requires a new managerial approach to questions of location. Each stage has its own problems, and the entrepreneur has to adapt his or her attitude and behaviour accordingly. The table also underlines the need for research into the decision-making dynamic in relation to location, based on the work of Filley (1978), Steinneetz (1969), Gasse (1989a; 1989b), and Marchesnay and Julien (1989). All the above have two main weaknesses: a lack of data on the situation preceding the actual startup, and not enough detail on the characteristics of the site chosen. Much empirical research is needed to fill out the schematic outline of Table 3.6.

At the third stage, the business can be required to change its location because of competition from other entrepreneurs who have seized on the opportunity to manufacture a similar product (the mimicry process). At this stage, the entrepreneur is more aware of the financial stakes in the sector of activity, has more experience, has often established a team of competent staff, and has developed a business network, and therefore can base a relocation decision on a greater number of elements. The decision will often be made jointly as a result of the delegation of power and functional decentralization characterizing the second stage of development, or will be based on outside advice. This is also the stage at which location becomes an independent variable for maximizing business profits, whereas in earlier stages the state of the business often determines location. This is the kind of research hypothesis that needs to be verified.

In addition to the analysis of location according to the stages of a business's development, especially small manufacturing businesses, another field in which work is needed is the *identification and assessment of the reasons for selecting a location using a more precise classification of business types*. Traditional classifications based on the type of industrial product produced lack definition, and are of little use in describing and gauging the various location factors. Typologies based on input and output are more relevant, but have lost some of their empirical power. A more useful, although far from perfect, type of classification could be based on a series of criteria including geographical market categories (local, regional, national, international and planetary), the degree of market dependency (sub-contracting, proximity requirements), product transportation difficulties, technological level attained, type of network (network of small manufacturing businesses associated for production purposes, technological network, research centres, international cooperation, as discussed in Chapter 2), degree of product specificity (market niche), and services to businesses (venture capital, transportation links).

These observations bring up the problem of the conceptual approach adopted for small businesses, especially small manufacturing businesses. Can the approach be renewed in order to isolate elements stable enough to guide the actions of future entrepreneurs and suggest new decision-making methods? This is the question that will be examined in the next chapter.

4.3   Methodological considerations for small business location studies

To better address the small business location theme (especially in the field of geography), there is an urgent need to review the conceptual approach for small businesses by analyzing the relationship between entrepreneurs and their environment. One question often raised in conventions and symposiums is this: what role is played by territorial structure in the creation and development of small businesses? The question, as it stands, is badly formulated and contains a measure of ambiguity, and so cannot be properly dealt with. It would be easier to address if posed as follows: what kind of relationship does an entrepreneur have with his or her immediate and more distant environment (in the extended meaning of the word)? This removes the simplistic, geographical and environmental determinism. Both environment and territorial structure may be essential conditions for the emergence of entrepreneurship, but they are by no means the only conditions. The actual environment is in fact less important than the perception that entrepreneurs have of it, taking into account their culture and the tasks facing them within the business. Attention must be given to the transactions between entrepreneurs and the environment, with or without the help of a network. The available, accessible information must be filtered, since the processing of that information is limited by the complexity of the factors to be taken into account, the range of possibilities for weighting the factors, the difficulty of measuring them, and the abundance of data to be collected, among other things. In this context, entrepreneurs rely on multiple strategies, and change them over time according to their own development and that of their business and the environment. The concepts of players and systems must be introduced if the question of location is to be properly understood (Crozier and Friedberg, 1977). Researchers must consider the whole player/entrepreneur dynamic in relation to the environment, since they are in fact performing strategic management functions that reflect the development of the business and changes in the environment. The teaching of strategic management skills is essential to studies of industrial location. As defined by Louis Jacques Filion (1990), this type of management is "the group of decisions and activities that determine the progression of the business in relation to its environment".

Since the type of relationship with the environment depends on the entrepreneur's own representations, the compulsory filtering of the relationship through the various functions of the business cannot be neglected (Graph 3.10). The entrepreneur is at the meeting point of the resources of the community and the opportunities of the market, thanks to a combination of the specific resources needed to ensure the future or the expansion of the business. To identify location factors and develop models, information collection must be centred on entrepreneurs, rather than on a uniform space as in traditional location theories. Instead of developing a group of theoretical postulates concerning space, we must substitute a group of hypotheses concerning the representations, attitudes and behaviour of entrepreneurs in environments that can vary greatly in terms of quality and quantity, since they establish a global relationship (neither total nor analytical) between the variables of the environment and the characteristics of their current or projected business. The proper operation of the business guarantees the unity of their analytical approach to the environment. To expose the relationship, the researcher must count more on interviews with entrepreneurs than on the aggregates of variables by industrial group or sector of activity provided by government services and professional associations.

Graph 3.10
Environmental perspective of the entrepreneur

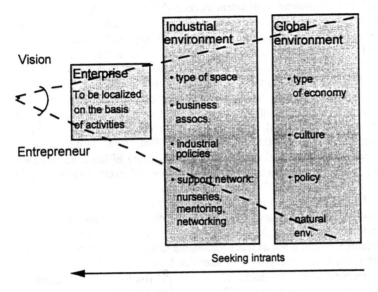

Small business location studies, then, together with distribution studies, must take into account the multiple relationships of entrepreneurs with their environment, not only as regards the use of resources (input) and the market (output), but also in terms of their representations, the way in which they analyze information, their decisions, and their strategy for action. Once these relationships have been studied, it will be easier to identify the reasons for small business location decisions, especially at the initial startup stage. An emphasis on the decision-making process will produce a more detailed, less structural approach to small business location and to the wide variety of solutions existing in this field.

4.4   New fields of study

A large amount of research will have to be undertaken to correct deficiencies observed in the small business location literature, not only along the lines discussed above, but also to take recent industrial mutations into account.

The first reason for the existence of these deficiencies lies in the changes that have occurred in the industrial environment of businesses.

The last fifteen years have seen major industrial re-deployment, a decline of traditional industrial zones (sometimes to the benefit of new industrial nations), an opening up of world markets (North American free trade and post-1992 Europe), the creation of new industrial zones (business incubators and nurseries, industrial motels, high-tech business parks), and technological evolution. As one example, the incubator phenomenon has resulted in a reduction in the risks associated with small business location, and the data on small business survival should be updated.

A second reason for the current lack of understanding of small business location results from the fact that the importance of the main location factors most frequently cited in the literature has been in constant decline for the last thirty years. Tight flows to cut down on inventories, small business flexibility, and quality of life considerations for workers, have become part and parcel of every entrepreneur's location concerns.

Lastly, the fact that researchers are moving on from deterministic and mechanistic conceptions should be mentioned. A new, more open approach means that the object of the research must be redefined. For example, would it not be more reasonable to study location reasons (with reference to the entrepreneur) rather that location factors (with reference to resources and the market)? Should not (human) organizations be considered before factories? The word organization evokes evolution over time, and a possible location/relocation cycle (migration). Space and time, then, (the location and development of the business) constitute the two complementary dimensions to be developed. With respect to time, numerous business life-cycle studies exist, but they have not been matched by far-reaching empirical research (Dainow, 1991). The limits of this approach were discussed in the introduction. As Dainow states,

"Although there is evidence that companies become more formal in their structures and procedures as they age and grow (Mintzberg), there are no empirical studies known to the author which have demonstrated a method for selecting companies at the same life cycle stage in order to verify that theorized changes are, in fact, taking place". (p.7)

There is a need for a comparative study of the different stages in a business's development and its location/relocation decisions. Every location study should, in principle, be based on a minimum knowledge of business development, although development is not always synonymous with growth from small to big business.

Very small and small business share a common characteristic that merits attention: their survival rate in the years following establishment.

What role does location play in survival rates and business closures? More location analyses exist for businesses that have survived the first few difficult years (as one might expect), despite the fact that more small businesses in fact disappear. Several studies, including that by Kirchhoff (1992) seem to show that their is no link between survival and location.

Lastly, an analysis of the literature shows that there is a need for location models for small manufacturing businesses. Many studies have been produced on small businesses in the tertiary sector, and researchers have identified many items to fuel the decision-making process. In contrast, the existing literature contains no coherent framework for reasons influencing the location decision of small manufacturing businesses. Empirical research is also needed into the actions of the owner-operators and entrepreneurs behind small manufacturing businesses to attempt to establish a typology taking into account, at the very least, business development stages and client strategies.

5.   Conclusion

This analysis of small business location is obviously incomplete, since several activities such as farming, mining, construction, finance, and transportation and storage have not been dealt with. For businesses in the tertiary sector, a quick review of the literature has revealed that effective models do exist, but the distribution and location of small manufacturing businesses contains many unknown factors. More detailed research could probably lead to the establishment of an empirical typology of small manufacturing businesses using a combination of location factors. Priority should be given, however, to location analysis rather than to distribution studies. Another field of research that offers interesting possibilities, especially in Western countries currently experiencing a dismantling of the welfare state, is that of local public services.

These suggestions for possible future research are not intended to lessen the importance of the points made by Ron Shaffer (1989) in a book about small communities:

"This decision process reflects a mixture of objective and subjective weights for the various factors in the decision. As the firm's location decision moves from the general region to the more specific community level, the subjectivity of the decision-making increases."

Location factor studies enumerate critical influences in the location decision. These critical factors vary by level of selection (regional vs.

site), type of business (manufacturing vs. non-manufacturing), and type of location change contemplated (new start, branch, or relocation). Firms can be categorized as input-oriented or market-oriented or somewhat indifferent. Orientation means that certain characteristics become extremely important in the location decision and are prerequisites to the plant's profitable existence. Failure to meet prerequisites means that the firm will not locate at a particular site (Shaffer, 1989, p. 70).

However, the most important progress made in the last ten years is constituted, in our view, by the theoretical and methodological advances summarized in the last part of this chapter.

4 Entrepreneurship: entrepreneurs and small business owner-managers

"My book is still a book. Except that when I start renewing it to prevent purchasers from leaving empty-handed, I make it my duty (as it is only a poorly-laid mosaic) to add some additional thing. These are only extra weights, which do not negate the initial form, but which give a special lift to each of the following forms, by means of some ambitious subtlety." Michel de Montaigne, "Essai".

1. Introduction

Any discussion about small business requires a discussion about small business owner-managers, and we cannot talk about small business owner-managers without also talking about entrepreneurs. The approaches and methods used have varied between countries and between continents. In Great Britain for example, from Bolton (1971) until the 1980s, much was said about owner-managers (Stanworth, Westrip et al., 1982; Stanworth and Gray, 1991), but since then attention has shifted increasingly to entrepreneurs (Burns and Dewhurst, 1989; Birley, 1989; Deakins, 1996). In the United States both subjects are addressed, but entrepreneurs have gained favour as a research field (Kent, Sexton et al., 1982; Sexton and Smilor, 1986; Sexton and Kasarda, 1992).

More than 1000 publications now appear annually in the field of entrepreneurship, at more than 50 conferences and in 25 specialized journals. A number of speciality areas have been developed, including innovation and creativity, venture creation, start-up and closure, company growth, self-employment and micro-enterprises, franchises, the various dimensions of the entrepreneur (behaviours, activity systems, entrepreneurial process, intrapreneurship and corporate entrepreneurship, technopreneurs), regional development, ethnic entrepreneurship, entrepreneurship support systems and government policies, cooperative entrepreneurship, entrepreneurship education, women entrepreneurs, and finally small business research and its consequent functional approaches, including finance, marketing, operations management, human resources management, information systems and strategy, all of which are addressed in other chapters of this book.

This chapter is aimed at beginners and experts alike. Obviously, it does not attempt to cover all the components of the field of entrepreneurship listed above. Its goal is to describe and discuss the core elements of current knowledge on entrepreneurs and small business owner-managers. It will begin by examining the world of the entrepreneur as seen by the pioneers of the field, the economists, and then by the behaviourists, who have shown a considerable interest over the years. It will then describe, with examples, the explosion of the field and its subsequent spillover into almost every discipline of the soft sciences and management sciences. Later sections examine some typologies of owner-managers, and propose another. This latter is the product of a taxonomy and is described in the appendix. The impacts of the proposed typology on small business strategy are briefly examined, and some attempts at theory, especially during the last decade, are considered and commented on. Finally, the chapter proposes a definition of the entrepreneur that is representative of the traditional research trends in the field.

2.   The world of the entrepreneur

People working in the field of entrepreneurship are convinced that there is a remarkable level of confusion surrounding the definition of the entrepreneur. We prefer the term "difference". Researchers tend to perceive and define entrepreneurs using the premises of their own disciplines. Taken from this standpoint, the confusion is perhaps not as great as people would have us believe, because similarities in the perception of the entrepreneur emerge within each discipline. For example, the economists have associated entrepreneurs with innovation, whereas the behaviourists have concentrated on the creative and intuitive characteristics of entrepreneurs. We will look more closely at these two standpoints in the following sections.

First, we must qualify the popular belief that entrepreneurship originated from the science of economics alone. A careful reading of the first two authors usually identified as the pioneers of the field - Cantillon (1755) and Say (1803; 1815; 1816; 1839) - reveals that these authors were interested not only in the economy but also in companies, venture creation, business development and business management. Cantillon was basically a banker who, today, would be described as a venture captitalist. His writings reveal a man seeking business opportunities, with a concern for shrewd, economic management and obtaining optimal yields on invested capital.

Vérin (1982) examined the origin and development of the term "entrepreneur", revealing that it acquired its current meaning in the 17th century. Although the term was used before Cantillon, it is clear, as Schumpeter (1954: 222) pointed out, that Cantillon was the first to offer a clear conception of the entrepreneurial function as a whole.

Some authors have associated Cantillon with one school of thought or another. However, Cantillon was an individualist, and it is unlikely that he had any such affiliation. Although the circumstances of his life did not enable him to put down roots in any particular country, he nevertheless showed the same interest in economic issues and the need for rationality as many of his European contemporaries. The Cantillon family came from Normandy, and emigrated to Ireland during the reign of William the Conqueror, who appointed them as managers of a small territory roughly the equivalent of a county. They were thus members of the gentry. Richard, whose date of birth is not known - and who should not be confused with his uncle, the knight Richard Cantillon who also lived in Paris - fled from Ireland to Paris in 1716 following the fall of the Stuarts in Great Britain. Paris had a large community of Irish immigrants, and Richard Cantillon became one of its patrons. He lived on private means, and sought out investment opportunities. He also travelled a lot. His descriptions of India's tea plantations are remarkable. He was able to analyze an operation, to see which elements were already profitable and which could be made more so. His writings show him, to some extent, to be a forerunner of Taylorism[1] . In the early 18th century,

---

1   As is also the case with Olivier de Serre, 150 years before Cantillon, as seen in Théâtre d'agriculture et messages des champs, 3rd edition, 1605.

he even invested in trading post operations in the Mississippi valley[2]. Cantillon was known to be tight-fisted, if not a miser. There was a rumour among his contemporaries to the effect that the cook who caused the fire in his London home actually did so deliberately, following Cantillon's obstinate refusal to increase his salary. The fire led to Cantillon's death in 1734. His manuscript was published posthumously more than 20 years after his death, with corrections by the editor, after being widely distributed in Paris and London.

Jean-Baptiste Say was the second author to take an interest in entrepreneurs. He regarded economic development as the result of venture creation, and hoped the English Industrial Revolution would spread to France (Say, 1816). He has been described as an economist because at that time, and in fact up to the second half of the 20th century, the management sciences did not exist. Consequently, anyone who took an interest in organizations or talked about the creation and distribution of wealth was bound to be classified as an economist. In today's terms, he would be much closer to Peter Drucker than to Kenneth Galbraith.

We can thus see from the writings of Cantillon and Say that their interest in entrepreneurship meant that they were difficult to categorize in a given discipline. This would subsequently be the lot of almost everyone who took an interest in the field. They would look at entrepreneurship from the premises of a specific discipline, but as soon as they ventured an opinion, they stepped over the boundaries of that discipline, found it difficult to go back and never received as much recognition from their peers.

Cantillon and Say regarded entrepreneurs as risk-takers basically because they invested their own money. In Cantillon's view, entrepreneurs bought a raw material - often a farm product - at a certain price, in order to process it and resell it at an uncertain price. Entrepreneurs were therefore people who seized opportunities with a view to making profits, and assumed the inherent risks. Say drew a distinction between the entrepreneur and the capitalist, and between their profits (Say, 1803; 1827: 295; 1815; 1816: 28-29; Schumpeter, 1954: 555). In doing so, he associated entrepreneurs with innovation. He saw

---

2   The same trading posts as the Perreault family of Quebec City and Trois-Rivières, in Canada. The father of François-Joseph Perreault went to live in St. Louis in the Mississippi Valley after the 1760 conquest of Canada by Britain. François-Joseph Perreault is considered to be one of the fathers of education in Quebec, having created the first private schools in the early 19th century.

entrepreneurs as change agents. He himself was an entrepreneur, and became the first to define the boundaries of what makes an entrepreneur, in the modern sense of the term. Schumpeter (1954) admitted that a major part of his own contribution was to tell the Anglo-Saxon community about the world of the entrepreneur as described in the writings of Jean-Baptiste Say. As Say was the first to lay a foundation for the field, we have described him as the father of entrepreneurship (Filion, 1988).

It is perhaps interesting to note that what Say did was basically to draw together two major trends of thought of his time: that of the physiocrats and that of the Industrial Revolution in Great Britain. He was a great admirer of Adam Smith, whose ideas he brought to France, and of the English Industrial Revolution (Say, 1816). In fact, he tried to establish a framework of thinking that would enable the Industrial Revolution to move across the Channel to France. He applied the liberal thinking, proposed by Quesnay, Mercier de La Rivière, Mirabeau, Condorcet, Turgot and other physiocrats in order to develop farming, to the entrepreneur.

However, it was Schumpeter who really launched the field of entrepreneurship, by associating it clearly with innovation.

> "The essence of entrepreneurship lies in the perception and exploitation of new opportunities in the realm of business ... it always has to do with bringing about a different use of national resources in that they are withdrawn from their traditional employ and subjected to new combinations."
>
> (Schumpeter, 1928)

Not only did Schumpeter associate entrepreneurs with innovation, but his imposing work shows the importance of entrepreneurs in explaining economic development.

In fact, he was not the only one to associate entrepreneurship with innovation. Clark (1899) had done so quite clearly some time before, and Higgins (1959), Baumol (1968), Schloss (1968), Leibenstein (1978) and most of the economists who took an interest in entrepreneurship after him also did the same. The economists were mainly interested in understanding the role played by the entrepreneur as the motor of the economic system (Smith, 1776; Mill, 1848; Knight, 1921; Innis, 1930, 1956; Baumol, 1968; Broehl, 1978; Leff, 1978, 1979; Kent, Sexton et al., 1982). From this standpoint, the economists saw entrepreneurs as "detectors" of business opportunities (Higgins, 1959; Penrose, 1959; Kirzner, 1976), creators of enterprises (Ely and Hess, 1893; Oxenfeldt, 1943; Schloss, 1968) and risk-takers (Leibenstein, 1968; Kihlstrom and

Laffont, 1979; Buchanan and Di Pierro, 1980). Hayek (1937; 1959) showed that the role of entrepreneurs was to inform the market of new elements. Knight (1921) showed that entrepreneurs assumed a risk because of the state of uncertainty in which they worked, and that they were rewarded accordingly by the profits they made from the activities they initiated. Hoselitz (1952, 1968) spoke of a higher level of tolerance that enabled entrepreneurs to work in conditions of ambiguity and uncertainty. Casson (1982) made an interesting attempt to develop a theory linking entrepreneurs with economic development. He insisted on the aspect of resource coordination and decision-making. Leibenstein (1979) had already established a model to measure the level of efficiency and inefficiency in the use of resources by entrepreneurs.

Entrepreneurs are mentioned in economics, but they appear very little - and sometimes not at all - in the classical models of economic development. Where they are present, they are represented by a function. The economists who took an interest in entrepreneurs were usually marginals, as was the case in other disciplines. If we were to summarize the main economic trends of thought on entrepreneurship, we would probably accept the standpoint of Baumol (1993), who proposed two categories of entrepreneurs: the entrepreneur-business organizer and the entrepreneur-innovator. The former includes the classical entrepreneur described by Say (1803), Knight (1921) and Kirzner (1983), and the latter the entrepreneur described by Schumpeter (1934).

It is never easy to introduce elements of rationality into the complex behaviour of entrepreneurs. One of the criticisms that could be levelled at the economists is that they have not been able to make economic science evolve. They have also been unable to create a science of the economic behaviour of entrepreneurs. Casson (1982) went as far as it was possible to go in terms of what is quantifiable and acceptable in economic science. The economists' refusal to accept non-quantifiable models clearly demonstrates the limits of this science in entrepreneurship. In fact, it was an element that led the world of entrepreneurship to turn to the behaviourists for more in-depth knowledge of the entrepreneur's behaviour.

2.2   *The behaviourists*

For the purposes of this chapter, the term "behaviourists" includes the psychologists, psychoanalysts, sociologists and other specialists of human behaviour. One of the first authors from this group to show an interest in entrepreneurs was Max Weber (1930). He identified the value system as a fundamental element in explaining entrepreneurial behaviour.

He viewed entrepreneurs as innovators, independent people whose role as business leaders conveyed a source of formal authority. However, the author who really launched the contribution of the behavioural sciences to entrepreneurship was undoubtedly David C. McClelland.

2.2.1 McClelland

In the 1950s, there was a good deal of interest in the rise of the USSR, and people began to wonder if *Homo sovieticus* would replace *Homo americanus*. This led David C. McClelland to study history for explanations of the existence of the great civilizations. This remarkable work led him to identify a number of elements (McClelland, 1961), the main one being the presence of heroes in literature. Subsequent generations took these heroes as models and tended to imitate them in their behaviour. The heroes overcame obstacles and extended the limits of the possible. According to McClelland, the people trained under this influence developed a very high need for achievement, and he associated this need with entrepreneurs. However, he did not define entrepreneurs in the same way as the rest of the literature. His definition was as follows:

> "An entrepreneur is someone who exercises control over production that is not just for his personal consumption. According to my definition, for example, an executive in a steel-producing unit in the USSR is an entrepreneur."
>
> (McClelland, 1971; see also 1961: 65)

In fact, McClelland's (1971) work concentrated on managers of large organizations. Although he is strongly associated with the field of entrepreneurship, a careful reading of his writings shows that he never made a connection between the need for achievement and the decision to launch, own or even manage a business (Brockhaus, 1982: 41). McClelland also identified the need for power, but he paid less attention to this aspect in his later work, and it is less well-known. A number of researchers have studied the need for achievement, but no-one seems to have made conclusive findings concerning any connection with entrepreneurial success (Durand and Shea, 1974; Hundall, 1971; Schrage, 1965; Singh, 1970; Singh and Singh, 1972).

Some authors found that the need for achievement was insufficient to explain venture creation (Hull, Bosley et al., 1980), while others found that simply developing a need for achievement was insufficient to explain entrepreneurial success (Durand, 1975; Neck, 1971; Patel, 1975;

Timmons, 1971). Timmons (1973), however, found that more of the people who had attended training sessions to enhance their need for achievement went on to create businesses than was the case in other groups. Gasse (1978) noted that McClelland had restricted his research to economic activity sectors. This point seems to be a particularly relevant one, because the need for achievement will be expressed according to the predominant values of a given society. In the former USSR, this could have meant becoming an influential member of the Communist party; in feudal Europe, joining the nobility; in 19th century Quebec, playing an influential role in the Catholic hierarchy. Thus, if the need for achievement is to be channelled towards entrepreneurship and venture creation, the ambiant social values must recognize and place sufficient value on business success to attract the people with a high need for achievement. Following the work of Gunder (1969) and Kunkel (1965), Gasse (1982) observed correctly that McClelland's theory of the need for achievement is inadequate, because it does not identify the social structures that determine individual choices. In other words, it is difficult to explain the choice to create a business or succeed as an entrepreneur based solely on the need for achievement (Brockhaus, 1982).

A second criticism of McClelland's theory of the need for achievement concerns its simplicity. McClelland attempted to explain social development and prosperity using just two main factors: the need for achievement and the need for power. However, it is far from certain that the behaviour of societies - or indeed, that of individuals and organizations - can be explained by just one or two factors. Marx (1844, 1848) emphasized the role of ideologies, Weber (1930) and Tawney (1947) the role of religious ideologies, and Burdeau (1979) and Vachet (1988) the role of the liberal ideology. However, Kennedy (1988), Rosenberg and Birdzell (1986) and Toynbee (1976) clearly showed the wide range of factors that explain the development of societies and civilizations.

Brockhaus (1982) underscored the fact that the connection between small business ownership and a high need for achievement has not been proved. However, McClelland did show that the human being is a social product. It is reasonable to think that human beings tend to reproduce their own model. In fact, we know that in many cases the existence of a model plays a key role in the decision to launch a business (Filion, 1988, 1990a and b). It may thus be the case that, all other things being equal, the more entrepreneurs a society has, and the greater the value it places on existing entrepreneurial models, the higher the number of young people who will choose to imitate those models by choosing entrepreneurship as a career path.

2.2.2   The school of personality traits

After McClelland, the behaviourists dominated the field of entrepreneurship for 20 years, until the early 1980s. Their goal was to define entrepreneurs and their characteristics. The behavioural sciences were expanding rapidly, and there was more consensus than in other disciplines regarding the most valid and reliable research methodologies. The movement was reflected in research on a number of subjects, including entrepreneurs. Thousands of publications described a whole series of characteristics attributed to entrepreneurs. The most common are shown in Table 4.1 below.

Table 4.1
Characteristics most often attributed to entrepreneurs
by behaviourists

Innovators	Need for achievement
Leaders	Self-awareness
Moderate risk-takers	Self-confidence
Independent	Long-term involvement
Creators	Tolerance of ambiguity and
Energetic	uncertainty
Tenacious	Initiative
Original	Learning
Optimistic	Use of resources
Results-oriented	Sensitivity to others
Flexible	Aggressive
Resourceful	Tendency to trust people
	Money as a measure of
	performance
Hornaday, 1982	
Meredith, Nelson et al., 1982	
Timmons, 1978	

125

All this research produced highly variable and often contradictory results, despite the fact that it used impeccable methodologies. So far, it has not been possible to establish an absolute scientific psychological profile of the entrepreneur. There are a number of reasons for this, not least being the differences in the samples. It is probably true that the function creates the organ, and that a characteristic develops with practice. Thus, a sample of entrepreneurs who went into business two years ago will not produce the same profile as a sample of entrepreneurs who went into business 20 years ago. Training and previous employment will also have an impact, as will religion, the values of the educational community, family culture and so on. Moreover, every researcher proposes his or her own definition of the entrepreneur. For some, an entrepreneur is someone who creates a business, while for others it is someone who creates a business that grows. For researchers of the Schumpeterian school, an entrepreneur is someone who introduces an innovation. On closer examination, it becomes clear that some research samples actually contain a mixture of small business owner-managers, franchisers and self-employed people.

We are not yet at the point where we can assess a person and decide with certainty whether or not he or she will succeed as an entrepreneur. However, we can establish whether or not that person has the characteristics and aptitudes most often found in entrepreneurs. Although no absolute scientific profile has been established, research has provided a number of guidelines for would-be entrepreneurs, to help them situate themselves. Research on successful entrepreneurs (Filion, 1991a and b) allow practising and potential entrepreneurs to identify the characteristics on which they must work if they are to succeed.

Lorrain and Dussault (1988a) showed that behaviours are better predictors of success than personality traits. After a short period in the limelight, the school of personality traits now seems to be on the way out. Kets de Vries (1985) suggested that entrepreneurs are poorly-adjusted individuals who need to create their own environment. A number of researchers have found the same thing, suggesting that entrepreneurs create businesses not simply because they want to work for themselves, but as a result of being unable to adjust adequately to their previous working environment (Bannock, 1981; Chell, 1985; Collins, More et al., 1964; Collins and Moore, 1970; Du Toit, 1980; Scase and Goffee, 1980; Stanworth and Curran, 1973). Other researchers have observed a higher degree of neuroticism among entrepreneurs than among the general public (Eyesenck, 1967; Lynn, 1969). This is understandable, because the nature of the entrepreneur's activities produces a constant state of personal unbalance. It has often been observed that a high level of emotional stability is required to function well as an entrepreneur.

In reality, one of the conclusions to be drawn with respect to the characteristics of entrepreneurs can be summarized as the social being. Human beings are products of their environment. A number of authors have shown that entrepreneurs reflect the characteristics of the period and the place in which they live (Ellis, 1983; Gibb and Ritchie, 1981; McGuire, 1964, 1976; Newman, 1981; Toulouse, 1979). Seen from the standpoint of entrepreneurial behaviour, entrepreneurship seems first and foremost to be a regional phenomenon. The cultures, needs and habits of a region fashion behaviours. Entrepreneurs integrate, assimilate and interpret these behaviours, and this is reflected in the way in which they act and construct their enterprises. In the electronic age, the larger entrepreneurs obviously exercise an influence that goes beyond the bounds of their region and even their country. Nevertheless, relationships between entrepreneurs and the population are still most frequent at the local level. And local entrepreneurs generally reflect the cultures of their own communities. They are often good conductors of regional cultures, and can even cause those cultures to change. The same phenomenon can also be seen in ethnic entrepreneurship (Toulouse and Brenner, 1992).

Many authors have shown that people have more chance of becoming entrepreneurs if they have a model in their family or environment (Filion, 1988, 1991a and b). When people become entrepreneurs, the nature of the activity leads them to practise and develop certain characteristics. For example, they have to be tenacious and creative if they want to stay in business. Thus, in addition to the social aspect, human beings who learn while practising a trade play a role with respect to the entrepreneurial characteristics. For example, entrepreneurs can be regarded as people who define projects and identify what they will have to learn to be able to realize those projects. From this starting point, entrepreneurs become people who must continue to learn in order to adjust to a trade, the activities of which lead them into a state of constant evolution, and not just people who define learning needs. Entrepreneurs must not only define what they have to do, but also what they have to learn to be able to do it (Filion, 1988). For example, Rotter (1966) always considered locus of control as an acquired characteristic. It is easy to understand why. When a person is in a position of leadership, he or she must exercise a certain amount of influence on people if things are to happen where desired. This is one of the elements that makes that person's leadership exist and develop. Thus locus of control, a characteristic often attributed to entrepreneurs, is first and foremost a

127

skill that is gradually learned and acquired by someone who wants to ensure that his or her wishes are realized. We know that successful entrepreneurs generally have a high locus of control. However, the characteristic is not exclusive to entrepreneurs, and is found in several other categories of leaders and successful people. Researchers have also observed that entrepreneurs have a strong need to control their environment (Filion, 1991a and b; Kets de Vries, 1985).

To conclude this section on the research of the behaviourists in the field of entrepreneurship, it is clear that we have not yet established a scientific profile that allows us to identify potential entrepreneurs with any certainty. However, we know enough about entrepreneurial characteristics to enable would-be entrepreneurs to situate themselves. In fact, the scope of the term "behaviour" has been extended, and it is no longer the exclusive province of the behaviourists. Research is tending to move towards other spheres, such as the skills required for a person to function well as an entrepreneur, and the personal and organizational learning methods required to adjust properly to changes in the activities related to the entrepreneurial trade.

3.   The explosion of the field of entrepreneurship

In the 1980s, the field of entrepreneurship exploded and spilled over into almost all the soft sciences and management sciences. The transition was marked by two events: the publication of the first-ever encyclopaedia containing the state of the art in the field (Kent, Sexton et al., 1982), and the first major annual conference (the Babson conference) dedicated to research in the new field.

The table of contents of the proceedings of annual conferences such as the Babson conference, entitled *Frontiers of Entrepreneurship Research*, and the ICSB (International Council for Small Business) conference provide some interesting information on the themes most often discussed (see Table 4.2).

The table shows the 25 dominant themes in the field of entrepreneurship. In one of the most complete bibliographies published on this subject, Harold P. Welsch (1992) identified 27 in all.

Table 4.2
Main themes of entrepreneurship research

- Behavioural characteristics of entrepreneurs
- Economic and demographic characteristics of small businesses
- Entrepreneurship and small business in developing countries
- The managerial characteristics of entrepreneurs
- The entrepreneurial process
- Venture creation
- Business development
- Risk capital and small business financing
- Business management, recovery and acquisition
- High technology firms
- Strategy and growth of the entrepreneurial company
- Strategic alliances
- Corporate entrepreneurship or intrapreneurship
- Family business
- Self-employment
- Incubators and entrepreneurship support systems
- Networks
- Factors influencing venture creation and development
- Government policies and venture creation
- Women, minorities, ethnic groups and entrepreneurship
- Entrepreneurship education
- Entrepreneurship research
- Comparative cultural studies
- Entrepreneurship and society
- Franchises

It is interesting to note that the development of entrepreneurship as a discipline did not follow the same pattern as other disciplines. In fact, large numbers of researchers, each using a culture, logic and methodology established to varying degrees in their own fields, began to take an interest and work in the field of entrepreneurship and small business.

The first doctoral graduates in entrepreneurship appeared in the 1980s. Nevertheless, the vast majority of those interested in the field were from disciplines other than entrepreneurship, and the study of entrepreneurship was not their main field of activity. Now, however, more people are devoting time and effort exclusively to entrepreneurship. The number of venture creations is growing, and the share of GNP attributable to small business in all countries is increasing every year, as we saw in Chapter 1. To follow the evolution and needs of their students and clients, many professors are having to learn more about entrepreneurship and small business. Thus, the assimilation and integration of entrepreneurship into the other disciplines, especially the soft sciences and management sciences, is unique as a phenomenon, and has never before occurred to such an extent in the paradigmatic construction of any other soft science discipline. Table 4.3 shows the main blocks of entrepreneurship research.

Table 4.3
Entrepreneurship research

Clients	Subjects	Specialists	Methodologies
Political system	Government policies Regional development	Economists Sociologists	Quantitative
Entrepreneurs Potential entrepreneurs Educators	Characteristics of the entrepreneur Entrepreneurial environment	Behavioural sciences Sociologists Anthropologists	Quantitative and qualitative
Entrepreneurs Potential entrepreneurs Educators Entrepreneurial advisory services	Business practice Management activities Financing Leadership Strategic thinking	Management sciences	Quantitative Qualitative

It is often said that confusion reigns in the field of entrepreneurship because there is no consensus on the definition of the entrepreneur and the boundaries of the paradigm. However, the reverse may also be true - entrepreneurship is one of the rare subjects that attracts specialists from such a wide range of disciplines, leading them to discuss and observe what others are doing in related disciplines and question how they are doing it. In fact, the confusion seems greatest if we compare the definitions of the entrepreneur between disciplines (Filion, 1987, 1988). On the other hand, if we compare the definitions produced by specialists within the same field, we find a quite astonishing consensus. The economists tend to agree that entrepreneurs are associated with innovation, and are seen as the driving forces of development. The behaviourists ascribe the characteristics of creativity, persistence, locus of control and leadership to entrepreneurs. Engineers and operations management specialists see entrepreneurs as good distributors and coordinators of resources. Finance specialists define entrepreneurs as people able to measure risk. For management specialists, entrepreneurs are resourceful and good organizers, develop guidelines or visions around which they organize their activities, and excel at organizing and using resources. Marketing specialists define entrepreneurs as people who identify opportunities, differentiate themselves and adopt customer-oriented thinking. For students of venture creation, the best elements for predicting the future success of an entrepreneur are the value, diversity and depth of experience and the skills acquired by the would-be entrepreneur in the sector in which he or she intends to operate.

In conclusion, the field of entrepreneurship has attracted the interest of specialists from almost all the soft science disciplines in the last decade. The apparent confusion basically reflects the differing logic and cultures of these disciplines. It seems likely that, in the coming decade, entrepreneurship will become one of the main gathering points of the soft sciences, because it is one of the rare subjects that has attracted such a large number of specialists from such a wide range of disciplines.

4.   Typologies of entrepreneurs, small businesses and small business owner-managers

We cannot examine the field of entrepreneurship without taking a look at entrepreneurial typologies. Typologies are of interest to researchers and teachers alike. They are especially useful and stimulating when used as part of entrepreneurial case studies, and enable analysis of the elements of consistency to be taken much further. This is extremely valuable in a field that has such a wide variety of cases. Many different typologies exist, and we will consider some of them here. Our own (Filion, 1988) is presented in an appendix to this chapter.

Cole (1959) established three types of business operation: innovation, imitation and repetition. Collins, Moore et al. (1964) and Collins and Moore (1970) drew a distinction between the "administrative entrepreneur" and the "independent entrepreneur". Smith (1967) first identified two types of entrepreneurs: the craftsman and the opportunist or business entrepreneur. He considered the technological entrepreneur to be in a separate category. Smith and Miner (1983) then considered the effects of each type on the type of business that would result. Lorrain and Dussault (1988b) analyzed the management behaviour of each type, and found that of the opportunist entrepreneur to be the most balanced. Following research by Miner, Smith et al. (1989), Miner (1990) observed certain differences between three types: entrepreneur, growth-focused entrepreneur, and manager. Laufer (1974) suggested four types of entrepreneur: the manager or innovator, the growth-oriented owner-entrepreneur, the entrepreneur who refuses growth but seeks efficiency, and the craftsman entrepreneur. Glueck (1977) drew a distinction between three types of self-employed people: the entrepreneur, the small business owner-manager and the family business leader. Gasse (1978), in his business and managerial ideology assessment grid, developed two types of entrepreneurial ideology: the ideology of the craftsman entrepreneur, and the ideology of the business entrepreneur. Chicha and Julien (1979) classified small businesses into three types: traditional, entrepreneurial (promotion-oriented) and administrative (or professional). Scase and Goffee (1980) also established enterprise categories. Schollhammer (1980) established five types of corporate entrepreneurship: administrative, opportunist, acquisitive, incubative and imitative. Vesper (1980) identified at least 11 types of entrepreneurs: (1) The Solo Self-employed individuals, (2) Team builders, (3) Independent Innovators, (4) Multipliers of existing models, (5) Economy-of-Scale Exploiters, (6) Capital Agregators, (7) Acquirers, (8) Artists who buy and sell, (9) Conglomerate builders, (10) Speculators, and (11) Manipulators of apparent values. Filion (1988) proposed two categories of small business: the classical and the comet. He also proposed six types of small business owner-managers (1988): the lumberjack, the seducer, the player, the hobbyist, the convert and the missionary (see Appendix 1) and two types of entrepreneurs: the operator and the visionary (1996a). Ibrahim (1994) suggested a relationship between strategy type and small business performance. Using the work of Miles and Snow (1978) as a basis, Julien and Marchesnay (1996) considered the innovation criterion and proposed four types of entrepreneurs: the prospector, the innovator, the follower and the reactor. They also considered the action logic and proposed two types of owner-managers: the PIG type (perpetuation, independence, growth) and the GAP (growth, autonomy, perpetuation) (Julien and

Marchesnay, 1987). These types are discussed in more detail in Chapter 5.

Julien (1990) also proposed a multi-criteria typology of small business, discussed in the first part of this book. He begins by describing the criteria underlying the main small business typologies in the literature, and goes on to suggest a continuum of qualitative and quantitative criteria to define small business. The main criteria used are size, sector, market, level of independence and centralization, type of strategy and type of technology. Lafuente and Salas (1989) established a typology of new entrepreneurs creating businesses in Spain, based on entrepreneurial aspirations and composed of four types: craftsman, risk-oriented, family-oriented and managerial. Woo, Cooper et al. (1991) assessed and discussed the impact of criteria on the creation of entrepreneurial typologies.

Obviously, no typology is complete enough to cover all types of entrepreneurs and owner-managers. Every case can be said to be unique. However, what typologies do is to provide a basis for understanding the anchor points as well as the values and thinking systems of entrepreneurs, and guidelines for understanding the overall behavioural consistency of the players.

5.   Trends for theory building

In every discipline, there is a desire to understand trends and formulate universal laws around which knowledge can be structured. The fields of entrepreneurship and small business are no exception to this. In this chapter, we have drawn a distinction between the two fields. Our discussion will begin with a brief look at small business, and will continue with entrepreneurship.

Great Britain was one of the first countries to realize the importance of small business in economic growth. After the First World War, in 1919, research groups were created to examine the phenomenon. Researchers had already identified the fact, which still holds true today, that small businesses create most new jobs (Birch, 1983; Peterson, 1977). New study commissions were formed, beginning during the economic crisis of the 1930s and culminating in the Bolton Commission, in 1969. The Bolton Report, published in 1971, shows among other things that small businesses exist where economies of scale are not automatically available to large corporations. They also exist because of the presence of entrepreneurs and an environment favourable to venture creation. Bolton (1971) and its successors (Stanworth, Estrip et al.,

1982; Stanworth and Gray, 1991) provide excellent summaries of the state of the art of small business. They have been reviewed elsewhere (see Filion, 1992) and will not be reproduced here. However, it is worth noting that Stanworth and Gray (1991), in their chapter 7, embark on an interesting discussion of the state of the art on owner-managers. They note that no consensus has been reached on the behavioural characteristics of small business owner-managers. Nevertheless, they conclude that people have a better chance of going into business in Great Britain if they are male, middle-aged or pre-retirement age, married, from a family environment where one or preferably both parents had a business activity, have studied in some field or other, and are from an ethnic group originating in the Indian sub-continent or the Mediterranean countries.

David J. Storey (1982) made an extensive study of the conditions explaining venture creation and development. He proposed the following equation:

$$E = f\,(\Pi, BE, GR, C)$$

where E = entry, Π = profits (+), BE = entry barriers (-), GR = growth (+) and C = concentration (-) (1994: 61).

For every small business that exists, there is an entrepreneur who created it. In this respect, the area of small business, like the area of self-employment, is one of the parameters of the wider field of entrepreneurship. In entrepreneurship, we have reached a point where many people are calling for a robust theory based on universal axioms, such as that which exists in physics, for example. The theory would be based on rigorous quantitative models and would be obtained by means of wide-ranging quantitative research that would incontestably prove the nature of the entrepreneur, entrepreneurial activity and its effects on economic development. At the same time, thousands of teachers are faced every day with the need to produce material to train entrepreneurs for entrepreneurial practice. To do this, they use qualitative methods to develop models and tools that will help actual and potential entrepreneurs to practise their profession competently. This tension between academics who write for other academics on the one hand, and academics who write for practitioners on the other, is strong enough in the field to deserve attention here.

Many attempts at theorizing have been made. The most frequently quoted include Amit, Glosten et al. (1993), Baumol (1993), Bull and

Willard (1993), Bull, Thomas et al. (1995), Bygrave (1989a and b), Casson (1982), Collins, Moore et al. (1964), Collins and Moore (1970), Covin and Slevin (1991), Gartner (1985, 1990), Gartner, Carland et al. (1988), Hébert and Link (1982), Hofer and Bygrave (1992), Leibenstein (1968), Low and MacMillan (1988), Peterson and Ainslie (1988), Reynold (1991), Sombart (1928), and Stevenson and Jarillo (1990). Wortman and Birkenholz (1991) summarized and attempted to classify many of these studies. When we look at all these theory-building efforts in the field of entrepreneurship, it becomes clear, as Mulholland (1994) pointed out, that the link established by Schumpeter (1928, 1934) between the entrepreneur and innovation has remained a dominant feature of the discipline, especially among the economists. In an earlier section of this chapter we considered the explosion of the field of entrepreneurship and the appropriation of relevant elements by the various soft science disciplines. It is this situation that led to the emergence of such a wide variety of definitions and methods of addressing the subject. For the economists, the innovation-based definition and approach developed by Schumpeter to explain the entrepreneur are sufficient to develop a theory of entrepreneurship (Kirchhoff, 1992, 1994). Julien (1989) has already pointed out the difficulty of aligning economics with the other soft sciences. In fact, when we compare the standpoints of Baumol (1990, 1993) and Casson (1982), the fundamental differences existing even between the economists themselves becomes obvious.

In the following paragraphs, we will examine the work of some of the authors who have thought about structure and theory in the field of entrepreneurship. Béchard (1996) suggested three approaches: the praxiological approach, the disciplinary approach and the epistemological approach. Cunningham and Lischeron (1991) suggested that the field of entrepreneurship is being structured around six points: the "great man" school, the psychological characteristics school, the classical (innovation) school, the management school, the leadership school and the intrapreneurship school. Blawatt (1995), using these and other characteristics, proposed that a conceptual model of entrepreneurship should include the performance criterion. He observed that most of the models proposed by the school of personality and others are generally static. He aligned himself with authors who have studied entrepreneurs in the field, and observed that entrepreneurs work in an evolving context where activities and roles change gradually. Entrepreneurs learn from what they do (Collins and Moore, 1970; Filion, 1988, 1989a and b, 1990a and b, 1991a and b), and because the nature of what they do changes, they too must change. They therefore have to learn to play different roles as their business evolves.

Two of the most interesting papers in entrepreneurial theory were written by a specialist in the field with doctoral training in both physics and entrepreneurship, and who has worked as both a scientist and an entrepreneur. The author in question is Bygrave, who showed first that entrepreneurship should break away from the paradigm of physics and quantitative approaches to find its own logic. He suggested that what we need most is qualitative field research to understand what entrepreneurs do (1989a). He then (1989b) proposed the chaos theory in physics as an interesting basis for a theory of entrepreneurship, but nevertheless warned that chaos is "no more than a mathematical metaphor because the accuracy of measurements necessary ... are unattainable in process" (1993).

Déry and Toulouse (1994) analyzed the themes addressed and the references used in one of the most frequently-quoted journals in the field of entrepreneurship, the *Journal of Business Venturing*. They observed that more than half the references were books. Similar research in the field of strategy, based on an analysis of quotations in the *Strategic Management Journal*, showed that more than half the references were academic papers. This seems to suggest that the field of strategy is now mature enough for researchers to have reached a certain consensus. In entrepreneurship, according to Déry and Toulouse, we are still in a developing paradigm where no consensus has yet been reached as regards the theoretical construction of the discipline. It may also be that the field of entrepreneurship is being structured theoretically in a different way from the other soft sciences, including strategy. While psychology emerged from philosophy (Miller, 1962), and psychoanalysis from medicine and psychology, the field of entrepreneurship is rooted in practically all the soft sciences and management sciences. Entrepreneurship research addresses both theoretical and practical elements. It would therefore not be surprising if theories were to emerge from sets of applied research. However, meetings with a number of researchers in the field of entrepreneurship have led us to believe that these people are already overworked as a result of requests to develop courses, programs and applied research, so that even if they were interested in constructing a theory, it would not be one of their priorities. Those who decide to take up the challenge must be imaginative, and should not limit themselves to a unidimensional approach, as has been the case in many scientific fields. Is it really necessary to point out that the soft sciences are composed mainly of flexible interpretative models, and that any theory of entrepreneurship must be flexible and multidimensional, to reflect its multidisciplinary roots?

6.   Definition

Obviously, we cannot hope to write a summary of entrepreneurship without defining the term "entrepreneur". Interestingly, some of the key words used in the modern vocabulary of management science are taken from the French language. For example, the term "manager" comes from the Old French "ménager", which meant careful housekeeping or organization. Defining the entrepreneur is a perpetual challenge, given the wide variety of standpoints used to study the phenomenon. Cochran (1968) observed that, for the economists in particular, the entrepreneur presented a kind of "incongruity of a human element that cannot be measured in a theoretical structure". In fact, whatever the definition used, there is always a danger that someone will not agree. The definition we propose here is intended to be a fairly broad common denominator, covering as wide a spectrum as possible. It reflects the main trends in entrepreneurial literature. Hélène Vérin examined the development of the term "entre-preneur" throughout history. In the 12th century, it was used to refer to a "supporter of squabbles" (Vérin, 1982: 31). In the 17th century, it described someone who undertook and managed a military action. It was not until the late 17th century and early 18th century that the term came to refer to someone who "formed and carried out projects" (1982: 33) or "created and managed enterprises" (1982: 32). In Cantillon's day, when the term took on its modern meaning, "entrepreneur" was used to describe someone who bought raw materials, processed them and sold them to someone else. The "entrepreneur" was therefore someone who had identified a business opportunity and taken a risk by deciding to process and resell a raw material. The element of risk thus appeared in descriptions of entrepreneurial activity as early as the beginning of the 18th century. The definition we propose here is also intended to be both a description and an interpretation of what entrepreneurs do. It is based on a study of approximately 60 of the most common definitions in the literature (Filion, 1987, 1988). It takes the standpoint used by Pinchot (1985), who described intrapreneurs as "dreamers who do".

Like many others, Lynn (1969) showed the parallel existing between entrepreneurs and creators. We have included this aspect in our definition, believing it to be fundamental in understanding entrepreneurial behaviour, i.e. the behaviour of creative people with active imaginations. We have observed that entrepreneurial imagination functions at two levels: entrepreneurs imagine the situation and scenario in which they will work and build their enterprises, and they also imagine a significant number of alternatives for the way they will organize and do things in order to realize their visions.

The first part of our definition therefore reads as follows:

"An entrepreneur is an imaginative person ..."

This imaginative person likes to set goals that he or she is sure of achieving. The goals are not always written down, but they exist, and constitute the main thread or vision around which the entrepreneur organizes all other activities. Entrepreneurs take action in order to achieve their goals, and develop the characteristics of tenacity, locus of control and creativity that have often been assigned to them in the literature.

The second element of our definition expresses this aspect:

"marked by a capacity to set and achieve goals ..."

Another aspect commonly found in the literature is the link between entrepreneurs and opportunity detection. This suggests that entrepreneurs develop a high level of environmental awareness. We have expressed this as follows:

"... who maintains a high level of environmental awareness in order to detect business opportunities."

In fact, as long as entrepreneurs continue to detect business opportunities and take action to exploit them, they continue to play an entrepreneurial role. Entrepreneurs are people who must continue to learn, not only about what is happening in their environment, in order to detect business opportunities, but also about what they do, so that they can adjust accordingly. In fact, as long as they continue to learn, entrepreneurs continue to play their role and act entrepreneurially. They live in a process of constant evolution. However, the main focus of their learning is always opportunity detection, to enable their entrepreneurial role to continue. This aspect has been included in our definition as follows:

"An entrepreneur who continues to learn about possible business opportunities ..."

Entrepreneurs do not play Russian roulette with their businesses. They initiate projects, usually business projects. To succeed, they minimize the risk associated with their decisions. Research has shown that entrepreneurs are people who tend to take moderate risks and minimize uncertainty in their decision-making processes. This aspect has been expressed as follows:

"... and to make moderately risky decisions ..."

In addition, Jean-Baptiste Say and, later, Joseph Alois Schumpeter both linked entrepreneurs to innovation. Entrepreneurs are change agents; they do new and different things. People can only be regarded as entrepreneurs if they contribute something new. This aspect has been included in our definition as follows:

"... aimed at innovating will continue to play an entrepreneurial role."

Our complete definition thus reads as follows:

"An entrepreneur is an imaginative person, marked by an ability to set and achieve goals, who maintains a high level of environmental awareness in order to detect business opportunities. An entrepreneur who continues to learn about possible business opportunities and to make moderately risky decisions aimed at innovating will continue to play an entrepreneurial role."

We have summarized this definition, retaining its essential elements, to arrive at the following:

"An entrepreneur is a person who imagines, develops and realizes visions."

(Filion, 1991b)

This short version includes all the elements of the longer definition. Imagination is obviously required to imagine visions. The term "vision" denotes the ability to set and achieve goals. The difference between a dream and a vision is that the vision is a realistic and achievable form of dream - in other words, a desired image of a future state. It also requires a high level of environmental awareness to detect business opportunities. If a vision is to develop, the entrepreneur must continue to learn about the environment. To realize a vision and stay in business, he or she must also make moderately risky decisions. These decisions must include new elements. A vision implies something new that will motivate the members of the organization and attract interest from the market. As long as an entrepreneur continues to imagine, develop and realize the visions that form the thread around which business activities are organized, he or she will continue to play an entrepreneurial role. Someone who invents something will always be an inventor in the eyes of the world. However, entrepreneurs will usually be regarded as such only for as long as they continue to play an entrepreneurial role. When someone sells a business, people will tend to say: "He (or she) was an entrepreneur."

At this point, it is important to draw a distinction between entrepreneurs and small business owner-managers. Many people will in fact play entrepreneurial roles without ever becoming small business owner-managers, either by working within large corporations (as intrapreneurs or corporate entrepreneurs) or by becoming self-employed without creating a company. At the other end of the scale are the small business owner-managers who buy companies instead of creating them, who do not make any significant changes, who have no vision of what they want to do, who have not developed new products or new markets, and who manage from day to day, making decisions on run-of-the-mill management activities without having a vision, overall plan or specific goal. Such people cannot be regarded as entrepreneurs. They are small business owner-managers who do not play a particularly entrepreneurial role.

Obviously, all definitions place limits on our perception and understanding of the subject. However, in a text such as this it is useful to define at least the key terms.

7.   Reflections and prospects

In the 1980s, the field of entrepreneurship exploded and spread into a number of other disciplines. Organizations and societies were forced to seek new approaches to incorporate rapid technological change into their dynamics. As the development of the communist countries levelled off, it became clear that societies could not evolve without entrepreneurs. The main asset of any society is its human resource, but this resource must be mobilized by and around entrepreneurial projects. After the collapse of the USSR, the shift towards performance - following or leading others - seemed to intensify (Fukuyama, 1992). This latter author also suggested that prosperity and its underlying force, entrepreneurship, was the result of a state of trust existing between the individual members of a society (1994).

Not only did entrepreneurship research extend to most disciplines, but the number of institutions offering entrepreneurship courses, as well as the number of courses offered, doubled in the space of a decade (Vesper, 1985, 1993). As was the case in many countries, Quebec witnessed the emergence in the early 1980s of a plethora of annual regional business galas where the most effective companies received awards: entrepreneur of the year, best marketing, best exports, best environmental protection, best human resource management, and so on. We thus witnessed the glorification of the entrepreneur and an acceptance of certain social models for prosperity.

Beyond all this, entrepreneurship can also be regarded as a new step towards the acquisition of freedom. Today's entrepreneurial society seems to be undergoing a far-reaching transformation, where entrepreneurship is expressed in smaller organizational forms. Thus, society has evolved from the expression of entrepreneurship in large corporations at the beginning of the century, on a shrinking continuum that began in the 1970s. The small business form emerged in the 1920s, and became the main focus of entrepreneurship in the 1970s. Since the early 1990s, increasing numbers of entrepreneurs have chosen the form of self-employment (Filion, 1996b).

In all these different forms of entrepreneurship, two categories can be distinguished: the voluntary entrepreneurs and the involuntary entrepreneurs (Filion, 1996b). In fact, the involuntary category is a product of the 1990s. It is composed mainly of new graduates and people laid off following corporate closures and restructuring, who have been unable to find jobs and are thus forced to create their own. The training and preparation needed by this group differs significantly from that used so far for the voluntary group. Involuntary entrepreneurs tend to choose self-employment, but they are not entrepreneurs in the generally-accepted sense of the term. They create a business activity, but are not drawn by the innovation aspect. While the key words used to define the entrepreneur are innovation and growth, those used to define the self-employed are personal ecology and balanced lifestyle.

Another phenomenon that pushes entrepreneurial expression towards smaller organizational forms lies in the changing meaning of the notion of success (Filion, 1996b). In fact, success is now defined by a growing number of younger, better educated entrepreneurs on the basis of intrinsic criteria related to self-fulfilment, rather than extrinsic criteria related to performance and status.

In addition, as the rate of change speeds up, large corporations become more difficult to manage. Learning (L) and its creative (CR) implementation (I) must be greater than the rate of change (C) if an individual, organization or society is to adapt and keep up with environmental change. In fact, this formula expresses one of the fundamental aspects of entrepreneurship:

$$[(L+CR) \, I > C]$$

The expression and success of entrepreneurial practice depend on many elements, two of which have received very little attention: management of space and management of time. Entrepreneurs must learn to manage internal and external space. They must learn to identify, define and establish a space to be occupied on the market. The notion of environmental organization is addressed in Chapter 5. As most business activities are cyclical, space and time become key elements in explaining success, for example at the level of stock and cash management.

In addition to market space, entrepreneurs must define a physical organizational space, and individual psychological spaces for their collaborators, depending on their perception of the capacities and abilities of the people around them. Their method of managing space will have an enormous impact on time. The more accurately they are able to allocate individual space and select market space, the more time they will have to devote to the identification and definition of other spaces.

As well as managing space, entrepreneurs must also manage time. The length of time a space remains open on the market is becoming shorter with the years. Similarly, given the speed of change, it will be easier for individuals to adjust their methods if they have more space of their own. The more fully people have accepted the organization's culture and rules, the more trust and the more space they will earn. And the more space they have, the better able they are to function quickly, because the number of people with whom they must transact in order to do what they do will be proportionally less.

In fact, we have come to a point where the speed of technological change is directly related to the ability of individuals and organizations to manage entrepreneurially, i.e. creatively and quickly. We are unlikely to return to a situation where the members of an organization spend many years doing the same repetitive tasks. Firms employing more than 5,000 people, divided into units of more than 200 people, are unlikely to remain in a position of leadership for much longer. This is easy to understand; the larger the organization, the more time it needs to learn and change. Beyond a certain size, the time required for internal change is greater than the speed of external change (see Chapter 1).

Accordingly, the coming era is one in which entrepreneurship will flourish. However, the greater the increase in the speed of technological change, the more likely it is that entrepreneurship will be expressed in smaller organizational forms. This is a direct result of the formula presented earlier. The relationship is inversely proportional. The companies most likely to succeed and grow will be those that make widespread use of subcontracting and different forms of franchising. All kinds of new forms of entrepreneurship will develop - for example, self-employment in peer and complementary networks (Filion, 1996b). As society moves towards a situation in which every individual will be responsible for himself or herself, whether voluntarily or involuntarily, we are taking a new step towards the acquisition of more freedom by more people. And here, research in the field of entrepreneurship takes on a new meaning, by offering tools that will help a growing number of people to act in their own terms, to be themselves in their activities, and to share that with others.

8.   Conclusion

We have seen that entrepreneurship was first identified by the economists as a useful element for understanding development. Subsequently, the behaviourists tried to understand the entrepreneur as a person. However, the field is currently in the midst of an explosion, in that it has spread into almost every other soft science discipline.

We agree with Mulholland (1994) and Rosa and Bowes (1990) that the field is still dominated by the positivist-functionalists, and that there is an urgent need to open up new perspectives in order to understand what entrepreneurs are and what they do. Particularly worthy of mention is the remarkable work of one researcher, Pierre Cossette (1994a and b), who has opened up a new avenue for research by his use of cognitive mapping to examine the entrepreneur's strategic logic. It may also be interesting to do further work on the concept of entrepreneurial vision (Filion, 1991a and b), and on the concept of self-space perceived, developed and acquired by the entrepreneur (Filion, 1993, 1994).

In light of the above, the field of entrepreneurship can be defined as the field that studies entrepreneurs. It examines their activities, characteristics, economic and social effects and the support methods used to facilitate the expression of entrepreneurial activity. No academic field can allow itself to neglect theory. However, to create a theory of the entrepreneur, it will probably be necessary to separate applied research from theoretical research by establishing a new science, entreprenology. This new science could create a theoretical corpus composed of the convergent elements of theoretical studies of entrepreneurs by entreprenologists in the various disciplines. Entrepreneurship itself would continue as an applied research field, producing results of interest to practising and potential entrepreneurs. However, several thousand more publications will be published, and perhaps several decades will have elapsed, before we finally reach this point.

Appendix 1
Six types of small business owner-manager

We have identified six types of small business owner-manager:

- the lumberjack
- the seducer
- the player
- the hobbyist
- the convert
- the missionary

The lumberjack
Lumberjacks do not like crowds. When they have to talk to people, they feel as though they are wasting their time. They are ambitious, with the ability to work hard. They like doing things. In fact, when they work for an employer, they produce twice as much as anyone else. As a result, they become convinced that they should work for themselves. They like sharpening the saw and chopping wood. They do it well, better than most other people. They do it from dawn until dusk.

When the people who buy their products want more - especially because of the quality - lumberjacks will hire staff to cut the wood. They will usually be dissatisfied with both the quality and the quantity of work done by the people they hire. They prefer people who work hard, for long hours, as they themselves do. The organizational culture is production-oriented.

When they reach a certain point in their careers, they may stop focusing on the trees, and cast an eye at the forest. If they reach this first level of strategic thinking, the company can perhaps begin to grow. Usually, they will attack the related product market, and it is here that development becomes possible.

The lumberjack is the most common type of small business owner-manager. Some successful lumberjacks go on to become missionaries.

The seducer
Seducers throw themselves heart and soul into their business, but their enthusiasm never lasts. They launch businesses, and then sell them. They buy companies in difficulty, and then sell them. They like things to happen quickly. They can judge a company's strengths and weaknesses and its potential markets with equal accuracy. They are

highly sociable, and have a lot of acquaintances. When they see a company in difficulty, they immediately start thinking which of their acquaintances could buy part of the production, who could subcontract the production, and who could subcontract a specific component. They invariably know someone who has created a method that would reduce distribution costs in one of the operational sectors, and someone else who would buy large quantities of a particular product if it were changed slightly. And so on.

However, things have to be constantly on the move, otherwise the seducer loses interest and begins to look elsewhere. As they meet a lot of people, they never lack opportunities. They look at everything from a very specific standpoint: where and how to make a profit with the least possible effort. When they look at companies, they see dollar signs. And in their minds, a little computer is constantly calculating how much profit would result if such or such an adjustment were to be made.

Seducers are rather like artists as regards their work: their styles, tastes and interests change over time. Nevertheless, they are always stimulated by novelty. When they are older, if they decide to stay with a particular company, they will often become players.

The player
They like leisure activity. They view sport as a vital element of their lives. The sport to which they devote the most time will vary with the years, and will also depend on their current relations system.

They see the company as a financial support, a means of gaining enough money to be able to do what they really want in life. Often, they will choose seasonal or cyclical fields, where they work very hard for certain periods, and not at all for others. Nevertheless, they are not emotionally committed to what they do, in contrast to the convert. They try to limit what they do to what is profitable, so that they can devote as much time as possible to the activities they really love, even though they have to work in order to earn sufficient resources to continue doing so. The business is seen as a means, and sometimes even a constraint, that enables them to do what they really love.

Often, players come from wealthy families where most of their youth was spent practising sports or other leisure activities. Sometimes, they are the third or fourth generation to own a family business.

Some players will gradually replace their sporting activities with social and political activities.

The hobbyist

Hobbyists devote all their energy and free time to the business. They will often have another, "official" job, but keep it only as a financial cushion or as a means of contributing financially to the business. The business is their hobby. It is here that they see the possibility of self-fulfilment. Consequently, they invest all their available resources to develop it as much as possible.

Hobbyists are always split between activities that require a very different operational logic. In their "official" jobs, they work at a relatively low, or at best intermediate, level. They do not have to solve complex problems or make complex decisions.

Because of this, they do not learn from experience how to distinguish between the different levels of decision-making, which makes them into owner managers who, in the long run, find it difficult to formulate strategic decisions, because they are conditioned by their main activity to make administrative decisions.

In fact, they often take a long time to make their first major strategic decision: to leave their "official" job and devote all their time to the business. They will thus continue for many years to work against two different levels of logic: their "job" and the management of their small business.

Some hobbyists will become lumberjacks, and others converts. However, they will all, at some point, exhibit some features of the player, because they will have acquired a double or multiple method of functioning, where they perform one activity in order to support another, in which they can truly fulfil themselves.

The convert

Converts have found "the thing", and everything in their lives evolves from this one fundamental discovery. This generally means the start of a new career. They had been looking for something for years - the thing that would truly enable them to fulfil themselves and make positive use of their potential. At long last, they have found it. And now it has become an obsession.

Beware of what you might say about the new business that your convert friend has just launched or bought. It has acquired a sacred status, and your convert will have a very deep emotional investment in it. Converts build a rigorously consistent logic that explains everything that happens. This logic seems to surround "the business" with a protective halo. Infidels, believers in other religions, and even innocent bystanders must be careful of what they say. They may become the target of the convert's celestial thunder!

In fact, converts soon learn to regard the world as being divided into the "fors" and the "againsts": the people who like and support what they do, and all the rest. Converts tend to over-value people who think and do as they do, and are sceptical of everyone else. Perhaps these other people are not totally honest ... because they do not think in the same way. Who knows what they might be hiding? In any case, all these people have not yet found "it". They do not know what they are missing.

Converts much prefer doing things rather than seeing the results, because in everything they do, they are convinced that they are taking a step - however small - towards the improvement of humanity.

They see themselves as being particularly gifted, and feel they have a duty to make these gifts available to society. They like to be in control. Consequently, it is difficult for them to delegate, at least until the other person has proved worthy.

Many creators and inventors fall into this category. In fact, the converts who come from R&D and marketing/sales backgrounds seem to succeed best. Many end up as missionaries.

The missionary
Missionaries have usually launched the business themselves. If not, they have acquired one and made substantial changes. They know their product and market well. They are devoured by a true passion for what they do. They are convinced that what they do is a major asset for the community. In some ways, they are converts who have achieved a certain degree of maturity. They are less emotionally involved than converts. They have managed to cut the umbilical cord that attaches them to the business, and can see the overall picture much more clearly.

In fact, they usually organize the business fairly quickly, usually when it is still fairly small, so that it can function without them, or at least without their presence on a daily basis.

Since they have passed the stage of survival, they no longer feel as threatened as before, and are much more open to new ideas. They see the business as a living organism. The evolution and learning of the individuals who work there is important. Their employees have to be happy, because they will condition the evolution of the business itself, and thus with its capacity to remain competitive and develop. Missionaries maintain a high interest in the harmonious evolution of their employees, because they have understood that a business is a social system. The results do not depend solely on individual performance, but on the ability of the people to work together.

147

Although they are very task-oriented, over the years they become much more concerned with human relations. Almost all their time and energy is devoted to the business. They tend to hold conservative values, have stable personal lives, usually focused on the family, and adopt a realistic approach to business practice. What interests them is not so much to develop a business, but to build a team - often in the image of the family - in other words, to build a social fabric with an open organizational culture in which people are fulfilled and can progress, and where interpersonal exchanges enable the organization to learn.

Missionaries delegate everything they can. They try to devote most of their time to preaching, communicating, and taking part in task force activities where they can listen, discuss, and exchange - in other words, where they can be the stimulators who bring a healthy attitude and common sense to group life. They preach by example. They communicate their enthusiasm to the people around them. This pays off, because their employees are always highly motivated, and act in such a way that the company goes from success to success. It may even become a multinational and "the word" can then be "spread" abroad. A word to the wise: if you do not share the religion, or if you do not want to become totally committed, go and work somewhere else.

The table below suggests the type of strategy that seems to be the most logical for each type of owner-manager.

Table 4.4
Types of small business owner-managers and strategies

Type of owner-manager	Company's *raison d'être*	Type of strategy
Lumberjack	Survival-success	Continuous
Seducer	Pleasure	Radical
Player	Leisure	Rational
Hobbyist	Self-fulfilment	Evolutionary
Convert	Security	Revolutionary
Missionary	Conquest	Progressive

Very few owner-manager types exist in their pure state. As is the case for all typologies, the owner-managers encountered in real life often have a profile that combines two or three types.

The typology was developed following in-depth field analysis of more than 100 small business owner-managers (Filion, 1996b). Between 1988 and 1996, the typology was applied to approximately ten case studies per year in the classroom. Thus, more than 80 owner-managers have so far been classified using it. It has proved useful for establishing the value system and intention of the person concerned, and for understanding that person's decision-making mode, strategic orientations and the development of the visionary process. Interestingly, some owner-managers change category in the course of their careers.

5 Strategic management

"In the eighteen years that I have been governing property, I have not been able to prevail upon myself not to see either my titles or my principal affairs, which by force of need pass through my knowledge and by my care." Michel de Montaigne, "Essai".

1. Introduction

The literature on the various aspects of small business strategy is abundant, to say the least. Space restrictions prevent us from attempting to deal with the subject's many facets in this chapter. Our objective is more modest, but equally ambitious: to provide some avenues for reflection on previous work in the field of small business strategy.

Researchers are confronted with what can only be described as a veritable diversity in two main areas: the definition of small business, debated at length in the introductory chapter, and the definition of strategy itself, which will be examined here. The development of strategic thought in the 1980s helped strengthen the primacy of decision-making processes over procedures, thus placing the emphasis on small organizations and strategists, rather than large planning structures.

To understand the meaning of this development, we will begin by reviewing the main trends in strategic thinking.

According to Mintzberg (Mintzberg, 1990), "in the beginning was LCAG"[1]. The Design School emphasized the implementation of a set of objectives fixed by general management and the board of directors, with a view to maximizing shareholder wealth. These objectives were chosen logically, by a careful analysis of the firm's strengths and weaknesses that was used subsequently as a basis for identifying the activities required (Andrews, 1987). Emphasis then shifted to the conditions in which these strategic choices were implemented, through strategic planning, similar in some ways to strategic management, and personified by Ansoff (Ansoff, 1984). During the 1970s, consulting firms designed strategic matrices based on this mainly academic work.

This body of work still constitutes the basis of most academic strategic management courses, manuals, books and papers (e.g. Johnson and Scholer, 1989). Yet, this particular perception of strategy has been criticized both academically and politically, to a point that some French

---

1 The famous Harvard manual, written by Learned, Christensen, Andrews and Guth, and re-edited many times since.

150

authors have talked of "the splendour and misery of strategic matrices" (Carrance, 1988). The main criticisms can be summarized as follows:

- Traditional strategic analysis is interested only in the corporate sector. It often leads to "mimicry of gigantism": "good" firms, whatever their size, must adopt the strategic management principles defined for their very large or giant counterparts. Moreover, the same kinds of firms are always cited: American, in the manufacturing sector of the second industrial generation, with a focus on economies of scale and/or variety, and M-shaped rather than U-shaped, to use Williamson's (1975) terms - in other words, multidivisional, diversified and centralized (and multinational rather than global). Even Michael Porter, the strategic management guru of the 1980s, fell into the same trap as his predecessors before his 1991 change of direction.

- Traditional strategic analysis is interested only in strategy implementation, not strategy design. Goals are defined by market forces such as price, expected profit, industrial structures, and so on. Consequently, excessive emphasis is placed on planning procedures, contrary to Ansoff's earlier ideas on the problems of limited rationality in organizations (Ansoff, 1987). "Good" firms must thus plan, just as "strategic" firms must plan growth. The adverse effects of planning are well-known: excessive bureaucracy in management control, useless refinements, and the inability to adapt to changes in the environment.

- Traditional strategic analysis is based on a linear, analytical process: goals, analysis of strengths and weaknesses, choice of actions, implementation, control and review. Yet, the behaviourist school had long questioned the relevance of this process, which is completely isolated from the decision-making reality of organizations. The strategic decision-making process seems to be dominated by the limited rationality of the players, which leads them to adopt a heuristic approach, where the dominant features are intuition, the ability to adapt to unexpected situations, and the consideration of interrelated problems. The heuristic trend includes the work of Herbert Simon (Demailly and Le Moigne, 1986) and Mintzberg (Mintzberg, 1990; Mintzberg and Quinn, 1991).

Together, these limits were sufficient to justify an in-depth questioning of the whole field in the 1980s. Bygrave and Hofer (1992) have clearly described the reasons for this. The development of strategic research thus came to focus on the following two goals:

- Going beyond excessive pragmatism in an attempt to identify more general models, using more "robust" research methods (to avoid the term "scientific"), based in particular on industrial economy.
- Relativizing the scope of operational models. Thus the famous "SOWT" model (strengths, opportunities, weaknesses, threats) could no longer be considered "the" best solution, but simply a tool within a more general analysis grid.

The consequences of this dual focus had an impact on both the internal and external aspects. Internally, the "basic resources" approach showed that business competitiveness was a function not only of the ability to bend to the dictates of the market, but of proper use of the various types of resources available (including managerial ability) to establish a competitive advantage (Marchesnay, Perez and Reix, 1984). This resource-based approach is illustrated by Abell (1980) and Hofer and Schendel (1978). At the same time, Porter helped relativize the notion of competitive positioning by reasoning in terms of sector or industry rather than market (Porter, 1981). He emphasized the fact that many different competitive positions were equally possible within a sector, the major problem being that the strategy chosen should result from a "fit" between the organization with its abilities and the environment with its opportunities.

In the 1980s, a double shift occurred. First, the main business functions gradually became aware of the increasing strategic component in their basic problems; as operational management methods progressed, concerns of a higher order (i.e. more fundamental, wider in scope, more open to the environment) had to be addressed, mainly marketing at first, but then finance, technology and finally information systems and human resources. At the same time, managers were also becoming aware of the interdependency of strategic functional decisions, and thus the need to relativize them by linking them to a higher order level that would serve as a reference point. However, this overall strategic paradigm had yet to be discovered.

Finally, it was also during the 1980s that strategic analysis came to consider enterprise size and sector of activity. The reasons for this are well-known (Julien, Chicha and Joyal, 1986). In a restructuring world, in constant evolution, medium-sized, small and very small businesses resist best, in specific sectors such as services, and especially business services. As has often been pointed out, small businesses are no longer considered to be future big firms, except by a nostalgic minority of strategic traditionalists. Moreover, small and medium-sized firms have turned out to be more innovative and better job-creators, as we saw in

Chapter 1, and more competitive. However, standard deviations are also greater, demonstrating both the extreme vulnerability and the extreme diversity of these firms.

2. The strategy of small businesses or entrepreneurs

In the last ten years, research on small business strategy has gradually emerged as an independent area. Until then, small business was still considered a multidisciplinary field rather than a discipline in itself (Gibb, 1992). The result was a variety of thinking, originating in different fields (economy, geography, sociology, psychology, management, technology and so on), on the causes, consequences, methods and means of improving small business performance, through creation, start-up and development strategies. This emergent phase of small business research produced the following changes:

- A growing restriction on the "size" assigned to small businesses. For obvious reasons, the research object came to include small firms (less than 50 employees), then very small firms (less than 10 employees), and finally micro-firms (between 1 and a handful of people). In France, for example, the Statistics Institute became aware of deficiencies in its small business inventory, and from 1985 onwards increased the number of samples with less than 10 employees.

- An increasing awareness of the special features and management or decision-making processes of smaller units. People began to pay more attention to the role of the entrepreneur and special forms of organization and competition, based on a new type of relationship with the environment. With respect to the latter point, the Porterian approach, generalizing the notion of groups or strategic maps, confirmed that it is possible to obtain a competitive advantage regardless of size[2]. One thing that emerged from all this was that small businesses were not necessarily bound to become big. The new success stories were small firms that had remained small, rather than those that had grown too quickly or too far from their roots.

- A curious relationship between small business strategy research methods. Initially, we saw an increase in the amount of normative research, based on dominant strategic analysis at the end of the 1970s (Ansoff's LCAG models, matrices), and empirical research aimed at identifying emerging small businesses. In both cases, researchers

---

2   Although in Porter's work, "small businesses" employ several thousand people.

153

tended to concentrate on medium-sized firms, and certain corporate sector precepts and prejudices were extrapolated - for example, the need to plan, grow, structure and manage "scientifically". Subsequently, more refined, less normative and more exploratory work was carried out, as researchers became aware of the extreme heterogeneity of the small business sector and realized that it was unrealistic to attempt to constitute a "representative" sample.

Consequently, the thinking on small business strategy, which had increasingly become thinking on small business itself, came to be expressed through in-depth research methods (case studies, action research, organizational ethnography, etc.). Methods such as these, mainly exploratory, highlighted the relative or contingent nature of strategic choices, and also their complexity within a management system that reflected their various characteristics (teleonomy; regulatory interactivity between action variables, control variables and state variables; dynamic induced by the chosen vision, and vulnerability to the environment, etc.).

Remarkably, these features of strategic analysis in the small business sector were then taken up by the new trends in strategic management, as shown by the research programs announced by Mintzberg in "Management" (Marchesnay, 1992) and by Porter in the special issue of the Strategic Management Journal mentioned earlier (Porter, 1991), suggesting a systemic diamond-shaped analysis grid.

- Finally, a growing priority of process over procedure in strategic management. Since decisions are made mainly by individuals faced with a need to solve complex problems, thus requiring an appropriate information processing system, economic analysis gave way to psychological analysis, cognitive styles, character components and so on. Implementation procedures became part of the thinking on psychosociological process, as conceived in their earlier form by Ansoff: acceptance of the decision, learning process, etc. Strategic variables were no longer "objective" data to be gathered (strengths, weaknesses, etc.), but representations linked mainly to the personal characteristics of managers. This explains the importance of research on the spirit of enterprise and the distinctive features of enterprise leaders, grouped under the heading of "entrepreneurship research". The latter increasingly came to include environmental aspects in venture creation support, development, financing, innovation and training systems (Sandberg, 1992, Julien and Marchesnay, 1992).

The environment was now seen as a source of opportunities and outsourcing. Research on small business strategy thus drifted towards a more complete consideration of the relationship with the environment, which is more decisive for small businesses than for their larger counterparts. This work also responded to a major social demand: public and parapublic action to improve small business competitiveness was increasing, and its effectiveness and relevance had to be measured. To quote the title of a recently-created journal, "entrepreneurship" became tied in with "regional development"[3].

The different approaches to strategic thinking can be summarized using "Mintzberg's clock" (Hampden-Turner, 1990; Sandberg, 1992), with some personal modifications (ERFI, 1991).

Diagram 5.1
"Mintzberg's clock"

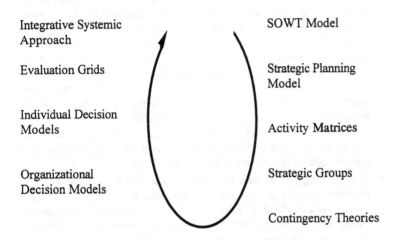

Integrative Systemic Approach

Evaluation Grids

Individual Decision Models

Organizational Decision Models

SOWT Model

Strategic Planning Model

Activity Matrices

Strategic Groups

Contingency Theories

This diagram calls for some comments:
- The theories or models to the right of the diagram are mainly concerned with decision-making procedures and tend to classify "good" strategic decisions as the result of a logical analysis of existing, supposedly "objective" situations. This type of positivism is still present in contingent theories of strategy (technological models,

3   The Irish journal "Entrepreneurship and Regional Development".

155

organization-environment fit), as shown by Crozier and Friedberg in "The Actor and the System" (1977). The theories or models to the left use a more descriptive or exploratory approach, attempting primarily to describe decision-making processes by examining the "whys", i.e. the goals, as well as the "hows", i.e. the methods. However, as we move up the left-hand side, we reach a pragmatic desire to help strategic decision-making by questioning the relevance of a "guided" heuristic approach by the maker or assessor of the strategic decision. This leads to an awareness of the complexity of the problem defined by the number of relevant interacting variables. We can thus speak of a true strategic management system, similar to Mintzberg's configuration approach.

- As the hands of the clock turn, they point to problems that touch increasingly on the concerns of decision-makers, and also of researchers, in the area of small business strategy. In fact, the realistic method is that used by individuals in situations of limited rationality, i.e. a heuristic approach based on innate or acquired mental schema, which enables them to consider a set of complex, interactive variables, each with its own strategic importance at a given time, and thus to modify the management system. It is interesting to observe, as Marchesnay (1992) pointed out, that Mintzberg, at the end of his recent book on management, moves quickly on the basis of reflections generated by his interpretation of the strategic decision towards an analysis of small and medium-sized organizations.

  Based on the process and classifications of Mintzberg and Quinn (1991), the strategic decision-making process can be divided into two separate phases (Julien and Marchesnay, 1991).

- A *triggering* phase, with two "generating factors". First, a strong external stimulus produces a response from the entrepreneur. This process is described as *reactive*. Second, without any apparent, strong, immediate or significant stimulus, the entrepreneur decides to make a strategic decision. In this case the process is described as *proactive* or reflexive.

  Clearly, it is sometimes difficult after the event to know whether or not a stimulus was present. In such cases the decision will be "more or less" reactive or proactive (especially in the case of a potential threat from a competitor).

- A *process implementation* phase. The process may be "gradual" (or incremental, to use Mintzberg's term), or "radical", involving a broader review of strategic options.

156

Consequently, we have four main types of process, as the following table shows:

Table 5.1
Strategic system

	Gradualist	*Radical*
Reactive	Improvement of the quality of customer service in the face of market disintegration	Sudden abandoning of a product or activity, lay-offs, sudden renewal of technology (new machines, new qualifications) in the face of new competitors or innovations
Proactive	Implementation of a training and immaterial investment policy covering a period of several years	Launching of a new activity Venture acquisition Closure

What we now want to develop is this kind of systemic approach, to highlight the special features of the strategic process in small businesses.

The strategic system can be illustrated as shown in Figure 5.1. The following comments are required:

- First, the diagram should be interpreted as a system. This means that the key variables are interactive (a decision initially affecting one of the key variables, or any spontaneous modification, will have repercussions on the other variables). In other words, the purpose of the system is expressed through management's goals, vision and plan of action, even if not formalized. This means that the system is open, that it is subject to outside influence and adapts to it. It also means that the system is dynamic, and must be placed in a temporal evolutionary perspective - which involves the phenomena of learning, discontinuity, spontaneous change and assisted change.

- Second, the diagram should be interpreted as an analysis grid - that is, a means of decoding the specific problems of each individual enterprise. However, beyond purely normative and pragmatic considerations, the grid is based on notions and concepts that fall within the framework of current research on small business strategy, as we will see later. There is therefore no antagonism between "academic" research and "goal-oriented" research - on the contrary, the concerns are the same. Moreover, the diagram allows all small business strategic analysis problems to be situated within a more general context, thus highlighting the necessarily contingent nature of research in the field, as many researchers have noted (Gibb, 1992), and as we will see in the last chapter. It would be foolhardy to give one particular strategic variable a determining or deterministic role over the others.

- Third, it is worth reviewing the key variables. In fact, they cover the different concerns in small business strategy research. First, the goals of the managers, related to their profiles among other things; next, the organization of the firm, including all kinds of configurations, to use Mintzberg's (1990) term; then the activities, their nature and their number; and finally, the environment, or rather the types of environments that affect small business strategy.

This diagram can easily be related to the main themes of strategic analysis:

- The upper part concerns what has been referred to as "corporate strategy" - in other words, general policy (Bower et al., 1991). This includes the problems of legitimacy (role in society), culture (values and standards within the firm, however small it may be) and vision as described by Louis Jacques Filion (1991) - in other words, an image of the firm in the future.

- The lower part concerns what has been called "business strategy", or "activity strategy" - in other words, strategic management or operational strategy, as it appears at the level of the main managerial functions. This includes the craft-mission pairing (Koenig, 1990), which generates problems in the marketing and technological strategies, as we will see in later chapters, and the action plan, or what replaces a "plan" in a small business, in that it must be analyzed more in terms of processes than procedures (Julien and Marchesnay, 1992).

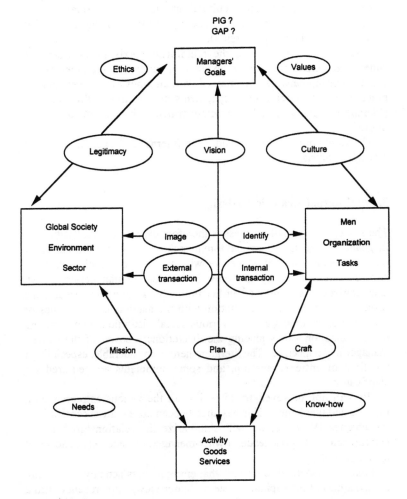

Figure 5.1
Strategic system and competitive base

- The middle zone covers the problems of the relationship between the firm's identity and image, leading to communications strategies that affect the representations of the firm. In fact, the firm's identity is based mainly on its values (culture) and its know-how (craft), while its image depends on its role in society (legitimacy) and how well it satisfies specific needs (mission).

It is also relevant to add the relationships existing between the "internal organization" and the "external organization" - in other words, the relationship networks maintained with all kinds of partners. As the practice of outsourcing develops, firms create "transaction spaces" (Marchesnay and Julien, 1990) within which their own boundaries are blurred.

The following sections consider the internal and external levels of strategic analysis.

3. Internal strategic analysis

The strategy of a small business is therefore expressed initially through its goals. The goals are first and foremost those of the decision-maker, or business leader (at this stage we will not use the ambiguous term "entrepreneur"). They are thus the product of that person's own characteristics, as mentioned earlier in this book. But they are also the result of a process of confrontation with the aspirations and values of organization members and the various social institutions that surround the organization - thus placing the discretionary power of the owner-manager in perspective. The literature here is considerable, especially in the field of entrepreneurship, and some comments are required for clarification.

We will not, however, try to review all the various entrepreneurial theories and typologies. This has already been done quite successfully in the chapter IV. Here, we will summarize the relationship between entrepreneur, enterprise leader, owner-manager, manager, etc., and small business strategy.

First, it is essential to define what entrepreneurs actually are, within the dynamics of the capitalist system. In our view, entrepreneurs fulfil a triple function:

- They are responsible for mobilizing financial capital (not necessarily their own - they are simply the agents) in order to make a profit, which Knight said was the fruit of risk and uncertainty. We will call this the "capitalist entrepreneur" function.
- To do this, they mobilize resources (material, human, technological, financial and information) within an organization that they must make effective (achieving goals - effectiveness - through economy of means - efficiency - with the greatest possible satisfaction - effectivity; Marchesnay, 1991a). We will call this the "manager entrepreneur" function, as originally conceived by Jean-Baptiste Say.
- However, in a market economy, profitability can be achieved only if the entrepreneur creates a rupture in the economic circuit through innovation, thus contributing to the dynamics of economic change. This is the Schumpeterian "innovator entrepreneur" function.

Very few enterprise leaders have the qualities required to fulfil all three functions. The "entrepreneur" is thus something of an ideal - an emblematic figure in a market economy (the economy of businesses and entrepreneurs), likely to be transformed into an archetype and then a stereotype. In the early 1980s, the French magazine "*Autrement*" described the people responsible for the venture creation wave as "the heroes of the economy". In fact, the "heroes" in question had very different levels of entrepreneurial fibre, and the stereotype conveys a number of irritating expectations. For example, the entrepreneur is supposed to be a risk-taker (which is not always to the liking of the people supplying the funds), when research has shown that venture creators and other company leaders have an aversion to risk very similar to that of ordinary people (Gibb, 1992), as we saw in Chapter 1.

In all, company leaders and owner-managers will exhibit different levels of "entrepreneurial aptitudes" (Carrier, 1992). These appear in their psychological characteristics, or specific features, as described and identified by authors such as Timmons (1990) and Gasse (1982), in frequently-cited research (Ricard, 1992). However, such lists give the impression of a kind of "superman" somewhat removed from real life: a taste for risk, decision-making autonomy, lucidity, vision, adaptability, leadership and negotiating skills. Yet, practical tests on groups of venture creators rarely produce such individuals. Moreover, even if they did exist, it would be no guarantee that their businesses would be successful, or that they would not make mistakes.

In reality, the notion of entrepreneur corresponds to the need in economic theory for an ideal model, like "the representative firm", to provide a general explanation of how the market economy works. To use Baumol's (1968) metaphor, while the entrepreneur may bring Macbeth back to centre stage, it is only in the form of a soulless statue subject to the pressures of a given environment. Even in more fully developed theories, such as the evolutionist approach to technological innovation (Gaffard, 1990), the strategic behaviour of individual entrepreneurs is conspicuous by its absence.

For this reason, small business strategic analysis requires a more in-depth knowledge of the real behaviour of decision-makers, which explains why the literature on entrepreneurship, as early as the 1960s, attempted to classify enterprise leaders on the basis of their "spirit of enterprise". This led to the development of many well-known typologies, the most famous being Norman Smith's (Smith, 1967). Rather than listing these typologies, we will simply describe the main groups and their common criteria.

- The first type is the "entrepreneur" owner-manager, who combines the qualities of innovator, risk-taker (investment of personal capital) and organizer. Few typologies use this "ideal" type as an observed fact, but refer to it when ranking the empirically dominant types.
- The second type is the "innovative" owner-manager, who usually innovates in the areas of product or market, rather than technologies or processes. Innovation can occur either when the business is created or during its development, and may take place with a view to renewal or change.
- The third type is the entrepreneur who is also a technician, low-level innovator and manager seeking an average, stable performance.
- The fourth type emphasizes the owner-manager's "organizer" characteristics, and is referred to as "manager" or "professional" as the case may be. This type is driven by a concern for organizational performance and proper resource planning, with fixed objectives and stable products.

These are the main types of "entrepreneurs" existing in the literature. Despite the imagination of researchers, the typologies are markedly prescriptive in type. For example, "technical craftsmen" are supposed to have few entrepreneurial characteristics, which causes them to be non-competitive, while "innovative" entrepreneurs lie at the other end of the scale. However, prescriptivism can be illustrated even more clearly. For example, the small business growth models mentioned in the introduction to this book state that, as the firm grows, it crosses certain thresholds (some authors have listed eleven "steps") that require organizational change and concurrent changes to the owner-manager's own profile - from being an innovator, he or she must become a manager. This supposes that the "entrepreneur" is driven by the sole aim of seeing the enterprise grow in size, to a point where it will have to be sold. Only the technical craftsmen would resist this suicidal approach, "constrained" to non-growth by their limited capacities. This hypothesis seems increasingly heroic. In fact, as we have said, it has become obvious that most small business leaders avoid growth, for a variety of reasons including narrow markets, lack of capital, lack of scale effects, risk of loss of control, or quite simply a desire to stay small in order to satisfy other personal objectives.

The prevailing feeling now is that it is somewhat risky to use these typologies to explain effective strategic behaviour by business leaders. In fact, they are mainly idealistic in nature, drawn from the traditional strategic management literature with its emphasis on growth strategies, the pursuit of critical size (as in the PIMS model - Profit Impact of Market Strategies), the portfolio grid developed by the Boston Consulting Group (BCG, 1984) and the use of formal planning. They prescribe an "optimal" strategy on the basis of a given type, when in fact we should perhaps be trying to do the opposite, and attempt through exploratory, clinical, empirical studies to observe strategic behaviour, using the observations to create categories.

In fact, researchers are now facing a dilemma:

- They can seek ideal types or holistic categories (Casson, 1991), and risk empirical non-relevance. For example, Caroline Woo (Woo et al., 1991), in a recent study, noted that Smith's opportunist craftsman typology became irrelevant as additional classification criteria were added. It is thus reasonable to think that the same would apply to all typologies.
- Or they can remain as close as possible to actual behaviour and establish typologies on the basis of individual problems. For example, a typology could be established on the basis of aptitude for innovation and the type of organization required as a result. Recently, Smith suggested enriching his typology by dividing the opportunist and innovator categories (Smith et al., 1992), as shown in the following Table 5.2:

Table 5.2
Organisation

		Informal	Formal
		Informal	Formal
Innovation	Low	Craftsman	Manager
	High	Innovator	Opportunist

The risk of this type of approach is that it would increase the number of typologies without providing a general reference framework. Instead, it would produce a kind of analysis grid, used to classify attitudes to the perception and solution of management problems, including the contingent variables likely to have an effect. What such constructions gain in description, they lose in prediction - a criticism often directed at contingency approaches (Crozier and Friedberg, 1977).

3.2   The economic goals of entrepreneurs

Existing knowledge of the effective behaviour of small and very small firms is so poor that we need to go through this exploratory stage before proposing more general models.

We have therefore suggested two types of entrepreneurs, based on current strategic behaviour. Obviously, this is a systematization, not an idealization (there is no normative or prescriptive judgment) of the realities observed (Julien and Marchesnay, 1992).

Our aim was to identify the goals likely to have a major impact on strategic choices, with emphasis on goals of an economic nature, but including and crystallizing the personal and social components of the decision-maker (character, aptitudes, entourage, etc.).

The literature on "entrepreneurial" typologies revealed three main goals (Marchesnay, 1986): perpetuation and survival, independence and autonomy, growth and power. In the 1930s, the theorists of imperfect competition (Hicks in particular) distinguished the "stickers", seeking long-term profit from an activity, from the "snatchers", seeking quick profits even if it meant changing activity (Andrews, 1964). Clearly, the priority order of the goals will depend on personal considerations that can be identified in personality tests, and also on social considerations such as the culture of the sector and the local or national environment, identifiable through implicit or explicit codes of behaviour. In fact, we could offer the hypothesis that the choice of priority order will have an impact on the strategic choices and their application.

We can thus identify a type of "entrepreneur" (owner-manager) whose priority goal is to perpetuate the business. This group want to remain in the same sector, and confine any innovations to that sector (they will thus tend to make process innovations rather than market innovations). They are often concerned with the issue of succession or handing the business on, either to family members or to outside successors. They take great interest in their sector's future, and their field of vision is "long" but "narrow" (Kepner-Tregoe, 1990). Their action logic can be summarized as property accumulation. In extreme cases and true to the typology, this will be expressed through a marked preference for material investments such as land and buildings, and a dislike of immaterial or intellectual investments such as training, research and promotion (Guilhon, 1992). In the same logic, the need for independence tends to take the form of a need to dispose freely of accumulated assets, exhibited through stock ownership and avoidance of long-term debt. This desire for financial independence can easily be identified by researchers and observers through the owner-manager's opinions of external funding sources, costs, and the risk of dependency or loss of autonomy.

The result is, naturally, that these owner-managers will limit business development on the basis of their own financial capacity. This does not mean that the business will not grow. However, growth will tend to be reactive, emergent and gradual, to use Mintzberg's terms (Mintzberg, 1991; Julien and Marchesnay, 1992). For example, the sector may continue to expand, or the firm's products will earn spontaneous recognition. A number of authors (Marchesnay, 1988, Lorrain, Perreault and Dussault, 1992) have confirmed that this type will show little interest in marketing-related activities, and will focus more on technical or organizational problems. From this point of view they resemble Smith's craftsmen-technicians. However, there is nothing to prevent these owner-managers from having good business experience and good qualifications, like the opportunists. This type of behaviour is particularly common among the creators of high-tech companies.

This category can be referred to as the "PIG" group (perpetuation, independence, growth). They would have a better chance of prospering in mature activities, where success depends more on exploiting an existing market than seeking to extend it through innovation and diversification. Thus, as a product reaches maturity, new "PIG"-type enterprise leaders emerge; or do existing managers simply change their behaviour and move towards this profile as the question of perpetuation arises?

The second type of entrepreneur is called the "GAP" type (growth, autonomy, perpetuation).

GAP entrepreneurs have an action logic focused on quick enhancement of invested capital. They will therefore tend to prefer sectors where anticipated profit margins are high, even if this means more risk. They will select activities with a shorter product life cycle, or at an early stage in the life cycle, or with entry barriers (even if temporary - licence or patent, specific know-how, etc.). Their main problem may be to build a customer base or a market for their product (product and/or specific service). The firm's competitiveness is mainly conditioned by the manager's interest in marketing issues, as confirmed by Lorrain, Perrault and Dussault (1992). Would opportunist owner-managers, with their focus on technical problems, need to find collaborators or partners with a market focus, or should they train themselves to do this?

The GAP group seems more concerned with decision-making autonomy than true independence. Their main problem is to maintain a certain flexibility in strategic decision-making. In this respect, they resemble Miles and Snow's (1978) "prospectors", in that they have to seize environmental opportunities in order to pursue fast-growth activities (in this sense, they are more "opportunist" than Smith's so-called "opportunist entrepreneurs", who prepare their market entry over a long period). For this reason, they will not hesitate to go into debt or to use outside capital as well as their own. For them, business means other people's money, provided they can maintain their decision-making autonomy and choose their own products and markets. This behaviour is all the more justifiable because they are working on activities with high (if temporary) profitability, and can be expected to have a major financial lever effect. If we take this to the extreme, we can say that GAP personalities should accumulate as little capital as possible. In fact, we know they have a marked preference for immaterial investments. This particular characteristic emerged very clearly in research on organizational change by industrial enterprise leaders in the Aix-Marseille region of France (Guilhon, 1992). The GAP group also has a higher propensity for outsourcing organizational activities, although they will hire qualified people to perform key activities within the organization (Naro, 1990).

Finally, and logically, the GAP group is not motivated to perpetuate the business. On the contrary, "typical GAP" entrepreneurs will tend to change their corporate name as their markets reach maturity and thus provide lower profit margins. This requires intense scanning activity, quite consistent with their preference for immaterial investment. However, as observed earlier, GAP entrepreneurs can change. They may accumulate property, start a family, develop a stable customer base and know-how that gives them a distinctive competency, and so on. In other words, GAP entrepreneurs can become PIG entrepreneurs (the reverse is less likely, because it would mean dissuasive irrecoverable costs; the business would have to be absorbed into another, or wound up, and the entrepreneur would have to start up new activities).

Clearly, then, the decision-making process of the GAP group differs considerably from that of the PIG group. The field of vision (Filion, 1991) is shorter, but broader. The GAP group seeks emerging activities, and does not seem to be affected by obstacles such as acquisition of know-how through learning (they will use other people who have the know-how). However, they have to cover a field that is sufficiently broad to enable them to seize opportunities. Their strategy thus seems to be emergent rather than deliberate, because they find it particularly difficult to establish long-term plans - and yet, they make many strategic decisions!

Overall, this classification is subject to the same criticisms as the others. The PIG and GAP groups represent extreme cases. However, they have the merit of revealing the inconsistencies in the goals of many owner-managers, and highlighting the conflicting goals of stockholders, usually members of the same family (if the father is PIG, the son will usually be GAP, as in the "Fer de Lance" case - ERFI, 1989). Similarly, the classification raises but does not answer the question of what will happen when, for example, a "PIG" entrepreneur finds himself or herself in an emerging activity more suited to a "GAP" entrepreneur (for example, a "GAP" entrepreneur may be able to regenerate a "mature" activity, by identifying new needs or proposing new services, while a "PIG" entrepreneur may help stabilize a turbulent activity).

In fact, this classification is of interest only as one element of the strategic system, whose other elements will now be discussed. Within the "corporate strategy", the strategic behaviours of enterprise leaders are influenced by, and influence, the dominant values in the environment and within the organization. This generates certain problems related to legitimacy and culture, which we will now consider.

4.   External strategic analysis

Legitimacy is a function of dominant social values. Society endows its institutions with social responsibility. The more highly valued this role or responsibility, the more legitimate the institution. In the 1980s, the legitimacy of small business was considerably strengthened, for the following reasons:

- First, the difficulties inherent in large corporations revealed that large size, related to the rhythm of the "critical mass", was not an end in itself.

- Second, the 1980s were marked by a phase of anomie, to use Durkheim's term; in other words, a questioning of dominant values, both in North America and Western Europe. In the early 1980s, the phrase "small is beautiful" was quoted frequently, and sometimes to excess (Marchesnay, 1982). Towards the middle of the decade, the social legitimacy of small business (personal fulfilment factor, job creator, user friendly, etc.), fed by myths, was replaced by economic legitimacy, as we saw in Chapter 1. Small businesses were more flexible, more innovative, and created interesting jobs, in both the high qualification (business services, manufacturing sector) and low qualification (individual services) areas. Small businesses, more in touch with their customers' needs, added value to products, and their competitive advantage lay in the service they provided. Moreover, they played a key role in local development (Chapter 3). In short, they were one of the leaders in the creation of new dominant values in society, focused on competition based on shared, cooperative values. They played a growing role in intermediary systems (so-called "meso-systems": groups of firms, regions, localities, channels and sectors), in particular through the formation of networks, with the Marshallian district playing the role of "carrier myth" (special edition of RIPME: V.A., 1989).

4.1   Social legitimacy

It is therefore not surprising that legitimacy of action became a major strategic asset for small business owner-managers, as an integration factor and an image-enhancing factor. In fact, because small firms are located mainly in very fertile environments, they have always had to consider the opinion of environmental players (customers, suppliers, bankers, public institutions, etc.).   However, the essential change was undoubtedly a reversal of public opinion. Even though the corporate sector was supposed to be more effective, doubts began to be expressed. For example, the problems of pollution were attributed mainly to "big business", and the development of business ethics courses, financed by large industrial groups, provided evidence of their guilty conscience and loss of legitimacy.

In this atmosphere of anomie, small business had to be able to take strategic action aimed at strengthening its legitimacy. The vectors of such action were to be job creation, insertion in the local economic and social fabric, personalization of outside relationships, use of local savings, satisfaction of local needs (of businesses and individuals), compliance with a local economic and cultural tradition, and so on. To this obtain greater legitimacy, the goals and values of the owner-managers had to be consistent with the development of surrounding cultural values, despite the context of globalization, which might force them to adopt a globalization strategy (Marchesnay, 1992). The notion of "new entrepreneur" was created (Sweeney, 1982) to convey these new values. Most venture creators were now graduates (Smith's self-taught craftsman became rare, even in the manufacturing sector). This implied a certain level of shared culture and values, between owner-managers and the people working with them. Unfortunately, with the exception of Gert Hofstede (1987), who worked on large global corporations, very few researchers have taken an interest in these cultural aspects of small business. More systematic work is therefore needed on the ethical attitudes of owner-managers, and the repercussions of such attitudes on strategic behaviour (V.A., 1990-1991, Serwinek, 1992; Longeneker et al., 1989).

4.2   *Organizational culture*

Another important question concerns the match between the values of the owner-manager and those of the other members of the organization, which we refer to as the "culture" in its broad sense. In fact, as we saw in the introduction, the smaller the business, the more personalized it tends to be (Mahé de Boislandelle, 1988). Also, the level of formality and task differentiation tends to decrease with size. Personalization is a product of the owner-manager, but also of strong interpersonal relationships. Conflicts are more frequent, but are usually solved better than in large corporations.

The owner-manager's values emerge at different stages of the strategic decision-making process:

- First, in the management and control style, as shown by management authors such as Blake and Mouton. While we might agree that decision-making is fairly centralized in small businesses, we must also accept that several decision-making processes exist (autocratic, deliberative), depending, if we follow Mintzberg's classifications (1990), on the owner-manager's style (ad-hoc or paternalistic).
- Second, in the choice of the functions considered to be essential within the organization. This aspect has been highlighted in a number of entrepreneurial typologies. For example, the "PIG" group would certainly be more concerned with the capitalistic functions (production, transportation, warehousing) involving tangible assets. In contrast, the "GAP" group would be more likely to concentrate on "intangible" functions (marketing, promotion, innovation, training), and outsource the capitalistic functions - although in reality, the situation tends to be a much more complex combination of the two (Guilhon, 1992).

However, owner-managers are themselves influenced by organizational values:

- First, the members of the organization can influence the owner-manager quite considerably. An example would be the role of the spouse or the accountant. Similarly, if the owner-manager is surrounded by people qualified in the areas in which he or she is not an expert (the case of the "modernist" as opposed to the "traditionalist"), these people will have a strong influence on the owner-manager's decisions and impose their own values.
- Second, the owner-manager must consider the firm's identity, usually related to its history and sector of activity. This is especially the case for family businesses, or businesses that are well-established in their region or sector, with their myths, heroes, values and "in-house spirit". This may translate into inter-generation conflict in cases of succession (Handler, 1991) or qualification conflicts in cases of technological renewal in the profession. Clearly, such problems will be exacerbated if the business is bought or taken over by an individual or another firm with a different culture.

Overall, the "corporate strategy" of the small business is a strategic subsystem within which the values of the owner-manager, the environment and the organization interact. In reality, the relationships are extremely complex, and they have a much greater influence on both the style of decision-making and the type of strategic decisions made than would be the case in a large corporation, where interpersonal, eventually emotional relationships (social, professional and family) are less common. This would, if there were any need, plead in favour of a different approach to strategy in small businesses. As the firm grows, aspects more common to large corporations could be re-introduced (see introductory chapter).

In the end, the small business owner-manager's strategic capacity will be judged on the relevance of the strategic choices, as they appear in the "business strategy" (Ansoff, 1969), a sub-system that corresponds to the lower part of the diagram proposed earlier. Consequently, the strategy corresponds here to the choice of activities, based on the internal capacities possessed or required (the "know-how") and the possibilities offered by the environment, in terms of needs to be satisfied (the "know-how-to-satisfy").

Although the two sub-systems have been separated here for the sake of explanation, the same does not apply to real-life decision-making. In real life, give-and-take is the rule, especially where the strategy is the result of an incremental, gradual and emerging process. In such cases, performance and information on resource use (efficiency), satisfaction within the organization (effectivity: Friedlander and Pickle, 1968), and the level of achievement of the objectives (effectiveness) mean that goals are challenged and the linear process of *diagnosis - choice of objectives - control - review of objectives* is avoided. In fact, owner-managers rely heavily on representations rather than "objective" analyses of "reality" - in other words, on what they perceive, because they remember it and because it corresponds to their mental pictures. Thus, the role of experience and intuition (common-sense or sixth-sense) is a key element in the process of learning and knowledge acquisition (Ricard, 1992).

A further consequence is that all information and all action may be strategic in nature whenever it is likely, through one of its elements, to challenge the strategic system in its current, more or less concrete state. This can be considered another characteristic of small business, one that explains its extreme flexibility in the area of strategy.

5.   The strategic system

If we now look at the strategic aspects of small business organization, a number of points need to be made.

First, and perhaps paradoxically, the smaller the organization, the more difficult it is to define its boundaries. Very small businesses, composed of one or a handful of people who are generally members of the same family, are so completely blended with the family patrimony that, for national accounting purposes, they are treated as households or simple consumers! In larger firms, the most striking feature is the importance of relations with outside collaborators (accountant, suppliers, sub-contractors, distributors, transporters and so on), to such a point that the decision-making unit may be difficult to locate, especially if the firm is highly dependent on a single order-giver.

5.1   Business networks

A further point can be added here. Given the widespread development of increasingly specialized activities aimed at satisfying increasingly narrow market segments, it is possible to foresee a reduction in external transaction costs. Whatever its frequency, the transaction will be less uncertain (because of the market structure) and more idiosyncratic (because of offer segmentation). As a result, and in accordance with the "basic resources" trend (Schendle, 1991), small businesses would do well not to invest resources to obtain capacity at a lower market opportunity cost; there is capacity avoidance (Julien and Marchesnay, 1990). We know that a consequence of this could be the introduction of business networks, where member firms supply each other with goods and services, half-way between the market and the hierarchy (Fourcade, 1991). In fact, as we saw in Chapters 1 and 3, the literature on small business networks refers mainly to districts, technopoles and highly specialized regions. The empirical evidence suggests a need for extreme prudence in generalizing meso-systems into networks. For example, in activity parks, sometimes described as a "network (or reticular) process", there is practically no relationships between members, in England and in France. However, beyond the "sublime" network form, it is clear that outsourcing of activities or functions:

- challenges organization boundaries, because strategic decisions interrelate;
- challenges the idea that small businesses are condemned to grow if they are successful, because many owner-managers expressly refuse to go beyond a certain size, in order to maintain their financial independence or decision-making autonomy, even if it means adopting a development approach involving the creation of legally independent units, or the constitution of tiny groups. These groups cannot exceed a certain size, for control reasons. The term "hypofirms" already exists to describe firms whose effectiveness depends on their small size; we now have "hypogroups" (Marchesnay and Julien, 1990);
- challenges the idea, rooted in classical management, that an organization must have all the functions and develop them

harmoniously. One of the contributions of the "basic resources" approach used by Michael Porter is to have shown that a firm, in its value chain, must emphasize its own distinct competencies, to promote its competitive advantage. It must master the know-how that gives it this advantage, even if this means outsourcing some functions (Porter, 1991). Thus, alongside the value chain argument, we have the economic benefits of hypofirm status;

- also challenges the idea that owner-managers should surround themselves with highly qualified resources. For example, if we base our arguments on agency theory, in particular the model of Jensens and Meckling (1986), it is easy to show that hiring highly qualified people generates agency and internal transaction costs that may dissuade owner-managers and encourage them instead to use outside consultants, or intrapreneurs (Carrier, 1992), or even "shared executives" (advisors paid on results, shared between several firms and responsible for long-term projects).

Second, and as a result of the foregoing, the competitive base of small firms deserves special attention. It is built on a specific skill, or know-how. However, the key know-how in the competitive advantage is likely to be challenged over time, due to evolving technology and needs. It is up to owner-managers to identify and even anticipate whether or not they have the entrepreneurial aptitudes to meet these changes. Discontinuities may arise when the competitive base changes radically - for example, automation removes the need for certain technical know-how. When this happens, the whole strategic system is challenged, including the owner-manager's own goals, behaviours and motivations. It is thus clear that organizational change is a highly complex area within the field of small business, since it cannot be separated from the whole strategic aspect of the corporate and business strategy.

5.2   The firm's mission

The same interactivity occurs with the mission. The mission means the type of basic need satisfied. For example, a chair could satisfy a need for rest, or comfort, or aesthetic beauty, or prestige, and so on. Depending on the need satisfied, a corresponding "craft" is required, for example the ability to produce large quantities, the ability to market, the ability to design, the ability to restore, and so on. Similarly, depending on the mission, the proposed range of activities will differ, as will the nature of the services included in the products.

The problem of defining the mission is especially important for small firms, which almost inevitably find themselves in relatively narrow market segments, or niches. They must specify the type of competitive advantage generated by their craft, which in turn corresponds to their competitive position. Dominant needs evolve with society, and they are subdivided on the basis not only of socio-professional categories and income levels, but also lifestyles and other cultural aspects. The fit between the position and the advantage will occur basically through the services attached to the product offered, which will themselves depend on the generic strategy adopted: low costs, high differentiation, narrow specialization (bearing in mind that many firms opt for mixed strategies, and succeed quite well). We know that the niche strategy is often recommended for small firms. However, they must be able to obtain a key competitive advantage from it, and their advantage must be based on a craft mastered by the owner-manager and the organization.

Consequently, the evolution of a small firm's activity strategy is linked to the parallel evolution of the environment and the organization. This generates some delicate problems in the area of organizational change, together with strategic piloting, which is based on technological and commercial scanning (to be discussed in Chapter 7). It is thus easy to understand that small business owner-managers have neither the interest nor the ability to undertake strategic planning in any case - and there are many - where this may result in exposure to changes that they can observe but not control. However, owner-managers do have a certain "visionary" ability (Filion, 1991); in other words, they can express as clearly as possible the situation in which they wish to be at a given future time, based on the major changes they intend to make in their environment and in their organization, resulting from future changes in their goals and activities. Strategic advisory support should thus concentrate mainly on the initial visionary process, revealing possible contradictions in the strategic system. Again, such an approach uses a methodology based on both decision heuristics and systematics, since it involves reaching a viable solution (the vision) following adjustments through repeated iteration in the strategic system. For example, it may be dangerous to use a linear process, without proper feedback, and especially without interaction between the stages, as is currently recommended (for example, Ibrahim, 1992). Such an approach also has the merit of being based on the mental processes of owner-managers, and reproducing their own intellectual approach. As stated at the beginning of this chapter, this avenue is gathering growing support in the main strategic thinking trends (Mintzberg and Quinn, 1991).

Notwithstanding this - and to complexify matters even further - the environment is not restricted to the market alone. We know that the sector, as defined by Porter, includes the components of the channel (upstream suppliers, downstream customers and distributors), potential competitors and close substitutes, in accordance with industrial analysis (Marchesnay, 1991a). A broader analysis of the economic environment would include all contributors of information and decisions likely to influence owner-managers in their strategic decisions. As a result, small firms find themselves in very different, interindividual, institutional and sometimes vital relations networks. We know, for example, that it is from these relations networks that small firms obtain most of their technological and commercial scanning information. As we will see in more detail in Chapter 7, such networks include "tutor" networks (administrations, chambers, professional unions, etc.), "expert" networks (various consulting services), and "partner" networks (mainly customers and suppliers), where many of the relationships are mixed. In view of the importance now ascribed to regional development, the "network" aspect has become particularly significant and deserves separate attention (Marchesnay, 1991c; Dubini and Aldrich, 1991).

Overall, depending on the layer, the competitive environment in the broader sense generates a number of strategic problems that can be separated into three levels in the "meso-environment": the activity sector, the channel and the competition.

- At the activity sector level, the most important risk, in our view, is vulnerability (the extent to which the firm's strategic system is disturbed by environmental disturbances). Such disturbances affect enterprise performance and measure sensitivity to unfavourable external factors. A small firm is even more vulnerable if:

- its activity sector is complex; the level of complexity is defined by the number of players or variables and the number of relations (especially two-way) between the players or variables. Here, the firm runs up against a problem of information control or system control: the more information it has and the simpler its sector, or the more the sector is simplified by the owner-manager, the less vulnerable the firm will be to changes in its environment.

- its activity sector is turbulent - in other words, subject to frequent and/or significant variations (in technology, in tastes, in product design, etc.). The more turbulent the sector, the greater the need for the owner-manager to scan and observe the key aspects of change. If the sector is stable but complex, vulnerability is reduced; if it is simple but turbulent, vulnerability is also reduced (the owner-manager will necessarily be able to obtain information more easily; the same applies to a subcontractor for an order-giver).

- its activity sector is fairly easily accessible, as a result of lack of entry barriers, ease of imitation, interest in the sector, and so on. The more accessible the sector, the less easy it will be to control what happens in it, and the more vulnerable the firm will be. Generally, accessibility goes hand-in-hand with increased risks of complexity and turbulence.

- At the channel level, the risk is one of dependency, either upstream (on suppliers) or downstream (on customers and distributors). In a given transaction, the risk of dependency is increased if the transaction is concentrated with one or a few suppliers, if the partner(s) are difficult to replace, or if the transaction is essential to the firm's strategic system. This situation is common enough for the dependency criterion to have become an indicator of dominant position and anti-competitive practice in French legislation on competition.

Faced with this risk of dependency, we know that firms should diversify their supply sources and distribution channels. However, several strategic situations are possible, in terms of the vulnerability-dependency pairing.

Table 5.3
Vulnerability

		High	Low
Dependency	High	Unfavourable situation E.g. Craftsmen Capacity subcontractors	Dangerous situation Pursuit of other customers or suppliers E.g. small firm with a handful of large customers or a single customer (frequent in spin-offs)
	Low	Risky situation Strong actual or potential competition Need for strategic flexibility Activities at the mercy of fashion, climate or technology	Apparently very favourable situation Risks related to maintenance of niche Fix an adapted generic strategy (need for notoreity)

For each of these situations, it is important to seek the best possible fit between craft and mission, and to specify the generic strategy to be used (pursuit of lower costs, or differentiation, or specialization).

- Finally, at the level of competition, the degree of hostility or aggression constitutes a basis for the strategy, which can reinforce or alleviate problems related to dependency and vulnerability. In extreme cases, we could imagine relatively friendly competition or even cooperation through professional syndicates, such as that which exists in certain endangered sectors. Similarly, the level of aggression plays an important role in sector penetration. A firm entering a sector, faced with perceived (or real) aggression, may in turn adopt an aggressive strategy, or an adaptive strategy (the "follower" in games theory), as T. Covin and J. Covin (1990) showed.

Overall, environment-related strategic situations are particularly complex for small businesses, which are rarely masters of the game. Moreover, small business owner-managers find themselves in a situation of imperfect and limited information. They usually have to rely on perceptions whereas large corporations suffer from information

177

overload, especially figures. This explains the strategic importance of personal relations networks, which far exceeds the importance of "orthodox" planning and strategic diagnosis procedures, as several authors have shown (Martinet and Ribault, 1989; Julien et al., 1997).

The main problem is undoubtedly the link between "corporate strategy" (general policy) and "business strategy" (operational strategy). It is not possible, in small business, to talk of strategic planning in the way that the term is used in the corporate sector. However, on a prescriptive level, it seems that the task of the strategic board, once the goals and lines of action have been established, is to implement and mobilize them by means of an action plan. The action plan must necessarily include the following:

- clarification of the vision; that is, a desired state at a given future time (for example, in three years). The vision should take account of problems of consistency in the strategic system, and feasibility (technical, financial commercial, etc.);

- the introduction of material and immaterial investment plans, with the latter usually complementing the former (for example, introduction of new machinery, new processes, pursuit of new customer groups, etc.);

- the creation of a strategic scanning system based on information gathering processes as similar as possible to those of the owner-manager;

- the creation of a directional system based on indicators familiar to the owner-manager.

Since the strategic process is usually and naturally gradual, the action plan should be reviewed frequently, to reflect the information gathered by the owner-manager or his/her advisor.

Alongside the notion of "action plan", it is useful to develop a "communication plan", even if it turns out to be somewhat sketchy. In fact, external communication depends on two not necessarily consistent representations of the firm:

- the identity of the firm, composed of the values and know-how (craft) considered dominant by the members of the organization. The identity is a result of internal representations;

- the image of the firm, on the other hand, is a result of external representations. Outsiders will perceive the firm on the basis of the services it provides to the community on the market or elsewhere, through goods, services and external factors of all kinds (mission), and on the basis of its social role - in other words, on the mission-legitimacy pairing.

Clearly, there will be some discord. The communication strategy will aim to reduce it, either by better explaining the firm's identity (improving its image), or by changing the identity to suit the wishes of the environment (adapting its image). In view of the growing need for small firms to meld with their local environments, this strategic dimension is likely to become increasingly important, even for very small firms (Marchesnay, in Fourcade, 1991).

As we said earlier, the aim of this chapter was above all to throw some light on the specific features of strategic management in small firms. These features are even more acute in the case of small and very small firms. While new ventures tend to be smaller in size, the vast majority want not to grow but to be competitive on their own scale. It is therefore clear that research on strategic management in very small firms will develop significantly in the coming years.

In our view, the basic questions that need to be asked are the following:

- It is important to know more about the learning and decision-making processes. Here, psychologists have a clear advantage over economists! This direction is fully consistent with the general concerns of strategy theorists, as this chapter has tried to show.

- It is important to know more about the process of increasing competitiveness and the basis of competitiveness in small businesses. Here again, the reversal of strategic models in favour of "small strategic groups" should facilitate future research.

- More thought is required on the role of small business in the third industrial generation society. More specifically, we should question the place of small business on global markets, and the nature of their globalization strategies. At a broader level, small business development will demand new forms of regulation in industrial systems, thus challenging traditional government industrial policies.

If the future is not what it once was, the arrival of small competitive businesses is undoubtedly part of the reason.

6 Small business marketing

"I am of the opinion that the most honourable vocation is to serve the public and be useful to many. Fructus enim ingenii et virtutis omnisque prestantiae tum maximum accipitur, cum in proximum quemque confertur. (We never better enjoy the fruits of genius and virtue and of any superiority than when we share it with our neighbour.)" Michel de Montaigne, "Essai".

1. Introduction

This chapter addresses the subject of marketing in small and medium-sized businesses. Our aim is to identify the elements that differentiate it from corporate marketing, as regards various forms of planning and development of marketing strategies and tactics.

Researchers have only recently begun to pay attention to the various functions of small businesses. The marketing function first attracted interest in the early 1980s, when the trend was to study marketing on the basis of firm size, i.e. large versus small. Stasch and Ward (1987) suggested three elements to explain the special characteristics of the marketing function in small firms:

1. the difference in marketing and competition circumstances;
2. the differences in management, due to the influence of the owner-manager who is often also the founder;
3. limited financial and organizational resources.

Marchesnay (1988) identified the following distinctive features of small businesses:

- highly personalized management;
- significant sensitivity to the environment;
- the specific features of their activities.

According to Hills (1987), the lack of academic interest in small business marketing may have been due to the fact that researchers viewed the term "small business" as having a connotation of mediocrity, stagnation and failure to grow, which made research into the phenomenon somewhat unexciting. Hills goes further than Stasch and Ward, believing that several variables must be considered when studying marketing in small businesses:

- the firm's size and life cycle;

- economies of scale;
- resource constraints;
- limited geographical presence on the market;
- weaker image;
- lack of customer loyalty;
- small market shares;
- decision-making based on less complete information than in large corporations;
- limited time available for management;
- the scarcity of professional managers;
- a mixture of personal and financial objectives not necessarily aimed at maximizing resources or organizational efficiency.

In firms exhibiting several of these variables, as we saw in the introductory chapter, we might expect the marketing function to be *perceived* and *performed* somewhat differently than in large corporations (Hills, 1987, p.5).

However, marketing can play an important role at three separate levels:

Corporate marketing: consists, from a customer and competitor standpoint, in establishing a "business unit" portfolio and allocating resources to each unit;

Strategic marketing: consists in establishing how each unit will compete by identifying a competitive advantage.

Marketing management: consists in developing and implementing marketing programs for every product/market pairing of each business unit.

In an exploratory study of executives in small manufacturing businesses, Laforge and Miller (1987) shed new light on the role of firm size as a moderating variable in the relationship between environment and strategic marketing (the second level).

They identified two types of *environmental factors*: *industrial factors* and *market factors*. The former category is composed of eight factors, including the number of firms and employees, growth of employment in the sector, the entry of new firms, concentration and intensity of competition, and import competition. The second category includes market size, growth, the arrival of new purchasers, market fragmentation and heterogeneity.

The 13 *strategic dimensions* are geographical coverage of the market, segmentation, a full range of products, speciality products, new product development, the variety of product characteristics, product quality, brand identification, response and delivery time, service, low prices, position based on cost, and price competition. The *enterprise factors* related to size include number of employees, sales and market share.

Laforge and Miller's results are interesting, in that firm size was found to be a predictor of strategy in only one case out of thirteen, but was a moderator for eight of the thirteen strategic dimensions, thus suggesting that size should definitely be considered in research on marketing strategies, even though it does not explain the strategic decisions made.

A new research trend emerged in the mid-1980s, when researchers suggested that it may be possible to understand the specific features of the marketing function in small firms by studying the entrepreneurship/marketing interface. Since 1987, five symposiums have been held on the subject, generating a number of contributions and some interesting debates. Since the winter of 1990, the biannual conferences of the American Marketing Association have included a marketing/entrepreneurship division. Readers will not be surprised to find several contributions from these conferences in this chapter.

The chapter first presents a conceptual framework illustrating all aspects of the marketing function within a business. The subsequent literature analysis is divided into three parts, the first dealing with the overall marketing process, the second with some of its specific aspects, and the third with international marketing. The chapter concludes with some suggested avenues for future research.

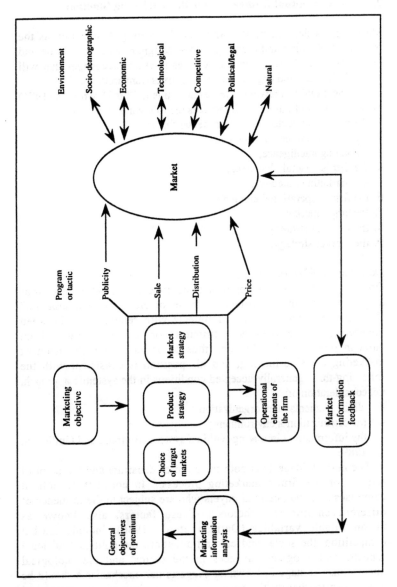

Figure 6.1
Downing's (1971) model

183

2. A conceptual framework for the marketing function

Marketing is defined by the American Marketing Association as the process of planning and carrying out the design, pricing, promotion and distribution of ideas, goods and services to create exchanges that will satisfy individual and organizational objectives (Iannarelli, 1987).

A conceptual framework often used in this field is Downing's (1971) model, shown in Figure 6.1. It includes the following elements:
1. the market subjected to environmental forces;
2. feedback from the environment;
3. marketing intelligence;
4. the firm's general objectives;
5. the marketing objectives;
6. the firm's operational elements;
7. the target market;
8. the product strategy;
9. the market strategy.

Downing's (1971) Model
Downing used a systemic approach to describe the marketing process as a system that can be defined as "a set of elements in interaction" (Bertalannfy, 1956), "a set of objects with relationships between themselves and between their attributes", or "the unit resulting from parts in interaction". Downing thus proposed an overall vision of marketing decision-making, and his position is consistent with the following three generally-accepted conditions in the systemic approach, i.e. consideration of:
- all the elements in an organization;
- the organization's environment;
- the information circulating within a system (Bertrand and Guillemet, 1989).

The market (stage 1) is both the point of departure and the point of arrival for the firm's marketing process. In constant turmoil, it comprises real and potential buyers who are subject to the influence of different environment factors. These factors, also known as uncontrollable variables (Darmon et al., 1986), include market competition, the social and cultural situation, the political and legal aspects, technological advances in the sector, and the ecological dimension. At stage 2, Downing suggests that mechanisms should be established to identify the behaviour and reactions of consumers, and their adjustments to the different environmental forces.

The aim of stage 3, marketing intelligence, is to give meaning to the information gathered at the previous stages, and to interpret the data available. This phase is vital in the subsequent overall development of marketing strategies and tactics. Interpretation requires statistical processing and the use of mathematical models or other quantitative or qualitative methods.

Stages 1 and 2 are thus concerned with information gathering (secondary data at the first stage, primary data at the second). The first three components of the model are related to the firm's marketing information system, which must be constantly on the lookout for changes in the environment and in individual behaviour. The environmental forces provide input for feedback, whose output becomes marketing intelligence input.

Two filters affect data interpretation: the general objectives (four in all) and the firm's operational elements (six in all). In small firms, the general objectives are often the owner-manager's personal objectives, values and priorities. The operational elements include the firm's production capacities, human resources, marketing expertise and financial resources - in other words, its strengths and weaknesses. Marketing intelligence output (marketing objectives, strategies and tactics) must be consistent with the two filters and must be of a kind that will help the firm achieve its general objectives within its specific limits.

The commercial offer that results from marketing intelligence is composed first and foremost of the choice of target market - "*WHO*" - which consists in identifying a segment of the market analyzed. The product - "*WHAT*" - best suited to the needs of the segment chosen is then identified. These two stages are classified at the level of strategic marketing (Lambin, 1994). They are long-term decisions whose effects are felt later (Ayral, 1988). They are virtually irreversible, and a bad choice of product/market pairing could threaten the firm's survival.

The market strategy corresponds to operational marketing (Lambin, 1991), and consists in deciding "*HOW*" the firm will intervene in the competitive environment, based on the product/market pairing established previously. The marketing mix, or the variables that can be controlled by the firm, is composed of the product, price, publicity, promotion and distribution strategies (Darmon et al., 1991). Such decisions are usually less restrictive than the previous ones, and their effect is mainly short-term, although distribution-related decisions may also have longer term effects because of the duration of agreements with network partners. The effect of market globalization has been to increase the strategic aspect of distribution for the firm.

The implementation of marketing strategies (tactics) serves as market input, disturbing the market and triggering adjustments by competitors, consumers and other players (for example, the government may legislate to control new commercial practices). The model illustrates the dynamic aspect of the marketing process.

It also highlights the importance of information in marketing, and uses systemic notions, where a system is "... a dynamic whose elements are interrelated and interact" (Bertrand and Guillemet, 1989, p.39). It also uses notions of cybernetics, "the science of communication and control processes in living bodies and machines" (p.25). Overall, the model as used to study small business marketing is intended to be descriptive rather than prescriptive.

3.   The literature on the general marketing process

A number of authors have examined the overall marketing function, while others have concentrated on specific elements. This part of the chapter looks at contributions in the former category.

3.1   Research on the marketing function as a whole

We will begin by outlining what we consider to be a major contribution to current knowledge of the role of the marketing function for small business owner-managers. A longitudinal study (Ellis and Jolibert, 1991) using a sample of small and medium-sized businesses in Brazil over the period 1976 to 1986 revealed a correlation between survival and executive knowledge of the marketing concept, and between executive marketing attitudes and marketing activities. Generally speaking, the correlation seemed to be stronger for medium-sized firms than for small firms.

For example, for the period studied, the overall survival rate of small and medium-sized firms in a developing industrial region was found to be 60% (62 survivors out of a total of 106 new ventures). Firms were considered "young" if they were less than seven years old when data was first gathered. Age was not found to be a discriminatory factor for survival, while size, defined by number of employees, was. Small firms (10-49 employees) exhibited a survival rate of just 46%, compared with 78% for medium-sized firms (50-500 employees).

The authors divided their results by surviving firms, and by executive knowledge of the marketing concept. In the first case, given the impact of size on survival, the profiles of survivors and non-survivors were compared separately for the small and medium-sized categories. In the second case, the results were calculated for the sample as a whole. The differences in the profiles of small survivors and non-survivors is interesting. The results are shown by marketing activities (Product-Publicity and Promotion-Price-Distribution), and then according to the marketing attitudes or orientations of the senior managers interviewed.

Product
All the survivors had changed their product lines. This was particularly true of medium-sized survivors, where the variation was highly significant. Although the variation tended in the same direction for small firms, it was not significant.

Moreover, the managers of surviving firms were more motivated (28% compared with 6%) by satisfaction of customer needs to make changes or additions to their product lines.

As far as knowledge of the marketing concept was concerned, two senior managers out of three had a "production orientation" rather than a "marketing orientation". It is interesting to note that firms in the former category added to or changed their product lines only half as frequently as firms in the latter category (30% as opposed to 60%).

Publicity and promotion
The survivors did not seem to differ significantly from the others in terms of the type of publicity and promotion used. However, a major difference was observed in their use of a variety of media, rather than just one or two possibilities. This distinction was particularly clear in the case of medium-sized firms, where the survivors used an average of 2.7 advertising media, compared with 1.2 for the non-survivors.

The use of publicity and promotion did not seem to differ significantly over time. However, a change was observed in the combination of media used. For example, advertising and the use of samples decreased, to be replaced by publicity leaflets, catalogues and sales representatives.

Firms with a "production orientation" used an average of 2.1 types of publicity and promotion, compared with 3.56 types for firms with a "marketing orientation".

Price
Most of the firms studied fixed their prices on the basis of expected costs and benefits, without reference to the prices charged by competitors. This was particularly noticeable among the survivors in the small firm category (68% as opposed to 47%), while the reverse was true

for medium-sized firm category (50% as opposed to 30%). The authors suggested two possible explanations for this: first, the larger firms dominated their local markets to a greater extent and were thus less concerned with competition; and second, the segment in question was not sensitive to price. We believe that both these explanations are equally plausible. The number of firms that set their prices using more than one approach increased during the second round of data gathering (1986-1988), indicating a development in this area. More than 80% of the firms with a "marketing orientation" said they used comparison with competitors as the method of fixing their prices, compared with 45% of firms with a "product orientation".

Distribution

More survivors than non-survivors used in-house distribution channels (i.e. control), although the differences were not significant. In contrast, the number of channels used seemed to increase the rate of survival. In fact, the number of survivors using multiple networks was almost double the number of non-survivors. Firm size did not seem to affect the number of channels used.

The second round of data gathering revealed that the distribution methods used by survivors had shifted towards the channels over which they had more control. For example, direct selling was used in 89% of cases, compared with 54% in the first round, corporate stores in 33% of cases, compared with 8%, wholesalers in 29% of cases, compared with 38%, and agents in 11% of cases, compared with 17%.

Managerial attitudes

When asked "What are you main marketing problems?", senior managers identified a variety of external and internal problems. The former consisted mainly in worries about competition in general and substitute products. External problems were mentioned more by survivors (34%) than non-survivors (9%).

Internal problems such as evaluation of promotional costs and recovery of accounts receivable were mentioned more by non-survivors (34% as opposed to 19%). Managers with a "marketing orientation" also seemed to be less worried by internal problems (39% as opposed to 68%).

The results of Ellis and Jolibert's longitudinal study suggest a correlation between firm survival on the one hand, and the marketing activities and attitudes of senior management on the other. This was more clearly visible in the case of medium-sized firms.

According to the authors, the marketing orientation of senior small business managers and the practice of marketing itself had an impact on the survival of industrial firms in a developing region where knowledge and application of marketing concepts were generally deficient. The major points to be remembered are that the firms which survived between 1976 and 1986 were those that:

- made more changes to their products, more frequently, in response to the needs expressed by the market;
- made greater and more diversified use of the publicity and promotional methods available;
- used a multiple distribution network;
- had identified major problems that were external to the firm and associated with the competition;
- had been influenced by the competition when fixing their prices.

Also of interest in terms of the overall marketing function is a pilot study by Kinsey (1987a), who looked at how and to what extent marketing was practised in small Scottish firms with less than 100 employees. A sample of fifty CEOs (owners and/or managers) agreed to take part in the survey. The questionnaire included sections on the firm's history, and comprehension and use of marketing, planning and management.

The results revealed that most of the firms produced less than five products, and that half of those products had changed during the last five years, in response to customer demand. The firms did not seem to have a system for anticipating future changes, and their reading of the environment seemed somewhat muddled. Nearly 70% of respondents did not know their firm's market share. Those that did were local market leaders.

Current customers had been obtained by the sales force, personal contact, word of mouth and, last of all, publicity and promotion. When it came to attracting new customers, the firms all said they wanted to make more use of the sales force, to rely less on word of mouth, and to use their own retail outlets and potential customer lists.

Competition seemed to be considered mainly with respect to prices, and the buying habits of customers were rarely considered. Twenty of the fifty respondent firms exported their products, but for 75% of these, exporting was the result of chance or luck rather than planning. Similar observations were made by Brisoux et al. (1992), while Brochu's (1991) findings were contradictory, showing that nearly eight small firms out of ten were interested or very interested in exporting, and were taking steps to do so successfully (Joyal, Julien and Deshaies, 1995).

The main strengths that respondents listed for their firms were product quality, service reliability, price and personal contact with customers. The main weaknesses were the financial aspect (working capital) and personnel management, identified by 30% of respondents, with marketing ranked third, mentioned by only 15% of respondents. Kinsey (1987b) attributes this to the fact that owner-managers tend to underestimate the importance of marketing. A handful of respondents (7%) admitted they were unable to interpret information obtained from the market.

As regards the controllable variables (the marketing mix), prices were fixed mainly on the basis of costs, very little on the basis of competition and demand, and even less on a combination of the three. Publicity and promotional expenses tended to be low - in fact, one firm out of every four carried out no advertising or promotion. Emphasis was firmly on the sales force. The firms questioned attributed relatively little importance to product conditioning, and changes were generally infrequent. Distribution, however, was considered to be a very important factor.

The research also revealed a planning deficiency in small firms, which tended to concentrate on solving everyday problems, as we saw in Chapter 4. For example, 80% of the sample firms had no formal planning process. Although they seemed to spend a lot of time on marketing (more than 40% of the time for 40% of the firms), marketing budgets were nevertheless small - less than 5% of the total budget in 60% of cases.

Some of the general conclusions drawn from this study were the lack of planning of the marketing function, the low level of sophistication and the lack of financial support. These results should, however, be viewed with some caution, for three main reasons: the small sample spread over a large number of different sectors, the fact that some of the products in question were industrial products, and the fact that some of the firms were family firms that had existed for many years.

3.2   Financial limits and the practice of marketing

It has often been observed that small firms have very limited marketing budgets. For example, Weinrauch et al. (1990), in their exploratory study, looked at how such firms managed to market their products or services despite budget constraints. They emphasized the realistic attitude that marketing consultants must adopt when choosing strategies and tactics for small and medium-sized firms.

The first set of results from this study, which used a sample of 52 retailers and 47 manufacturing and service firms, revealed that the technique most used (by three-quarters of the sample) was point-of-sale promotion, followed in descending order by "Yellow Pages" advertising (71%), price reductions (68%), window displays (65%) and cooperative publicity (53%), i.e. the division of publicity and promotional costs between different distribution network channels. Although 20% of respondents used catalogues, they did not offer customers a free telephone line because of their limited resources. Sponsorship and publicity leaflets were used more commonly by service companies.

The measure of effectiveness of the methods used, shown as feedback in Downing's model, should be of constant concern to small business owner-managers (Perreault et al., 1990). According to Weinrauch et al. (1990), marketing managers perceive customer newsletters, brochures, window displays, point of sale promotions, price reductions and Yellow Page advertising as the most effective methods for increasing sales.

Owner-managers face many different problems in marketing. It is important for researchers and socioeconomic players alike to be aware of these problems if they are to help small firms overcome them. The main problems highlighted in the study were:
- lack of planning;
- failure to complete projects undertaken;
- lack of marketing control;
- failure to account for some tasks;
- poor understanding of the importance of marketing in achieving the general objectives;
- poor synchronization in test activities;
- lack of patience with the marketing program.

The literature suggests that the first five years are of key importance in small business survival, success and strategies (Timmons, Smollen and Dengee, 1985). This issue was the subject of a study that attempted to identify the techniques most commonly used by small firms less than five years old. It was found that, over time, the use of window displays declined, while the use of the Yellow Pages increased. Changes in promotional techniques seemed to occur when the firms had an established customer base. It was not surprising to find that sponsorship became more common after five years. A condition for sponsorship success is that the sponsor already enjoys a certain reputation, and the sponsorship activity serves merely to remind consumers of the brand, product or service.

3.3   Marketing and business success

Since it is generally accepted that marketing is one of the most critical functional areas for entrepreneurial success, Ram and Forbes (1990) attempted to identify:
1. the level of difficulty associated with some marketing activities;
2. improvements required in the elements of the marketing strategy;
3. the success criteria for small and medium-sized businesses;
4. success and/or failure factors.

The authors used a case study approach, with a sample composed of 20 entrepreneurs who had all attended the University of Arizona's entrepreneurship program. All were founders and directors of small business operations. Six firms were at the creation stage, three at start-up, ten had reached maturity and one had been sold. The firms were divided almost equally between services and product innovation. The results of the research showed that:
1. Generally speaking, marketing activities were perceived as difficult by the entrepreneurs. Those perceived as most difficult were the development of a distribution network (80%), product conditioning (73%), a good product/service mix (67%), the development and reputation of the product or service (58%), and market research (53%). For products, prototype development and distribution seemed to present the most problems.
2. According to the respondents, some aspects of the strategy needed to be improved. On a scale of 1 to 5 (1 for no improvement required and 5 for major improvement required), marketing as a whole seemed to require some improvement (2.85). The areas where the most improvement was needed were publicity and promotion (3.20), market research (2.84), distribution (2.61), product or service (2.52), sales force (2.47) and price (2.37). The price variable seemed to be neglected by marketing managers. They did not believe much improvement was needed, and other research has shown that they do not consider identification of price-fixing formulas to be important.
3. Some elements of marketing were thought to be success criteria for the firm - in other words, a basis for measuring the firm's success. This was the case for customer loyalty (30% of respondents) and market share (20% of respondents). However, profit was ranked first among the success criteria by 75% of respondents, followed by total sales (30%) and growth rate (15%).
4. Respondents listed the reasons for their success as the product (for manufacturers), and staff and sales force (for service firms). Other important factors included positioning, overall marketing strategy,

192

good management and customer service. Not surprisingly, promotion and distribution were not listed as success factors, since the respondents were not satisfied with their performance in this area, and felt that a considerable improvement was needed.

This exploratory study, despite certain limits due to the size and nature of the sample, produced some interesting results on the role of marketing in business success.

3.4   The problems of growth stages for firms

Kraft and Goodell (1989) linked certain marketing problems with growth stages, although this approach has its limits, as we saw in the introductory chapter. More than 750 owner-managers took part in the research. The sample was divided into three groups: firms aged 0 to 2 years, firms aged 2 to 5 years, and firms aged 5 years or over.

Regardless of age, the most important problem categories were almost all connected with the firm's external environment (five of the first six). Marketing ranked seventh of the fourteen problem categories identified as major or critical by the respondents. The sample owner-managers thus seem to be fairly confident of being able to operate adequately with the marketing methods at their disposal.

Sales forecasts, market research and testing of new products or new ideas were among the most common problems for the owner-managers questioned, while the choice of a marketing consultant, the choice of advertising media, the sales force, distribution and segmentation seemed to be of less concern. It is interesting to note that the perceived severity of certain problems varied according to the firm's age. For example, "what makes it sell" was perceived as a crucial problem by 14% of new firms (0-2 years), but as critical by nearly a quarter of the firms aged three to five years.

A control group of 33 small business experts was formed, and their perceptions of the crucial problems facing small businesses was compared with the perceptions of the owner-managers. Marketing was perceived as the fourth most important problem by the experts, and seventh by the owner-managers. Like the authors of this study, we think, on the basis of these results, that small business owner-managers are perhaps not aware of their deficiencies in the area of marketing, and underestimate the problems this creates.

Cohen and Stretch (1989) also attempted to identify the problems faced by small business owner-managers. It is difficult to compare their results with the results of the preceding study, since in this case the authors obtained their information from firms seeking free consulting

193

services from a non-profit organization with the mission of helping firms in need.

The authors examined more than 120 requests for help from firms, and discovered that marketing problems were the most common (based on frequency, not severity). Their results showed that most of the problems encountered were related to the firm's internal environment, not the external environment, as Kraft and Goodell (1989) had found. Three of the four most frequently-mentioned problems - increasing sales, publicity and promotion, accounting and book-keeping, and market research - were related to marketing. Respondents thus seemed to be aware of the need to organize their sales properly in order to remain in business, and this had become a central concern for them.

3.5   Crucial activities and time as a resource

The above studies considered the owner-manager's perception of the importance of the various company activities and compared it with the perception of small business experts. Teach and Tarpley (1989) went on to study how entrepreneurs behave towards the activities considered crucial. They decided the best way of approaching this question was to look at how the entrepreneurs used their most precious resource, time.

Previous studies by the same authors in the micro-computing field showed that success, measured as sales, varied according to the planning process, and that marketing planning was more likely to bring success than general planning.

Of the 119 senior managers who took part in Teach and Tarpley's study, most said they spent the majority of their time on general company management (63 hours per month). However, they spent an average of 47 hours per month on marketing, ranking it at the top of the list of enterprise functions.

The authors divided their sample into two groups, one composed of firms aged eight years or less, and one composed of firms over eight years of age. Only four activities differed significantly between the two groups in terms of their perceived importance for the firm. They were:
- publicity, market research and price, which were perceived as more important in the early years;
- financial management, which was perceived as more important for "mature" firms.

These results confirm the importance of some activities for small firms, in terms of both the owner-manager's perception and the time actually spent on them.

3.6   Types of entrepreneurs and management behaviour

Lorrain and his colleagues (1989, 1990, 1991) studied the management behaviour of 70 small business owner-managers during the first year in business. Their work has shed light on the management practices of two types of entrepreneurs: the craftsman and the opportunist (Smith, 1967). The former are not well-educated but have good technical skills, work is their main focus of interest, they have a paternalist attitude to the firm and are not growth-oriented. The latter are better educated and usually have considerable and wide-ranging experience, they are less paternalist and are not afraid of losing control of the firm. The limits of Smith's analysis have been criticized in Chapter 4. However, it remains valid as a preliminary approach.

Business knowledge prior to venture creation was measured using 11 statements ranging from knowledge of major market trends to sources of financing in the environment. The groups differed significantly with respect to four elements. The "opportunists" were better-informed about the break-even point, competitors and sources of financing, while the "craftsmen" were more knowledgeable about the role of innovation in the sector.

Table 6.1 shows that the behaviour of the two groups can be distinguished significantly (05) by the managerial functions of planning, organization and control, and by all the administrative functions.

With respect to the marketing function, Table 6.1 also reveals significant differences between the two groups for nine of the 16 marketing dimensions proposed (market knowledge, identification of potential new markets, knowledge of competitors, formulation of marketing objectives, knowledge of competitors' marketing objectives, carrying out of a marketing plan, knowledge of sales by product line, cost of sales, and knowledge of product cost price). These activities were performed more frequently by the opportunist entrepreneurs. However, for all respondents, knowledge of market share, use of publicity and control of publicity were very weak.

Table 6.1
Administrative and management functions

	Total Sample			Craftsman				Opportunist				U/P
	N	X	SD	N	X	SD	RG	N	X	SD	RG	
Administrative functions												
Production	69	3.63	.78	39	3.34	.77	29.01	28	3.86	.80	40.95	351.5/.006
Marketing	70	3.15	.82	39	2.89	.77	26.37	28	3.69	.73	44.63	248.5/.000
Human resources	46	2.83	.80	27	2.18	.95	20.83	24	2.90	.85	31.81	184.5/.004
R&D	43	3.06	.84	25	2.85	.76	18.34	16	3.26	.89	25.16	133.5/.037
Finance	70	3.15	.97	39	2.79	.89	27.60	28	3.57	.96	42.91	296.5/.001
Managerial functions												
Planning	70	2.92	.76	39	2.61	.71	26.91	28	3.67	.73	43.88	269.5/.000
Organization	70	2.97	.80	39	2.04	.89	27.00	28	2.82	.90	43.75	273.0/.000
Commanding	43	3.92	.50	27	3.17	1.24	23.23	24	3.76	.72	29.23	246.5/.142
Controlling	69	3.15	.78	39	2.73	.78	27.92	28	3.30	.80	42.46	309.0/.003
Mean		3.18			2.73				3.37			

Source: Lorrain et al., 1990.

196

Table 6.2
The marketing behaviour of craftsmen and opportunists

Marketing statements	Total Sample			Craftsman				Opportunist				U/P
	N	X	SD	N	X	SD	RG	N	X	SD	RG	
Market	70	3.99	1.22	39	3.69	1.28	29.64	28	4.32	1.09	40.07	376.0/.021
New markets	70	3.34	1.60	39	2.97	1.51	29.22	28	3.82	1.63	40.66	359.5/.014
Customer needs	69	4.25	1.17	39	4.03	1.31	31.23	28	4.50	0.92	37.86	438.0/.116
Purchasing habits	68	3.85	1.46	39	3.64	1.71	33.38	28	4.00	1.16	34.86	522.0/.742
Competitors	70	3.90	1.34	39	3.62	1.35	29.46	28	4.29	1.30	40.32	369.0/.016
Market share	69	1.77	1.26	39	1.62	1.22	31.18	28	2.04	1.32	37.93	436.0/.098
Marketing objectives	70	3.27	1.49	39	2.80	1.47	27.78	28	3.96	1.35	42.66	303.5/.001
Marketing objectives of competitors	70	3.23	1.61	39	2.64	1.51	27.08	28	4.00	1.47	43.64	276.0/.000
Marketing plan	70	2.91	1.58	39	2.46	1.54	28.81	28	3.54	1.53	41.23	343.5/.008
Information gathering	69	4.12	1.16	39	3.95	1.23	31.19	28	4.36	1.03	37.91	436.5/.008
Sales by product	68	3.12	1.62	39	2.60	1.45	28.54	28	3.71	1.68	41.61	333.0/.005
Cost of sales	64	2.77	1.65	39	2.24	1.60	29.25	28	3.11	1.60	39.27	370.5/.028
New product penetration	69	3.17	1.44	39	3.00	1.34	32.42	28	3.29	1.65	36.20	484.5/.423
Costs	69	3.62	1.44	39	3.31	1.36	28.40	28	4.14	1.38	41.80	327.5/.004
Publicity	68	1.90	1.22	39	1.74	1.02	32.99	28	2.00	1.36	35.41	506.5/.576
Advertising effectiveness	69	2.07	1.42	39	1.97	1.41	32.64	28	2.18	1.44	35.89	493.0/.455

Source: Ibidem.

197

A more recent study (Lorrain and Perreault, 1992) was performed on a sample of "young entrepreneurs" under 30 years of age. The sample was composed of individuals who had received financial support from the Quebec government's "Young Promoters", "Business Grant" and "New Entrepreneurs" programs. Other names were obtained from the regional offices of Quebec's Department of Industry, Trade and Technology. The final sample totalled 2,210 young entrepreneurs, to whom the questionnaire was sent by mail. In all, 606 completed questionnaires were returned, and used to compile the statistical data.

Table 6.3
Problems encountered before start-up

Problem	Mean[1]	Standard deviation
Government sluggishness and paperwork	3.1	1.7
Obtaining funding	3.0	1.5
Preparation of business plan and project planning	2.7	1.4
Lack of business experience	2.6	1.3
Suppliers' prices and credit conditions	2.5	2.0
Obtaining customers in advance	2.5	2.0
Doubts about success	2.4	1.4
Finding customers	2.3	1.4
Obtaining personnel	2.3	2.3
Wariness of elders	2.2	2.2
Finding suppliers	2.1	1.8
Lack of moral support	2.0	1.6
Finding premises	2.0	1.8
Relations with partners	1.7	2.3
Family opposition	1.4	2.4

Note: 1. Scale from 1 (no problem) to 5 (significant problem).

Source: Lorrain et Perreault (1992).

As Table 6.3 shows, marketing planning ranked second (after financial planning) as the aspect of most concern to the sample entrepreneurs in preparing their business plans. In business plan implementation, no activity really stood out from the others, except perhaps the time required for organizing premises.

The research identified two types of problems: first, the problems encountered during implementation of the enterprise plan, and second, the problems encountered during the survey, i.e. during operations. In the former category, two marketing elements seemed to be of moderate importance: identifying customers, and the art of convincing customers. In the latter category, as shown in Table 6.4, the major post start-up problems were almost all marketing-related. The most serious problem was increasing the number of customers to achieve sales and profit objectives, using the marketing mix variables. Even at this stage, the enterprise leaders were aware of the need to introduce new products or services.

Table 6.4
Problems encountered after start-up

Problem	Mean[1]	Standard deviation
Increasing the number of customers	4.4	0.9
Meeting sales objectives	4.3	1.0
Meeting profit objectives	4.3	1.1
Publicizing product or service (i.e.) publicity-promotion)	4.0	1.2
Improving product-service	3.9	1.4
Selling to new customer groups	3.8	1.3
Satisfying demand	3.7	1.4
Distribution	3.7	1.4
Selling a new product-service	3.7	1.4
Attracting competent personnel	3.6	1.5
Extending sales territory	3.6	1.4
Finding reliable suppliers	3.5	1.5
Developing an accounting system	3.4	1.4
Obtaining financial support	3.1	1.5
Defining roles and policies	3.1	1.4
Insufficient number of suppliers	2.4	1.4
Insufficient number of external advisors or internal members for the board of directors	2.0	1.3

Note: 1. Scale from 1 (no problem) to 5 (significant problem).

Source: Idem.

4. Some contributions concerning specific aspects of marketing

To our knowledge, very few researchers have considered specific marketing activities in small businesses. So far, as we saw in the last section, most have tended to concentrate on the marketing process as a whole, and the changes resulting from enterprise growth. Nevertheless, there is a body of work on small business market research, which we will present in the following paragraphs.

According to LaBarbera and Rosenberg (1989), one of the most serious problems at the start-up stage is assessing market potential. Many entrepreneurs tend to overestimate demand (Hills, 1985). Moreover, market research seems to be of no use (Spitzer et al., 1989), and negative information that contradicts the business project is often ignored or set aside. Some entrepreneurs carry out research simply to comply with bank requirements. However, LaBarbera et al. (1989) presented three case studies to show that even simple, fairly limited surveys, using purposely-selected samples, can be extremely useful for small firms. Both consultants and business leaders should therefore be innovative and use their common sense, to adapt sophisticated tools to a less extravagant level.

The market information available to small business owner-managers seems to be insufficient and fragmented. This is especially apparent among young firms (Marchesnay, 1988). Formal market surveys are not used, either in the industrial sector (Schlegelmilch et al., 1986) or the service and trade sectors (Weinrauch et al., 1991).

Moreover, according to Meziou (1991), small American businesses devote very little effort to discovering the needs of current and potential customers. Reagan and Gavin (1988) and Lorrain et al. (1989) observed slightly more awareness of this element among their samples, but their results did not show what methods the entrepreneurs used to obtain the information.

According to Spitzer et al. (1989), a formal marketing plan is required if market research is to be fully appreciated. In our opinion, it is likely that entrepreneurs who have undertaken a formal planning process will have a higher regard for market research, since they will have a better grasp of the importance of the information it provides.

Marketing planning in small businesses

Marketing planning can be considered the most classical way of coordinating marketing activities (Hermann, 1993). Some contributions in this area are worth noting. For example, Carson and Cromie (1990) observed that 40% of their sample of 68 small firms at the start-up stage had done some marketing planning (described as the "implicit level"), while all the others had made no effort whatsoever (described as "non-marketing"). None of the sample firms exhibited marketing behaviour that could be described as "sophisticated". The authors concluded that more than half of all small firms did not carry out marketing planning, at least in the generally-accepted sense.

Other work by Carson (1990) using a sample of 80 very different small firms revealed that respondent firms usually did not adopt long-term reasoning, and tended to emphasize short-term or immediate marketing problems. Similar results were obtained by Chéron and Cheyssial (1992), who observed that the marketing actions of small manufacturing businesses were badly prepared and badly organized, and often bore little or no relation to the firm's overall activities and marketing efforts. The owner-managers thus seemed to exhibit reactive behaviour, adopting a fire-fighting approach instead of preventing fires through more elaborate planning and better coordination.

Coordination of marketing action can also be observed through the control methods introduced by small businesses. The author of this chapter studied the marketing control system of small businesses using four main indicators: marketing planning, feedback, corrective action and evaluation of personnel. The results showed that three-quarters of the small firms studied had not implemented specific coordination activities that were observable in marketing planning or control terms.

The market orientation and small businesses
In our view, the market orientation is an interesting concept for observing the coordination of marketing and all other activities in the firm. As Gauzente (1995) pointed out, the market orientation requires a customer focus based on coordination within the marketing department and between the other departments, and also profitability. More specifically, according to Kohli and Jaworski (1990), market orientation is "... the production, at the level of the organization, of relevant market information related to the current and future needs of the customer, the distribution of this information to all departments and the capacity, within the enterprise as a whole, to react and respond to the information elements". In Navar and Slater's (1990) view, the competition also had to be considered. These latter authors defined market orientation as an enterprise culture whose effects were customer satisfaction and organizational profitability.

We know of no specific work on market orientation in small businesses as operationalized by Kohli and Jaworski (1990). We believe, however, that the concept will be helpful in understanding the marketing activities of small businesses. As Gauzente (1995) observed, market orientation is "a strategic vision, in that it represents a voluntary movement by company management leading to far-reaching, sustainable changes at the organizational level".

5.   International marketing

Globalization of the economy and the opening up of new Eastern markets may provide opportunities for small businesses operating in already saturated markets. However, their ability to seize these opportunities depends on how well they can follow a formal international marketing decision-making process (Brisoux et al., 1992).

Several of the stages and elements in the decision-making process proposed by the literature (Dennis, 1987 and De Leersnyder, 1982) include five major decisions:

• the decision to develop internationally;
• the decision concerning choice of markets;
• the decision on market penetration methods;
• decisions concerning the marketing mix;
• the decision concerning the layout of organizational structures.

Some perceived constraints may, however, cause small firms to give up the idea of international activity. For example, Cort (1987), in a study of 51 entrepreneurs in different industries, identified certain constraints associated with small business presence on international markets. They included lack of management capacity, size of management team and a negative attitude to international business. Overall, the entrepreneurs did not seem prepared to face the music, and lacked confidence in their own abilities.

Two recent studies in Quebec (Brochu, 1991; Brixoux et al., 1991), using samples of small firms exporting to the United States, showed how the decision-making process operated. Brochu's sample contained 65 owner-managers of small manufacturing businesses in an outlying area of Quebec, close to the American border, working mainly in the metal and furniture sectors. The second study (Brisoux et al., 1991) used a sample of 30 firms from the Greater Montreal area, operating in the metal products and machine manufacturing sectors. Although the conceptual frameworks were not exactly the same, we will attempt to compare the decision-making processes observed in the two cases.

1. The results of the two studies are contradictory with regard to the decision to develop foreign activities. For example, in Brochu's study, 80% of the firms were interested or very interested in international business, whereas international business was a chance affair for 80% of the firms studied by Brisoux et al. The latter findings mirror Kinsey's (1987) research, which revealed that chance played a major role in 25% of cases.
2. In the study by Brisoux et al., market proximity and similarity of needs and distribution systems were the main reasons given by the owner-managers for choosing the American market, whereas in Brochu's study, general market conditions were more important.
3. As far as the elements of the marketing mix were concerned, the Greater Montreal entrepreneurs ranked product first, then price and distribution, and finally promotion. The latter element was not measured in Brochu's study.
4. Access or penetration of the foreign market was generally very limited. The entrepreneurs questioned by Brisoux et al. had investigated an average of only 2.7 of the 19 available exporting formulas. Both studies showed that commission agents and importer-distributors were the channels most commonly used, and Brochu also noted that one firm in every four used a salaried representative.
5. According to Brisoux et al. (1992), more than half the firms had introduced organizational changes, especially those with more recent export experience and those that exported a larger percentage of their production.

It therefore seems that access to foreign markets is a chance affair for a large number of small firms (Kinsey, 1987; Brisoux et al., 1992). Market proximity is an important selection criterion, product and price are the most frequently used variables, very few different penetration formulas are used or even considered, and small firms actually do make the organizational changes required by internationalization. However, for the better-organized small firms, referred to as "professional exporters" in the literature, export demand tends to be better planned (Joyal et al., 1995). Brochu investigated the existence of a relationship between the choice of access routes to foreign markets on the one hand, and the characteristics of the market, the firm and the product on the other. Such a relationship, based on models designed for the corporate sector (De Leersnyder, 1982), was not found.

6. Conclusion

As we conclude this chapter, we should remember that Downing's model was proposed as a descriptive and not a prescriptive model of small business marketing. Knowledge of the field is still far too limited to establish a prescriptive model adapted to the small business context. The prescriptive aspect of a model resembling Downing's would probably differ in terms of the nature of the links and relationships between the variables, rather than in the removal or addition of variables.

We have nevertheless been able to observe that the marketing process begins with market knowledge, which in turn is dependent on market research (primary and secondary data) on the target customer group and all other aspects of the market. This particular aspect seems to be neglected by entrepreneurs, who consider it of secondary importance (Hills, 1985; Spitzer et al., 1989; LaBarbera et al., 1989).

It is not difficult to see why owner-managers find it difficult to interpret insufficient and often absent data (market intelligence) when planning the firm's activities. The literature review revealed a flagrant lack of formal planning (Marchesnay, 1988; Kinsey, 1987a; Kraft et al., 1989) in the marketing function. The result is that marketing efforts are not always properly coordinated by the marketing people themselves or with their colleagues in other enterprise functions.

A number of authors (Statch and Ward, 1987; Hills, 1987; Marchesnay, 1988) have described the two filters in Downing's model. These are the objectives and characteristics of the entrepreneur and the operational elements of the firm. These two aspects are potential moderating variables in understanding marketing strategies and tactics. It is clear that small business marketing strategies and tactics, while somewhat less intense than in large corporations, are nevertheless sufficient to ensure the perpetuation and survival of the firms (Ellis and Jolibert, 1991). It is important that any prescriptive model used should not be geared to the level of intensity found in large firms.

The literature review also suggests some avenues for future research in the field of small business marketing. For example, very few researchers have looked at how market research is performed by small and medium-sized firms. We believe that work is needed on the "marketing information system" of small firms, to identify the links between information gathering, interpretation and planning. We also believe that enough work has been done on listing, comparing and counting the marketing tactics used by entrepreneurs. It is now time to pay more attention to the strategic aspects of marketing, as opposed to the operational aspects. New measuring instruments will be required to achieve this objective, since existing instruments are more suited to operational marketing. A better understanding of corporate and strategic marketing will also be useful to socioeconomic officers working with small businesses, as we saw in Chapter 4.

Finally, more research is needed to understand the special features of marketing concept implementation within small firms. Here, the work of Kohli and Jaworski (1990) and Narver and Slater (1990) provides some interesting avenues in the area of small business marketing.

7 New technologies

"Moreover, it is not the right way to examine only the side wall and the moat; to judge the safety of a place, one must be able to see where the attacker may come from and in what condition he is." Michel de Montaigne, "Essai".

1. Introduction

The dynamism of an industrial economy is obviously dependent on the productivity of its businesses, both large and small. As Howard (1990) points out for the United States, small businesses make as great a contribution to national competitiveness as large corporations, because of the numerous links between the two levels, especially in the field of subcontracting. According to Womack, Jones and Ross (1990), the poor competitiveness of small US businesses in certain sectors, compared to their German and Japanese counterparts, explains the difficulties experienced by sectors such as the automobile industry, whereas the productivity of large US companies compares favourably with that of similar businesses in Germany and Japan.

Whatever the links existing between small and large firms, and despite the fact that, in industrialized economies, the importance of small businesses in terms of numbers of production units is recognized by both researchers and governments, as discussed in the first chapter, there is a need for small businesses to maintain and even improve their competitiveness if they are to survive in an evolving economy.

In the last few years, many small businesses have made a serious attempt to modernize their means of production, which explains the increasingly large share of national added value and employment for which they are responsible. But market globalization (in conjunction with a certain segmentation of national and regional markets[1]), the

---

1   The concept of "market globalization" needs to be treated with caution. For example, some products have always been sold in practically all countries around the world, and raw materials have long been the foundation of international trade. In contrast, despite the emergence of economic blocks, certain limited natural alliances have reformed. For instance, with the extension of the European Economic Community, the medieval links between Catalonia, Provence and Piedmont have been re-established as an alternative to, or in parallel with, broader-scale ties. Similarly, North American free trade is leading to a re-establishment of north-south ties between, for example, Quebec

growing interpenetration of national economies, and an increasing interdependency of the key players in various types of networks, among other factors, are perhaps modifying the conditions that led to the dynamism of existing small businesses, or at least creating conditions in which dynamism becomes dependent on the need to increase competitiveness in order to avoid adverse effects on economic performance (Julien and Morin, 1996).

A wide array of competitive strategies are used by small businesses, depending on business types and locations. As discussed in Chapter 5, many strategies are possible, according to business size, the objectives of the owner-managers, market type and sector, the level of competition, the economic situation, and so on.

Despite the number of strategies available, many small businesses, especially those whose competitive strategy is based on pricing, will have to modernize in the medium or the long term in order to stay in production. Businesses that are exposed to foreign competition, in particular, cannot escape this requirement, and their number is likely to grow as trade barriers disappear. Although specific needs vary, modernization is essential and necessarily involves some kind of technological innovation in the area of management, information systems, production, or work organization and distribution. For a business, mastering technological change means implementing and coordinating a series of actions to obtain technological information and adapt it to the business's needs, investing in appropriate technology, transforming the means of production in line with new technologies, and managing the whole process.

Technological information can be provided by various sources, such as an in-house R & D department, public and university-related research centres, consulting firms, and so on. Information can be transmitted via networks, for example technological cooperation networks, technological parks, and technopoles, and each business must devote resources to technological scanning and financing in order to purchase new technologies at the appropriate time.

This chapter is designed to provide answers, as far as possible, to the various questions raised by the above topics, by:
- specifying how small businesses must prepare for the introduction of new technologies, especially as regards the *material investment*

---

and the New England states and British Columbia and the Western U.S., to the detriment of the Canadian "coast to coast" ideal (see P.P. Proulx, 1990), while large-scale decentralization is also becoming common.

required, together with other facilitating conditions such as new management techniques and technological scanning, which constitute the *non-material investment*;

- identifying technological management elements, as regards both production and strategy, especially those relating to training;
- examining the question of how work will be organized following the introduction, often gradual, of new technologies.

2. Small businesses, new technologies and their distribution and introduction

The expression "new technologies" refers to a variety of techniques and tools used in complex management and production operations that often vary widely from one business to another. No two businesses, in fact, share exactly the same technological needs. Most possess several types of machinery or equipment corresponding to the various stages of production, beginning with the reception of raw materials, primary processing or assembly, secondary processing or assembly, and so on up to the finishing, packing and dispatching stages. Each stage can require machines and techniques of varying degrees of modernity, employees with varying degrees of specialization, and management techniques of varying degrees of sophistication. Generally, in small businesses, the modernization of a factory begins with the purchase of a first modern piece of machinery, to which the older machinery is adapted, improved where necessary by ad hoc or spontaneous innovations. The production process is reorganized, and later a second, digitally-controlled piece of machinery is purchased. Management practices are revised to take account of the new need for better-qualified staff, either by ad hoc training programs or the hiring of new employees such as technicians or even engineers. The whole production line is gradually transformed as part of a continuous learning process, rendered necessary not because the modernization is fundamentally different from the automation phases of the 1950s and 1960s, but because the links between production control and production itself have been transformed. The production process now generates information (the machinery has been "computerized") that can be dealt with directly by management staff or that has a direct impact on management[2]. The examples provided by CAD/CAM (computer

---

2 This is why one of the positions the most at risk in the computerization process is that of the middle manager, e.g. foreman,

assisted design/computer assisted production) or, even more radically, by CPS (computerized production systems) illustrate the change, especially the new complexity of the management and production processes.

Nevertheless, even in cases where production can be entirely assigned to new plant, many small businesses retain traditional tools or machinery for short or one-off production runs. This is why the same technologies are not necessarily used by all the small businesses working in a given sector, and why massive, uniform re-tooling for different small businesses does not occur.

Several studies have shown that small businesses take relatively more time than larger firms to invest in new equipment, use new production technologies, or adopt technological scanning and improve workforce qualifications - in other words, to make non-material investments. These results must be treated with caution, however, and in certain sectors, and for certain technologies, the gap is closing.

2.1   The introduction of new technologies into small businesses

Where the introduction of management technologies is concerned, the gap between large and small businesses is slight, since even the smallest businesses tend to be relatively well-equipped in this area. OECD (1991), for example, points out that, in many industrialized countries, over 90% of small manufacturing businesses, including the very smallest, had at least one micro-computer. Raymond (1985) has shown that various computer-based operations such as accounting and stock management were also spreading quickly among small businesses, as we shall see later. In France, studies by the ADEPA (1992) obtained similar findings.

The gap is greater, however, where production technologies are concerned. In 1983, for example, over 30% of firms with 1,000 or more employees in France, Japan and Great Britain used micro-computers for production, compared to less than 10% of firms with less than 100 employees (D'Iribarne, 1986). In Canada in 1984-85, 80% of large businesses possessed at least one piece of CADCAM equipment[3], whereas during the same period, only 31% of small businesses with less

---

since senior management can now control the production process directly.

3   CAD means computer assisted design; CAM means computer assisted manufacturing.

than 200 employees had at least one NCMT[4]; the rate was only 5 percentage points higher in 1989 (Lefebvre et al., 1985).

However, the gap is closing rapidly. A study of three contrasting Quebec business sectors (sawmills, plastics factories and machine shops) carried out in 1988 showed that 19.4% of small businesses had at least one digitally-controlled piece of machinery, 7.7% used computer-assisted manufacturing and 2.8% used robots. In all, 38% used at least one piece of modern equipment[5], compared to 17% in 1985 (Julien, 1991).

In 1989, the CADCAM Association redistributed major extracts from the 1988 questionnaire, but this time in connection only with computer technologies in a sample of businesses of various sizes working in eight different sectors. The results showed that 23.2% of firms used at least one computer production technology, 6.6% used two and 5.7% used three or more.

In February and March, 1992, the Quebec Manufacturers' Association carried out a new telephone survey (with interviews lasting roughly 32 minutes) of more than 400 small businesses (employing between 5 and 250 people) in ten business sectors. Diagram 7.1 compares the 1989 results for businesses of all sizes with the 1992 results for small businesses only. By 1992, 28.8% of small businesses had one computer production technology, 11.5% two, and 16.7% three or more. A further survey was carried out, two years later, for ten other industrial sectors with a strong small business representation. By then, 18.2% of small businesses had one computer production technology, 16.7% two, and 49.8% three or more (Julien and Carrière, 1994). Thus, in the space of five years, and taking into account the fact that the 1989 survey included large corporatoins, the number of small businesses using three or more computer technologies had increased tenfold, while the percentage of businesses using no computer technology at all fell from 65% to 15%.

The gap between large and small businesses, if it exists at all, also varies according to sector and business type. For example, a survey carried out by the CADCAM Association in 1989 showed that, in the clothing industry, only 22% of Quebec firms used computer equipment, compared with 70.7% in the electrical products industry, 49.9% in the plastic products industry, and 42.3% in the transportation equipment

---

4   NCMT means numerically-controlled machine tool.
5   Including "high-tech" but not numerically-controlled techniques, such as injection moulding, filament winding, double-screw extruding, etc. (for plastics), plasma rebuilding, laser welding (in machine shops), or optimal log use studies (sawmills).

sector. In the 1992 study, we demonstrated that the penetration rate for new technologies is often greater where a smaller range of new technologies is required. Diagram 7.2 shows a lower percentage for the aeronautics component sector, which uses a large number of new technologies, and a higher percentage for the milk products industry, where fewer new technologies are used.

Diagram 7.1
1989 penetration rate of new computer production technologies in businesses in eight industrial sectors; 1992 and 1994 penetration rates in small Quebec businesses in ten industrial sectors*

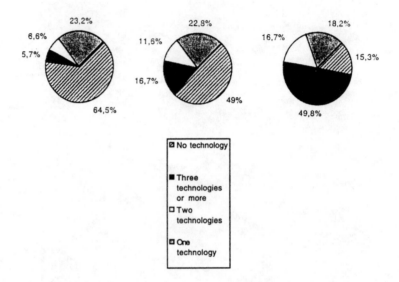

* For 1989, the sectors were as follows: plastic products, textiles, wooden furniture, clothing, transportation equipment, metal products, mechanical products, and electrical and electronic products; for 1992: dairy products, textiles, clothing, doors, windows and other woodworking, household furniture, machining, aircraft and aircraft parts, automobile parts and accessories, electrical products, and pharmaceuticals; for 1994: meat and poultry processing, plastic products, leather and related products, sawmills and planing mills, commercial printing and photoplate making, die stamping and die forging, machinery and equipment, communications equipment, and scientific and professional equipment.

Source: CADCAM Association, "Tendances et degré de pénétration. L'informatisation et l'informatisation de la production", Montréal, CRIQ, 1989; P.A. Julien and J.B. Carrière (1994), "L'efficacité des PME et les nouvelles technologies", *Revue d'économie Industrielle* no.67, p. 120-135. P.A. Julien and J.B. Carrière, "Profil technologique de la PME manufacturière québécoise 1995", CEFRIO, Quebec 1995.

The gap is thus slight, or non-existent, in the "engineering" sectors, and in certain segments of traditional sectors. Some studies have also shown that small businesses have certain advantages over big businesses that tend to facilitate the penetration of new technologies or to compensate for technological weakness (Meredith, 1987; Acs and Audrestch, 1990).

Diagram 7.2
Introduction rate of computer technologies for small businesses in the aircraft parts and dairy products sectors, 1992

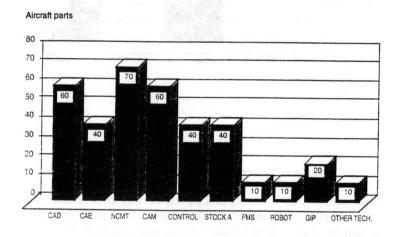

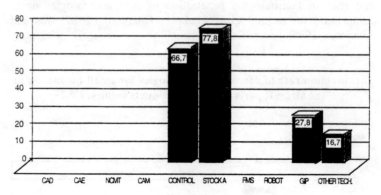

Milk products

Source: Ibidem.

2.2 Why do small businesses introduce new technologies?

Various reasons have been suggested to explain why the penetration rates of new technologies vary from sector to sector and firm to firm. Some reasons are based on macro-economics, and others on the internal dynamics of each firm.

From a macro-economic point of view, the availability of a given technology is an important factor. In some sectors a wide range of CAD and CAM techniques, and even robots, is available, whereas in other sectors only traditional machinery with a few new digital controls can be purchased. The "engineering" sectors (electrical and electronic products, equipment and machinery, transportation products, etc.) dispose of the widest range of new technologies and have the highest rates of use. Other sectors lag behind, because of the type of products involved or the dispersion of production sites. Some types of technology designed for large businesses have not yet been adapted for the needs of small businesses or for short production runs. In many cases, the expected rate of growth of a sector or a specific market does not justify modernization, or not until the economic climate changes (Julien and Thibodeau, 1991).

The relative dynamism of the economy also affects the use of new technologies. Dynamism is dependent on strong growth, a highly-developed technological culture, the presence of workforce training facilities and sources of information, and the availability of other complementary resources such as savings and venture capital to support investment. For example, the spread of new technologies can be facilitated by basic or on-going training programs centering on change and the transfer of scientific and technological information, by specialized magazines to inform business leaders, by trade fairs, by networks bringing together the manufacturers and distributors of new technologies with specialized consultants, by partnerships between small and large businesses, and by government support programs designed to spread information about applied technology and its transfer to small businesses, and to support the diffusion of new technologies.

From a micro-economic point of view, a number of points have been identified: the sometimes excessive cost of the new technologies, especially for small firms, their inappropriateness for the needs of small businesses, a low level of awareness and use among small firms, a lack of input from the technological information network or its inability to make technologies better known, etc. (Garsombke and Garsombke, 1989).

However, several studies have shown that the two main factors affecting penetration rates, or the fact that some small businesses use new technologies while others rely on more traditional equipment, are the sophistication of the management staff and their ability to obtain and process technological information. In other words, small businesses which use new production technologies tend to be those headed by well-educated owner-managers, often university graduates in a technical field, or those with a well-trained management staff, that use more complex management techniques involving, for example, market surveys and management committees. These businesses are often larger in size[6]; they have more links with the outside world, through their exports or their ties with foreign suppliers. Above all, they seek out outside sources of varied technological information, at specialized trade fairs, for example, or in private or public research centres, as discussed below.

The cost variable, or the need to finance new equipment, is not the primary variable; or rather, for businesses that already use numerically-controlled equipment, the variable is considered from a dynamic point of

---

6 The average size of 42 employees in our studies carried out in Quebec and 100 employees in the Algoe report (1988) in France, is not fortuitous, since the effects of national and international competition often begin to be felt when a firm's production, and markets, expand.

view (in terms of the "insufficient foreseeable return on new machinery"). For businesses that use only traditional equipment, owner-managers emphasize their "insufficient financial resources", the "excessive cost of conversion" and the "excessive financial risk" equally (Julien, Carrière and Hébert, 1988). The financial factor can thus be seen as one *condition* among many, rather than as an obstacle for modern businesses.

2.3   The importance of technological scanning

Information on new technology is thus a central element in the information strategy of small businesses, and may be more or less refined: firms already using new technologies tend to have a complex "technological scanning" process, and also rely on organized networks to gather technological information.

Technological scanning is a relatively new research concept, but it is known to exist in a number of particularly dynamic small businesses, in either an implicit and/or sporadic form, or an explicit and organized form. It allows businesses to observe the evolution of competing firms and to remain on the lookout for new technologies to maintain or increase their own *competitive* capacity and respond to various needs for innovation, besides allowing market trends to be observed. It involves gathering, selecting, analyzing and summarizing information, and transmitting the results to the decision-making authority for immediate action or inclusion in a long-term strategy. It is based on a directed search for outside information, generally repetitive in nature.

The first condition is that the owner-manager feels the need for change (in products, equipment, organization, etc.). The feeling may result from competition, the success of a leading-edge firm, or a visit to a trade fair; it may also be stimulated by an information network or a key staff member, especially a "technological gatekeeper". It may take shape slowly or quickly, and can be compared with and enriched by further information gained directly or via the network. Checks are made to assess advantages and disadvantages, and feasibility. Feasibility, and the difficulties to be overcome, are checked with suppliers, professional associations, and sometimes even competitors in other markets. A range of possibilities is explored: patent purchase, cooperative agreement, R&D in collaboration with a support organization, etc., depending partly on the firm's experience and available skills. At a later stage, tests may be carried out in a public or private research centre or by a trustworthy consulting firm. Formal internal or external analysis can be used to support the results. In most cases, though, the process is implicit or non-structured, although in retrospect a certain logic can be detected.

Technological scanning relies primarily on access to sources of specialized information, not necessarily all found in the same location. The choices are dictated by circumstances. It should be noted that technological scanning is often carried out in conjunction with commercial scanning, since technological changes are often required by or closely linked to market changes.

The first necessity is therefore a range of sources for technological information. It is known that firms rarely limit themselves to a single source, first because their needs are varied, and second because no one source can supply all the applicable information (Meyer and Goes, 1987; Planque, 1987). Table 7.1, taken from an investigation of 344 small manufacturing businesses, shows the relative importance and breakdown of various sources of information, and the frequency of consultation. Clients, followed by specialized magazines and employees, are the most important sources of information, and the most frequently consulted. The initial sources also tend to be "personal" and are generally consulted informally (Julien, Jacob et al., 1995).

A major 1985 survey by the National Research Council and the Italian Statistics Institute (ISTAT) on technological innovation in 24,000 manufacturing businesses with more than 20 employees, which achieved a 69.3% response rate, provides a rich source of information about technological innovation in businesses of all sizes, but especially small manufacturing businesses. For example, the survey shows that small businesses in Italy with over 50 employees were almost as likely to innovate as large businesses, whatever the industrial sector, and that 60% of firms with between 20 and 49 employees innovate, except in textiles and clothing (52.1%), chemicals and pharmaceuticals (57.2%) and metal products (58.0%). However, the sources for technological innovation varied according to business size, as shown in Table 7.2.

The type of innovation also varied according to business size. For example, large firms were more likely to implement organizational changes, a predictable result, whereas innovations or improvements in production techniques were more evenly spread. According to a recent French study, small businesses that seek out information systematically behave only slightly differently from their larger counterparts as regards possible internal and external sources of information (Table 7.3).

In addition, small businesses are wary of single sources of information, and prefer to double-check the information received. They tend to suspect consulting firms and suppliers of trying to impose inappropriate equipment to boost their own sales, and are suspicious of public and semi-public research centres whose fields of interest may not match their needs exactly, or whose results are biased from contact with larger firms or firms with completely different needs.

Table 7.1
Characteristics of sources of technological information (1)

Relative importance of sources (2)			
Clients	4.01	Subcontractors	2.33
Specialized periodicals	3.58	Internal databases	2.30
Production staff	3.48	Government organizations	2.24
Management staff	3.39	Consultants	2.21
Suppliers	3.34	Reference books	2.14
Sales personnel	3.34	Sector associations	2.11
Brochures and catalogues	3.31	Other staff	2.11
Industrial fairs and		Research centres	2.07
exhibitions	3.12	Government publications	2.06
Commercial fairs and		Board of directors	2.01
exhibitions	3.03	Financial institutions	1.93
Business periodicals	2.98	Universities and colleges	1.85
Agents and representatives	2.80		
Placers of orders	2.73		
Newspapers	3.62		
Competitors	2.50		

Frequency of use of personal sources (3)			
Informal sources		Formal sources	
Clients	3.58	Consultants	2.01
Production staff	3.43	Government organizations	1.96
Management staff	3.31	Research centres	1.83
Sales staff	3.16	Financial institutions	1.61
Suppliers	3.14	Universities and colleges	1.54
Agents and representatives	2.59		
Placers of orders	2.42		
Sub-contractors	2.07		
Competitors	1.96		
Board of directors	1.89		
Other staff	1.88		

Frequency of use of non-personal sources (3)			
Written sources		Oral sources	
Specialized periodicals	3.39	Industrial fairs and exhibitions	3.00
Brochures and catalogues	3.18	Commercial fairs and	2.77
Business periodicals	2.95	exhibitions	1.87
Newspapers	2.63	Sector associations	
Internal databases	2.20		
Reference books	2.00		
Government publications	1.94		

Number of sources used			
Informal		Formal	
Informal	8.62	Written	5.90
Formal	3.74	Oral	2.48
Total	12.38	Total	8.40
Frequency of source use (3)			
Personal		Non-personal	
Informal	2.70	Written	2.65
Formal	1.81	Oral	2.56

Notes: (1): Averages
(2): 1 = not important to 5 = very important
(3): 1 = seldom to 5 = frequently

Source: P.A. Julien, R. Jacob, L. Raymond and C. Ramangalahy, "La veille technologique dans les PME manufacturières", *Research Report, Bombardier Chair*, June 1995.

Table 7.2
Sources of technological knowledge by business size

Size category	Internal (2)	External (3)	R&D	Industrial projects	Patents	Economic community (4)	Purchases (5)	Patent purchases (5)
20-49	0.79	0.95	0.70	0.84	0.74	0.94	1.00	0.64
50-99	1.05	1.02	0.99	1.04	1.11	1.05	0.99	0.98
100-199	1.27	1.06	1.32	1.25	1.29	1.08	1.00	1.43
200-499	1.53	1.12	2.03	1.36	1.48	1.12	1.03	1.81
500 and +	2.04	1.22	2.69	1.65	2.44	1.12	0.98	3.75
All firms	1.00	1.00	1.00	1.00	1.00	1.00	1.00	1.00
Variation coefficient (6)	0.36	0.10	0.52	0.25	0.45	0.07	0.02	0.71
Number of responses	12337	21049	2714	7039	2584	8062	11554	1433

Notes: Sources based on average response (1)
1) Where the response from firms in a given size category was close to the average for all firms, they obtained the score 1.00; a tendency to specify particular sources raised the score (and vice-versa).
2) R&D, industrial projects, internal patents.
3) Purchases of equipment and intermediate goods, purchases of patents and knowledge.
4) Professional organizations, technical centres, trades fairs, clients, etc.
5) Purchases of equipment or intermediate goods, purchases of raw materials, etc.
6) Typical variation/weighted average.

Source: D. Archibugi and S. Cesaretto, "Piccole imprese e combiamento technologico. Modelli teorici e risultati del l'indagine Cnr-Istat sull'innovazione technologica nel settore manifatturiero italiano", *Piccola Impresa*, No. 2, 1989, pp. 45-75.

Table 7.3
Internal and external sources of information by business size
(% of businesses)

Business size	Internal sources				External sources				Technological intrants		
	Inter-nal R&D	Studies	Patents	(1)	Group R&D	Exter-nal R&D	Rights/Patents	(2)	Innova-tive use of goods	New materials invested	(3)
20-49	40.0	70.9	20.0	79.4	18.4	42.6	17.0	56.0	71.7	57.5	82.8
50-99	51.5	78.7	27.8	87.6	28.2	45.7	20.1	63.7	72.8	59.4	83.1
100-199	61.8	85.6	36.0	92.6	37.5	47.9	22.2	69.6	78.9	68.2	88.5
200-499	72.2	86.7	43.7	94.9	45.9	53.5	31.4	76.6	81.3	65.6	89.5
500-999	80.5	90.4	58.4	97.1	69.2	60.6	39.4	85.8	85.8	75.7	93.4
1000-1999	89.4	92.6	70.7	97.9	69.7	62.8	40.4	88.8	89.4	78.2	94.1
2000+	91.4	95.3	76.6	99.2	78.1	71.9	55.5	96.9	93.0	88.3	96.9
TOTAL	50.3	76.7	28.1	85.1	28.1	45.9	20.9	62.8	74.4	60.9	84.6

Notes: (1)   businesses using at least one type of internal source
        (2)   businesses using at least one type of external source
        (3)   businesses using at least one type of technological intrant

Source: Survey EAE 1990 - SESSI, Department of Industry and External Trade (France), 1991.

The search for effective sources of information requires the gradual development[7] of relationships of trust. For this reason, information must be available within a reasonable distance, in geographical and sector terms, of small businesses (Guesnier, 1984; Savi, 1988), unless the sources are highly specialized and referred by a network or by recognized "champion" firms[8].

The presence of one or more research centres in a given region is one effective means of spreading innovation, unless the centre was founded and is controlled by other firms, as sometimes occurs in certain Italian industrial districts or in the case of industrial associations (Tinacci-Mossello and Dini, 1989; Maillat and Perrin, 1990).

An investigation carried out by the Battelle Institute[9] in Emilio-Romany found that the external technological information used by small businesses in the region originated mainly in cafés and restaurants and was rarely transmitted by formal organizations providing technological information. Our own studies have shown that the most important external sources of technological information are order-givers, followed by trade fairs (Table 7.1).

2.4 The importance of networks

In fields in which change is rapid, external sources of information are a necessity. However, many small businesses have neither the capacity to obtain the correct information when it is needed, nor to use it adequately. Either their links with the technological information network are too tenuous, there is no appropriate network, or the network is not designed for use by small businesses (Lambooy, 1986). The cost of acquiring information may be prohibitive, acquisition may be subject to conditions, or the information may be limited to marketing techniques and exclude production. The information may be provided for exclusive use and/or for a given territory; it may be permanent or subject to revocation. For all these reasons, many small businesses need assistance in gaining access to information and in using it.

---

7 A study has shown that even if advice for small businesses is less available in outlying regions than in major centres, it is nevertheless better known, either directly or via networks. The advice is, however, less specialized, often limited to management and computing, and ineffective as regards production techniques (Thibodeau, 1989).

8 "Champion" firms, like "champion" innovators, are the leading firms that other firms tend to follow.

9 Cited in a study by the German Ministry of Research and Technology (MFRT, 1989).

222

One of the main means used by small businesses to gather knowledge, assess it and use it appropriately is the network, as discussed in chapters 2 and 5. Several studies have shown that the most successful small businesses tend to develop in osmosis with one or more networks that provide information and help assess or "validate" it, thereby adding the element of "trust"[10] necessary in non-systematic transactions (GREMI, 1986). The networks filter "free" information and, when organized in a partnership system, provide access to "shared" information. If the partnership is highly structured, for example through a system of affiliation or franchising, it provides some or all of the required "controlled" information.

Networks are one of the most important sources of information for small businesses, because they add the element of trust needed if the quality of the information is to be assessed. Networks are implicit or explicit associations, groups or other agglomerations of agents, businesses in manufacturing or services, and institutions, working in often complementary fields and intended to bring together various resources, especially information resources, to develop relationships of trust between members, and to reduce the costs of obtaining information, thereby reducing short and long-term uncertainty about market effects.

A network may be based on contracts of varying degrees of formality and varying duration, often involving upstream partners. It allows information, often unavailable on the open market, to be obtained at lower cost, reducing uncertainty and creating synergy between network members (Perrin, 1990). It can reduce the costs of transactions that are carried out sporadically, are difficult to assess and to foresee, and are thus sources of uncertainty. The network of a small business may include the members of the board of directors, if any, specific suppliers, a business association, a consulting firm, quasi-competitors, "close" sub-contractors or the placers of orders, and so on.

A network may be based on contracts of varying degrees of formality and varying duration with partners in strategic alliances. It can reduce the costs of transactions that are carried out sporadically, are difficult to assess and to foresee, and are thus sources of uncertainty. Small business networks, however, generally involve flexible, sporadic relationships according to immediate needs. The more strategic and permanent a network, the more effective it will be.

---

10 The importance of trust in economic transactions is beginning to be taken into account by researchers as they seek to go beyond "rational" economic theories. See, in this connection, Sabel (1990) and Lorino (1989).

Networks can take several forms, with more or less well-defined boundaries. They are often concentric; in other words, when the answer to a question cannot be provided by the primary, inner network, access to another more specialized network can be gained through an affiliated member to obtain part of the required information, and from there to another more distant network, until all the required information has been obtained. This is shown in Illustration 7.1.

In general, the primary network is consulted first, and most often, even though it provides information that tends to be more general or more traditional; second and third level networks are consulted less often, but provide information that is more specialized and often more useful. Information is a cumulative phenomenon, as regards both learning and information sources (from the closest to the furthest, from the most simple to the most complex) (Birley, Cromie and Myers, 1991; Aldrich and Zimmer, 1985); (Estimé, Drilhon and Julien, 1993).

Illustration 7.1
The personal network of a small business

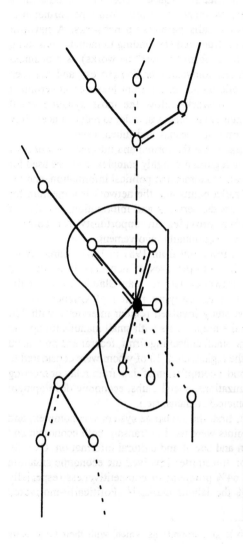

Key:
● : the focusing entrepreneur
○ : colleagues, friends, and other network members
——— : instrumental ties
— — — : emotional ties
·········· : moral ties
⌐⌐ : the boundaries of the local network, according to local community organisation

Source: B. Johannisson, "Network strategies: management technology for entrepreneurship and change", *International Small Business Journal*, Vol. 5, No. 1, 1989, p. 26.

Small business networks are often informal (friends, social and professional acquaintances). They are "personal" networks existing in a relatively well-defined "transaction space". They can become more structured through the development of various forms of partnership, leading to what Marchesnay calls partnership networks. A network becomes more complex and structured (expanding to include consulting firms, research centres, etc. to form "expert" networks) as a business develops and organizes its technological scanning process, and can even include public or para-public bodies at different levels of government ("mentoring" networks). Networks allow the most dynamic small businesses to *organize*[11] their environment in order to reduce uncertainty and prepare for the long term (Marchesnay and Julien, 1990).

Joseph Szarka (1989) states that the formal and informal networks of small businesses in outlying regions are highly complex; they are used for the transfer of technological, economic and political information, and for social relationships. As Szarka points out, the network is a medium for the exchange not only of goods, services and information, but also of ideas and values; it often provides an opportunity for control, coordination, cooperation and community involvement.

In a longitudinal study carried out from 1981 to 1987, Marc-Urbain Proulx (1992) analyzed the multiple uses of networks in a study of utilitarian information networks (what Jean-Claude Perrin calls "horizontal networks") in an outlying region of Quebec with a population of 26,000. The study involved regular interviews with 220 core decision-makers (local entrepreneurs with small manufacturing and service businesses, mayors, small consulting firms, federal and provincial civil servants working in the region, etc.), 10 of whom were considered to be key decision-makers, and a compilation of data from relay or meeting points (professional organizations, social clubs, economic development agencies in the region, municipal councils, etc.).

The study showed that, first, the exchange system was complex, and second, the same relay points were used to transmit both economic and technological information and social and cultural information. Overall, 33.41% of the information transmitted involved the economic situation and economic trends, 18.64% problems of competitiveness (especially technological), and 6.3% the labour market[12]. Politically-motivated

---

11 In a manner similar to large corporations which, with their large-scale resources, can influence their environment.

12 The percentages were calculated on the basis of the principal subject discussed during meetings between decision-makers. In the study, the density of relay points, according to the total number of meetings

information accounted for a further 21.07%, for a total of 79.4% of the information exchanged via the utilitarian networks. Examples of information involving competitiveness included aid programs for business modernization and workforce training programs, sub-contracting relationships, transportation between the region and the nearest urban area, and so on.

The remaining information involved public administration in the region and subjects relating to culture, social problems and land use planning.

Networks can also be organized in whole or in part by public authorities, as is the case in business incubators, technopoles and State or university technology parks.

2.5 Small businesses, innovation, workforce training and new technologies

As we have already said, the mere introduction of new technologies is often not sufficient to improve the competitiveness of a small business; it must be associated with product innovations and workforce training, which, together with technological scanning, constitute the non-material investments.

With respect to innovation, several studies, such as those by the CNR/ISTAT in Italy (Archibugi and Cesarretto, 1989), the IFO Institute in Germany (MFRT, 1989) and the INSEE in France (Bernard and Torre, 1994), have shown that almost 60% of small businesses in the manufacturing sector, whatever their size, innovate regularly. Innovation is generally gradual, and mainly involves the production of new products or the improvement of existing products (Belhumeur and Nguyen, 1989), but also involves the upgrading of equipment (often purchased second-hand), specific ways of reaching certain customers, etc. Ten percent of the small businesses studied had nevertheless implemented major innovations, a higher proportion than among large corporations (Mansfield, 1981; Fisher and Nijkamp, 1988).

In the case of very small firms, an investigation was carried out on a representative sample of 1,016 small firms in France with a pre-tax turnover of less than one million Francs, and less than 10 employees. The investigation identified several different types of innovative businesses, drawing a distinction between businesses that simply incorporated outside technologies and those that innovated regularly or in an organized manner. The results observed depended on the sector of

---

versus the number of months of existence of the relay point, was also taken into account.

activity involved, but nevertheless showed that between 25% and 64% of small businesses, depending on the sector, have a medium to high rate of innovation, as shown in Table 7.4. Very small businesses tended to innovate more in processes than in products, in contrast to small businesses in general.

Such data does not, however, necessarily provide a true picture of the situation. A large number of material and non-material innovations in small businesses go unrecorded, simply because they are designed to answer a specific, limited need within the business and are not considered to be actual innovations, but rather as responses to particular problems. During our own field investigations, we have found that entrepreneurs only admit to having innovated in a given case when pressed with questions.

It is also clear that the R&D underlying innovations in small businesses is generally spontaneous (applied as needed) or sporadic. It is normally under the responsibility of management staff, assisted by one or more technicians and/or engineers, and is thus dependent on the dynamism of the management staff and its tendency to innovate. In contrast to the R&D of large businesses, which is generally part of a routine process, small business R&D reflects entrepreneurial-style behaviour patterns based on action to meet immediate needs. Where small businesses carry out research systematically, however, they devote proportionally more resources to it than do large companies.

With respect to human resources, several studies have shown that small businesses have a workforce that is relatively less educated, although certain studies have also shown that highly innovative or "leading edge" small businesses have a greater proportion of qualified staff than do large businesses working in the same high-tech sectors. Their human resources organization is more flexible, new initiatives are more easily introduced, and the mission of the business is more easily shared. Workforce upgrading takes longer than in large businesses, and few small businesses, in general, implement systematic training programs, although training is increasingly considered an important factor. Differences exist between countries. It would appear that training is better organized and more systematic in Germany and Japan, and that training is more often internal than external. The larger the business, the more emphasis is given to training, as we shall see in Section 4.

Table 7.4

**Innovative capacity of smaller manufacturing businesses in France
(less than 10 employees)**

	5-position innovation rating				
	1	2	3	4	5
General machinery	11.6	16.4	21.9	31.1	19.0
Agricultural equipment	28.6	22.0	18.9	19.7	10.9
Professional supplies	12.3	11.1	12.3	31.2	32.9
Timber industry	17.6	23.7	16.4	25.8	16.6
Textiles - Clothing	27.5	16.9	17.8	27.5	10.3
Consumer goods	21.3	14.3	18.7	26.8	18.8
Electrical installations	29.8	26.5	17.1	19.9	6.8
Climatic engineering	25.4	26.7	23.3	19.2	5.3
All activities	19.7	18.4	17.8	26.4	17.7

Column 1: *Totally non-innovative businesses* (rating of 0).

Column 2: *Passive* businesses, non-innovative but occasionally required to integrate technologies forming part of the materials or components used (rating between 1 and 3).

Column 3: *Copycat* businesses, active in redistributing technology but with no independent capacity for innovation (rating between 4 and 7).

Column 4: *Businesses with a low to medium rate of innovation*, in products or production processes, generally using gradual improvements (rating between 8 and 14).

Column 5: Champions of innovation, *leading edge firms*, both in products and production techniques, on an on-going basis (rating of at least 15).

Source: J.L. Médus and J.C. Pacitto, "L'innovation technologique dans la TPE: un premier bilan", *Research Notebook* No. 94-11, University of Paris Val-de-Marne, September 1994.

In short, new technologies alone, however up to date, cannot increase productivity. To take full advantage of them and ensure their effectiveness, the operation of the business must be changed gradually by improving the training of some of the workforce or hiring technicians or an engineer, by splitting production between old and new machinery, and by changing the work organization. Above all, a strategy must be developed to manage technological change. Too many firms have suffered because they failed to plan the introduction of new technologies properly, or because new machinery was introduced without any other changes.

3. Technology management

Several strategies can be employed to meet national and international competition or to maintain and develop competitiveness, some of which allow the introduction of the latest technologies to be delayed in the short or medium term. In some sectors, little leading-edge technology is not available, or else it is not appropriate to the needs of the firm or cannot be justified economically speaking.

For example, the UK Production Engineering Research Association, after examining 5,200 projects, calculated that roughly one quarter of small businesses in the manufacturing sector operated in such specific markets that they did not need advanced services; and that the types of services provided to those businesses that did use them varied considerably. Similarly, a study recently completed on the behaviour of some small businesses in three regions of Quebec, whose products were particularly affected by the Canada-US Free Trade Agreement, has shown that 15.7% had a market that was too small or produced specific products, and that 38.8% were protected by various market niches; only 45.5% had any reason to be concerned by an increase in competition resulting from the lowering of customs duties between the two countries, either by countering the competition or by trying to benefit from it (Julien, Joyal and Deshaies, 1994).

However, as we stated above, systematic use of new production technologies is essential for a large number of small businesses if they are to meet increasing international competition. Use of new technologies is dependent on a favourable socioeconomic climate generated by appropriate public policies, in particular to encourage the production and distribution of scientific and technological information. It also relies on a set of internal and external elements to allow each firm to manage technological change as new technologies arrive on the market and new needs become apparent.

These internal and external elements can be divided into four groups: elements relating to the decision to introduce new technologies or implement technological change, elements affecting the decision-making process within the business, elements relating to organizational capabilities and, lastly, elements bringing businesses into regular contact with external technological information, and that relate to the businesses' technological culture.

3.1   Strategic decisions

A strategic decision to change technology, whether tangible or intangible, begins with an analysis of the strategic advantages to be gained. The analysis can be triggered by various environmental factors, such as a specific customer order, a drop in sales caused by a relative lack of competitive capacity compared to other businesses, information from a supplier, new environmental regulations or standards, and so on. Other factors can be internal to the business: a need for cost reductions or improved product quality, problems ensuring supplies, delivery problems, the implementation of a just-in-time system to meet the needs of a placer of orders, and so on.

As we have seen, in small businesses the quality of any such analysis depends on the technological skills of the owner-manager, perhaps assisted by key managers or employees. The skills only come into play, however, if management is open to technological change and is able to seize opportunities, which implies that the management staff must possess sufficient technological know-how, which is not always the case, and that the decision-making process is already primed for technological change.

3.2   The decision-making process

The decision-making process must take into account the main equipment already in operation, including computer systems, product design and development capabilities, and the main technological skills of the workforce or readily-available outside resources. The first element that must be established is whether the technological skills available are sufficient to achieve the hoped-for strategic advantages, and the second, whether these technological skills are available only within the business. The possibilities may be analyzed in a more or less intuitive, or structured, fashion, depending on the process followed.

The type of process depends on how the business perceives and deals with the elements of the analysis and uses its organizational capacity. Every decision must take the firm's characteristics into account (Sethi et al., 1985). For example, the introduction of new technologies must not run counter to the firm's other advantages, especially its flexibility, as we saw in Chapter 1.

3.3   Organizational capabilities

The success of the analysis will depend on the firm's general strengths. In a very small business, the decision-making process is almost totally centralized. As the business grows and its organization develops, responsibility for analysis is shared, although final decisions are generally made by management.

Obviously, a business's ability to manage technological change will be the reflection of its general, fundamental capabilities in other areas. Technology-related decisions automatically bring about changes in the firm's general strategy, affecting, for example, the general financing structure and debt load, the hiring of new employees or training of current employees (which may in turn bring about a reorganization of personnel and/or equipment), the firm's marketing capability, and so on (Gold, 1983).

The firm's general capabilities also allow new equipment to be introduced alongside existing equipment, and the provision of on-going feedback to management and thus to the organization. Effective management of technological change requires a monitoring of the technology already in use, in order to gain the information needed to foresee future changes and modifications, and allows internal information to be assimilated or converted into knowledge that will drive the search for new outside information and its application as needed. Often, there will be a need to train management staff, in addition to supervisory and production staff.

The way in which the firm is organized will also affect the rate at which new technologies are introduced. Cohn and Turyn (1980), for example, have shown that an organization that is decentralized[13], complex (with some high-quality staff from various backgrounds) and relatively de-structured, will foster technological innovation. In the next section, we will see that new ways of organizing human resources must be encouraged to maximize the use of new technologies in small businesses in an on-going process.

If technological change is pursued systematically, it will tend to encourage organizations and structures, both inside and outside the firm, to obtain and manage information. One sign of this structuring process is technological scanning, with the links it creates to existing information networks, as we saw in the previous section.

---

13 The decentralization is, of course, relative in the case of small businesses which are, by definition, centralized.

Technological scanning allows information to be located, sorted and analyzed. Information is, in fact, the raw material for technological change and creation, leading to internal change in the business and further innovation. Information is the trigger for change, and also for an increase in competitiveness. It can involve scientific data, patents, experimental results, new products, new equipment or new ways of using products, production equipment or processes, standards, management methods and procedures, organization, and so on. The availability of information depends on the output of the various research organizations, and also on the level of penetration and use of information by other businesses and competitors. Besides scientific and technical information, information on competing businesses and their level of technological development, or on the capacity of the market to absorb or respond to the changes resulting from the introduction of new technologies, is also useful (Estimé, Drilhon and Julien, 1993).

The more turbulent the business sector, the more essential technological scanning becomes; this is often the case in the so-called high-tech sectors. In other areas, the pace of change is slower, and there is more "stability"; technologies evolve slowly and change is easier to foresee. Covin and Slevin (1989) describe small business environments as "hostile" or "receptive", adding the scale of competition to the level of turbulence resulting from technological change. Within a business, scanning allows the planning of training and the improvement of the business's technological culture. Our studies have shown that the first and last group of elements are the most useful in delimiting various types of management approaches to technological change. In other words, the various management approaches are based essentially on the ability to recognize and use market opportunities, and respond to them by changing the technological organization of the business (Julien et al., 1994).

In short, current research has shown that small manufacturing businesses rely increasingly on computers, used in increasingly complex ways. Several elements indicate that small businesses are closing the gap with their larger counterparts as regards the use of at least one computerized technology. More specifically, they are turning to a wide range of material technologies in complex production processes, associating them with organizational technologies such as just-in-time techniques or new non-material control processes for total quality.

Such change must, however, be accelerated in an economic system that is becoming more open to international competition. Small businesses implementing technological change must be systematically encouraged to manage that change as efficiently as possible. Management approaches should include:

1. the presence within the business of a technological culture, centred in particular on the owner-manager, but also on key personnel members;
2. a true understanding of the business's current technological level, compared to its chief or potential competitors;
3. efficient technological scanning, linked to at least the first level of a technological information network, and through it to other more complex networks;
4. a range of possible technological innovations obtained through the scanning process that can be implemented as required;
5. internal resources that can be made gradually, or that are potentially, available (financing, organization, etc.);
6. external resources that are potentially available (advice, financing, etc.), including links with dynamic networks and possibilities for various alliances;
7. an effective strategy, and the ability to make diagnoses to meet the needs of the strategy as the environment changes.

The manner in which these elements must be implemented if increasing numbers of small businesses are to be able to meet the challenges facing them, especially as regards the mobilization of human resources within each business, must now be studied.

4.   Technological change and the human factor

As we have seen, technological change, meaning the introduction of new production processes and/or equipment based largely on micro-computing (Alsène, 1988), leads to a potential increase in flexibility and in production, and to a potential reduction in costs. How, though, do new technologies affect human factors? Do they also generate potential improvements in social development and in the personal commitment made by each worker, or in other words, do they create a desire among workers to make a personal contribution towards the implementation and use of new technologies?

These questions are important since, in keeping with a distinctly reductionist view of human beings in the workplace (White, 1987), workers have come to be seen as determinate, objectified units and, in the past, new technology has been introduced according to the principles of order and the scientific organization of work, in other words in line with the dominant classical model of management science. However, many studies have demonstrated that this approach limits the range of possibilities offered to most workers (Pettersen and Jacob, 1992). This is especially true when feedback and the knowledge gained through experience are neglected, along with the creative potential and intelligence of each worker (Laborit, 1985; Aktouf, 1989). In connection with this last point, work carried out by North American and European researchers in the field of work psychopathology has led to an major finding: a scientific, Taylorian organization of work is the most important factor in the negation of workers as human beings (Dejours, 1987).

As Sainsaulieu has stated (1987, p.290), "with the introduction of new technologies, work organization is faced with an imperative choice, between a return to well-known structures on the one hand, and a genuine invention of a new type of organization, on the other". The underlying questions, in this connection, are whether new technologies bring with them new opportunities for workers in terms of reorganized workplaces and increased recognition for their role, whether workers can contribute towards optimizing the introduction of new technologies, and what the terms of their participation will be.

Until recently, research into technological innovation and the human factor in the North American context has generally been articulated as follows: an examination of impacts, monocausal explanations, unidirectional effects, and the exclusion of context and human volition (Kling and Lacono, 1988). Technological innovation is treated as an independent variable whose effects are measured against a set of dependent variables, such as job types, working conditions and productivity (Filion and Bernier, 1987). This approach precludes study of the decision-making process underlying organizational and technological choices (Majchrzak and Davis, 1990). When considered in studies as an intangible, technological innovation necessarily produces conflicting empirical results that, in turn, lead to polarized attitudes ranging from utopian euphoria to fatalism (Proulx, 1984). Optimists tend to consider that social progress is an inevitable result of technological revolution and posit freedom through machines, that the characteristic alienation of a mechanized world will be abolished in a computerized world. Pessimists, on the other hand, point to the expropriation of workers' knowledge and the disqualification of the workers themselves, and consider that no action is possible except through radical change as defined by Burrell and Morgan (1979). For actual workers in the workplace, however, it is unlikely that such oppositions will give rise to new, organized relationships.

The strict determinism of this approach has been strongly criticized. Morin (1985, p. 13) summarizes the criticism, noting that the positions of the optimists and the pessimists "are based on unidimensional, unidirectional perspectives that must be treated with caution", thus setting limits on studies of technological innovation that can be compared to those arising from similar criticism in the fields of pure and social sciences (Maruyama, 1974), organization theory (Burrel and Morgan, 1979; Morgan, 1986) and management (Aktouf, 1989). The unitary paradigm is being called into question in all fields, and determinism is being replaced by a volition-based approach to organizations.

Given this context, technological innovation will be discussed here not as an effect to be measured, but rather as an opportunity, a point in time at which choice is possible. The decision-making process, as it relates to the introduction of new technologies, will be examined more closely in the following section, in light of the technological culture described above.

4.1   The introduction of technological innovation: a reference framework

Applied documentation in the field of management clearly identifies the process leading to the introduction of technological innovation as a fundamental factor having a major impact on the workplace, whether in economic, organizational or social terms, and on the optimization of technology within organizations (Vallée, 1986; Gagnon and Nollet, 1990; Sankar, 1991). The same studies suggest that the authoritarian introduction of new technologies should give way to other methods allowing the persons affected by technological change to have real input, but without spelling out how this is to be achieved or the objectives and results of the process.

A review of the existing literature on worker participation within organizations, including the work of Dachler and Wilpert (1978), Loveridge (1980), Cordova (1982), Strauss (1982), Long and Warner (1987), Cotton et al. (1988), has allowed us to develop a reference framework to assess the managerial practices presently being applied in the field in relation to the introduction of new technologies. Three dimensions have been selected for presentation here: the level of control over the decision-making process, the availability of information, and the phases of the introduction process.

The level of control over the decision-making process reflects the degree of worker input. It ranges from simply being informed of a decision made unilaterally by management before the actual introduction of the technology, to consultation and negotiated collaboration. More specifically, the consultation level is the level where managerial decisions are made after, for example, surveying worker opinions in the matter. Negotiated collaboration, based on democratic dialogue (Gustavsen, 1985) and diagnostic-oriented methodologies such as the soft systems approach of Checkland (Hirscheim, 1985), and necessarily involving the informing and training of users at the various stages of the introduction of a technological system, leads to a "local theory" (Elden, 1983) of the organization and use of technological innovations in a given workplace. Local theory essentially relates to the appropriateness of the workplace.

The availability of information refers to the nature of the decisions made. There are three levels: the long term selection of technological innovations in keeping with the firm's general strategy, the operational level or conceptual dimension relating to the conditions governing the organization of technological decisions (such as work organization and division, task definitions) and lastly, the operational level, relating to conditions of adaptation (for example, training, recycling, transfers, wages, and work schedules).

It is possible to establish, in actual cases, a link between the availability of information and the time selected for and various phases of the introduction process. Three phases will be discusses here: the initiation phase (corresponding to feasibility studies), the design phase (corresponding to an examination of technical and organizational alternatives and the final selection of one alternative) and actual introduction (corresponding to the action taken in conjunction with various management practices).

Until now, a lot has been said about participation, but little about human nature. Can participation, in the ontological sense, constitute an opportunity for workers to rehabilitate their role as key players? If so, what types of participation provide the best opportunities?

Aktouf (1989) addressed this question following anthropological work comparing participation in standard manufacturing businesses with that in so-called "innovative" businesses, in particular the Cascades company case. He concluded that workers see themselves as key players following a double appropriation: appropriation of the factory (where workers are involved in the production process, in other words in the understanding, design and final production of the product) and appropriation of their own right to provide input. The result is an authentic relationship between those directing and those directed.

From another standpoint, Martin (1981, p. 69) suggests that authentic collaboration involves "behaviour in a given situation that allows the player to become involved in the solving of problems he considers to be relevant, with results he can actually help to design and control". Authentic participation is thus a true transformation of power

237

relationships, as is also demonstrated in the work of Pateman (1970) and Bernstein (1982). Borzeix and Linhart (1988) address the question of the type of decisions that are involved when workers gain the right to participate. Work psychopathology, as stated above, provides a clear answer: the organization of work is at the very centre of the constraints imposed on workers, and consequently of the repression of volition, one of the constitutive acts of the self.

Using all the above materials, it is possible to organize theoretical and empirical observations into a reference framework in order to observe the link between the process of introducing technological innovation and the role of the user-operator as object or subject (Diagram 7.3). The reference framework shows that the more the process tends towards negotiated collaboration, the more it introduces an element of discussion as regards technological choices. The more workers become key players in the process of technological change, the more the workplace is subject to appropriation, as understood in local action theory, reflecting the wishes of the persons affected by the technological change. From the point of view of the business itself, an appropriated technological change mobilizes staff, not only as regards their acceptance of technological innovations, but also, and especially, as regards the fuller use made of the innovation in the short and medium term.

The reference framework will thus be used to examine, not the theoretical aspects, but rather the actual ways in which technological change is implemented in the field, drawing on the available data from Canada for both small and large firms. The presentation of the data will be completed by observations taken from other overseas studies.

Diagram 7.3
Links between the level of control over the decision-making process, types of information and the phases of the process to introduce technological innovations, and the role of the owner-manager

Phases	Initiation	Design	Implementation
Level of control ╲ Type of information	Strategic	Conceptual	Operational
Information	—	—	Object
Consultation	—	Object	Object
Negotiated collaboration	Subject	Subject	Subject

Key: ―― : no role

4.2 The introduction of technological innovation: trends in small and large businesses

This examination of the different ways in which technological innovation is implemented will be mainly based on data from various surveys, which will then be compared with the reference framework presented previously.

A survey of automation prepared for the Economic Council of Canada by Betcherman and McMullen (1986), covering 946 businesses of all sizes, showed that the main players in the planning of innovation projects were senior managers and outside consultants, in 96% and 42% of the cases reported, as compared to 24% and 15% for worker groups and employer-employee committees. Furthermore, among the unionized businesses in the same sampling, 46% reported negotiations relating to technological change. A majority of the negotiations involved adaptation to the new conditions with respect, mainly, to training, remuneration, job security, seniority, and health and safety. With respect to control over the decision-making process, the negotiations involved prior notice and consultation mechanisms in, respectively, 30% and 20% of the businesses concerned. Significantly, the survey showed, however, that conditions were modified less often when the negotiations involved changes to be made to decision-making mechanisms, either through joint committees or under management power provisions (p. 45).

Similarly, a survey of all the collective agreements covering 500 employees or more in Canada showed that 38% contained technological change provisions concerning prior notice/consultation, and 14.6% contained provisions relating to employer-employee committees on matters relating to technological change. Although these percentages varied from one sector to another, the tendency towards a sharing of responsibilities was widespread. When business size was introduced as a factor, the survey showed that the trend is more marked in small businesses (Economic Council of Canada, 1987).

Other studies reflect a similar situation. A study by Desjardins (1985) of a representative sample of 2859 collective agreements including technological change clauses showed that the mechanisms almost exclusively addressed the question of workforce retraining. Only 9% of the collective agreements in the sample provided for joint committees on technological change. The union position remained ambiguous. While showing openness towards the negotiation of technological change, and thus proving their awareness of the strategic importance of new technologies, the real attitude of the unions was shown by Gagnon and Landry (1989a) to be largely defensive. Negotiations focus essentially on retraining conditions.

The same trends can be observed in an exploratory study of technological change in 40 businesses of all sizes in Quebec (Vallée, 1986). Information and consultation programs were reported in, respectively, 21% and 5% of the cases surveyed. When business size was factored in, and when only the nineteen small and medium-sized businesses in the sample were considered, it could be seen that only two businesses actually used this type of program. In no case was there any participation in the decision-making process. In fact, the main means of involving the workforce when new technologies are introduced remains, even today, a training or retraining program, in other words a worker adaptation measure. A recent OECD report (1991, p. 48) on new technologies shows that educational and training activities and expenses vary widely from one business, industry or workforce category to another, and are generally concentrated in large businesses, high-tech businesses and more highly-qualified worker categories. The same report states, however, that large businesses invest four times more than small businesses in structured training activities although, even so, only 30% of large businesses and 10% of businesses with 99 employees or less invest in this area. We should add, though, that surveys of training in small businesses present the same difficulties as surveys of their R&D capacity.

From another point of view, surveys of the attitudes of business leaders regarding the role that should be played by workers during technological change have shown that they remain unconvinced that actual involvement, as meant by the term appropriation, of the people affected by the change is necessary (Vallée, 1986; Guimond and Bégin, 1987), despite the example of innovative businesses that have succeeded in this area (Betcherman et al., 1990). Decision-makers are aware that worker participation improves implementation and the rate of return on new technologies but, in practice, tend to rely more on information and consultation than on negotiated collaboration based on genuine participation (Gagnon and Nollet, 1990).

Using the reference framework presented in Diagram 7.3, we can thus observe that examples of the implementation of new technologies seem to show little involvement of workers as subjects, whether in small or large firms. This has also been the finding of a recent analysis by Quebec's council for science and technology (1990), and ties in with the observations of Gagnon and Landry (1989a) in their studies of technological change. For comparison purposes, the recent empirical data collected by Sandberg (1992) from 200 small Swedish businesses show similar results; the technocentric approach remains the main way in which technological innovations are introduced in the manufacturing sector. Another major survey on participation, covering businesses in twelve European Community countries, shows that the situation is similar: non-participation and information strategies remain the norm, followed by consultation strategies. Only the data from Denmark and Germany break away from the pattern by showing a reliance on negotiation and joint decision-making (Gill, 1991).

Other observers point out that even when participation takes place, it is passive and instrumental. This is the case, in particular, where technology is introduced following information and consultation only, and where only adaptation conditions are addressed, essentially as illustrated by the formal actions identified in the surveys presented above. This point will be discussed in the next section.

4.3   Criticism of instrumental participation

Lobet-Maris (1984) summarizes the interests underlying instrumental-type introduction strategies, which are of two kinds: technological and psychosociological. In the first case, the involvement of the user-operator is important in order to obtain an increasingly fine-grained analysis of the existing situation, in reaction to the large numbers of failures caused by overly abstract models (Kling, 1980). This is also the ideal time to codify informal aspects and thus to better control, as part of a power relationship, the practical knowledge of future user-operators (Borzeix and Linhart, 1988).

At the psychosociological level, the ability to manage resistance to change must be developed, to the extent that resistance would be a barrier to the effectiveness of the technological project. Essentially, an instrumental approach involves gaining acceptance for a technico-organizational choice without changing its predetermined content significantly. Gagnon and Landry (1989b) point out that designers, after consultation, are little influenced by their exchanges with user-operators as regards potential consequences for the latter group. The instrumental approach thus includes an a priori component. Pichault (1990) concludes that the main negative force is that exercised by the postulates held by management representatives, resuming the situation as follows: "the innovation process, and recognition of the workers' capacity for social and technical imagination, constitute important points that have not always been clearly reflected in management terms" (p. 214).

To give an example of the instrumental approach to the introduction of technological change, let us focus on one of the most frequent conditions of adaptation - training - and ask the following question: Does training lead beyond technical proficiency to a genuine taking in charge of reality by user-operators?

In a vast majority of cases, training centres on the acquisition of the operational aspects of technological innovation, and can be termed short-term adaptive training (Le Goff, 1987). With respect to training strategies, it is possible to state, based on the work of Lesne (1977), that training for new technologies is generally structured around a learning process designed to transmit a set of predetermined standards, in which the experience of the workers undergoing training is expected to submit to the ideal provided by the expert. The workers must show, at each stage, that they have learned what they were supposed to learn. Does this type of training, however, really lead to the acquisition of the technical culture needed to appropriate reality, or in other words to become a player in the mastering of a new technology? Probably not, since such a culture represents the thought processes used by user-operators to capture technological innovation. The goal, for user-operators, is thus not just to acquire techniques, but to grasp the logic lying behind the new technology and thus "to appropriate the skills they will have to deploy in practice, because they will have theorized practice; they will know why they do what they do, and what the goal is" (Orofiamma, 1987, p. 107). D'Iribarne (1983, p. 149) goes even further by introducing the idea of a learning process that can begin at the same time as the process to introduce technological innovations: "the mastery of a technique implies the ability to understand its nature, its evolution and its functions, to reflect on its meaning, the extent of its use and development, to transfer applications to other fields of knowledge, and to be able to carry out a critical analysis to improve the technique or reject it on specific grounds" (our translation).

The technological and psychosociological interests tied to information and consultation practices, and the type of training provided, point to the conclusion that instrumental participation in the process to introduce technological innovation is a symbolic approach rather than a real opportunity for genuine participation.

Are the new tools and specialized vocabulary of this enlightened form of management not an attempt to develop a new worker identification with the organizational system and its own instrumental logic? For several observers, this identification is fundamental, given the intrinsic characteristics of the work carried out using current technological innovations, such as tasks that cannot be defined by a specific operational mode, a maximizing of the use of automated equipment (and a corresponding shift from work-time to machine-time), the obligation to produce results which refers to the capacity for analysis and the accountability of the workforce (Veltz, 1986; Stankiewicz, 1988). Is it not utopic to believe that such an identification could occur? A number of analyses have shown the limits of this approach to organization, taken as an identification with a single organizational culture (Jacob, 1990). The most likely hypothesis is a return to existing manager-directed social relationships, before the introduction of a technological innovation. Such relationships will, however, always be biased against those directed in almost all cases. The rewards will continue to go to those at the top of the hierarchy, and the resistance so feared by the decision-makers will continue to surface in opposition rather than involvement.

5.   Tentative conclusion: successful technological innovation and the double-loop learning cycle

Most observers agree that the economic benefits deriving from new technologies are associated, mainly, with the innovations connected with work organization (OECD, 1991; Jacob and Ducharme, 1995). A lack of genuine involvement, though, of the persons affected by a technological innovation, or a reliance on instrumental participation during the process to introduce a technological innovation, both contribute to the maintenance of a narrow ideology of rationality, thereby limiting the range of possibilities as regards work organization. Workers, the user-operators, are stuck in a subordinate situation that limits their chances of emancipation. In this connection, Dumont (1987, p. 116) has pointed out that enlightened management tends to "broaden its technique rather than question its principles".

Despite calls from practitioners and researchers to recognize the importance of a true involvement of the persons affected by technological change to ensure its full development, and despite recent empirical results that provide a rich source of information regarding the factors influencing a successful introduction of new technologies into small businesses (Garsombke and Garsombke, 1989; Schroeder et al., 1989; Raymond et al., 1990; Raymond and Julien, 1994), two observations, tending to support the trend described above, must be retained for any study carried out in the field of small business:
- The system of knowledge and reasoning (the paradigm) of a majority of owner-managers and designer-consultants is overly dependent on a technocentric representation of technological change (in which technical and economic feasibility overrides considerations of organizational and social feasibility) and a mechanical representation (rational conception) of their organization;
- Owner-managers and designers are largely unable to question their own fundamental hypotheses (their paradigms) about technological change (they remain impervious to socio-technical representations) and management (they are unable to appreciate a systemic, political and cultural view of their organization).

These observations also apply to the representatives of the workforce. Their practical attitude, as shown in the work of Gagnon and Landry (1989a), is still marked by a classical approach to labour relations, and a new approach, for most players in the field, has to be developed.

Our two observations can be reduced to a fundamental idea: whatever the normative prescriptions that are developed (in connection with methods), in a large majority of cases new technologies only bring with them the potential for economic and social development if the decision-makers involved are able to open their minds to a complementary way of considering existing managerial and organizational situations, in other words the concepts and theories that support the introduction of new players in the workplace as part of material and non-material technological change. The new players must be able to understand the limits of their representational model of reality, since these are the models that will condition the strategic selection of new technology and the selection of patterns of work organization and workforce adaptation, and thus the decision to consider workers as either subjects or objects (Clegg and Kemp, 1986; Landry et al., 1989). Argyris and Schön (1978) have clearly demonstrated that few people understand or are aware of the knowledge system, or paradigm, that they generally use. It is clear that this phenomenon constitutes a major barrier to assessing alternative approaches to technological change.

The updating of knowledge systems and the acceptance of new ways of conceiving existing managerial and organizational factors requires the completion of a double-loop learning cycle (Guilhon, 1994). The empirical observations of Eraly (1989) have shown that neglect of such learning generally leads an organization to integrate new technologies according to existing managerial practices that, in the main, reflect a classical view of organizations.

Negotiated collaboration, of the type discussed earlier, is fundamentally based on the learning of a new approach to management (Morgan, 1986; Sainsaulieu, 1987; Aktouf, 1989; Crozier, 1989). This paradigm, a complement rather than an alternative, has been presented from the standpoint of complexity (Séguin-Bernard and Chanlat, 1983), heterogeneity (Maruyama, 1980) and emergence (Lincoln, 1985; Audet and Bélanger, 1989), and introduces concepts such as self-organization, local theory, flexibility, polyocularity (the updating of new knowledge through the confrontation of expert knowledge and experiential knowledge), open dialogue and the cultural acquisition of new organized patterns. Regarding the process for change, socio-technical and problem-resolution methodologies are mentioned, including soft system methodology, training-action and negotiated diagnosis, all of which can be applied from the strategic planning stage of a technological innovation project.

Actual intervention on fundamental hypotheses, in the manner, for example, of Argyris and Schön (1978) or Bartunek and Moch (1987), would seem to be an important condition for success in a technological change based on appropriation (by workers) and optimization (of technology). For the players involved, this means understanding how they acquire knowledge about technological change, and then renewing their knowledge systems in order to introduce different, complementary approaches. In this connection, Leavitt and March (1988, p. 324), while summarizing organizational learning and change, comment as follows: "one of the most efficient approaches to organizational change consists, first, in working on the transformation of fundamental hypotheses, ideas, and concepts through awareness-raising techniques, double-loop learning, and paradigmatic reflection".

It must not be forgotten that an organization, its equipment and technology notwithstanding, is a social construct brokered through the representational systems of the players concerned. However, regarding management practices and strategic choices, a movement to re-negotiate this social construct must be assumed by those responsible for a firm's orientation (Aktouf, 1989). Since the role played by owner-managers is vital to the introduction of new technologies into small businesses, because technological strategy is intrinsically linked to the owner-manager (Solé Parrellada, 1990), they should be the first target group for attempts to inform and train using a double-loop learning cycle. To complement the previously-mentioned work on factors affecting the successful introduction of new technology, applied research work is needed into the implementation of these approaches to technological change in small businesses. The links between implementation and knowledge systems are important, since currently the involvement of employees in the introduction of technological innovation is being addressed in theory only, both by directors and workforce representatives. Concrete action calling the fundamental hypotheses of classic management theory into question has, in a majority of cases, yet to occur. Current attitudes, however, seem to indicate a willingness to undertake double-loop learning cycles.

246

8 Operations management

"...to whom some could reproach that, since they do not see either end of the joining line between too much and too little, long and short, light and heavy, near and far, and since they recognize neither its end nor its beginning, they judge very uncertainly about the middle." Michel de Montaigne, "Essai".

1. Introduction

1.1 Definition of operations management (OM)

Nollet, Kélada and Diorio (1986) gave the following definition of operations management: "A set of planning, organization, command and control activities, to which are sometimes added assurance activities, applicable to production operations. The management activities are aimed at helping achieve the firm's strategic goals or objectives, through optimal use of the tangible and intangible resources at its disposal. In doing so, the activity managers consider the various internal and external constraints to be respected" (our translation).

These same authors, at the beginning of their book, state that they have used the terms "production", "operations" and "production operations" synonymously. Rather than embarking on a discussion of the terminology, the author of this chapter has preferred to suggest that many of the *activities* and *functions* of a manufacturing production firm are closely linked, and that most cannot be isolated, in whole or in part, without some difficulty. In addition, to simplify the organization of this chapter on *operations and production management*, we propose to classify the various small business operations management activities as follows:

1. The activities under the more direct authority of senior management, performed at more or less regular intervals, depending on the environment, and generally affecting the firm as a whole; these activities, usually known as strategic planning activities, are concerned

with the location or relocation of production units, identification of market niches, product range analysis, enterprise financing, human resources management methods, and so on. Although all these activities undoubtedly have an influence on everyday operations in small firms, they do not fall within the scope of this chapter, and are dealt with in more detail in Chapter 5.

2. Ad-hoc activities, performed on an occasional basis, usually alongside everyday production operations. They include, among others:

- new product design;
- reorganization of the shop floor and workstations;
- determination of new working methods;
- choice and justification of new production equipment;
- implementation of new management approaches such as tight flow, just-in-time or total quality.

These aspects of life in small manufacturing businesses will be mentioned occasionally in this chapter, and were addressed in part in the preceding chapter.

3. Finally, the everyday manufacturing production operations in small firms, taking for granted that the human, physical and financial resources are well established, and that the production manager is required to use them productively to respond to production demand emanating directly from customers or based on the forecasts of the marketing function, seen in Chapter 6. These activities include:

- demand forecasts;
- the creation of a certified (integrated) production plan, in light of product families, human resources and overall plant capacity;
- the creation of a master schedule showing, for a given planning horizon, the quantity of products to be manufactured, the time at which production will begin, and the date on which production and assembly, if any, is expected to end;
- the creation of a material requirements plan (MRP), describing raw material and purchased component requirements together with the date required, based on the master schedule;
- the creation of a production program specifying master schedule demand for production machinery and equipment;
- manpower assignments for the master schedule;
- a production schedule, showing the list of operations and the time at which they will be performed on each machine;

- control activities, i.e. the activities performed to ensure that the master schedule (and production schedule) is carried out as specified, or that corrections are made where necessary;
- raw material and finished goods inventory management;
- activities related to quality management (e.g. inspection operations), which must be planned at the same time as production.

These activities, as performed in the small business environment, are examined in greater detail in the following sections.

1.2 History of operations management

The history of operations management in manufacturing enterprises can be summarized around the following major reference points:
- the industrial revolution, which transformed the production system from a craft operation to an organized high volume operation;
- Taylorism (late 19th century) which, although much disparaged, made a number of suggestions concerning the scientific organization of work that are still used today in discussions of manufacturing productivity;
- information technology (mid-20th century), which facilitated and led to the implementation of better production management techniques (Sadowski, 1984);
- the Japanese influence (last quarter of the 20th century) which, among other things, highlighted the importance of workers and their opinions within the system, and advocated production system flexibility.

1.3 The importance of operations management in small firms

The importance of operations management in small manufacturing firms can be seen through the example of a highly entrepreneurial person who has an idea for a new product that he or she believes would sell well. This person, if a go-ahead type, will devote time to designing, producing and selling the product. We can therefore say with certainty that the basic functions of a manufacturing enterprise created with a production rationale will be product design, product fabrication and product marketing. The other functions can be said to be auxiliary or support and management functions.

In the early stages, most of a small firm's energy will be devoted to the basic functions, since the other functions require relatively little effort. As the firm grows, however, the other functions will become more important as the volume of activity increases. Unfortunately, this sometimes causes the basic functions to be neglected.

To survive and grow, a small manufacturing business must not lose sight of its production rationale. As the business grows, production management problems will multiply, and the firm must take steps to maintain its performance in this area. Unfortunately, small firms do not give enough importance to this function. This may be due to a shortage of the required resources, or to a lack of vision on the part of management. Small business owner-managers must realize that enterprise productivity depends to a large extent on the productivity of its production operations, and thus on operations management, although at the same time they must not lose sight of the importance of the other functions.

2.   Models of the operations management function

Operations management may take a number of very different forms, depending on the industrial sector and the size of the firm. The relative importance of each element of the operations management function will therefore vary considerably between firms. The following pages contain three conceptual diagrams of the function as it is seen in the literature and in practice.

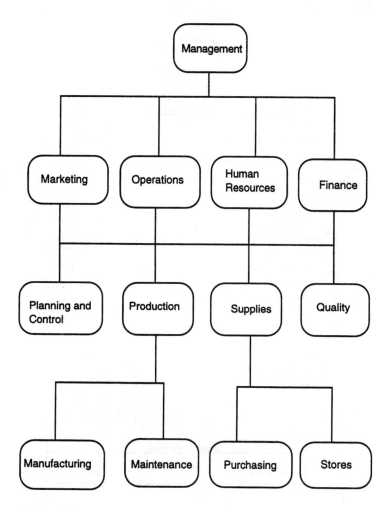

Figure 8.1
Organizational model

251

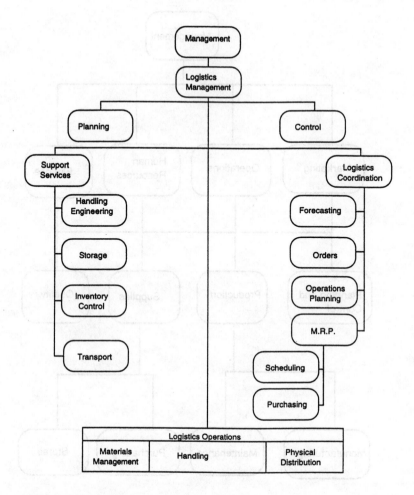

Figure 8.2
Logistics model

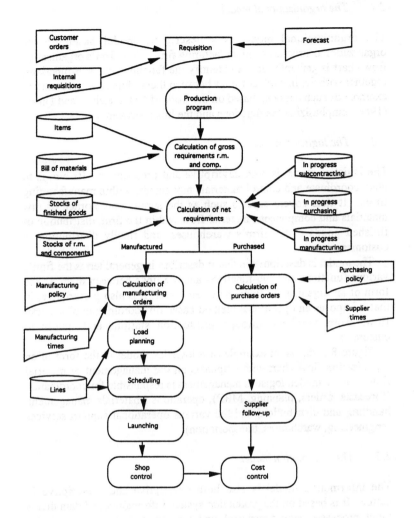

Figure 8.3
Information model

2.1 The organizational model

The organizational model is a descriptive model based on the organizational structure of manufacturing firms. The firm's organization flow chart is generally used to identify the functions and sub-functions, together with the line or staff links between them. Figure 8.1 presents an example of such a model, based on the work of Nolet, Kélada and Diorio (1986), emphasizing the functions and the links between them.

2.2 The logistics model

The logistics model is both descriptive and prescriptive. Its aim is to plan, coordinate and control materials movements within manufacturing firms. It thus covers aspects such as the supply and storage of raw materials and components, material flow within the firm, distribution of finished goods to the firm's warehouses, and finally distribution to customers.

The model is descriptive in that it describes in general terms the firm's various functions and sub-functions and the links between them, in the form of an organization flow chart. However, it is also prescriptive, in that it imposes an operational method based on coordination of material flows from suppliers, through production stations and finally to customers.

Figure 8.2 shows an example of a logistics model in the form of an organization flow chart with emphasis on the management of material flows. In the model, logistics management is responsible for coordination (forecasts, orders, planning, MRP), operations (materials management, handling and distribution) and the various operational support services (engineering, warehouses, transportation).

2.3 The information model

The information model is also both descriptive and prescriptive in nature. It is based on the production system information and data that is input, processed, stored retrieved, updated and used by management for decision-making purposes. The model is descriptive in that it describes both the data and information and their points of entry and use. It is prescriptive in that it sets out the dissemination and use of information within the system, and the input, processing and updating operations required if the information is to fulfill the role assigned to it.

Figure 8.3 shows an information model for the planning, scheduling and control of manufacturing operations. The model applies mainly to

254

batch production firms. At regular intervals - normally of several weeks - the status of customer orders, shop requisitions and inventories is examined and compared with sales forecasts. On the basis of the comparison and in light of production capacities, new shop requisitions are planned. The new requisitions trigger the process of raw material ordering and production planning. The loop is closed by the control activities.

3. Operations management practice: the state of current knowledge

In this section, we will look first at the main production management approaches and techniques, and then at examples of their implementation and discussions of their applicability taken from the literature.

3.1 Production management approaches and techniques

The planning-scheduling-control approach

This is the traditional production management approach, comprising three clearly identified phases in the management process: planning, scheduling and control. The various approaches and techniques described below apply to one of these phases (e.g. operational research techniques), or to all three along with the supplies needed to meet the production schedule (e.g. manufacturing resources planning: MRP II), or more comprehensively to the firm's production management environment, including related functions like quality management. This is the case of the so-called "world class" manufacturing approach, the most modern of the approaches that allows the firm to compete throughout the world.

The *planning* phase consists in establishing, for a given time span, the quantities of products to be produced, generally by sub-periods within the time span. The period for which production is planned depends on two factors: first, how detailed the planning is, and second, the type of production process.

Aggregate production planning is carried out for sets or groups of products from the firm's product range, without reference to the distribution of each of the resources (products, components) within the groups. At this planning level, overall production capacity alone is considered and not the capacity of individual workstations. Detailed planning will then be performed to establish the quantity of each item to be produced. The aggregate planning horizon will thus be in the longer term, while the detailed plan based on the aggregate plan will cover the short term. Adjustments are possible before proceeding with detailed planning, to reflect possible changes in the aggregate plan as a result of the market situation.

Two elements of the production process have a major impact on the planning horizon: the production cycle and the type of market. The production cycle is an inherent characteristic of every manufacturing production system, and comprises the average time between the planned date (or time) of a shop order, and the time at which the order is ready for delivery, either to the firm's warehouse or to the customer. The type of market refers to the distinction between a company producing to order, i.e. producing only firm customer orders (e.g. a machine tool shop) and one producing for inventory, i.e. producing more than the quantity shown in the order book (e.g. a furniture producer). For example, a small machine tool shop producing components requiring little work, to order, will have a planning horizon of only a few days, while a medium-sized firm in the furniture or door and window sector, producing for inventory, will have a planning horizon of several months, depending on seasonal or other fluctuations.

In the *scheduling* phase, all production operations are scheduled at the various workstations. In situations where the scheduling plan is established in advance and assigns all operations on all workstations for the coming days, this activity is considered to be a planning activity. In other production environments, however, it may be an everyday operations management activity. Once production begins, shop floor management will schedule operations as production progresses. This second approach, although obviously leaving more room for error, is nevertheless used by many small manufacturing firms.

In the *control* phase, application of the plan (detailed production plan, scheduling plan) is monitored. The control cycle (measurement-evaluation-action) includes production of the initial and terminal operations reports by the plant, comparison of the reports and plan by the production manager, and corrective action by the production manager where appropriate.

In this traditional approach, and until the advent of the material requirements planning approach (MRP), inventory management was typically separate from production management. The warehouse manager functioned fairly independently, viewing the plant as a customer that ordered raw materials and components, evaluating the demand pattern for each stock item, and managing supplies in consequence.

256

Operational research techniques

Operational research (OR) is concerned with system optimization. In the operational research approach, the system/problem is modelled, including the constraints, operational postulates and optimization objective, and algorithms or heuristics are used to identify the "best" solution or a "good" achievable solution. Since operations management often gives rise to problems well-suited to modelling, OR techniques have been applied in several cases, with varying levels of success depending on the problem and the assumptions required to arrive at the algorithmic solution. For example, Satish (1990) gives the following list of applications:

PROBLEM	POTENTIAL TECHNIQUES
Forecasting	Moving average, exponential smoothing, time series
Inventory management	Reorder points, periodic reviews, simple material requirements planning (MRP)
Mix of products, resource allocation, capacity calculation, location, distribution	Linear programming, transport algorithms
Scheduling	Assignment, Johnson's algorithm, priority rules
Adjustment	Load balancing techniques
Quality control and customer service	Statistical process control techniques and tools (SPC)
Failure forecasts	Analysis of ratios, factors, profit analysis

Simulation is also classified by many people as an OR technique, partly because it also includes modelling, and is used to address many of the problems addressed by OR. A typical simulation project would be a systems analysis, modelling, programming of elements from the model, and testing of various operational alternatives using a computer. Simulation has been, and still is, used frequently to analyze or design various elements of the production system, including inventory management, planning, scheduling, assignment and so on.

Materials Requirements Planning (MRP) first appeared in the early 1970s, when it was considered revolutionary, for a number of reasons.

First, the approach defined two types of stock items: those subject to *independent* demand, mainly the products sold by the firm, and those subject to *dependent* demand, mainly the raw materials used to manufacture products. This basic distinction led to the definition of two methods of inventory management: the traditional method for independent demand items (i.e. forecasts, economic quantities, reorder points, etc.), and the MRP method for dependent demand items, where supplies were managed according to demand for the parent products on which they depended.

Second, the MRP approach required planning of production *and* supplies of dependent demand items by time buckets, in contrast to the traditional approach (forecasts, economic quantities, reorder points, etc.).

The MRP approach can thus be summarized as follows: the firm first formalizes all its production data, including the items list, bills of materials, product structures, process sheets, lead times, manufacturing and assembly times. Then, based on the production plan and technical data, the (dependent) requirements for raw materials, components and sub-assemblies are established. MRP output takes the form of a list of supplier orders and shop orders, spread over time, to carry out the plan - hence its name, materials requirements planning.

Although MRP has been comparatively successful in general terms, some of its applications have nevertheless failed, for a variety of reasons. First, MRP is based on technical production data, which must be accurate and continually updated. This is not the case in many firms. Second, the approach cannot necessarily be applied in every type of production environment. It is very useful in repetitive production environments, with well-defined product ranges that remain relatively stable over time. However, because it is so well-known, some firms have unfortunately tried to implement it in less suitable production environments. Third, MRP is a first step towards integration of enterprise functions (production, supplies, engineering, etc.), which usually did not exist before MRP implementation. Moreover, the MRP approach requires a fairly powerful computer system, used by a number of different people throughout the firm. When MRP first appeared, reliable, user-friendly systems were not common, and firms often ran up against human user problems when they introduced fairly complex technical tools not designed for ordinary people like warehousemen with no computer training. Finally, MRP was based on infinite capacity - in other words, when manufacturing, assembly and supply schedules were drawn up using technical data and the production plan, it was assumed that production capacity would always be sufficient. When the time came to implement the schedules, and capacity was found not to be sufficient, the credibility of the approach was challenged.

Manufacturing Resources Planning (MRP II) is a natural extension of MRP. It was quickly realized that the technical database used by MRP was of interest to many people within the firm. In particular, when attempts were made to overcome the problem of infinite capacity planning in the early days of MRP, it was found that the software had to include a technical description of all production workstations, including availability, performance, production rates for operations assigned to them, assembly time, etc. Workstations are operated by people, which meant that a detailed list of the firm's direct labour, together with assignment and availability, also had to be included. As the field of information systems developed, it became fairly easy to build a huge technical production database, used by various people throughout the firm for equally various reasons. For example, if the "production control" component of MRP II software contained data on production time per employee, only a small additional step was required to obtain salary details for those same employees. Similarly, raw material use and direct manpower hours were stored directly in the MRP II system to place shop orders, and only a small additional step was required to obtain the unit cost price of the products ordered.

Development - thanks largely to progress in the information systems field - took place around two focal points: the type of data stored in MRP II systems, and the applications added. Figure 8.4 shows a typical layout (data and applications) for commercial MRP software.

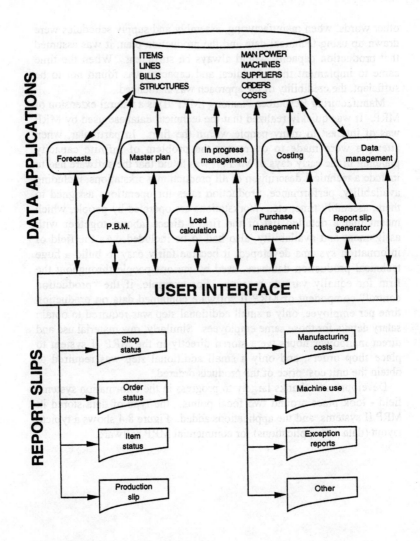

Figure 8.4
Diagram of an MRP II system

260

MRP II is first and foremost a huge computerized database, used by different application modules to support planning, organization and control of production, and also by other enterprise functions. However, it is additionally an *integrating approach* to operations management, where success is measured by data integrity and consistency with the corresponding values of the real system. The approach covers most of the enterprise functions that have a strong link to production, from human resources (assignment) to storage of the finished goods (distribution).

Implementation problems were also experienced with MRP II software. In particular, most MRP implementation problems were carried over to MRP II, with the notable exception that computer systems were by that time more user-oriented and the interfaces more user-friendly. On the other hand, as MRP II packages covered a variety of enterprise functions, data integrity and coordination problems tended to be greater. Moreover, the size of MRP II systems was an obstacle to their use in small firms, because of the human resources required.

Optimized production technology (OPT)

Optimized production technology is both an operations management approach and a powerful production planning and scheduling package. The OPT method, developed by Eliyahu M. Goldratt (1986), appeared towards the end of the 1970s. The production management philosophy underlying it has been explained in detail by its creator. It can be summarized as follows: in every manufacturing production unit (workshop, plant), workstations can be divided into two separate groups: bottlenecks and others. The bottlenecks are the workstations that are used to capacity, or almost to capacity, during production. They will thus regulate the productivity of the unit, and production management must take this into account. A corollary of this is that the non-bottleneck stations must be managed according to but differently from the bottlenecks.

This approach, like MRP, was seen as a revolution in the production management world. Although bottlenecks were traditionally well-known in small firms, management tended to "live with" them, rather than managing production in consequence. In OPT, on the other hand, they are the exclusive focus.

The approach is based on the following eight basic rules (Courtois, Pillet and Martin, 1989):

- flows, not capacities, must be balanced;

- the use of a non-bottleneck is determined not by its own potential but by other constraints in the system;
- use of a resource and full employment of a resource are not the same thing;
- an hour lost in a bottleneck is an hour lost for the whole system;
- an hour gained in a non-bottleneck is only an illusion;
- bottlenecks determine both output flow and stock levels;
- the transfer batch should not always be equal to the production batch;
- the sum of local optima is not the optimum for the whole system.

OPT obviously requires the same technical production data as MRP-MRP II: items list, bills of materials, product structures, process sheets, lead times, etc. Based on the production plan, the software package produces a detailed scheduling plan, by means of an algorithm, described as "secret and sophisticated", which applies the above basic principles. The software tends to be used mainly by large production firms, since it is fairly expensive. On the other hand, the philosophy on which it is based can be a source of ideas for production planning in small businesses.

Pull or "just-in-time" production

Pull or just-in-time (JIT) production is a Japanese approach developed by Toyota (Winston and Heiko, 1990). It is both a production management technique and an enterprise philosophy. Its creator summarized it as follows: "In a word, it is a production system based on the complete elimination of waste, aimed at achieving maximum rationality in working methods".

From a *production management technique* standpoint, JIT is characterized mainly by the fact that production is literally pulled from the upstream station by the downstream station, according to finished goods requirements. An order for finished goods triggers a shop requisition for product assembly. The assembly station uses parts and components and requisitions replacements from upstream stations. In turn, the stations immediately upstream dispatch semi-finished components and requisition replacement components from the next upstream station. This upstream use-requisition-replacement sequence continues up to the raw materials store, and ultimately up to the raw materials supplier. Requisitions between production units are made by means of signals. For example, production of a given component will begin only on receipt of a signal from the ordering unit. The most frequently used signal is the *kanban*, a voucher identifying the material required, the quantity and the two stations involved.

With the traditional production management approach, a shop requisition for finished goods or provisional scheduling in anticipation of a requisition for parts triggers an issue of raw materials from the store. The materials are then pushed to the next station, and so on, up to the assembly station - this is known as the "push" approach. System production levels are monitored, and resulting work-in-progress measured. By maintaining the work-in-progress at a slightly higher level than necessary, the impacts of unknown production factors can be minimized. JIT also uses a form of provisional scheduling. However, it is controlled on the basis of work-in-progress levels, and production levels are measured to obtain feedback. It is sometimes said that MRP uses a "pull" approach, since it triggers supply and production (manufacturing, assembly) orders over time, so as to obtain only what is required at a given moment. Although this principle does in fact underlie MRP, the comparison stops there. The "push" approach is still used to manage production progress, and it cannot therefore be described as pull production.

With respect to the *enterprise philosophy* of JIT, this is a reference to the set of operational elements in the production system aimed at achieving the overall JIT objective. Although the list of such elements varies according to the authors, the variations are due mainly to the fact that some authors refer to the specific objectives themselves, and others to the means used to achieve those objectives.

Winston and Heiko list the seven general concepts of JIT, as identified by the American Production and Inventory Control Society (APICS):

- production to customer orders;
- perfect quality;
- zero waiting time;
- elimination of waste;
- development of the productive potential of people;
- ongoing quest for improvement;
- flexibility.

In addition, Inman and Mehra (1990) identified the critical elements that facilitate operationalization of JIT in firms:

- quality circles;
- preventive maintenance;
- diversified employee training;

263

- outside consultants for implementation;
- reduction of production run change time;
- reduction of batch size.

There are several constants in the elements that constitute JIT philosophy. They can be summarized as follows: in an *ideal* JIT environment, production would be by the unit, workers would be able to perform several different tasks, the parts/products would have no defects. and the time taken to make production run changes on the machines would be insignificant as a percentage of the total production cycle. The Japanese have left their hallmark on the process through the element of employee participation, in ensuring perfect quality, carrying out preventive maintenance, overseeing regular materials flows in the plant, and solving ad-hoc problems - not an easy task, as we saw in the last chapter.

Computer integrated manufacturing (CIM)

Computer integrated manufacturing is generally referred to by its acronym, CIM.

Integrating production using a computer system is not in itself a production management technique. Carpenter (1984) described the CIM approach in small business as using the benefits of a series of extremely rapid calculations. These tools are used in product design, equipment and product manufacturing, capital management, process monitoring, data handling and so on.

Ideally, only one CIM database is built, containing information on the firm's finances, suppliers, customers and human resources, together with technical design and production data. The database is used by the various people involved in the CIM process, at all levels and for all functions. The integrated computer system also contains a series of applications software packages and user interfaces. The system thus integrates enterprise data and enterprise functions. For example, the design engineer could develop a component using a computer-assisted design module, and prepare the program for a numerically-controlled machine using another module. When the time comes to produce the component, a third production management module will transfer the program to the machine so that production can begin. A production monitoring module will inform the system of the progress made, a cost price module will establish the direct production cost, and then add the overheads percentage, which it obtains from the database.

MRP II systems are themselves a simple form of CIM, for the production element. There are, however, three basic differences, at least in their original concepts. First, CIM was originally intended to integrate design *and* production directly - in other words, to connect the machine controls to the production management system. This was not the case for the original MRP II. Second, MRP II had to use MRP to plan production, whereas CIM used a completely different technique. Finally, the initial CIM concept incorporated enterprise functions more broadly than MRP II, in particular the manufacturing operations.

"World class" manufacturing

Eisenhower (1990) defined the so-called "world class" manufacturing as the capacity of some firms to carve out a niche on world markets and maintain their position by continually improving already superior product quality and cost. The challenge is created by the competitive forces that disrupt world markets.

Krause and Keller (1988) identified the following key elements in world class manufacturing:

- employee involvement in the process;
- implementation of JIT;
- introduction of quality control techniques;
- use of preventive maintenance;
- rapid, ongoing improvement.

World class manufacturing is not a production management technique, but a company *philosophy* which will force the company, among other things, to improve its production (and production management) continuously, in order to remain competitive in a context of market globalization. It is this philosophy, for example, that will lead the company to introduce JIT or one of its components, or to develop computer integrated design and production. According to Eisenhower (1990), it is thus an approach involving ongoing improvement of quality, cost, customer service and flexibility. In this respect, it is farther from manufacturing operations management than the techniques and approaches described previously. Nevertheless, it needs to be mentioned in this chapter because it may cause a company considering foreign markets to follow developments in operations management techniques and adapt the latest innovations to its own environment.

3.2   Operations management in small businesses: a survey of the literature

Bibliographical research was carried out on a computer database, using key words from the various techniques and approaches discussed above. The research was directed particularly towards small business, and a special effort was made to identify papers describing the results of research that had used samples of several small firms, to obtain an overview of the OM question in this type of business. The following paragraphs contain a sample of the results, by type of technique or approach.

Planning-ordering-monitoring

Sharp et al. (1990) described the results of a survey of 3,000 small businesses in Great Britain. Their aim was to identify the core production management activities considered to be an acceptable minimum for effective production management. The firms were also asked which of the activities would require computer support. All respondents were responsible for production in their respective firms.

The four activities on which respondents said they spent the most time were, in order of importance:

- materials control, which for the purposes of the survey included control of materials on the shop floor, and control of raw materials and finished goods stocks;
- production planning;
- shop floor monitoring;
- costing.

Many of the respondents said their main computer support requirements would be satisfied if they had a system that covered the following core activities:

- forecasts;
- production planning;
- production and materials control;
- costing.

All these activities are covered by MRP II software application modules.

Satish (1990) said that small firms have the same, fairly complex problems to solve as large firms, and suggested that they should use the same OR techniques. However, he added that the techniques should be used competently and rigorously, which is perhaps difficult in the small business context. He provided a list of typical problems and corresponding OR techniques. The list is shown in the preceding section.

Alpar and Reeves (1990) carried out a survey of 495 small technology-oriented firms to identify the factors that encouraged them to use OR techniques. One of their initial observations was that OR would be used if more conventional techniques were well established. Other factors that influenced the use of OR were the presence of appropriate skills to develop, modify and maintain the software, and the size of the firm.

MRP, MRP II

Much has been written about MRP and MRP II. Some authors have described and criticized these two approaches, others have produced case studies, and some have presented the results of user surveys.

A 1982 survey (Anderson et al., 1982) of 679 American manufacturing firms revealed that 433 (64%) used MRP. Table 8.1, drawn from Anderson's paper, shows the percentage of respondent firms using MRP, according to turnover. The results suggest that enterprise size has an impact on the use of the technique.

Table 8.1
Percentage of MRP use by respondents, by turnover

Turnover	MRP Users
$10 M and under	43%
$11 - $25 M	61%
$26 - $50 M	72%
$51 - $100 M	77%
$100 M and over	70%

The same questionnaire was used in 1986 (Laforge and Vanessa, 1986) with a sample of 107 firms in South Carolina, for comparison purposes. A total of 33 respondents (31%) said they used MRP or MRP II.

Interestingly, the average size of the respondent firms was not the same as in the first survey, although the geographical area covered was larger. In the first survey, the average firm produced 3,002 different products and employed 19 people in production and inventory management, compared to 1,836 products and 14 people in the second. This clearly shows that MRP and MRP II software tend to be used more in large firms than in small firms. In Laforge and Vanessa's research, only 28% of the firms with less than 100 end products used MRP, compared to 46% of those with more than 1,000 products. It is worth noting that the results of both surveys were probably biased upwards in terms of the percentage of firms using MRP, since the questionnaires were sent to firms via employees who were members of APICS, the American Production and Inventory Control Society. The respondent firms thus all had highly competent staff in charge of production management, which is not necessarily the case in small firms.

Oliver Wight (1981) described hundreds of cases of MRP implementation in firms of various sizes. An issue of *Industrial Engineering* (March 1991) dedicated mainly to MRP II described three cases of successful implementation in small American manufacturing businesses, one with a turnover of $20 million, the second with a turnover of $52 million and the third with an undisclosed turnover, each employing 150 people. The three cases all concerned successful implementation of MRP II software.

Kenneth Hartley (1991) observed that 53% of firms using MRP II had achieved better inventory control within a year. The results obtained by firms using the system included:

- better customer service;
- optimal production planning;
- fewer raw materials shortages;
- inventory management refinements;
- a shorter production cycle.

The OPT approach

Very little research has been done on OPT in small firms, probably because of the relatively high cost of these systems. Nevertheless, many firms base their production management systems design and review work on the OPT approach.

Ashcroft (1989) described the case of a small firm producing wooden furniture to order. The firm first analyzed its production process using basic OPT principles, and then applied the OPT approach to plan and control production on the basis of bottlenecks. The results can be summarized as follows:

- orders could be sent for production 24 hours after receipt, without disturbing work-in-process;
- the value of work-in-process was cut by 75%;
- the value of inventories was cut by 50%;
- the production cycle was cut from 20 days to 7 days;
- customer service was improved significantly.

JIT approach

Wight (1981) discussed the relevance of using JIT in small firms, according to their level of development. The author identified four phases in small business development: birth, development, maturity and decline. His main conclusion was that although many of the benefits of JIT can be obtained if the approach is implemented in any of the last three phases, the best results are undoubtedly produced if it is implemented at maturity, i.e. when sales are levelling off, either because of market forces or because this is what management wants. However, as we saw in the Introduction to this book, sales stability is rare and generally of short duration.

Manoochehri (1988) briefly described the main elements of JIT, and their applicability according to the type of production environment. In his view, the three conditions for JIT applicability are:

- fairly stable demand;
- small batch capability on a just-in-time basis;
- the ability to receive deliveries of raw materials at the right time and in the right quantity.

The first and last of these conditions are usually more difficult for small firms to meet, and the ease with which they are satisfied depends on the firm's relationship with its suppliers and customers. On the other hand, small firms have a distinct advantage over their larger counterparts with respect to the second condition, precisely because of their smaller size and greater flexibility.

The paper lists nine small American firms that had successfully introduced JIT, together with the benefits they had obtained.

Inman and Mehra (1990) reported the results of a survey of 114 manufacturing firms, 52 of which had less than 500 employees and were therefore described as small businesses. The firms were asked if they employed the following JIT elements:

- quality circles;
- services of an outside consultant;
- preventive maintenance;
- shorter production run changeover time;
- diversified manpower training;
- smaller production batches.

The study's main conclusions were as follows:

- All the elements considered important in JIT implementation existed to the same extent in small and large firms, except for the use of an outside consultant in the implementation process, which seemed to be exclusive to large firms.
- The benefits obtained by small firms were at least as significant as those obtained by large firms. In fact, the results of small firms were actually better in the areas of reduction of downtime and inventory turnover.

We can therefore say that JIT is both applicable and of benefit to small firms. Rafael and Antonio (1992), in a literature review, analyzed 38 publications (between 1982 and 1990) from the major journals. The main points identified were:

- generally speaking, the introduction of JIT principles is fairly easy and inexpensive compared with the potential benefits;
- the time needed to implement JIT varies, according to the firms questioned, from one month to ten years;
- it is not necessary for all the elements to be introduced at the same time - in fact, it is better to begin with a pilot project and move on gradually.

Every production environment is unique, and the JIT philosophy must be adapted to the prevailing context. Simply using a stock formula based on an ideal system may lead to failure. Like total quality, an ideal zero-inventory pull manufacturing system should be seen as the "ultimate objective", giving direction to ongoing improvement.

Computer integrated manufacturing (CIM)

The literature on CIM in small business is much less abundant. Carpenter (1984) discussed the elements of CIM, with emphasis on small firms, and went on to describe the procedure for implementing CIM in a small business context.

Odon (1984) described CIM implementation in a firm with a turnover of $50 million and 800 employees. His main recommendations were related to the involvement of senior management, monitoring of implementation by a multi-department committee, and employee training, which was considered onerous but essential to the success of the project. However, he said nothing about the importance of CIM in the small business context.

World Class Manufacturing

Krause and Keller (1988) described the implementation of the world class manufacturing and accounting philosophy in a small firm with 60 production employees. The firm identified the following elements as forming part of the philosophy:
- involvement of employees in the process;
- JIT;
- integrated quality management;
- total productive maintenance;
- rapid, ongoing improvements.

The authors' main observation was that although the implementation process is fairly long, it can nevertheless be applied in small firms. Employee involvement in ongoing system improvement is considered primordial.

4.   Contingency factors

A number of factors can hinder the development of operations management in small firms. As a result, while some small firms have no formal production planning process, others have been able to introduce most of the JIT constituent elements, often successfully, as we saw in the last chapter. In the following paragraphs, we will examine the main factors, although no attempt will be made to rank them by order of importance. The factors listed are those most often cited in the literature, and identified on numerous occasions by the author.

Management's will to introduce recent operations management techniques and approaches is of crucial importance. Projects proposed by production managers have little chance of success if they do not receive the wholehearted support of senior management. Whether the techniques in question are MRP II, JIT, OPT or CIM, it is clear from case studies and consulting reports alike that management must not only support them, but must be actively involved. This aspect is examined in the last chapter, where management, and in particular its technological culture, is identified as a core element in technology implementation by small manufacturing businesses.

Employee training is also a key factor, in two respects. First, the presence in the firm of people with good basic training in production management will encourage proper organization of the operations management function, will ensure that the firm performs outside technological search to detect trends and new developments, and will provide a major skill input during the implementation process. Second, and often neglected, is the need for users to be trained in the use of the new technique or in the method itself where a new philosophy is involved. MRP II failures are often due to lack of training. *Industrial Engineering* (1990) provides the following example: "employees come to work on Monday morning and discover strange machines sitting on their desks. The machines use strange and exotic software. At 10:00 a.m., management sends out a memo informing them that they are to be trained on the new MRP II system". Clearly, what should have happened here is that the employees should first have been *informed* of the MRP II project. They should then have *taken part* in defining the new system, and finally they should have been trained extensively on the new system *before* it was introduced, as we saw in the last chapter.

The *applicability* of the techniques or approaches is often not analyzed sufficiently prior to the decision to introduce a specific system. For example, both MRP II and the "pull" approach can be introduced much more easily in a repeat production environment with a standard product range that remains fairly stable over time. In any other type of environment, there is a risk that the system will fail if nothing is done to adapt it to the specific features of the firm in question. This also applies to the *level of development* of operations management in the firm. The basic activities (planning, scheduling, controlling) and the basic data (items, structures, times, etc.) must be properly implemented before more sophisticated techniques or approaches are even considered. A common mistake is to assume that the use of sophisticated software will compensate for inadequate operating methods or erroneous data. As far as production management support software is concerned, a common complaint of production managers is that commercial software is not necessarily suited to their firms. The software is often developed either for a specific type of application (e.g. for an industrial sub-branch) or in a more generalist perspective, so that it can be used in different industries. In both cases, before a small firm can use such software it will have to adjust its methods, and this may affect its productivity.

Users may thus lose confidence in the system, which will consequently not be used to its full capacity.

Small business owner-managers do not have sufficient access to *information* on the various production management techniques and commercial software. Whether this is because they do not invest enough energy to obtain the information, or because the information itself is not available in the required form, production managers and company leaders are often forced to make decisions based on incomplete or inaccurate information. In a survey of 61 small manufacturing firms in Quebec (Rochette, 1991), roughly two-thirds of respondents said that information on production management software was important or very important to them.

Finally, *cost* is a barrier to the use of new techniques or approaches in small firms. Whatever the technique selected - MRP, JIT, OPT or CIM - implementation projects are generally major, spread over a year or more, and demand a lot of time and energy from existing resources. If proper planning is carried out, if training is provided as it should be, and if man-hours costs are added to the cost of the system itself, then the project often runs to several hundreds of thousands of dollars. This is a major investment for any small firm. Moreover, while it is fairly easy to quantify the cash benefits of purchasing a new production machine, the benefits of better operations management are unfortunately more difficult to identify and quantify. It may thus be difficult to justify this type of operation from an economic standpoint.

5. Conclusion

5.1 Development trends

Operations management is subjected to the forces of *market globalization*. Small businesses must compete with companies not only from neighbouring regions, but from throughout the world. And the new global competition forces firms to follow new rules: quality, flexibility and rapidity. World class manufacturing is not just a phrase; it is a management method with an impact on operations management. JIT elements should be introduced into the production management function: production to order, perfect quality, zero waiting time, no waste, employee involvement, ongoing improvement and flexibility.

From the operational standpoint, this means, among other things, a drastic reduction in production run changeover times, total productive maintenance, smaller batch sizes, flexibility of manpower and production equipment, and tight production planning and control.

From the information standpoint, it means *integration*. Jain (1991) describes the "enterprise solution" as a pyramid with CIM at the base, linking the machines to the engineering and production management software, followed by a second layer composed of MRP II, for planning, scheduling and control of production and for related functions such as cost price, and finally a third layer comprising a management information system, extracting data from the other two layers and relaying relevant information to managers for planning and monitoring. The information-related elements of such an organization are discussed in Chapter 11. The speed at which computer systems and computer networking are progressing, together with decreasing costs, suggests that this type of integrated solution will soon be available for small firms.

5.2   Avenues for future research

An obvious avenue for future research is the applicability of the various techniques and approaches. On several occasions in this chapter, we have noted that a given technique or approach is easier to apply in a certain type of production environment. JIT is a good example of this. While some of its elements can be used by almost any firm, the "pull" approach clearly cannot. The boundary separating the types of environment in which "pull" can be used is not well defined. Nevertheless, hybrid approaches may be interesting. For example, the CONWIP approach originally proposed by Spearman, Woodruff and Hopp (1980) is based on principles taken from OPT, MRP II and JIT, and is in effect a bottleneck approach where production flows are pulled or pushed depending on the relationship between two production units.

A second avenue for research is the definition of a procedure for implementing the techniques and approaches. Again, implementation can take different forms depending on the firm, its type of production, its organizational structure, and so on. What the literature now provides is a kind of stock recipe to be followed regardless of the environment. It is interesting to note (GRIP, 1988) that the methods available for improving productivity, including technology and quality, do not have the same relative importance in all industries.

Finally, recent operations management techniques and approaches have a number of factors in common. An interesting contribution to the field of small business operations management would be the development of a world class manufacturing operations model incorporating these common elements, and reflecting the specific features of the different industrial sectors.

9 The financial problems of small businesses

"Oh what a bad and stupid endeavour to examine one's money, to take pleasure in handling, weighing and counting it. This is how greed begins its approach." Michel de Montaigne, "Essai".

1.   Introduction[1]

Financial problems affect firms regardless of size. In the case of small firms, however, such problems tend to be amplified or compounded by other difficulties, including the following, identified by Berryman (1982):

1. The firm's dependency on the owner-manager and the owner-manager's inability to delegate authority and introduce a formal structure.
2. Limited market power, mainly because small firms tend to move into sectors with few entry barriers and high levels of competition.
3. A higher business risk, given the cash flow problems, vulnerability and difficulty in competing usually experienced by small firms.
4. The lack of management skills of small business owner-managers.
5. Failure to review financial performance periodically, and absence of financial planning procedures.

This list includes two of the factors most often cited as explanations of small business bankruptcies, i.e. lack of management skills on the part of the owner-manager, and absence of a formal financial planning structure. These elements, in addition to the financial difficulties normally experienced by small business, provide a good idea of the reasons for bankruptcy, and may be useful in helping anticipate it. However, many so-called explanatory factors are in fact based on myth, not reality, and it is important that the two be clearly distinguished.

---

1   It was not possible to obtain the original papers of some authors, especially those from Australia. Where this was the case, their conclusions were taken from the book by McMahon et al. (1993), and the symbol * has been inserted after the publication year. The references are nevertheless shown in the bibliography at the end of the chapter.

2.   The financial problems of small businesses

According to some authors, *most* small firms encounter four types of financial problems that can cause them to be inefficient, and often lead to bankruptcy. In this section, we will look at how these problems have been addressed in the more recent literature, and we will criticize research conclusions based more on myth than on the reality of financial markets and small business financing.

Table 9.1

**Summary of research on small business access
to different sources of financing**

Author(s)	Research	Conclusions
Tamari (1980)	Identification of empirical research on financing in 5 countries	Small firms use more short-term debt, mainly in the form of commercial loans. Bank loan levels are significantly lower than in large corporations.
Renfrew (1982*)	Study of 10,000 firms between 1968 and 1978	There is a preference for lines of credit, which are used to finance investments. Owner-managers do not seem dissatisfied with the sources of financing offered by the capital market.
Calof (1985)	Survey of the financial preferences of 115 small Canadian businesses' owner-managers	Financial structures are due mainly to the preferences of the entrepreneurs and not to the inefficiencies of the financial markets. Small business debt levels are due to a lack of knowledge among owner-managers. The level of sophistication of the financial structure increases in proportion to the firm's financial needs and the owner-manager's knowledge.
Holmes and Kent (1990)	Survey of 391 metal sector manufacturing enterprises	The results do not seem to confirm discrimination against small businesses, in terms of either funding supply or cost. However, the sample is biased towards surviving small firms, since it contains no bankrupt firms or firms in financial difficulty.

277

Dunstan et al. (1992)	Survey of 425 firms of different sizes and from different industries	There is a difference in the cost of a line of credit, which is around 7 points higher for small firms. Other sources of bank financing are no more expensive. However, the cost of loan applications is much higher for small firms.
Baldwin et al. (1994)	Survey of the profile of 1480 growing Canadian small businesses	Growing small firms make relatively more use of long-term financing than short-term financing. They make more use of equity capital than debt capital, and reinvest a significant amount of their earnings.

2.1   Limited access to financial resources

The following extract from a paper by Tamari (1980) clearly shows the nature of the debate on small business financing and the consequent economic development problems it provokes.

"Small firms have limited access to the capital and money markets and therefore suffer from chronic undercapitalisation. As a result, they are likely to have excessive recourse to expensive funds which act as a brake on their economic development." (Tamari, 1980, p.20)

The difference between the financing possibilities of small and large firms, and the costs inherent in small business status, create what some authors have called the "financial gap", defined as the gap in the supply of funds available to growing small firms, which prevents them from moving serenely towards maturity. An example would be a growing firm that has reached a stage in its development where it is making maximum use of short-term financing but has not yet grown sufficiently to have access to long-term financing in the form of loans or equity capital.

The *financial gap* seems to have two main components:
- The *knowledge gap*: limited use of debt financing is a direct consequence of lack of knowledge about the different sources of financing and their advantages, disadvantages and inherent costs;
- The *supply gap*: funds are not available for small firms, or some financing sources are available but at a much higher cost than to large firms.

Of all the myths surrounding the alleged financial problems of small businesses, the *financial gap* is the one that has most often been cited as a cause of bankruptcy. As Table 9.1 shows, researchers have not really proved that such a gap in fact exists, in either the choice or the cost of financing.

The conclusions of these studies do not confirm the existence of a differential between funding available to small firms and that available to large corporations. However, the authors seem to agree that small firms make more use of short-term financing, which is less restrictive for owner-managers. We will come back later to the specific situation of growing small firms.

In a survey of 115 small Canadian businesses, Calof (1985) showed that financial structure depended more on the financial preferences of the entrepreneurs than on deficiencies in the financial markets. He concluded that the differences in financial structure were probably caused by the owner-managers' desire to maintain control of their firms and to obtain support from outside investors who would place fewer restrictions on their daily management activities, as we saw in the Introduction and Chapter 5.

Finally, most research on financing structure does not consider the development stage of the firms studied. This aspect, as we will see later, has an impact on the choice of funding. For example, Suret and Arnoux (1995) showed that very small craft firms (assets of less than $100,000) had higher debt levels than the others, because they had more profitability problems. Undercapitalization was no worse among small firms as a group than among large firms. When the authors separated the small firms by asset base, they observed an undercapitalization effect due to poor profitability, but only for a segment of their sample.

These conclusions suggest that care is needed when interpreting the results of research that treats sample firms with very different development, size and profitability characteristics as a homogeneous group. Undercapitalization does not seem to be systematic and, contrary to certain claims, small firms using debt financing rather than equity financing may actually have chosen this method as being best suited to the owner-manager's needs, or may have been forced to accept it because of profitability problems that prevented them from seeking a more suitable form of financing. The frequently cited funding supply problems for small businesses therefore do not seem to exist.

2.2 Financial risk and financial leverage

Financial institutions cite the higher financial risk of small businesses to justify the loan charge differential for small and large firms (McMahon et al., 1993) and the different constraints imposed in loan covenants.

Research results confirming the existence of this higher financial risk are somewhat mitigated, as we saw in Chapter 2.

In view of the different periods studied and the different samples and methodologies used by the researchers, the situation is far from clear, and we cannot say beyond a shadow of a doubt that small firms have higher average debt levels than large firms.

Ang (1992) observed that it is more difficult to explain the funding choices of small firms because of the problem of measuring the various structural components and, among other things, differentiating debt from equity. As examples, he mentioned items such as "advance from owner" and "loans from directors", and what he considered "quasi-equity capital", which he defined as follows:

"... debts held by individuals or institutions that have an implicit understanding with the small business owners (1) not to exercise the right to force bankruptcy when interest payments are delinquent, and (2) to share some residual claims when the firm is returned to profitability."

Small firms that make extensive use of quasi-equity capital are thus considered to be undercapitalized. Suret and Arnoux (1995) calculated that shareholders' loans represented a quarter of total funding in craft firms, but just 5% or 6% in large corporations. Thus, the size effect should be considered when measuring this particular form of funding.

Gagnon and Papillon (1984) and Suret and Arnoux (1995) showed that when small business financial statements were adjusted to classify the different funding sources properly (i.e. by classifying advances from owners as equity rather than debt), size had no significant effect on total debt levels.

These authors also observed that profitability has a much greater impact on capitalization than size. In fact, because large firms have better access to outside capital markets, they can more easily balance their financial structure in low profit periods. This is not possible for small firms, whose capital base is depleted by negative profits. The authors concluded that "*whatever the size of the firm, undercapitalization is first and foremost a result of poor profitability*" (our translation). Constand et al. (1991) also noted that debt and profitability are negatively related, suggesting that more profitable firms make greater use of internal funding.

Table 9.2

Comparison of the financial structure of small firms and large corporations

Significant Differences	No Significant Differences
Holmes and Kent (1991) found that small firms had a debt/equity ratio of 2.4:1 compared with 1.5:1 for large firms.	Dunstan et al. (1992) found no significant difference in debt/equity ratios.
Remmers et al. (1974) found that size was not an explanatory factor for level of debt in the United States, whereas in other countries small firms all had higher debt levels than their larger counterparts (France, Japan, Norway and Holland).	Chen and Balke (1979) found that neither industrial sector nor size had a significant effect on debt ratios.
Tamari (1980) found that small firms were less risky if the leverage was measured with long-term debt. They use more non-bank short-term debt.	Suret and Arnoux (1995) showed that where shareholders' loans are classified as equity, there is no linear relationship between enterprise size and capitalization. Profitability seems to have a greater impact on debt levels than firm size.
Pettit and Singer (1985) confirmed that small firms have higher debt levels than large corporations.	
Osteryoung et al. (1992) found that large corporations had higher debt levels than small firms and made greater use of short-term debt. However, they used a sample of small privately-owned firms.	
Paranque (1994) found that small French firms had higher debt levels than larger firms, but that this was due to more intensive investment in the renewal of production potential. Variance in small business debt levels was also higher.	

Cooley and Edwards (1983) asked 97 small business owner-managers to list the factors that influenced their use of debt financing. The factor ranked as most important was uncertainty about future profitability, while the restrictions imposed by creditors were the least important. Apparently, the firms with the lowest debt ratio were those that considered profitability to be important, while those with the highest debt levels tended to be more concerned with growth of turnover.

Overall, debt levels were no higher among small firms than among large firms. However, debt structure did seem to differ according to size. Small business debt was mainly short-term (line of credit and commercial loans). Supplier financing, which involves no interest charges and is less restrictive than bank financing, was much more prevalent among growing small firms (see Table 9.6). Suret and Arnoux (1995) observed that very small firms with apparently high debt levels are in fact suffering the direct effects of low profitability.

Churchill and Lewis (1986) attempted to see if the difference in the debt levels of small and large firms affected loan portfolio risk in a large American financial institution, thus justifying the higher charges to small firms. They divided the portfolio into two categories: small business loans (average turnover of $8.4 million) and loans to large corporations (average turnover of $450 million). They found that the small business category had higher administrative expenses and presented a higher risk level, but that revenues from the loans were also higher. Overall, loans to small businesses were considerably more profitable than those to large corporations, and the additional risk of default was offset by the additional revenues earned. Bank managers spread the higher portfolio risk over all firms in the category, which means that the better firms "subsidized" the others. This policy has the effect of equalizing the portfolio's risk and overall revenues. *And yet, this method is questionable.*

Levratto (1992) also argued that the loan conditions offered to small firms were less favourable than those offered to large corporations, but mainly because the former did not negotiate as systematically and rigorously with their lending institutions. This behaviour benefits the financial institutions, whose losses on small business loans are no greater than on loans to large corporations (with size as a constant). In short, as this author concluded, "Disparities in interest rates confirm the question of risk appraisal by enterprise category by lending institutions" (p.263, our translation).

In fact, it is not so much the higher risk presented by small firms that explains the differences in loan charges or covenants, but the nature of the agency problems involved. According to Pettit and Singer (1985), three such problems influence banks:

- **Asymmetric information.** The fact that small firms are often private companies means that information is available to a limited number of people, and sometimes only to the owner-manager. This exacerbates the problem of asymmetric information.
- **Transfer of wealth.** Because control of the firm lies in the hands of one or a few people, they are in a position to divert company resources for their own personal use, at the expense of outside investors. This situation considerably increases the uncertainty of lenders (and other investors).
- **Personal remuneration.** The owner-manager's freedom extends to the form of remuneration he or she takes from the firm's resources. Lenders do not like the owner-manager to take variable amounts, since this reduces the cash flow available to repay loans.

Barnea et al. (1981) stated that lenders will protect themselves and reduce agency problems by demanding additional security for loans and imposing constraints in loan covenants. The constraints will considerably restrict the owner-manager's freedom.

Apilado and Millington (1992) looked at whether or not constraints in borrowing covenants led to reductions in small business loan charges. Their survey of 23 American banks revealed that considerably more restrictions[2] were placed on small firms than on large corporations (18.2 as opposed to 10.8). A size effect was also observed between small and large banks. Large banks seemed to impose rather more restrictions than small banks, but linked the number of restrictions to the level of loan charges. For example, they appeared to reduce loan charges by an average of 1% for each series of 14 restrictions. The smaller banks, however, did not do this, with the result that they overcharged small firms by imposing two risk premiums.

In short, it seems that small firms are overcharged, either by the imposition of higher loan charges or by the inclusion of more restrictions

---

2   Examples of the kind of restriction found in borrowing contracts offered by financial institutions to reduce the risk of default include prohibition from purchasing shares in other companies, restrictions on salary advances and the use of guaranteed loans, the obligation to maintain some financial ratios at a level considered acceptable by the lender, prohibition from negotiating loans with other institutions, prohibition from paying dividends to shareholders for a certain period, payment of "fair" remuneration to directors, etc.

in loan covenants. Conservative lending institutions do more than simply protect their small business loans, and charge the "better" firms more to offset the risk presented by the others. This, as has often been suggested, is due to a higher business risk and not a higher financial risk.

2.3   Equity financing

The *financial gap* described earlier does not seem to have gathered unanimous support from researchers. Some authors have referred instead to an *equity gap*. The markets do not allow small firms to issue stock freely in order to increase their capitalization and be able subsequently to increase their debt. The relative absence of investors for small business stock is therefore considered to restrict their growth. Holmes and Kent (1991) used Myers' Pecking Order Theory, apparently well-suited to the small business context, to explain funding choices. According to these authors, small business owner-managers prefer internal financing to external financing (thus retaining a larger percentage of profit than large corporations) and, where necessary, debt financing to equity financing, since they do not want to share ownership and decision-making with other partners (these results were confirmed by Bird and Juttner (1975) and Renfrew (1982*)). In the case of debt financing, they prefer short-term financing with fewer constraints and restrictions on the firm's assets.

Holmes and Kent (1990) confirmed the link between this theory and small business by noting that small business owner-managers are entrepreneurs who do not want to share control. This view was supported by Calof (1985), who showed (in a survey of 100 small Canadian businesses) that entrepreneurs prefer internal financing to external financing, and external bank financing to external equity financing. The latter is perceived as highly restrictive, less clear and demanding too high a commitment for the owner-manager (on the firm's present and future prospects), in contrast to bank financing, where covenant terms and lender involvement is clear from the outset. Clearly, as we saw in Chapter 5, this is less true for growth-directed firms than for independence-directed firms.

Moreover, if external financing becomes necessary, the owner-manager will tend to opt for short-term financing, which is less restrictive and allows more latitude than long-term financing with covenant terms that may affect managerial freedom. Tamari (1980) also pointed out that, in short-term financing, small firms prefer commercial loans to bank financing, for the following reasons:

284

- small firms are put off by bank requests for detailed financial reports, repeated intervention in the everyday affairs of the firm, bank requirements for the use of assets offered as loan security, and the presence of bank representatives on the board of directors;
- supplier credit is fairly easy to obtain;
- it is easier to negotiate with a supplier than with a bank to spread payments over a longer period.

As this discussion shows, the existence of an *equity gap* is far from clear, and the reluctance of small firms to enter into partnerships by selling their capital stock is due more to their need for freedom and independence than to a dysfunction of the financial markets. A recent study by St-Pierre and Beaudoin (1995) showed that in small firms making initial public offerings, debt ratios drop significantly when the public offering takes place, and then rise significantly in the following two years. These results may well confirm Myers' hypothesis that small business owner-managers prefer debt financing to equity financing, even after they have gone public.

2.4   Cash flow and working capital problems

A number of authors have stated that small firms have considerable difficulty with their working capital, so that in most cases cash flow management remains a priority. A firm can survive for years without making a profit, but will soon disappear if it has no cash.

Various authors have compared the absolute and relative liquid assets of small and large firms. Again, their conclusions are not unanimous. Davidson and Dutia (1991), the Wilson Committee reports (1979*) and the SBA reports (1984*) all found that small firms generally have more liquid assets than large firms. However, some authors came to the opposite conclusion (Gupta, 1969*; Walker and Petty, 1978; Davidson and Dutia, 1991), and others found no significant difference (Tamari, 1972*; Elliott, 1972*; SBA, 1984; Oysteryoung et al., 1992). Chen and Balke (1979), who compared various small firm and large firm ratios, observed a significant difference only in the liquidity ratio (in favour of small firms), while Fieldsend et al. (1987) found that the liquidity ratios of small firms were higher or lower than those of large firms depending on the sector.

It is thus clear that the "typical" small firm does not exist, as we saw in the Introduction and in Chapter 5, and research into financial problems must take account of the widely different characteristics of these firms depending on their development stage, size, industry sector and profitability, and the amount of financial information available.

It also seems obvious that, generally speaking, small business access to financial resources is not limited, that these firms do not present a higher financial risk than large corporations (although they do present a higher business risk), that they do not suffer from lack of access to equity financing, and that if they do have a lower level of capitalization than large corporations, it is because they use the sources of financing that respond best to their needs, i.e. short-term rather than long-term.

3.   The problems of growth

The results of research into the financial characteristics of small businesses have clearly shown that it is difficult to compare small firms and large firms, even where sufficiently reliable and accurate financial data is available for the elements discussed above. One of the reasons for this is that small firms are not all at the same development stage or in the same situation when the research takes place. Growth seems to generate effects that have a significant impact on the data available, in particular on liquid assets and financial structure.

Hutchinson and Ray (1986*) identified the main differences between growing firms and others. The clearest differences were the goals of the owner-managers and the complexity of the information-producing systems.

1. Growing firms are more concerned with maximizing profits, operate with a more formal organizational structure, and keep financial records that enable them to assess their performance against certain standards on a regular basis (the "GAP" firms described in Chapter 5).

2. Control of non-growth firms lies in the hands of owner-managers who are more concerned with independence and authority, whose objectives do not include maximizing profits, who do not keep proper financial records, and who tend to accept market prices without argument (the "PIG" firms described in Chapter 5).

Table 3 shows the importance and frequency of forecasts for growing firms. Cash flow and profitability variables are key elements. As we will see later, this is a major determinant of enterprise success or failure.

In the same paper, Hutchinson and Ray (1986*) associated growth stage with type of financing and financial stress factors (see Table 9.4).

Often, a problem of undercapitalization from start-up will prevent a firm from moving on to the other stages of normal development. When the firm enters the growth phase it faces new difficulties, such as overuse of short-term commercial and bank loans in the growth/start-up phase, which creates regular cash crises. Fast growth plunges the firm into the financial gap described earlier, and an undercapitalized firm will have no choice but to obtain even more short-term financing. It will eventually grow to a size where the owner-manager is forced to share control if he or she wants the firm to continue to grow. Otherwise, growth is likely to slow considerably.

In short, if we are to address the financial structure of small and medium-sized firms or compare it with large firms, we must consider the supply of funds, which changes at every development stage. According to the theory, firms are confronted at each stage with different problems that modify the financial choices open to them.

Peterson and Shulman (1987) concluded that growing small firms should develop a more balanced, less costly financing structure through reductions in agency costs and a funding supply that offers a much greater range of choices.

A recent Canadian study by Baldwin et al. (1994) of 1,480 growing firms found, among other things, that the sample firms had balanced financial structures, and that the undercapitalization so frequently cited in the literature was not a dominant factor. The distribution of financing in growing small firms is as shown in Table 9.5, based on size.

Table 9.3
Financial attributes of growth and non-growth firms

	Growth Firms	Non-Growth Firms
Goals	Maximizing profits. Increasing turnover.	Owner-managers want to preserve their independence and do not seek to maximize profits.
Organizational structure	Line organization. Development of work teams.	Line organization in old firms, or flat structure.
Management style	Autocratic, becoming more advisory.	Paternal.
Financial data compilation system	Directed towards profit centres.	Directed towards cost centres.
Historical data	Monthly or weekly earnings and some key balance sheet items.	Monthly or weekly earnings and some key balance sheet items.
Data provided	Monthly forecasts, especially for cash flows.	Very few.
Key variables	Cash flows, profit margin, marginal contribution, sales.	Tendency to accept prices offered on the market and to submit to market development requirements.

These data also show that growth seems to be linked to a reduction in the relative importance of commercial loans and retained earnings, and to an increase in the relative importance of capital stock. The group of firms with assets of between $5 and $10 million differ considerably from the rest. With a debt level 10 points higher than the other four groups (67.5% as opposed to 55.5%), they seem to be undercapitalized.

To sum up, according to the literature the main financial problems experienced by small firms are of external origin, grouped around what is known as the financial gap. Research into the causes of bankruptcy should therefore have much to say about the lack of acceptably-priced financial supply for small firms as a major explanatory factor.

Table 9.4
Choice of financing and financial stress
by development stage

Stage	Finance Used	Predominant Financial Stress Factor
Inception	Owners' resources	Undercapitalisation
Growth 1 (take-off)	Owners' resources plus retained profits, trade credit, bank loans and overdrafts, hire purchase, leasing	Overtrading and recurrent liquidity crises
Growth 2 (rapid growth)	Owners' resources plus longer-term debt finance from lending institutions	Finance gap
Growth 3 (threshold)	Owners' resources plus equity finance from partnerships, venture capital sources and second board listing	Loss of control
Maturity	All sources available including main board listing	Maintaining return on investment
Decline	Withdrawal of finance, sale of assets, takeover	Falling return on investment

Source: McMahon et al., 1993, p.163.

4. Financial difficulties and bankruptcy

4.1 Definition of bankruptcy

Berryman (1982) gave several definitions of small business failure, a term used by many authors to mean bankruptcy:

1. insufficient profitability: a firm fails if it does not provide an adequate and continuous yield on its investments;
2. solvency criteria (defined by Dun and Bradstreet): firms that cease operations and legally declare themselves bankrupt; cause their creditors to lose money; close down voluntarily without paying all their debts; are involved in reorganizations; have negotiated voluntary repayment agreements with their creditors;
3. legal bankruptcy: often accompanied by winding-up;
4. repeated loss criterion: a firm that makes regular losses and is wound up to put an end to the situation.

As the definition of bankruptcy is clarified, researchers have less information to enable them to establish the state of the situation. In addition, bankruptcy rates seem to vary considerably depending on the definition used. The problem of definition should be borne in mind when examining the statistics on high bankruptcy rates among small firms. Bankruptcy must also be distinguished from closure, merger and temporary suspension, as pointed out in Chapter 1.

Watson and Everett (1993) showed that small business failure rates vary significantly according to the definition used by researchers, as shown in Diagrams 1 and 2 (the definitions used are similar to those described by Berryman (1982)).

Failure rates vary significantly depending on the definition used. Bankruptcy rates are well below the percentages regularly announced by government agencies. The difference between bankruptcy and failure is thus fundamental in reaching valid conclusions.

With such wide variations in failure rates, on a year-by-year basis and according to company age, care is required in generalizing explanatory factors.

Table 9.5
Distribution of financing (% of Assets)
by size of growing firms
(millions of dollars of sales in 1991)

Type of financing	< 1	1 to 5	5 to 10	10 to 25	> 25	All
S-t debt	13.2	15.8	18.7	16.6	16.5	14.9
Creditors	24.2	24.9	23.6	18.0	15.8	23.8
L-t debt	17.5	16.7	25.2	23.0	19.7	18.2
Retained earnings	34.0	31.8	17.3	20.7	13.6	30.0
Capital stock	5.1	4.8	7.5	15.2	23.4	6.3
Deferred taxes	1.5	1.6	2.1	1.8	3.2	1.7
Other	4.0	4.4	5.4	4.7	7.8	5.1

Source: J. Baldwin et al. (1994), *Stratégies de réussite: Profil des petites et moyennes entreprises en croissance (PMEC) au Canada*, Statistics Canada, No. 61-523F.

4.2 Causes of bankruptcy

Several studies on the causes of bankruptcy do not list undercapitalization as an explanatory factor for small business mortality.

Perry and Pendleton (1983*) estimated that 90% of small businesses bankruptcies are due to administrative deficiencies such as management inexperience or incompetence.

Williams (1987*) reached the same conclusion, finding that 60.5% of bankruptcies were due to managerial inexperience.

Larson and Clute (1979) did an in-depth study of 359 small American firms in the Chicago area that had asked for help before going bankrupt. From their study of the managers' attributes, the authors identified three factors that could be used to explain and, to some extent, anticipate bankruptcy. Their observations are summarized in Table 9.6.

The financial factors identified are concerned with deficiencies in financial management, and not external elements such as lack of funding supply.

In addition, Hall and Young (1991), in their study of British firms, found that 36.8% of the 231 reasons given by enterprise managers to explain bankruptcy were financial in nature: (1) undercapitalization (15%); (2) poor debt management (10%); (3) poor accounting management (6%); and (4) problems with capital suppliers (6%). Topping the list of reasons were operations management problems (40.26%). The main reason given in public bankruptcy announcements was also operational in nature - undercapitalization (51.42%) - leading to marketing, managerial and developmental difficulties. This conclusion is hardly surprising if the financial statements used to obtain the information were taken from the year of bankruptcy, since the equity of a firm in financial difficulty will obviously have been depleted by continual losses, and its debt level will thus be higher. These results led Hall and Young to conclude that government interventions in the area of planning and marketing advisory services should also cover operational aspects such as the choice and management of financing.

Gaskill, Van Auken and Manning (1993) made an interesting summary of the causes of small business bankruptcy and success, and identified certain similarities between the two states. The authors used factor analysis to classify the causes of bankruptcy identified from a study of 91 owner-managers of electrical appliance firms. Lack of management skills was ranked first, followed by financial management difficulties, especially financial planning and cash flow management. Although the sample was limited to one particular sector, the conclusions of the study highlighted a number of problems experienced by small businesses as identified by other researchers.

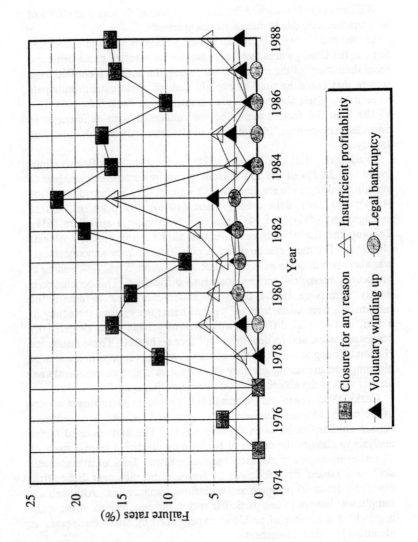

Figure 9.1
Changes in small business failure rates over time

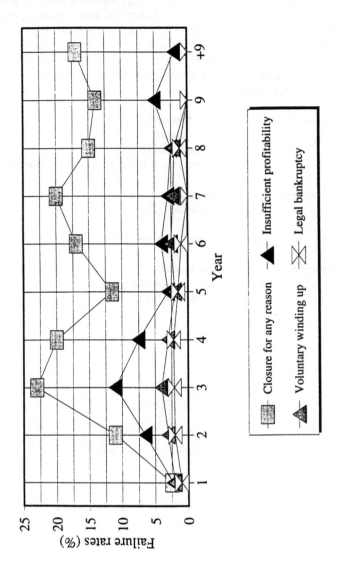

Figure 9.2
Small business failure rates in the year following creation

293

Berryman (1982), in a literature survey, identified many different small business bankruptcy factors and classified them according to the number of times they were mentioned, using the percentage of papers addressing a specific factors as the unit of measurement. Interestingly, only 28% of the papers mentioned undercapitalization, and elements related to the quality of financial management (finance, accounting) were cited much more frequently.

1. *Accounting:* Deficient loan management (50)
   Poor inventory control (39)
   No or inadequate bookkeeping (33)
   Insufficient analysis of liquid assets and cash flow (28)

2. *Marketing:* Poor location (22)
   General deficiencies (22)

3. *Finance:* Initial undercapitalization (28)

4. *Endogenous factors:* Lack of experience (22)
   Limited accounting knowledge (22)
   Excessive withdrawals (22)

Table 9.6
Personal attributes and managerial deficiencies
of owner-managers, and financial factors in bankrupt companies

Personal Attributes	Managerial Deficiencies	Financial Factors
1. Tendency to overestimate own management knowledge.	1. Weak or non-existent identification of market and geographical zone.	1. No inventory control.
2. Low level of education.	2. Non-existent identification of commercial zone.	2. Accounting books incomplete and book-keeping incorrect.
3. Resistance to change and lack of flexibility.	3. No objective techniques used to select location.	3. Failure to understand the importance of cash flow and liquidity.
4. Use of personal opinion as the standard.	4. Failure to understand the principles of delegation.	4. Inability to check accuracy of accounting information reported by staff (or consultants).
5. Decision-making process based on intuition and emotion.	5. Considers advertising to be an expense, not an investment.	5. Failure to use financial statements to plan the future.
6. Oriented towards the past, not the future.	6. No effective planning.	6. No control over incoming and outgoing funds.
7. Poorly documented on business develop-ments (newspapers).	7. Rudimentary knowledge of price-setting, strategies and tactics.	7. Failure to understand accounting terminology.
8. Resistance to suggestions from qualified people.	8. Failure to understand the principle of distribution channels.	
	9. Failure to motivate employees.	
	10. Belief that problems are exogenous and a loan will solve everything.	

Source: C.M. Larson and R.C. Clute (1979), "The Failure Syndrome", *American Journal of Small Business*, Vol. 4, No. 2, pp. 35-43.

In short, although some of the research on the causes of bankruptcy identified undercapitalization as a financial factor, elements such as management skills and financial management knowledge were found to be much more significant.

McMahon et al. (1993), in their chapter on the financial problems of small firms, identified two major categories of bankruptcy causes among small firms: (1) lack of management skills and (2) lack of short-term or long-term capital. In the following paragraphs, we will criticize this statement and illustrate the difference between a cause and a consequence of a particular state.

As we saw earlier, undercapitalization is not a chronic problem for all small firms. It would also be wrong to imply that it is a major cause of small business bankruptcy. On the other hand, undercapitalization may cause bankruptcy in some cases:

1. Very small firms: they may have a capitalization problem from creation, and insufficient profitability will simply exacerbate this. These are firms whose product or service is not sufficiently developed, where the owner has not injected enough funds, which carry out very little financial planning (see Dodge and Robbins, 1992), and with an inadequate organizational structure that does not enable them to overcome start-up difficulties. Firms such as these are doomed to bankruptcy, and proper initial capitalization, while perhaps prolonging their life, would not have changed this.

2. Small firms: in firms with chronic profitability problems, retained earnings and thus the relative importance of equity in the financial structure, will dwindle. These firms go bankrupt not because they are undercapitalized, but because they are not sufficiently profitable, due to a lack of planning, poor financial management (accounts receivable, stocks, accounts payable, cash flows) and an inadequate accounting system (that does not, for example, allow them to monitor costs and cost price).

To explain and anticipate the causes of bankruptcy, we should therefore concentrate on managerial skills, particularly in the area of finance.

A number of authors followed the classical work by Beaver (1966) and Altman (1968) by developing bankruptcy predictors based on small business financial statements.

McNamara, Cocks and Hamilton (1988) found that the RE/TA, TD/TA and SE/TD ratios were the main bankruptcy predictors.

RE/TA_{-1} = Retained earnings/Total assets 1 year before bankruptcy
TD/TA_{-1} = Total debt/Total assets 1 year before bankruptcy

SE/TA_{-2} = Shareholder's equity/Total debt 1 year before bankruptcy

- The RE/TA ratio is the most important and can be used as a measure of the firm's age. The older the firm and the longer it has been in business, the more earnings it will have accumulated and the less likely it is to go bankrupt. The ratio can also be used as a reserve, to enable the firm to survive during difficult and less profitable periods.
- The TD/TA ratio shows the firm's financial structure and level of financial risk. The higher the ratio, the higher the risk of bankruptcy.
- The SE/TA ratio shows the shareholders' contribution to enterprise funding. The greater the financial commitment of the shareholders, the greater the firm's chances of survival in difficult periods.

These results are hardly surprising, and could easily be predicted. In fact, retained earnings decline in proportion to financial soundness, thus increasing the ratio of debt to equity. These results do not explain why firms go bankrupt, but simply confirm the presence of financial problems.

Bankruptcy prediction models, which obtain their information from financial statements, are weakened by the fact that small business accounting data are unreliable.

For example, the following problems are often present in small business financial statements:

1. Owner-managers tend to manipulate information that they do not want to disclose to investors. This is especially true in firms experiencing financial difficulties.
2. Generally speaking, financial statements are not audited.
3. The financial statements are not detailed, and many items having a major impact in cases of bankruptcy are not necessarily disclosed.
4. Profitability measures are inaccurate, because owner-managers generally pay themselves out of irregular surpluses (related to the dividend policy). This practice introduces an element of uncertainty. To compare enterprise profitability, owner-manager remuneration policies and dividend policies would have to be constant.

More general models, using both financial and non-financial data, are thus needed.

The study by Keasey and Watson (1991), using financial and non-financial variables, was rather more comprehensive than that of McNamara et al. (1988). The liquidity ratio, the time taken to produce the financial statements and the presence of a lending bank were all found to differentiate bankrupt and non-bankrupt companies. The authors criticized the use of accounting information to measure the likelihood of bankruptcy because of the behaviour of the owner-managers of companies in difficulty and their tendency to camouflage the situation by manipulating the financial statements. In fact, the authors observed that the financial statements of companies in difficulty actually painted a more positive picture in the years immediately preceding bankruptcy. As we said earlier, they concluded that, in empirical research, it was important to distinguish the causes of bankruptcy from their financial consequences.

5.   Conclusion

The literature survey described in this chapter, together with the criticisms made, highlight a number of myths surrounding the issue of financial problems in small businesses. These same myths are used by many financial institutions to justify loan conditions that are often excessive in comparison with the level of risk involved.

Contrary to the beliefs of many researchers and public administrators, it seems that:

• Overall, small businesses have no trouble obtaining access to various sources of financing, which would explain why they sometimes seem to have higher debt levels than large corporations.

• Small businesses that make extensive use of short-term debt do so by choice, not by necessity.

• Small businesses do not present a higher financial risk than large corporations, and the higher credit charges they are generally required to pay enable the lending institutions to make abnormally high profits on small business loans.

• Overall, small businesses do not have cash flow problems that prevent them from growing.

• Small businesses cannot be studied without distinguishing their stages of development, sector, size and profitability.

• The factors explaining small business bankruptcies have nothing to do with dysfunctional financial markets that prevent the firms from building a financial structure enabling them to make profits.

Small business bankruptcy rates will be reduced not by increasing funding supplies and giving access to more capital, but by providing entrepreneurs with better training. In the prevailing economic context, where people will be required increasingly to create their own jobs, more companies are likely to see the light of day. If funding supplies are increased without improving the financial management skills of these new entrepreneurs, bankruptcy rates are also bound to increase.

Since most firms will progress through the various stages of development, success depends first and foremost on good general and financial planning.

As Levratto (1992) suggested, given the significant contribution of small businesses to employment and economic development, government authorities should help by keeping a close eye on the practices that allow banks to overcharge small firms in search of financing.

10 Information systems

"Even in these dreamings I fear the betrayal of my memory, which inadvertently may have made me record something twice. I hate to repeat myself, and only against my will do I go back to what I have once expressed. And there is no new thing to learn here." Michel de Montaigne, "Essai".

1.   Introduction

The innovations of the last ten years in the area of mini-computing and micro-computing, and the introduction of new related technologies such as automated office systems, telematics and production automation systems, mean that today even the smallest businesses are able to purchase and use computer-based information systems. This chapter is not intended to provide complete, definitive answers to the complex problems raised by information systems (IS) and the management of information technologies (IT) in small businesses. Rather, it will provide an overview of the current state of knowledge and an analysis of the main elements of a research area that has become essential to the understanding of small businesses.

The first section of the chapter provides a brief review of IS basics, in order to better understand the role they play in small businesses. The second section contains a proposal for and analysis of a conceptual framework relating to the introduction, management and use of information systems in small businesses. Lastly, the third section focuses more closely on the main topics of debate and the research challenges in the area of computer technologies in small businesses.

2.   Origin and nature of information systems research

An analysis of the evolution of information systems as a component of administrative science provides an interesting illustration of the progress of knowledge relating to IS. The work of Herbert Simon of the Carnegie Institute of Technology in the 1940s and 1950s provided the conceptual base on which the growth of information systems was founded. More specifically, an approach centred on decision-making underlined the importance of information, and thus of information systems (Simon, 1969). Before that time, classical theory, which posited the total "rationality" of the decision-maker, accepted no theoretical flaw or gap as regards the processing of information by individuals and organizations.

Simon proposed a new vision in which decision-makers were endowed with "bounded" rationality, and organizations and environments were ambiguous and tended towards disorder. Theorists and managers were prompted to develop self-defence mechanisms against the hazards that threatened the balance, efficiency and effectiveness of organizations (Katz and Kahn, 1966). From that time, the notion of uncertainty, or lack of control over the environment surrounding the decision-maker and the organization, became the ontological foundation that provided the nascent discipline of information systems, and its practical applications, with legitimacy. The main objects of study of the discipline are the individual and organizational weaknesses affecting the gathering, processing, storing and distributing of information.

2.1   Uncertainty: the raison d'etre of information systems

The work of March and Simon (1958) finally laid to rest the concept of the certitude of the rational decision-maker within an ordered, harmonious universe. The disappearance of perfect and absolute order as a postulate in organizational theory meant that a notion of uncertainty was needed, and indeed the relationship between individuals and organizations on the one hand, and between individuals and the environment on the other, can only be considered as a relationship of uncertainty. Uncertainty is probably the single most important problem faced by high-level managers in strategic analysis (Thompson, 1967).

Organizations thus seek to minimize uncertainty. Their main weapon has always been, and always will be, information and the systems and technologies needed to process, distribute and analyze it. Galbraith (1973) defines uncertainty as the difference between the level of information needed and the information actually available. The efforts deployed and investments made to integrate information technologies into organizations can only be interpreted as an attempt to combat and reduce uncertainty (Tushman and Nadler, 1979), although some researchers also consider uncertainty to be a perceptual phenomenon embodied in the information gathered and assimilated via cognitive mechanisms (Downey and Slocum, 1975).

2.2   Information systems and systems analysis

Besides organizational theory, which is based on the notion of uncertainty, the second main contribution made to the field of information systems is systems theory and the related analytical tools. Organizational phenomena relating to information can be better understood if the organization itself is considered as an "open" system in a constant state of exchange with its environment (Gingras, Magnenat-Thalmann and Raymond, 1986). Such exchange is both a source of danger and the foundation of the survival and continued evolution of the organization. Within this analytic framework, information flows are a vital component of adaptation, and the feedback of exogenous and endogenous information is one of the main indicators of system effectiveness and efficiency (Boland and Hirscheim, 1987).

An organization, considered as an open, dynamic system, adopts self-defence mechanisms that reduce the natural trend towards disintegration and disorder (Morgan, 1989). The renewal of inventory, the launching of new products, the implementation of training programs and the introduction of production- or management-related technological innovations are examples of such mechanisms. Information quality, variety, reliability and availability all directly affect the making of organizational choices (Child, 1972). An organization's ability to evolve in an increasingly complex environment is heavily dependent on the characteristics of the information it consumes, stores and distributes (Morin, 1977). These are the functions assumed by information systems and their technological tools, which have become vital elements for organizations large and small, private and public, whether in the manufacturing, commercial or services sector.

2.3   *Small businesses and information systems research*

As is the case for other areas in business management, research objectives in the area of information systems are both descriptive and prescriptive. The first aim is to better understand the ways in which a given organization adopts, uses and manages its information systems and technologies, using explanatory models tested against empirical studies. The knowledge obtained must then be applied by proposing various approaches, methods, techniques and tools to organizations to allow them to improve the management of information resources and thus to increase the effectiveness and efficiency of their use of information systems (Cooley, Walz and Walz, 1987).

Before the early 1980s, few researchers had carried out empirical research into the information systems used in particular by small businesses, and there was therefore a need to design and validate an appropriate set of standards (Raymond, 1984). Given the specific nature of small businesses, almost none of the results obtained in studies of mainly large businesses could be extrapolated directly, especially as regards the critical factors for the successful development, implementation and use of information technologies (Alpar, 1989; Raymond et al., 1990).

As a result of this situation, a number of researchers have turned their attention to the question of information systems in small businesses. In the beginning, only the size of the organization concerned (based on, for example, the number of employees) was used as a discriminatory variable to identify differences between large and small businesses for characteristics such as the involvement of senior management in the move to computers (Montazemi, 1988), the structure of the IS function (Ein-Dor and Segev, 1978, 1982), investment in hardware, software and human resources (DeLone, 1981), the sophistication of the computer system (Lehman, 1985), and computer use (Gremillion, 1984). It quickly became clear, however, that any attempt to explain the differences encountered had to be based on other environmental, organizational, human and technical variables, some of which, like organizational structure, were far more significant than the arbitrarily-selected criterion of business size (McGuire, 1976).

Once small and large businesses had been recognized as being, ontologically speaking, two different kinds of research subject, studies were designed to take the difference into account. A critical analysis of these studies must, however, be based on a recognized conceptual framework for research in the field of information systems that is sufficiently comprehensive to include all the specific characteristics of small businesses, and that can also be used to generate research hypotheses relating to the specific nature of small businesses.

3. Conceptual framework for research

The best-known conceptual framework for research in the field of information systems is that of Ives, Hamilton and Davis (1980), in which an organizational information system (OIS) is defined as a computer-based system designed to supply informational support for the operations of the organization and for the activities and functions of management. The system breaks down into a group of information sub-systems (ISS), or application systems (such as an inventory management system) defined by organizational or functional boundaries. Research into information systems is defined as being "a systematic investigation into the development, operation, use and/or impact of an information (sub) system within an organizational context".

Figure 10.1 shows a pictorial representation of the conceptual framework.

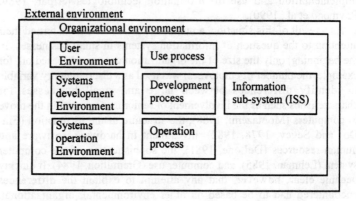

Figure 10.1
Conceptual framework for information systems research

Three types of variables can be distinguished, namely:
1. environmental variables defining the resources and constraints that determine the scope and shape of each ISS; they include:
- the external environment, including legal, social, political, cultural, economic, educational, industrial and commercial considerations;
- the organizational environment, defined by the objectives, tasks, structure and management style of each organization;
- the user environment, which surrounds and includes management staff making decisions based on ISS output, and the intermediaries responsible for filtering or interpreting the output;
- the OIS development environment, including ISS design and implementation methods and techniques, the development staff and its characteristics, and systems development and maintenance management;
- the OIS operating environment, including resources such as hardware, software, operating staff and computer operations management;
2. process variables defining ISS interaction with the environments described above, basically meaning performance measurements as regards system use by managers, and system development and operation;

3. characteristic ISS variables defining function, user interface, temporal dimensions and technical characteristics (administrative, managerial, decision-support, strategic, office automation, telematics and expert systems applications, etc.).

The model allow various avenues for research to be defined, since the researcher can focus on a single variable or on the relation between variables of a given type or of different types.

The research by DeLone (1981) referred to previously is an example of research linking variables of the same type, namely size (organizational environment) with the use of outside programming (OIS development environment), and size with expenditure on hardware and software (OIS operating environment). It should be mentioned, however, that the most relevant research is that which uses "process" type variables (performance measurements) as dependent critical variables. Several studies of information systems in small businesses have attempted to identify the organizational, informational and individual factors for success. Given the prescriptive objective of the studies, an alternative conceptual framework, more specifically centred on success factors, is more useful for practitioners and managers (Figure 2). Some of these factors are wholly or partially controllable, whereas others are wholly uncontrollable. Using this conceptual framework, Raymond and Bergeron (1992) have found that small business managers using systems to assist them in making decisions were more satisfied (success) the more their tasks were complex (individual factor), and when the system provided analysis and information capabilities (informational factor).

4. Information systems and the specific nature of small businesses

Given the managerial and strategic potential of information technologies for small businesses, the conceptual frameworks described above cannot be used unless the specific nature of small businesses as regards their environment, processes and systems is taken into account. Some researchers have attempted to measure the impact of these specific aspects on the assessment and introduction of information technologies by small businesses.

4.1   The specific nature of small businesses

Small businesses have to face specific problems that are not encountered by large corporations and that require specific management approaches. From a strategic and administrative point of view, small businesses are primarily "organic" in nature, and may be considered, fundamentally, as being an extension of the personality of their founder, as discussed in the introductory chapter. The structure of small businesses is typically informal and relatively uniform. A chronic lack of resources is reflected in their weakness in the areas of financing, planning, direction, training and information systems (Welsh and White, 1981), and small businesses have a higher mortality rate than large corporations because of both environmental and internal factors. On the other hand, though, small firms have other advantages, such as the ability to make quick decisions, their proximity to markets, and a capacity to adapt and change direction in the short term (Julien and Marchesnay, 1992). Some of these aspects specific to small businesses may affect the development, operation and use of information systems. They can be classified under environmental, organization, decision-related, psycho-sociological and information systems headings, as summarized in Table 10.1, completing the discussions presented in the introductory chapter and in Chapter 5.

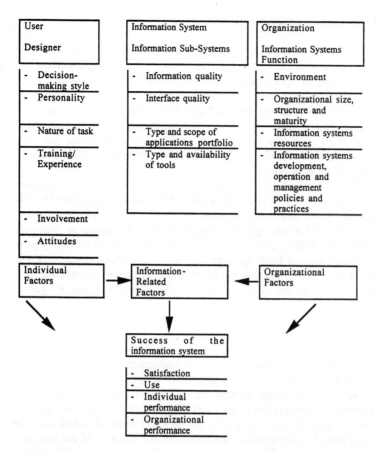

User Designer	Information System Information Sub-Systems	Organization Information Systems Function
- Decision- making style	- Information quality	- Environment
- Personality	- Interface quality	- Organizational size, structure and maturity
- Nature of task	- Type and scope of applications portfolio	- Information systems resources
- Training/ Experience	- Type and availability of tools	- Information systems development, operation and management policies and practices
- Involvement		
- Attitudes		

Individual Factors → Information-Related Factors ← Organizational Factors

Success of the information system

- Satisfaction
- Use
- Individual performance
- Organizational performance

Figure 10.2
Overall conceptual framework showing factors for a successful information system

4.2   Specific environmental aspects

Small businesses are generally characterized by a high degree of uncertainty with respect to their environment. For example, taxation, interest rates and government regulations have a greater impact on small firms than on large ones (see the preceding chapter). Uncertainty about the technological environment and competitive forces, however, probably has the greatest impact on the introduction of information technology in small businesses. By technological environment, we mean not only information technologies but also production technologies in the sector in which a firm is working.

With their lack of knowledge and experience, small businesses generally have to live with a high level of uncertainty as regards the new technological environment and the possible use of information technologies for strategic or competition-related managerial purposes (Raymond, 1988a). In some cases the use of information technologies is imposed on small firms by larger customers or suppliers, especially in the area of electronic data interchange (EDI), thereby increasing their dependency and reducing their freedom (Raymond, Blili and Bergeron, 1994).

4.3   Specific organizational aspects

Small businesses, as we have seen, are characterized by a simple, highly centralized structure. Centralization can be seen as a factor for success in introducing information systems into an organization, since it leads to a reduction in complexity (Moch and Morse, 1975). A simple structure should, in particular, facilitate the determination of needs and the coordination of information systems with the strategy of the business concerned, essentially the strategy espoused by one or more owner-managers (Dewar and Hage, 1978).

Small businesses often suffer from "poverty" in their human, financial and material resources (Welsh and White, 1981). They generally do not have the capacity to develop and manage information systems themselves, and rely on outside help (suppliers, consultants, service operators) that provide products and services of varying quality (Gingras, Rouette and d'Amboise 1985). This lack of control over the management of their information resources increases the level of risk facing small businesses, especially those that rely on such resources not only for their operation but also for their strategy. The challenge has, however, been met by some small businesses (Bergeron and Raymond, 1992b).

Table 10.1
Specific aspects of small businesses

Specific environmental aspects

- Uncertainty: about the technological environment;
- Vulnerability: towards competitive forces (customers, suppliers).

Specific organizational aspects

- Structure: relatively informal, undifferentiated;
- Resources: poor in terms of human and financial resources.

Specific decision-making aspects

- Strategic decision-making cycle: short-term, reactive (as opposed to proactive);
- Decision-making process: intuitive, experience-based, low use of formal management information and techniques, focused on physical flows (as opposed to information flows).

Specific psycho-sociological aspects

- Dominant role played by entrepreneur: low level of information sharing, low rate of decision-making delegation;
- Psychological climate: open attitudes but low expectations regarding information systems.

Specific information system aspects

- Information systems function: early stage of development, subordinated to accounting, lack of expertise, experience and training in information systems management;
- Complexity of information systems: emphasis on administrative applications (as opposed to managerial) based on software packages (as opposed to custom software), low technical expertise;
- Success of the information system: under-use of information systems, low impact on decision-related and organizational effectiveness.

4.4   Specific decision-making aspects

The strategic decision-making cycle, or time-frame, of small businesses is often a short-term cycle based on reaction rather than anticipation. The lack of planning, especially as regards information systems, leads to problems with the introduction, operation and use of information technologies that are specific to small businesses (Raymond et al., 1990). In addition, small businesses tend to make little use of management methods and techniques such as forecasting, financial analysis and project management.

The decision-making process of small business managers is generally considered to be more intuitive, more "judgmental", and less dependent on information and on formal decision-making models. Information technologies, therefore, can be introduced not only as part of the business's operational strategy, but also to contribute to the design and implementation of that strategy by the use of decision support systems (Raymond and Bergeron, 1992). In connection with small businesses, then, specific approaches and methodologies to identify needs and propose development possibilities are needed, that are simple, robust and flexible (Reix, Bergeron and Raymond, 1991).

4.5   Specific psycho-sociological aspects

Owner-managers obviously play a key role in the strategy, decision-making process and organizational climate of small businesses, and are not inclined to pass on information or delegate the making of decisions to their subordinates. They are often the only people in the business to have authority, responsibility and access to the information needed to identify possible applications of information technologies. Within a given business, the organizational attitude towards information systems is strongly dependent on the prior training and experience of managers and users. Training is often a weak point in small businesses, and experience in computer applications has only recently become widespread (Nickell and Seado, 1986). In general, then, initial attitudes towards information systems are unlikely to be critical, but expectations are low and centre mainly on increased productivity rather than greater effectiveness (Raymond, 1987c).

4.6   Specific information systems aspects

Information systems have only recently begun to appear in most small businesses; according to the incremental model proposed by Nolan

(1979), they are at the "initiation" or "proliferation" stage and not at the later stages (Raymond, 1985). Information systems are generally subordinate to the accounting function, and most organizations lack the necessary managerial expertise to plan, organize and direct the use of information resources.

The typical applications portfolio found in a small business relies heavily on administrative-type applications (such as receivables accounts) that produce operational documents and reports on a periodic basis (Rumberger and Levin, 1986). The programs are generally acquired as pre-programmed software packages, since the information systems function of the typical small business has a low level of technical expertise in developing and operating software applications (Mahmood and Malhotra, 1986). Systems used for strategic or managerial purposes, however, are by their very nature usually custom-designed and possess interactive query and analysis functions (Bergeron and Raymond, 1992b).

It would seem that under-use of organizational information systems is widespread in small businesses (Massey, 1986). In most cases, information technology affects only tasks incidental to the main business activity, such as accounting. The strategic applications of information technology, however, are primarily connected with key activities such as production and marketing and are designed to have a direct impact on the firm's performance. Analysis and planning methods will therefore have to take account of the specific aspects outlines above, and in particular the lack of resources and expertise within small businesses as regards computerized information systems.

4.7   Specific aspects of small businesses and factors for a successful information system

The empirical identification of factors for the successful introduction and use of information technologies in small businesses confirms the weight of the aspects specific to small businesses (Raymond, 1984) and allows a prescriptive framework to be sketched out. At the organizational level, improvements in the effectiveness of information systems involve:

- greater emphasis on the development and implementation of firm strategy using information systems, especially concerning opportunity analysis and information requirements;
- a shorter cycle for the introduction of information systems, based on user-developed applications and prototyping better suited to the short-term time-frame of small businesses;

- preservation of the advantages deriving from the simple structure of small businesses by using information systems instead of increased bureaucracy;
- an increase in the sophistication of small businesses in the area of information technologies, based on more systematic informational processes, the planning and management of information resources, an applications portfolio targeting support for management and decision-making and the use of "end-user computing" and 4th-generation (application generator) software.

From the point of view of the user, an organizational information system is only effective if:

- the importance of the training and communication roles of the project coordinator or consultant is recognized by management (rather than just the technical design role), in order to transform managers into users by overriding their resistance to change;
- the project designers stress the user-friendliness of the system/user interface and flexible approach to the various information search and decision-making styles of small-business management.

Figure 10.3 presents examples of research into the impact of aspects specific to small businesses on factors influencing the successful introduction of information systems.

Process	Development				Management	Use	
Success factors / Specific aspect	Analysis of opportunities and information requirements	Policies and practices	Development autonomy	User participation and management involvement	Sophistication	Training Experience	Diversification of applications portfolio
ENVIRONMENTAL ORGANIZATIONAL Lack of resources Centralized management Uncontrollable extraorganizational situation Lack of organizational maturity Ability to adapt	Montazemi, 1987 Bilii and Raymond, 1993 Bergeron and Raymond, 1993	Mahmood and Malhotra, 1986 Bilii, 1989 Bradbard et al., 1990 Bergeron and Raymond, 1992b	Raymond, 1987a Chen, 1989	De Lone, 1988 Raymond, Rivard and Bergeron, 1988 Raymond, 1987b	Raymond and Paré, 1992 Cragg and King, 1992 Raymond et al., 1994 Raymond et al., 1996	Raymond, 1988b Bilii and Rivard, 1990	Kagan, Lau and Nusgart, 1990 Montazemi, 1988 Weil and Broadbent, 1990
DECISION-RELATED Intuitive decision making Short-term time frame Lack of planning	Bilii and Raymond, 1988 Bilii and Raymond, 1993	Griese and Kurpicz, 1985 Raymond, 1983	Raymond, 1990a	Bilii, 1989	Raymond, 1990b Julien and Raymond, 1994a	Weber and Ticmeyer, 1981 Raymond, 1988b	Bergeron and Raymond, 1992b Fuller, 1987 Raymond et al., 1990
PSYCHO-SOCIOLOGICAL Dominance of the owner-manager Dependency on some employees or consultants	Bergeron, Bluteau and Raymond, 1991 Bilii and Raymond, 1988	Gable, 1990 Griese and Kurpicz, 1985	Kole, 1983	Raymond, 1988a Martin, 1989	Martin, 1989	Nickell and Seado, 1986 Raymond, 1984b	Fallery, 1983 DeLone, 1988 Dupuy, 1987

Figure 10.3
Examples of the impact of specific small business aspects on IS success factors

5.   Empirical observations

The research outlined above can be analyzed by matching the specific problems raised with the proposed solutions, in order to better understand the factors that determine the current level of organizational validity of information systems in small businesses and, in addition, the basis for the proposals made to improve their effectiveness (Raymond, 1989).

5.1   Organization and management of organizational information systems

Research has shown that information technologies are not one of the main concerns of small business management despite their growing importance for every firm (Barcet et al., 1984). Technological management of information and information resources is a concept based on a vision of the hardware, software, personnel and data of an information system as precious resources that must be effectively managed for the benefit of the entire organization (Malone, 1985). This concept has become vital in the current technological environment of small businesses, mainly for the following two reasons that have been confirmed by research findings.

First, information technologies and the ways in which they are applied to meet the needs of small businesses are expanding and evolving rapidly (Lees and Lees, 1987). This growth and evolution over time of an organizational information system can be seen in

- the increasing percentage of revenue invested in information resources;
- the increasing percentage of the information systems budget that is spent on software and personnel;
- the use of increasing numbers of strategic (such as EDI) and managerial (such as cost accounting) software, as opposed to administrative software (such as invoicing);
- the introduction of information systems in areas other than accounting (such as production);
- the greater independence of the OIS function from the accounting function;
- a greater reliance on the development of customized software, especially in the area of managerial applications, rather than software packages;

- a greater reliance on direct interaction between users and the information system, using dialogue-based software with a graphic user-system interface.

Second, the inadequate performance and unsatisfactory use of information systems applications and resources constitutes a major problem for many small businesses. The problem can become apparent in several different ways:

- the seriousness of information system operating problems that increases with the organizational complexity of the system;
- a low rate of use of applications introduced by managers, and the presence of resistance-to-change phenomena;
- a lack of planning concerning the evolution of the information system within the firm;
- a lack of control over the achievement of the objectives of the information system (IS evaluation) and of the outside environment (consultants, suppliers, service bureaus, the parent company);
- the absence of security measures and appropriate documentation, and insufficient training of the individual responsible for information systems.

In response, the firm's management must implement concepts and tools to plan, organize and manage the firm's information resources. Management must be able to answer certain key questions, such as:

- What is the current and potential contribution of the information system towards the short-term and long-term performance of the business?
- From a strategic standpoint, do certain aspects of the information system procure advantages for the firm?
- Has the firm over-invested, or under-invested, in information technologies?
- Does the firm have a realistic plan for the acquisition and development of applications to improve the effectiveness of its operations and decision-making process? Can it, in particular, identify the applications which, once implemented, would provide it with a specific competitive advantage?
- Are information system operations and development projects being managed appropriately?

The findings of several studies show that most small businesses surveyed cannot, at the present time, answer these questions. It is also clear that the limited resources of small firms, and their approach to

315

management based on a relative lack of structure, short-term vision and reaction rather than anticipation, imposes specific constraints that must be taken into account in any realistic information resources management policy.

Such a policy would include the following goals:

- minimizing the risks associated with the introduction of information technology by establishing realistic objectives for the firm's information system, defining the associated tasks and main activities, and structuring the implementation process to allow monitoring and assessment;
- maximizing the effectiveness of the firm's information system users and personnel by defining guidelines (such as training) and procedures (such as data security) to help them carry out their information system-related tasks;
- develop a strategy to facilitate the evolution of the information system, by defining future needs in connection with overall firm strategy and the resources required, using an anticipatory, adaptive approach (including, for example, hardware expansion capacity, software flexibility, needs for particular applications, etc.).

This type of policy must be implemented using tools that are accessible to small business managers, especially an instrument for "self-diagnosis" that could be used both as a framework for an analysis of the current situation of information systems within the firm, and as a reference framework for drawing up an information technologies management plan (Lesca and Raymond, 1993). Used by management alone or in collaboration with an outside consultant, the instrument would also offer the advantage of allowing the firm's management to participate in the information resources management process and thus to increase their awareness of the importance of information systems for the firm.

5.2   The implementation of information systems

The second major research finding is that the initial process by which information systems are introduced into small businesses is, all too often, totally empirical, whereas one of main the advantages of information systems lies in the process by which they are implemented (Blili, 1989). It is clear that the approach used by a firm to introduce information technology is crucial for the future success of the information systems. Research has shown that one major mistake at the introduction stage has repercussions on system performance that will be felt long into the future. Regarding this point, researchers and information systems professionals have concluded that a systematic approach to the introduction of an information system must include the following fundamental steps (Bergeron, Raymond and Reix, 1992):

- an examination of the feasibility of implementing an information system in relation to the problems and opportunities identified by the firm's management, and a plan for the proposed introduction (why? by whom? when?);
- an analysis of the information-related needs arising from the problems and opportunities identified;
- the functional design of an information system to respond to the firm's needs, including the determination of system objectives (what needs to be achieved) independently of any technical concerns;
- the physical design of the previously-defined information system (how to achieve what is needed), including a determination of the degree of computerization of the system, its operating characteristics, the concurrent systematization of management methods and procedures affected by the new system, and the acquisition of the required hardware, software and human resources;
- the start-up and assessment of the completed system.

It is clear that the real-life introduction of information systems into small businesses bears little relation to this model. Weaknesses are found in several areas, either because one or more stages of the process are omitted, because of a lack of planning or supervision at the introductory stage, or because of a lack of experience or knowledge affecting one stage in particular.

Given this situation, a participatory strategy (involving management, the person responsible for introducing information technology, and users) can be set up to allow the firm itself to take charge of designing the information system using the determination of its problems and needs, regardless of technical difficulties. The objective of such a strategy is to minimize the risks related to the introduction, while taking into account the limits of the resources of a small business.

The strategy is based on a definition of the roles of each person involved in the process, and on a systematic approach to the actions to be taken within the limits set by the size of the business. The first role is that of management, which must initiate the project once all problems and potential uses within the firm have been identified, designate a person to run the project, ensure that the objectives and introduction strategy of the new system are prepared and provide visible support and cooperation throughout the project.

The second role is that of the project coordinator, who must be one of the firm's key managers and either possess the necessary skills or have access to an external consultant. The coordinator plans the project, analyzes user needs and defines system objectives, besides preparing a systematic strategy for the introduction of the new system based on a consultative approach combined, initially, with a pre-programmed software package. The coordinator draws up the specifications for the new system, assesses the bids received from suppliers, trains users and supervises the implementation of the solution selected, and must possess communication and training skills and a sufficient knowledge of computers.

The last role is that of the users, who take an active role in the whole process (analysis of needs, assessments of software packages, training of other users, assessment of the new system) and become the new "owners" of the system.

5.3   Applications portfolios for small business information systems

A third finding is that information systems are perceived and used by small businesses simply as tools to increase productivity in certain areas, unrelated to the actual "heart" of the business. The contents of a firm's applications portfolio is one of the key indications of the role played by its information system (Cron and Sobol, 1983). The typical portfolio generally contains applications centering around financial operations, operational control and day-to-day management, whereas the information-related needs defined by managers concern marketing and production, management control and the   decision-making process, planning and analysis (Raymond, 1988a).

A part from the basic administrative applications, other software generally reflects the more specific needs of each firm, which, unless a software package is available, must develop or commission appropriate software itself. Such software often requires a higher level of computer resources, given the greater complexity of its functions and of the user-interface. In this connection, the development and use of decision support systems are significantly different from administrative systems. Prototyping and user-developed applications (user-computing) are particularly important for such systems.

In light of the above, information systems cannot be expected to play an important role in small businesses, in connection with the performance of individuals and of the firm itself, unless a more global approach is adopted to respond to the requirements of production, marketing and global firm strategy (Treadgold, 1989). The approach will bring with it, though, new constraints and higher levels of risk, since it involves the introduction of a new logic in the firm's structure and operations.

The new constraints include:

- the need to plan the introduction of applications in an integrated manner, rather than "piecemeal", given the strong integration of the various functions of a small business;
- the need to win the support not only of the firm's accountant or financial manager, but also of all management staff, in the planning and introduction strategy;
- the need to structure certain processes in order to gain access to non-accounting data (for example, the capture of production data);
- the need to analyze and structure certain decision-making processes (such as pricing decisions) in order to define information-related needs;
- the need to use information tools better able to integrate the information resources of the organization and provide support for decision-making (data bases, report generating software, electronic spreadsheets, etc.), while retaining the specific advantages of a small business, such as flexibility and the ability to reach decisions quickly;
- the need to use new methods to design systems based on an object-oriented approach allowing the "re-use" (components and generic models for businesses in the sector) of software and the "transposition" of the approach used by a group of similar small businesses to a specific small firm.

The risks include:

- an increased dependence of the firm's vital functions on information systems, especially on the support provided by a supplier or consultant;
- a larger investment in human, material and financial resources, even when the advantages of strategic and managerial applications are, a priori, less tangible and quantifiable than those of administrative applications.

Figure 10.4 summarizes the links between problems, success factors and the concrete solutions that have been proposed to increase the effectiveness of information systems in small businesses.

6. Computers and users

Since the early 1980s, the proliferation of micro-computers, combined with the increasing "user-friendliness" of computer applications (4th-generation software such as electronic spreadsheets), improved knowledge of computers among managers and the inability of information systems departments to meet increasing demands have resulted in the emergence of a phenomenon known as end-user computing. This is a process by which users (who are not computer experts) develop and operate their own computer applications, in contrast to the traditional process in which such activities are carried out by specialists (Rivard and Huff, 1988; Blili, Raymond and Rivard, 1996)).

End-user computing in large corporations runs parallel to the explosion of information systems development and operation activities. Traditionally centralized in an information systems department, decision-making powers and skills relating to computing are now distributed among other administrative units. This new organization of the information systems function has also appeared in small businesses, which were often only at the early stages of the computerization process (Raymond and Magnenat-Thalmann, 1982) and even in the early stages of their existence (Raymond and Lorrain, 1991). In this case, end-user computing is typically observed when budgeting, financial analysis and cost-accounting software in developed and brought into operation by managers, using software tools such as Lotus 1-2-3. The specific nature of small businesses once again plays an important role in identifying the factors for the successful implementation of end-user computing and its management.

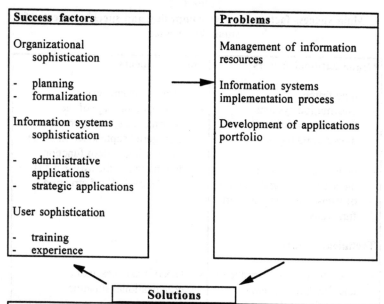

Success factors	Problems
Organizational sophistication - planning - formalization Information systems sophistication - administrative applications - strategic applications User sophistication - training - experience	Management of information resources Information systems implementation process Development of applications portfolio

Solutions

Realistic policy and management tools for information technologies (instrument for self-diagnosis) adapted to the specific nature of small businesses.

Participatory strategy for introduction, based on the systematic assigning of tasks to those involved (implementation guide).

Analysis of the information requirements and decision-making processes related to the strategy and key sectors of the business, such as production and marketing (integration of applications, 4th-generation software and data bases, inter-firm systems, expert systems, Internet, object-oriented approach).

End-user computing in the small business (training and consultation through outside organizations).

Figure 10.4
Problems, success factors and solutions for information systems in small businesses

Table 10.2
Main success factors for user-computing and specific aspects of small businesses

Organizational factors	Specific aspects
- time-frame - information systems function overload - user-computing policy - management support - hierarchic level and location of user-computing support functions	- decision-making cycle - development stage of the information system function - managerial sophistication of the information system function - domination of the owner-manager - simple, centralized structure
Technical factors	
- availability, user-friendliness and flexibility of user-computing tools - type and quality of technical support provided (by the information systems function, compucentre, supplier)	- lack of resources, extra-organizational situation - lack of resources, extra-organizational situation, technical sophistication of the information systems function
Individual factors	
- information systems/end-user computing training - information systems/end-user computing experience - user attitudes and expectations - type of task (autonomy, complexity, variety)	- lack of resources, extra-organizational situation, technical sophistication of the information systems function - stage of development reached by the information systems - managerial ideology, psychological climate - decision-making process

Compared to other information systems, end-user computing is simpler, more personalized, less formal, has a shorter time-frame and is based on effectiveness rather than on efficiency. In addition, end-user computing is characterized by its flexibility and amenity, and until now by the empirical and incremental way it has been managed by organizations (Sumner and Klepper, 1987). If organizational and information systems environments are to converge, the distinctive traits of end-user computing as compared to traditional computing offer many advantages that should lead to its introduction into small businesses (O'Shea, 1989).

Various organizational, technical and individual factors contribute towards the success of end-user computing in terms of user satisfaction, level of use, productivity and effectiveness (Raymond, 1990a). Table 10.2 summarizes the main factors studied empirically, and the specific aspects of small businesses potentially associated with them.

A valid question is whether the factors governing the success of end-user computing that have been identified empirically in large corporations are the same in the small business context, or if the specific aspects of small businesses affect the presence and relative importance of the factors.

An overloading of the information systems function in connection with the development of new applications is considered to the main organizational determining factor for the success of end-user computing, which means that the greater the overload, the more users will tend to develop and be satisfied with their own applications. However, the fact that information systems are generally either in the "initiation" or the "proliferation" stage in small businesses (Raymond, 1990b) means that overloading is rarely a problem, and thus would not be a determining factor for the presence and success of end-user computing.

Another crucial factor is the level of technical support for end-user computing that is provided by the information systems function, particularly as regards the type and quality of products (hardware and software) and services (training, consultation) offered by the administrative unit set up for that purpose, often known as the compucentre. The lack of resources and technical sophistication of most small businesses rules out the possibility of establishing a compucentre (Brancheau, Vogel and Wetherbe, 1985). On the other hand, external sources of support for user computing are available, such as small business help centres operated by universities, government agencies and suppliers. The availability and quality of this extra-organizational support thus becomes one of the determining factors in the success of end-user computing in small businesses.

Lastly, there is general agreement on the fact that training is one of the most important individual factors (Raymond, 1988c). Training obviously includes not only the prior training of end-users, but also the type of training offered; training can range from general knowledge and skills connected with the role of information systems within the organization and the development of such systems (such as a development methodology) to detailed training on a specific software tool (such as how to create a spreadsheet with Excel). Small business managers initially required the first type of training, given that they generally lack computer experience and training (Weber and Tiemeyer, 1982) and that their organization cannot provide the technical support needed for efficient end-user computing.

6.2   Managing end-user computing in small businesses

Given that end-user computing requires an increasing amount of resources and sometimes involves considerable risks for the business (Raymond et al., 1988), planning, organization and monitoring are essential. The prime objective is to minimize the risks involved, while maximizing the individual and organizational benefits. The end-user computing management strategies so far proposed have all been aimed at large organizations. It is, once again, necessary to ask if the strategies that have been presented are appropriate for small businesses, or if the specific aspects of small·businesses requires adapted strategies or new strategies designed specifically for small businesses.

In this connection, a first possible step would be the creation of "proto-strategies" for small businesses to meet the specific user-computing needs. Since each proto-strategy has its own user-computing vision and strategy which differs fundamentally from the others (Table 10.3), the efficient management of end-user computing will necessarily depend on finding the proto-strategy that best reflects the needs of the organization.

324

Table 10.3
Proto-strategies for end-user computing in small businesses

Proto-strategy	Vision of end-user computing	Objective	Stage of application growth
I Adopt end-user computing as an alternative to organizational information systems	As a means of overcoming a lack of resources and a dependence on extra-organizational resources	Increasing operational efficiency at minimum cost	Initiation, administrative applications developed by users and acquired as software packages
II Reject end-user computing as a threat to organizational information systems	As an obstacle to the maturity and continuing success of organizational information systems	Increasing operational efficiency and effective decision-making	Proliferation, administrative applications in the form of software packages, some customized managerial applications
III Adopt end-user computing as a complement to organizational information systems	As a means of seizing opportunities or solving problems outside the scope of organizational information systems	Increasing effective decision-making and organizational effectiveness	Control, managerial or strategic applications developed by users

The first proto-strategy applied by the management of a small business could be the adoption of end-user computing as a substitute for an organizational informations system, as the initial step towards introducing computer technologies. End-user computing can be seen as a way of overcoming a lack of resources and a dependence on extra-organizational resources, at least as a more feasible alternative to some applications (Raymond and Bergeron, 1992). A second possible proto-strategy could be to prevent all forms of end-user computing. The problems associated with the proliferation of applications provided by the organizational information systems function could be stemmed by management, in order to avoid making the system more complex and posing a threat to the managerial and technical sophistication of the information systems function (Raymond, 1987a).

Lastly, a third proto-strategy could be for managers to see user computing as a complement to organizational information systems. End-user computing can, in fact, be a means to respond to certain strategic opportunities or to solve specific problems that cannot be reached by the information systems function (Hayen, 1982). In light of this analysis, the following step would be to examine existing strategies and develop new ones, ensuring that each proto-strategy is designed to converge with the associated end-user computing management policies.

7. Towards a strategic use of information systems in small businesses

Research into information systems in small businesses has produced a number of observations and solutions to the major problems associated with the introduction, use and management of information systems. The general conclusion which may be drawn is that the contribution made by information technologies towards small business performance could be much greater than it is at present. The main obstacles to a more effective, more efficient use of information technologies are not technical in nature; existing hardware and software can meet all the needs of small businesses in terms of operations, information and decision-making.

The findings of most empirical studies tend to confirm that the obstacles encountered relate to organizations and individuals, since small businesses lack, above all, resources, methods, and management and training tools in connection with their information systems; external sources of assistance and consultation are therefore necessary (DeLone and Gray, 1991). In view of this, every solution proposed by researchers and practitioners needs to be simple and robust, and must take into account the constraints applying to small businesses while preserving their advantages of flexibility and speed of execution. For these reasons, end-user computing is one of the most obvious solutions for small businesses, including decision supportand the expertise needed when a firm is created, such as the design and drafting of a business plan (Raymond and Lorrain, 1991). Another approach has also been suggested, involving the application of artificial intelligence to management and training using expert systems and tutorial systems (Martin et al., 1991), which have the potential to remedy certain deficiencies in specialized human resources by providing a substitute for management consultants, training staff and other experts whose services are often too expensive and too unreliable for small businesses (Gordon and Key, 1987). The approach has been tested experimentally to produce a diagnosis of the environmental scanning process in a firm, and to provide related recommendations (Lesca and Raymond, 1994).

Ultimately, however, the main issues for small businesses that wish to improve their performance, maintain their position or simply survive, centre on the strategic and competitive application of information technologies (Blili and Rivard, 1990). Despite their sophistication and the resources they mobilize, these applications are even now within the reach of innovative small businesses (Bergeron, Buteau and Raymond, 1991). For example, EDI is an application that will probably spread rapidly through computer-to-computer network links to carry out transactions between commercial partners (Bergeron and Raymond, 1992a). Small businesses will have to adopt a proactive attitude rather than wait to have changes imposed on them.

One of the main objectives of researchers and practitioners, in this regard, is to identify opportunities for the strategic application, by small businesses, of information technologies by proposing appropriate analytic methods. To our knowledge, the only current method specifically adapted to the small business context is that of Bergeron and Raymond (1992b), based on an identification grid for strategic applications. It is shown in Figure 10.5.

The true impact of strategic information systems is still unknown in terms of the competitive advantage gained by the small businesses that have introduced them. The introduction of similar systems in large corporations can also be seen as a threat for small businesses. One example is the application of information technologies by large organizations to remove intermediaries by integrating their functions (Blili and Raymond, 1993). Similarly, new applications such as EDI can be imposed on small businesses by large corporations (Raymond and Bergeron, 1996), and can thus be used by one organization to subject its own partners (suppliers or customers).

Lastly, in connection with new information and communications technologies, it is impossible to ignore the impact of the "information superhighway" and, in particular, the Internet and the access network to hypermedia documents known as the World Wide Web. This network is currently generalizing the use of EDI and leading to the creation of network organizations or "shared" enterprises (Julien and Raymond, 1994) based on a shared computer infrastructure, an inter-organizational information system (Massotte, 1994). In a context of globalization, links between small businesses and large corporations here become inevitable.

8.   Conclusion

The introduction and use of information technologies by small businesses is a phenomenon that will inevitably gain momentum as we move towards the year 2000. Understanding and mastering this phenomenon are the major challenges facing those involved in research on information systems, and it is to be hoped that researchers will continue to address the specific aspects of small businesses at both the theoretical and practical levels to help them survive and prosper in an increasingly complex and uncertain environment, in which the mastery of information technologies has become a critical factor for success.

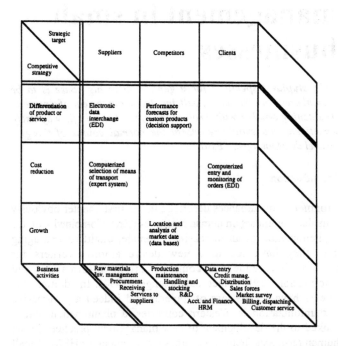

Figure 10.5
Identification grid for strategic applications in small businesses

11 Human resource management in small businesses

"The stupidest spectacle for a gentleman in his house is to be encumbered with the care of policing, talking in the ear of a servant, threatening another with a roll of the eyes; it should flow by itself, unnoticed, and should represent the normal course of things."
Michel de Montaigne, "Essai".

1. Introduction

The environmental disturbances described in the first chapter obviously have a considerable impact on human resources (HR). Combined with the Western phenomenon of an increasingly female, qualified and aging workforce, they have led to a new desire among workers for consideration, independence, communication, information and participation (Fabi, 1991; Audet and Bélanger, 1994). In addition, the last ten years have seen a loss of impetus and indeed a progressive decline of unionization in Western countries, a phenomenon that is closely linked to the development of new management practices in the area of human resources (human resources management, or HRM). Small businesses offer less scope for, and are often opposed to, union ideology, and the new jobs created in large numbers by small and medium-sized businesses have generally not been unionized (Bélanger and Mercier, 1994).

The growing emphasis on human resource issues has made HRM an essential component in the strategic process of each organization (Liouville and Bayad, 1995). In an international context that now requires a qualified, correctly-paid workforce, businesses have no other choice than to pursue dynamic objectives to mobilize and revitalize their personnel (Larouche, 1994). As a result, the HRM field has experienced strong growth and has given rise to a number of academic and praxiological developments with focus on the harmonization of different approaches.

In order to study the empirical data on HRM within small businesses, we have divided this chapter into six sections that form part of an overall conceptual and exploratory approach. An exhaustive synthetic framework is proposed for the interpretation of the relations existing between HRM practices and various contingency factors relating to the degree of formalization in small businesses. After the introduction, the second section underlines the importance of HR studies and their role in small and medium-sized businesses. In the third section, the analytical framework used to describe HR practices is defined, followed by a statistical summary of selected empirical studies dealing with HRM in small businesses.

The fourth section presents the main subject-matter of Chapter 11. It sets out, in eight subdivisions, the principal aspects of HRM that have been found empirically to exist in forms specific to small businesses: human resource planning (HRP); job analysis, recruitment, selection, and induction; compensation and benefits; personnel appraisal; training and development; organization and participation; and workplace health and safety (WHS). Unfortunately, a number of other major activities had to be excluded for reasons of specialization, homogeneity and space. Thus, HRM practices relating to problems of productivity (motivation, job satisfaction, absenteeism, etc.) and labour relations in small businesses (accreditation, negotiation, dispute settlement, etc.) have not been analyzed here.

In order to understand the phenomena relating to the existence and development of HRM practices in the small business context, the fifth section examines the formalization process, the key element of our analysis, in greater depth, establishes the importance of entrepreneurial vision, sets out the main contingent factors having an impact on HRM practices, and proposes a contingency model for HRM in small businesses. The conclusion defines several possibilities for future research centred on empirical verification of the model, which still contains several obvious weaknesses. The limits of our research, and the need to design innovative solutions adapted to the specific aspects of small businesses, are underlined.

2. Human resources and small businesses: diversity and flexibility

It is important to state, from the outset, that HRM should not be considered simply as an extension of other areas of management, but rather as an essential function at the heart of a business's strategic process (d'Amboise and Garand, 1995). HRM in small businesses has, until now, received little attention and has generally led to generalizations based on impressions and partial observations rather than on extensive research (Mahé de Boislandelle, 1988; Duberley and Walley, 1995; Bacon et al., 1996). It thus seems appropriate to examine the subject in greater depth in order to understand its particularities and, eventually, to suggest ways for small businesses to act more effectively and thus improve their competitiveness.

Several North American research projects have, in fact, clearly demonstrated the existence of management problems in small businesses, especially in connection with human resources. Although most entrepreneurs recognize the fundamental necessity and the importance of their workforce, a number of studies have shown that they experience ongoing difficulties in managing their personnel appropriately and systematically (Hoy and Vaught, 1980; Mahé et al., 1985; Deshpande and Golhar, 1994). According to several investigations, personnel recruitment and training are two of the three most important management problems facing small businesses; productivity and labour costs occupy the fourth and tenth positions, respectively (d'Amboise and Parent, 1989). Since entrepreneurs often have to take responsibility for HRM themselves, it seems reasonable to suggest that there is a clear need for assistance in this area.

However, these concerns have led to only eight major research projects (Baker, 1955; McEvoy, 1984; Mahé de Boislandelle, 1988; Hornsby and Kuratko, 1990; Scott et al., 1990; Benoit and Rousseau, 1993; Deshpande and Golhar, 1994; Duberley and Walley, 1995) that form the foundation for the empirical analysis of HRM practices in small businesses. This does not mean that the importance of HRM problems in small businesses was ignored in the period preceding the above research, since numerous articles did, in fact, appear on the subject, although most were normative or anecdotal in nature (Garand, 1993).

An overview of the above studies reveals that HRM management activities are more varied, and more extensively applied, in many small businesses, in contrast to most prevailing opinions. HRM practices do exist and are applied in small businesses, even though they are generally not formalized and extremely diverse, and thus resist generalization.

332

Although a majority of small businesses engage in only three basic activities, namely recruitment, selection, and compensation, others extend their HRM by means of one or more less traditional practices, such as personnel appraisal, training, and workplace health and safety. Obviously, the implementation of these practices also depends on the legal context and organizational constraints. For example, recruitment, compensation, training, working conditions, workplace health and safety, information and participation are sometimes governed by national regulatory provisions, and even if the legal rules are not always applied systematically by small businesses, their influence can be clearly felt in the actual HRM practices applied.

3. Methodological considerations

The HR function, because of its central position in the organization, constitutes one of the most diversified areas of management and therefore one of the most extended for research purposes. With its multiple links to other areas - engineering, sociology, law, psychology and administration - HRM includes a considerable number of activities that operate synergetically with the other functions of the organization. Needless to say, analysis must be circumscribed to certain specific practices to avoid superficial scanning of an excessive number of elements. The use of an analytical framework for HRM practices is essential in order to define the areas of activity that will be analyzed in the next section. This synopsis of HRM practices, as shown in Table 11.1, is in no way intended to provide an exhaustive summary of all the aspects of each practice, but rather to provide an overall reference framework to compare the range of HRM practices to those actually observed in small businesses.

The framework allows the main practice areas, among the wide range of activities ascribed in general to HRM, to be identified. The use, in this chapter, of the generic term "HRM practices" thus refers to the ten or so principal activities recognized as such in North American and European circles; operationally speaking, this typology corresponds to the main activities identified in most academic and educational textbooks in the HR field.

Table 11.1
Framework of analysis for HRM practices in small businesses

HRM Practices		Synopsis of main human resource Management activities in small businesses
Acquisition of human resources		
Planning of human resources	manpower needs organization charts decisions and strategic planning	hiring and dismissals; training; compensation
Job analysis	general job analysis individual job descriptions	job requirements
Recruitment, selection and induction	recruitment and selection in general	policies and procedures overview: recruitment, selection, induction
	recruitment	recruiting decisions and responsibilities sources of recruitment recruiting effectiveness and difficulties
	selection	selection decisions and responsibilities selection techniques references tests and validation selection discrimination final hiring decisions
	induction	arrival/orientation of new employee accompaniment, sponsorship, monitoring and feedback
Maintenance of human resources		
Compensation and fringe benefits	salaries and compensation	overview of compensation practices compensation decisions and responsibilities salary determination modes of compensation salary increases incentive plans
	fringe benefits	fringe benefits in general employee services, social and leisure activities
	compensation for managers	wage gaps between small and large firms
Personnel appraisal	overview of appraisals and evaluations objectives and content of evaluation assessors and responsibility for evaluation frequency of evaluation	evaluation methods and procedures evaluation information and training effectiveness of the assessment procedure
	staff movements	promotions, transfers and demotions

Table 11.1 (continued)

Framework of analysis for HRM practices in small businesses

Human resource development

Training and development	North American and Anglo-Saxon context	methods and techniques
	French context	training themes
	overview	assessment, efficiency and cost
	analysis of needs and objectives	training and development difficulties
	training and development responsibilities and training staff	promotion of training and development
Career planning and management	expectations, objectives and career progression	plateauing, plateaus and end of career
		career assessment
		orientation and counselling
		reassignment
	personnel movements	internal
		external (incoming, returns, departures)
Equity and employment	notions of equality, equity and discrimination	different forms of discrimination
	government legislation	affirmative action programmes

Work environment

Organization and participation	work organization	working conditions
	work timetables and schedules	
	information, communication and participative management	
Workplace health and safety	general health and safety	employee assistance programmes

As stated previously, most (81%) of the empirical studies dealing with HRM in small businesses were conducted in the 1980s and 1990s, except in the US where such concerns were triggered by the 1950 Small Business Act. In most countries, a wave of interest began in the 1970s as a direct result of a renewal of personnel management practices that quickly led, in the 1980s, to the emergence of HRM as a management field. The general outline of this movement can be clearly seen in Table 11.2; the concentration of the investigations, the academic status of the researchers (78%) and the variety of the media used for the dissemination of the results (50% academic or professional journals) should also be noted. In addition, it appears that the size of the samples selected for the studies as a whole follows a near-normal curve peaking around 100 to 200 businesses and/or individuals. Lastly, the 110 empirical studies analyzed represent roughly 15% of the literature consulted, a reasonable proportion for this type of qualitative meta-analysis.

Overall, the compilation demonstrates that research on HRM in small businesses is a recent occurrence (having taken place over the last 15 years), that there is a growing interest in these questions, that work has been carried out in many different countries, that a wide range of samples can be examined and that, whatever the origin or status of the researchers involved, they have assigned substantial importance to most HRM practices (Garand, 1993).

4. HRM practices in small businesses: the current state of knowledge

4.1 Human resource planning

Human resource planning (HRP) has never been considered to be a widespread practice in small firms, and is mostly encountered in medium-sized and large corporations in North America. The literature on manpower forecasting (hiring and layoffs), reflecting a mainly French outlook, shows that certain policies and procedures do exist in small businesses, despite their often informal and unfocused nature. Two opposing trends can be detected: one the one hand are the studies that conclude on the existence of relatively well-articulated HRP in small businesses (Naro, 1990; Bayad and Herrmann, 1991; Rowden, 1995), and on the other, the studies that demonstrate the lack or inadequacy of forward-looking management practices in small businesses (Hess, 1987; Larrivée and d'Amboise, 1989).

Most small businesses strive to manage their human resources in a forward-looking manner (Paumier and Gouadain, 1984) and their efforts, far from being superficial, are based on precise information obtained from different sources. Most businesses establish economic forecasts and forecasts concerning personnel movements, generally on time-frames of less than three years. However, few pre-established recruitment or transfer and promotion plans for managers and non-managers seem to exist, whether in small businesses or large corporations. Seventy percent of small businesses plan recruiting less than a month in advance, and 50% apply the same approach to promotions (McEvoy, 1984).

It is thus clear that a small business employment management strategy does actually exist, although it would appear to be reactive (structural constraints) rather than preventive or forward-looking (strategy or plan), acting as a parameter integrated *ex-post* into the management of a business and not as an *ex-ante* element, as is the case for technological strategy. The level of personnel management depends as much on the stage of development reached by, and the industrial maturity of, a given small business as on the type of production involved and organizational size (Bayad and Herrmann, 1991). Small business personnel management features a variety of practices; often informal, intuitive and unplanned, they come under the responsibility of the owner-manager who, alone or in collaboration with others, undertakes the direction, planning and implementation of recruitment-related tasks. No single behavioural model exists, but several important trends can be observed: an increasing reliance on outside staff, a relative lack of cases in which human resources are replaced by technical resources, and a tendency to use fixed-term contracts and overtime to respond to short-term fluctuations (Naro, 1990). In addition, rationalization strategies differ considerably between small and large organizations (Wassermann, 1989).

Table 11.2
Overall compilation of research dealing with HRM in SMEs
(frequency and percentage of total number of studies
for research as a whole)

	United States n	United States %	France n	France %	England, Ireland, Scotland n	England, Ireland, Scotland %	Quebec n	Quebec %	Europe & OECD n	Europe & OECD %	Canada n	Canada %	Overall n	Overall %
No. of studies used	41	39,4	26	25,0	13	12,5	11	10,6	8	7,7	5	4,8	104	100,0
Research period														
• 1950-59	1	2,4	0		0		0		0		0		1	1,0
• 1960-69	4	9,8	0		0		0		0		0		4	3,8
• 1970-79	5	12,2	2	7,7	4	30,8	1	9,1	2	25,0	1	20,0	15	14,4
• 1980-84	9	22,0	4	15,4	4	30,8	5	45,5	3	37,5	0		25	24,0
• 1985-89	13	31,7	16	61,5	2	15,4	4	36,4	3	37,5	2	40,0	40	38,5
• 1990-94	9	22,0	4	15,4	3	23,1	1	9,1	0		2	40,0	19	18,3
Author's status														
• University professor	64	91,4	16	47,1	25	96,2	12	57,1	12	75,0	6	85,7	135	78,0
• Professional-consultant	3	4,3	7	20,6	0		3	14,3	2	12,5	1	14,3	16	9,2
• Graduate student	3	4,3	8	23,5	0		6	28,6	0		0		16	9,2
• Research group	0		3	8,8	1	3,8	0		2	12,5	0		6	3,5
Nature of document														
• «Academic» journal	29	63,0	8	19,5	5	31,3	3	20,0	1	11,1	4	50,0	50	36,8
• Working paper	2	4,3	9	22,0	4	25,0	6	40,0	5	55,6	2	25,0	28	20,6
• Conference paper	9	19,6	5	12,2	1	6,3	3	20,0	1	11,1	1	12,5	20	14,7
• «Professional» journal	3	6,5	10	24,4	2	12,5	0		2	22,2	1	12,5	18	13,2
• Master's dissertation or doctoral thesis	2	4,3	6	14,6	1	6,3	2	13,3	0		0		11	8,1
• Book or chapter	1	2,2	3	7,3	3	18,8	1	6,7	0		0		9	6,6
Size of sample (Enterprises and/or individuals)														
• less than 20	1	2,4	4	15,4	2	16,7	0		0		1	20,0	8	8,0
• 20 to 49	3	7,3	9	34,6	2	16,7	1	10,0	2	33,3	0		17	17,0
• 50 to 99	13	31,7	5	19,2	3	25,0	2	20,0	0		0		24	24,0
• 100 to 399	13	31,7	4	15,4	2	16,7	6	60,0	2	33,3	1	20,0	28	28,0
• 400 to 999	5	12,2	3	11,5	1	8,3	1	10,0	0		1	20,0	11	11,0
• more than 1000	6	14,6	1	3,8	2	16,7	0		2	33,3	1	20,0	12	12,0

The total number of "n" may differ from the number of studies retained for each corresponding country.

The conclusions reached by Hess (1987), however, are diametrically opposed. The small businesses surveyed carried out no preventive personnel management, and their needs and resource analysis was either non-existent or embryonic. All the respondents carried out personnel forecasts, but using techniques that lacked formality; no small business had a recruitment and promotion plan; none carried out formalized predictions or produced forecasts. There was no short- or long-term forecasting for workers and employees, and only informal plans for managers and supervisors. Only a handful of small businesses had a personnel manager, since the tasks were performed by the owner-manager. In addition, the businesses surveyed experienced difficulties in estimating personnel needs and resources; future needs were assessed on the basis of past experience and personal appraisals of the future, and 83% perceived no gap between their current needs and their resources.

Organization charts are one of the fundamental tools used in HRP by small businesses, although they are not always formally integrated into the organization. Between 30% and 40% of small firms use a functional organization chart of their business, and the percentage seems to be directly related to business size (Amba-Rao and Pendse, 1985; Benoit and Rousseau, 1993). Since the organizational structure of small businesses is relatively simple and informal, it can be assumed that employees understand it well enough to dispense with a formal chart setting out status and functional authority relationships. Bayad and Nebenhaus (1993) report lower percentages, however, for small industrial firms: 84% and 65% for the two classes of firms most likely to practise HRP (larger firms), and 36% on average for the three other classes (small firms), creating a fairly direct link with organizational size, as shown in Table 11.3.

Table 11.3
Use of a functional organization chart

Business size	Number of employees	Percentage of use
Extremely small	0 - 19	less than 20%
Small	20 - 99	25% - 35%
Small to medium	100 - 249	45% - 60%
Medium to large	250 - 500	70% to 80%
Large	500 and over	over 75%

The human resource planning process also includes elements relating to the business's decision-making and strategic planning processes. The larger the organization, the greater the number of reporting levels, meaning that, for personnel managers,

- it often takes longer to get decisions, policies and procedures approved, amended or implemented;
- a number of signatures can be required for even the simplest problem;
- low-ranking employees in the human resource service (HRS) often hesitate to make their views known to their service heads, even though they work in the same department.

In addition, in a hierarchy the ultimate decision-maker for human resource decisions has seldom received any training in HRM, but is generally an executive manager whose responsibilities include HR and who makes decisions on the basis of expert opinions provided by lower-ranking managers. Personnel managers participate in 76% of decisions made by the managing board and 54.5% of the decisions made by the operational planning board. Over 50% of personnel directors are consulted by such boards on the firm's objectives and projects, while 20% are consulted about the introduction of new technologies or new products, and 40% about the main objectives in human resources. However, personnel directors are not as frequently consulted concerning objectives in other areas, although 90% are consulted during the preparation of a collective bargaining policy and when a settlement is proposed.

4.2   Job analysis

Job analysis has never been considered a priority in small businesses, and in many cases the owner-manager has no knowledge of this aspect of HRM. Often, the only element of job analysis used is the job description, mainly drawn up following a basic observation of the work of an employee and, to a lesser extent, interviews and specialized questionnaires (Hornsby and Kuratko, 1990).

The use and degree of formalization of job analysis techniques (such as the use of forms for applications and analysis) increase gradually with business size, especially in unionized firms. Jones and De Cotiis (1969) reported that, overall, 25% of respondents had no job analysis program and that only 33% planned to establish one. The most commonly-raised objections were that job analysis served no useful purpose, that no acceptable system could be found, that it was too expensive, and that it took up too much time.

Job descriptions are practically the only activity observed in small businesses in relation to this sector of HRM, and their use increases directly with firm size, as shown in Table 11.4. Several authors (McEvoy, 1984; Astrachan and Kolenko, 1994) report, respectively, that 63%, 35% and 47% of the small businesses studied possessed no written job descriptions and that the sources of information used by company directors were not sufficiently specialized.

Table 11.4
Use of job descriptions in small businesses

Business size	Number of employees	Percentage of use
Extremely small	0 - 19	less than 35%
Small	20 - 99	30% - 45%
Small to medium	100 - 249	40% - 65%
Medium to large	250 - 500	65% to 85%
Large	500 and over	over 80%

On the other hand, Le Louarn and Thériault (1984) and Mahé et al. (1985) report contradictory results: over three-quarters of the small businesses analyzed apparently used job descriptions, including 30% of firms with between 10 and 49 employees; management positions tended to be defined twice as often as other jobs. The job descriptions were used in hiring (advertising), staff assignments and replacements, the assigning of tasks and compensation, as well as in evaluations of functions and work to increase productivity.

4.3   Recruitment, selection and induction

The process of recruiting, selecting and receiving human resources is fundamental to all management and production activities. The quality of human resources, both in small firms and large corporations, has a continuous influence on the firm's success, and it is clear that the bigger the organization, the more it relies on formal recruitment and selection policies and procedures. Only half of all very small and small businesses use written procedures, compared to three-quarters of medium-sized and large businesses (Le Louarn and Thériault, 1984).

Recruitment

Recruiting decisions and responsibilities. Decisions about when to initiate a recruiting procedure seem to be split between owner-managers and management, depending on organizational size. The larger the firm, the more the owner-manager delegates authority to a supervisor, manager or director of production or, in a small number of instances, to the director of personnel (Mahé et al., 1985). Such delegation may involve the use of pre-established forms or of some procedure for initial recruiting decisions. The recruiting process generally begins when a need becomes apparent, but only after all the possibilities provided by internal resources have been exhausted. Given the strong centralization of the recruiting process on the owner-manager, the personnel department is never alone in decisions relating to the creation of a new position (Mealiea and Lee, 1980). Responsibility for recruitment is shared between the owner-manager, managers and the director of personnel, although the latter is often responsible only for administrative aspects, seldom makes decisions and is involved in primary selection alone.

Internal sources and methods. Despite the small size of the workforce, referrals made by the employees of small businesses (Marlow and Patton, 1993; Deshpande and Golhar, 1994), sometimes rewarded by a small bonus if hiring takes place (McEvoy, 1984), are one of the three main sources of recruitment, and are practically the only internal method used (Table 11.5). Significant qualifications are, however, made in a recent study by Deshpande and Golhar (1994), who assign first place to in-house advertising (1st place, with a frequency of use of 3.19 in small businesses and 3.62 in large corporations), promotion (3rd place - 2.54 in small businesses and 2nd place - 2.81 in large corporations) and the hiring of temporary or laid-off staff (4th place - 2.52 in small businesses and 3rd place -2.57 in large corporations)[1].

Employee referrals are used by 67% of small businesses, 75% of businesses with between 51 and 100 employees and 69% of medium-sized businesses with between 101 and 150 employees. They seem to be especially important in small firms, since the directors of large firms seem to be less ready to accept suggestions from their workers regarding recruitment. Since selection tools are largely unknown in small businesses, referrals from employees whose performance and attitudes are satisfactory give good results, especially where they help reduce the uncertainty resulting from the recruitment of new employees.

---

1   The rank obtained by nine recruitment sources (internal and external), based on the frequency of use of HRM practices as measured on a four-point Likert scale: from 1 (never used) to 4 (always used).

External sources and methods. The external methods, among the most used by businesses in general[2], that are encountered most frequently in small businesses are spontaneous applications (walk-ins), newspaper advertising and the personal contacts of the owner (Table 11.5). Public and private employment agencies constitute a second, less frequently used option, followed by educational institutions (cooperative programs, placement schemes, on-campus recruiting) and the placement services of professional or union organizations (McEvoy, 1984; Le Louarn and Thériault, 1984; Benoit and Rousseau, 1993). Lastly, small businesses with less than 50 employees rarely call on outside assistance for recruiting (Mahé et al., 1985).

---

2   This observation is partially contradicted (5th and 9th place) by the results of Deshpande and Golhar (1994).

Table 11.5
Sources of recruitment used by small businesses
(major trends observed)

Business size	Very small	Small	Small to medium	Medium to large	Large
Employee referrals	40-75 %	45-75 %	50-75 %	50-80 %	30-55 %
Spontaneous (walk-ins)	35-60 %	45-65 %	50-65 %	60-70 %	75-80 %
Newspaper advertising	25-50 %	30-60 %	50-65 %	40-70 %	70 %
Transfers and promotions			35-50 %		
Former employees			30-45 %		
Government employment agencies	20-40 %	20-35 %	25-50 %	30-45 %	25-40 %
Educational institutions	15-20 %	20-25 %	20-35 %	25-40 %	30-45 %
Private employment agencies	10-20 %	15-25 %	20-25 %	25-30 %	30 %

344

However, Hornsby and Kuratko (1990) add a level of nuance by stating that, in general, small businesses use a wider range of recruiting methods than might otherwise be thought, although very small businesses tend to rely on the least costly options, a result recently confirmed by Deshpande and Golhar (1994).

Selection

Selection techniques. As shown in Table 11.6, most research into selection techniques in small businesses reveals a heavy reliance on three main tools: interviews, job application forms (less evident in very small businesses) and resumes. Other selection techniques seem less common, although their use increases with organizational size: practical aptitude tests, psychological tests, weighted job application forms, etc. In small firms, the owner-manager has a clear idea of what kind of resources are needed and generally makes a selection from a limited number of candidates. As an organization develops, though, the number and the complexity of positions grows rapidly and the selection process, correspondingly more complex, is systematically delegated to a lower-ranking manager.

Over 80% of small businesses produce their own job application forms or analyze resumes, and the proportion increases with business size, ranging from 75% to 85% in very small businesses to 95% to 100% in medium-sized firms. In addition, over 90% of small businesses follow up with selection interviews, a percentage that remains constant for all sizes of business (McEvoy, 1984; Mahé et al., 1985; Hornsby and Kuratko, 1990; Deshpande and Golhar, 1994). In small and large firms, individual interviews are the norm (50%), whereas in medium-sized firms, both individual and committee interviews seem to be the most prevalent. Interviews are a little less structured in small businesses, where 54% are semi-structured in firms with less than 249 employees, and the number of interviews per person, one or two, is constant.

References. Almost 80% of small businesses require letters of reference (Table 11.6). Overall, the results obtained in the US and Quebec seem to point to an increasing use of references by small businesses; a percentage of between 56% and 74% was reported by Baker in 1955, followed by 71% to 75% (Le Louarn and Thériault, 1984) and 90% to 100% (Hornsby and Kuratko, 1990). The latter study showed that 90% of small businesses check the references supplied by job applicants, increasing to 100% in firms with between 51 and 100 employees and 98% in firms with between 101 and 150 employees. References are required in most cases, but are checked in only 50% of the businesses surveyed (Benoit and Rousseau, 1993).

Table 11.6
Types of selection used by small businesses
(major trends observed)

Category	Item		%	Trend
Examination of applications	job application form		70 - 100 %	↗
	resume		over 80 %	↗
	references:	required	over 80 %	↗
		checked occasionally	50 - 70 %	
		systematically	25 - 40 %	
Interviews	carried out systematically		85 - 100 %	↗
	type:	individual	35 - 50 %	↗
		committee	20 - 30 %	↗
		individual and committee	25 - 45 %	↗
		semi-structured	35 - 55 %	↗
		free/structured	25 - 40 %	↗
	average number: 1 or 2 per candidate		70 - 75 %	
	number of interviews per position		4 to 5 in SB / over 6 in LB	
Tests	medical examination (physical)		10 - 70 %	↗
	aptitude tests/simulation		25 - 45 %	↗
	intelligence/mental skills		20 - 40 %	
	personality		15 - 30 %	
	interests		10 - 20 %	
	drug use		less than 25 %	↗

Tests and validation. The use of tests as part of the selection process varies slightly according to business size (Le Louarn and Thériault, 1984; Thacker and Cattaneo, 1987). Tests are most prevalent in medium-sized firms with over 100 employees, since they are a selection tool that small businesses cannot afford (Hornsby and Kuratko, 1990)[3]. Overall, as shown in Table 11.6, roughly one quarter of small and medium-sized businesses use selection tests. Medical examinations (physicals), practical simulations and probation periods seem to be used by most respondents. Other possibilities, less frequently encountered, include (in decreasing order of use) intelligence, aptitude and mental skills tests, certain psychological tests, such as personality tests or personal interest tests, drug-detection tests and, lastly, appraisal centres (less than 20%) and lie-detector tests.

Other studies show that one-third of small businesses use no tests at all during the selection process. Even though 66% of respondents use some form of test, it is disconcerting to discover how little knowledge they have about validation: between 40% and 52% of respondents have never heard of the three types of validity (content validity, concomitant validity and predictive validity). Most use selection techniques without verifying validity (Thacker and Cattaneo, 1987). Once again, Deshpande and Golhar (1994) throw new light on the data with the finding that 51% of the small businesses surveyed used probation periods, compared to 29% of large corporations.

Discrimination in selection. The question of discrimination in small businesses mainly involves recruiting and selection procedures, and many irregularities can be observed in job application forms (Halatin et al., 1985). Analysis has shown that 20.7% of respondents use forms containing no "illegal" questions, but that 79% of forms include one or more poorly-phrased questions. In fact, small businesses routinely and constantly use illegal questions or use them in a discriminatory manner, probably through lack of experience or interest. The forms they use are often obtained from business form or office equipment suppliers on the understanding that they comply with legislative and regulatory requirements which, unfortunately, is not always the case. The checking of references, too, remains largely subjective and can sometimes lead to lawsuits for libel, especially in North America (Fenton and Lawrimore, 1992). Small businesses should, therefore, draw up a list of all potentially discriminatory elements and either eliminate them, redraft

---

3   Partially contradicted by Deshpande and Golhar (1994): the tests were used by 41% of small businesses and 33% of large corporations.

them in compliance with the appropriate regulations, or make answering them voluntary.

Decision-making and responsibility for selection. In small businesses responsibility seems to be centred on the owner-manager, both for routine selection activities and final hiring decisions, and in medium-sized businesses, on supervisors who carry out initial and final interviews. Small businesses assign more responsibility to the directors of their personnel services, where they exist, but the sharing of responsibility is often at an extremely low level because the hierarchical structure is less complex. The larger the firm, the more likely responsibility for final hiring decisions will pass from the owner or director to the supervisor or director of the personnel service, partly linked to business size (Le Louarn and Thériault, 1984).

Difficulties connected with the recruitment and selection process. Almost all small businesses experience difficulty in recruiting qualified workers, and the situation is compounded by a high turnover of staff which seems to be a point neglected by entrepreneurs (Mahé et al., 1985; Benoit and Rousseau, 1993). In fact, few firms have sufficient internal expertise in management, and this weakness constitutes a handicap in attracting and maintaining qualified workers (Deshpande and Golhar, 1994).

Larrivée and d'Amboise (1989) partially confirm these observations, stating that roughly 33% of entrepreneurs believe that their difficulties will continue for five years. The authors point to some contributing factors: the inability to pay high salaries (45%), the small size of the firm (34%) and its location (32%). External factors also cause recruiting problems: inadequate educational programs (49%), the weakness of the industrial sector concerned (45% and the impact of the general economic situation (35%). To reduce or eliminate recruiting difficulties, 75% of small businesses suggest that production planning should be improved, 59% that on-the-job training should be better adapted, 59% that formal manpower planning is needed, 45% that overtime should be increased, 23% that subcontracting is necessary, and 22% that better contacts should be maintained with schools.

Similarly, Laroche (1989) states that recruiting difficulties are the main HR problem experienced by small businesses, reporting that these firms face a clear structural problem: the difficulty of recruiting a qualified workforce, connected with the working environment and conditions offered, is a major concern for many small businesses and handicaps their development considerably. According to Laroche, small business leaders should examine their own shortcomings rather than automatically pointing to educational institutions and the non-availability of workers, as they have long tended to do. They should, for example, examine the quality of the jobs they have to offer and the associated working conditions.

Effectiveness of the recruiting and selection process. Few employers assess the relative worth of the various sources of recruitment used (Le Louarn and Thériault, 1984; Mahé et al., 1985), although the frequency of appraisal increases with business size. Hornsby and Kuratko (1990), as shown in Table 11.7, have found that the three most effective methods of recruitment used by small businesses are employee recommendations, newspaper advertising and spontaneous job applications, and that the least effective are government employment agencies and radio.

Table 11.7
Average effectiveness of recruitment sources for small businesses*

Employee referrals	3.37
Newspaper adverts	3.11
Walk-ins	3.05
Private employment agencies	2.94
Government employment agencies	2.76
Radio	2.58

*   Average effectiveness of HRM practices based on the perception of small business owner-managers recorded by a five-point Likert scale: from 1 (not at all effective) to 5 (extremely effective).

Hornsby and Kuratko go on to state that interviews and job application forms are far more effective than selection tests, and show that tests are, in fact, the least effective tool in the selection process (Table 11.8). Although their effectiveness increases substantially with business size, ranging from 2.61 to 2.81 and 2.99, it is surpassed by other methods (which have effectiveness ratings of 4.00, 4.04 and 4.15 in small, medium and large firms, respectively). However, although tests are used less frequently, they increase the effectiveness of the selection process and act as a useful complement to traditional interviews (Thacker and Cattaneo, 1987; Deshpande and Golhar, 1994).

Table 11.8
Average effectiveness of selection methods used by small businesses*

Interviews	4.60
Application forms	3.89
Reference checks	3.70
Intelligence and aptitude tests	3.05
Psychological tests	2.72
Drug tests	2.65

* *Ibidem.*

Induction

The last stage in the recruitment and selection process often receives little attention in small businesses. Although induction policies are not totally absent, they generally consist in lightweight methods or procedures (Mahé et al., 1985). In some small businesses, induction seems to be relatively systematic, depending on business size, with slightly higher rates in larger firms. Induction and integration can be summarized as follows: a tour of the business, a systematic program spread over time, an induction booklet, and coaching in firms of 50 employees or more. A large proportion of small businesses leave supervisors with the task of introducing new workers to their colleagues at the work site, sometimes accompanied with an explanation of various rules and products and, to a lesser extent, sometimes provide help in the form of a formal induction of the new worker. Very small firms use coaching by a coworker more often (Amba-Rao and Pendse, 1985; Benoit and Rousseau, 1993). In France, a majority of small businesses see no systematic need for the implementation of a formal induction program (Mahé et al., 1985).

4.4 Compensation and fringe benefits

Compensation

After recruiting its personnel, every organization must provide adequate compensation for the human resources it has acquired on an increasingly competitive market. Businesses large and small must comply with the prevailing standards in the country, region and sector of activity concerned. In contrast to other areas of HRM which can, in practice, be neglected by small businesses, no exceptions are permitted in the area of compensation: every employer must remunerate workers in return for the work they accomplish.

The perceptions of the directors and personnel managers of small and medium-sized businesses, concerning the relative importance they foresee for management and HR practices, shows that compensation and fringe benefits are given priority (arriving in 1st and 3rd position), especially in small businesses (Hornsby and Kuratko, 1990). Small firms must conserve a comparative advantage over their competitors in order to attract qualified workers or to satisfy needs that are not met in large corporations. However, small businesses must take one major constraint into consideration: their compensation schedules must always remain within the limits of their financial capacity. Each firm must have the actual capacity to pay its employees what it intends to pay them, and since its financial means are often limited, the owner-manager must always make a thorough analysis of the situation before making promises that cannot, in the long run, be kept.

Fay and Maurer (1986) underline the importance of maintaining absolute fairness in questions of compensation. Employees unfailingly compare their wages with those of their colleagues and friends in similar or different positions both inside and outside the organization. This comparison determines their perception of the equity of their own situation: external equity as compared to similar positions in other firms; internal equity as compared to other positions within the organization; and individual equity as compared to other employees holding the same position within the organization.

Unfortunately, in the first years of activity of a small business, the questions of staffing and compensation seem to be of little concern to entrepreneurs. This neglect often results in the departure of qualified personnel as soon as the firm has found its niche in the market, since it is easy for competitors to entice badly-paid workers away (Neiswander et al., 1987).

In France, the whole question of compensation and fringe benefits within small businesses is veiled in secrecy. Few firms are unionized, and the main claims of the unions in those that are concern, first, wages, followed by fringe benefits, which do not seem to constitute a priority for the labour movement in France. However, it would seem that premiums and various benefits are almost always offered to managers and employees in small French businesses, although they lag behind large corporations in the area of wages and employment conditions in general despite considerable effort in this direction (Mahé et al., 1985).

Decisions and responsibilities for compensation. Little data exists on compensation policies within small businesses, which often remain the private preserve of the owner-manager, although, as the business grows and administrative tasks are delegated, wage procedures often become more formalized (Benoit and Rousseau, 1993). More small businesses apparently use written compensation policies than other HRM practices (57%: Astrachan and Kolenko, 1994), and business size, especially in unionized firms, also seems to be a factor. The use of forms by small businesses for compensation-related tasks seems to be restricted, although they are generally found in unionized firms and firms with over 150 employees. Lastly, responsibility for compensation-related activities varies according to the type of task and the sector of activity. The drawing up of pay scales and overall compensation levels are the responsibility of the owner-manager, whereas responsibility for pay and personnel records is almost entirely delegated to different employees (Little, 1986).

Salary determination. Little use seems to be made of the various methods and tools available for fixing salaries (Mealiea and Lee, 1980), since only job analysis, salary scales and surveys are reported. According to Amba-Rao and Pendse (1985), small businesses should make their competitive advantage in terms of salary levels (where that is the case) better known among employees, using local information networks on salaries and employment conditions (magazines, employment centres, advertisements). In this way the various small businesses in a given sector can work to harmonize their wage levels and facilitate the fixing of their own salary levels.

Small businesses often fix their basic salaries using informal criteria. Firms with 500 or more employees are more prone to using formal salary surveys than smaller firms. The biggest users of directed surveys are firms with between 250 and 499 employees. Regarding job assessments, large corporations use formal methods, and firms with less than 250 employees use informal assessment (Thériault, 1986). However, certain small businesses use a wide range of methods, the most common being market rates, seniority, job requirements, performance assessment and the minimum legal wage.

A recent study by Deshpande and Golhar (1994) has produced some interesting results. In comparing small and medium-sized firms with large corporations, they place performance-based compensation in fourth place for small businesses, compared to second place for large corporations, with an average rating[4] of 3.53 and 3.76. Similarly,

---

4   Ranked among 17 HRM practices, based on the importance assigned by managers to each practice, measured on a five-point Likert scale from 1 (not important) to 5 (very important).

maintaining competitive salaries is ranked in fifth and third place (3.47 and 3.71), while skills-based compensation - an unprecedented finding among the studies surveyed - ranked seventh in small businesses and tenth in large corporations (3.31 and 2.76). Unsurprisingly, compensation based strictly on seniority ranked fourteenth in both cases, with minimal importance (2.30 and 2.10).

Job assessments. Job assessments for salary-fixing purposes are infrequent: 18% of respondents use some kind of job assessment system. It is extremely rare in very small businesses, occurring in between 3% and 20%; infrequent in small businesses (15% to 46%) and in medium-sized businesses (12% to 47%), and more common in medium sized businesses with 150 or more employees (between 27% and 60%; Hornsby and Kuratko, 1990). Small businesses do not use the conventional methods generally established in large corporations, except the traditional market-based points system. This practice appears to be widespread and is even a matter of little concern for directors, who often use a reactive approach in connection with compensation. Only one-third of respondents used some kind of job assessment method for internal job comparisons (equity) (McEvoy, 1984).

Wage surveys. Other methods are, however, used to fix salaries. The use of wage surveys increases with business size, and actually doubles. However, almost 50% of respondents use no wage surveys at all, either because they are not aware of them, because they feel no need to use them because of the size of their business, because they do not feel able to use them properly despite their availability or, lastly, because they do not consider them useful for as long as they are able to find qualified workers with no difficulty (Amba-Rao and Pendse, 1985). McEvoy (1984) reports a strong reliance on informal methods, since only 29% of his respondents carried out formal wage surveys of the markets concerned.

Modes of compensation. The sophisticated programs and systems used in large corporations require the presence of full-time specialists in the field of compensation. Small businesses, obviously, do not need the same level of administrative support since wage surveys and compensation management can be carried out at little cost. The basic services can be expanded as the business grows.

Salary increases. Salary increases can be calculated in various ways, but the operation need not necessarily take the form of straight wage increases, since other possibilities relating to work incentives and organization exist. Thériault (1986) has observed that there seems to be no significant difference between organizations of various sizes as regards the choice of criteria for salary increases, which include rises in the cost of living, the financial health of the business and comparative conditions on the market. As regards individual salary increases, the results of formal assessments of performance are more likely to be taken into account in large corporations, whereas in smaller firms the consumer price index and years of service take precedence. Responsibility for decisions on wage increases, in small businesses, lies with the owner-manager or the board of directors (or the equivalent).

Incentives and bonuses. As shown in Table 11.9, the compensation of employees and managers is not limited to their salaries alone. Firms of all sizes are increasingly using more sophisticated forms of compensation that allow them to differentiate, individualize and improve compensation levels in a competitive market. These new trends have led to the emergence of various types of performance incentives, bonuses for management and productions activities, and profit-sharing schemes. In many cases such payments represent more than 30% of the pay of senior managers. These incentives, formerly offered mainly to sales and production staff, now form part of most compensation schemes for all categories of managers, and in the last ten years a growing number of unionized and non-unionized employees have also been offered such programs.

Table 11.9
Incentive and bonus schemes offered by small businesses
(major trends observed)

	Average effectiveness (out of 5)	↗ ↗ ↗	↗ ↗
Bonus schemes			
Individual bonus	4.06	25 - 45 %	
Commission	4.15	25 - 55 %	
Performance bonus	•	30 - 40 %	
Group bonus	•	30 - 40 %	
Piece-work bonus	2.64	less than 15 %	less than 15 %
Incentive schemes			
Profit-sharing	3.51	less than 20 %	10 to 30 %
Shareholding	2.49	less than 10 %	
Compared to fixed hourly rates	3.90	10 to 15 %	

A clear increase in employee satisfaction can be observed after the implementation of an employee profit-sharing scheme (Christiansen, 1980). In addition, profit-sharing and performance-related bonuses develop productivity and a sense of responsibility among employees (Neiswander *et al.*, 1987). Furthermore, Mahé et al. (1985) report that bonus schemes, premiums and various benefits are offered by 77% of respondents in various forms, even though, in France, profit-sharing schemes are optional for small businesses with less than 100 employees.

A clear link can thus be observed in France between incentive schemes and worker participation in the management of the business, in contrast to North America and Great Britain where such schemes are a form of extended compensation, often used to attract or maintain qualified workers or dynamic managers (Shaw and Lang, 1985). Thériault (1986) also provides some interesting material concerning small businesses.

1. In very small and small businesses, bonuses are unusual and generally amount to less than $50, an amount that increases rapidly with business size. However, bonuses are uncommon, whatever the size of the business, and the limited sample available does not allow any significant conclusions to be drawn.

2. Schemes to share the results of increased productivity are also uncommon, whatever the business size.

3. Individual bonus schemes appear to be more common in small businesses with less than 100 employees and are related to individual performance, besides several other differences compared to the formulae used to determine bonuses in small businesses: they are almost always paid in cash (over 90%); they cannot be transferred or postponed; and they quickly reach a ceiling in small and medium-sized businesses.

4. Profit-sharing schemes are slightly more common in small and medium-sized businesses, and are often based on pre-tax profits. In addition, individual payments are essentially based on an individual's rank, status and salary; profit-sharing takes the form of cash bonuses, whatever the business size; the bonus generally amounts to less than 10% of an individual's salary in small and medium-sized businesses; and the postponement of payments seems more widespread.

5. Long-term maintenance schemes seem to be directly related to business size; they are uncommon in small and medium-sized businesses and fairly common in very large corporations; they generally take the form of share-purchasing schemes, for which several companies even provide financial assistance.

Once again, the results of Deshpande and Golhar (1994) provide additional information on the importance and effectiveness of incentive and profit-sharing schemes. Group incentive schemes are found in 13th and 12th position, respectively (2.42 for small and medium-sized businesses and 2.38 for large corporations)[5], whereas individual programs are found in last place. Profit-sharing schemes come in 11th and 14th, and are more common in small and medium-sized businesses (2.68 and 2.10).

Fringe benefits
Over the last ten years, businesses have had to redirect their compensation strategies towards more flexible, indirect means for a number of reasons, ranging from government controls to reduce inflation to increasingly stringent fiscal measures for all salary-earners. Fringe benefits are often designed to personalize the compensation of qualified workers to counter the manoeuvres of other firms competing to attract the same employees. Small businesses, too, have joined the movement to set up diversified programs: basic benefits, official fringe benefits (paid in cash or in time; immediate or postponed), close fringe benefits (often non-cash) and far fringe benefits (complementary and statutory). The administration of benefits has gradually become a highly complex task.

Overall, most businesses use fringe benefits, but the way in which they are applied and the limits of each scheme vary randomly according to business size, although several trends are apparent. As shown in Table 11.10, the most common benefits are paid holidays, leave and breaks, life and health insurance and pension plans, the latter benefit offered by 50% of respondents (McEvoy, 1984). In the US, fringe benefits represent 9% of the total compensation paid by small businesses and 13.2% of the total compensation paid by firms with over 100 employees, with an average of 11% (Sutton, 1986). Business size is a preponderant factor in the type of fringe benefits offered to employees, since a large number of differences can be observed between the insurance coverage and pension plans offered by small businesses and large corporations. Firms with less than 100 employees seem to offer their personnel a minimum of benefits.

---

5   See note 3.

Table 11.10
Fringe benefits offered by small businesses
(major trends observed)

Category	Benefit		Trend
Paid leave	Paid holidays	75 - 100 %	↗
	Social leave	85 - 90 %	↗
	Paid leave of absence	55 - 85 %	↗
	Sick leave (less frequent in workshops)	20 - 70 %	↗
	Mobile leave	25 - 30 %	↗
Insurance	Health insurance	70 - 100 %	↗
	Life insurance	50 - 95 %	↗
	Health insurance (family coverage)	50 - 90 %	↗
	Group insurance	45 - 90 %	↗
	Long-term disability insurance	40 - 90 %	↗
	Short-term invalidity insurance	35 - 90 %	↗
	Life insurance (family coverage)	25 - 55 %	↗
	Dental insurance	15 - 70 %	↗
	Vision insurance	5 - 40 %	↕
Pension plans	Very small businesses (0-19)	5 - 20 %	
	Small businesses (20-99)	15 - 50 %	
	Medium-sized businesses (100-249)	25 - 60 %	↗
	Medium to large businesses (250-500)	25 - 55 %	↗
	Large businesses (500 +)	45 - 65 %	
	Redundancy pay	5 - 20 %	
Main complementary benefits	Parking	55 - 70 %	↗
	Tuition fees for employees	40 - 85 %	↗
	Reduced-price products or services	40 - 60 %	↗
	Paid conventions and seminars	20 - 40 %	
	Extra maternity leave	15 - 50 %	
	Professional dues	20 - 35 %	
	Savings plan	10 - 30 %	
	Savings fund	average 20 %	
	... over twenty other benefits	average 15 %	↗
		less than 30 %	
		less than 20 %	↕

No significant difference can be detected as regards life insurance, although there is a slight but direct link with business size (Table 11.10). Premiums for short-term invalidity insurance are paid in a greater proportion by very large corporations than by smaller firms. These schemes are generally insured, meaning that benefits are paid by an insurance company rather than by the employer. There is a close link between dental insurance and business size: less than 30% of small businesses offer dental insurance, compared to 76% of firms with over 1,000 employees. Vision insurance (Table 11.10) presents only insignificant differences. A whole range of other benefits can also be observed, proving that there are no limits on the types of products and services that can be offered to employees and managers, whatever the size of a business or its sector of activity (Thériault, 1986).

The firms offering no fringe benefits are often more recently-established, smaller, employ more part-time staff and work in retail sales and services (Bagby, 1987). In addition, small businesses restrict the number of benefits offered to their staff. Hornsby and Kuratko (1990) stress the significant direct link existing between business size and the complexity of the of benefits offered. The differences are especially apparent when small and medium-sized firms and firms from two different sectors are compared. Manufacturing firms offer a better selection of fringe benefits as business size increases, and firms working in the retail sector and wholesale distribution of goods and services appear to be the least generous.

Management compensation in small businesses. Small businesses have, in the last ten years, had to compete increasingly with large corporations in the hunt for managers and executive officers. Successful recruiting depends on the intrinsic and extrinsic value of the compensation offered, and most studies report a relatively diverse array of compensation plans for small business managers and executive officers. Their compensation, in fact, differs little from that of their colleagues in large corporations, except perhaps concerning the range of items available and the actual monetary value of their salary. The small businesses that feel unable to match the offers of large corporations generally invoke the fact that small businesses do not generate enough money to offer the same benefits, that they cannot provide the same opportunities for promotion, and that their jobs do not involve the same kind of large-scale responsibilities for large numbers of individuals that justify a high salary. However, the existence of specific, deeper motivations among the executive officers of small businesses has been noted, and they often outweigh the attraction of money and thus compensate the pay gap (Bacon, 1970; Shaw and Lang, 1985).

It appears that, overall, small business salaries are between 30% and 40% lower than the salaries offered by large corporations. The gap narrows with business size, but even so remains at 25% for small businesses, 15% to 20% for medium-sized businesses and 10% for moderately large businesses, not to mention the considerable differences observed between countries. The employees of small German businesses, for example, whether white- or blue-collar, male or female, earn less on average than their big business colleagues, and the increase in average income in West Germany between 1981 and 1985 clearly demonstrated the existence of a direct link between business size and a gap in compensation between small firms and large corporations (Wassermann, 1989).

More finely-focused studies, however, such as that by the International Labour Office (1992), allow certain adjustments to be made to this widely-held belief. Most comparisons have been carried out regardless of industrial sector, location and non-monetary benefits. The salary of employees in the textiles and garment sector cannot be compared to that of workers in the pulp and paper or petroleum products industry. The salary gap between the employees of large and small firms in the same sector, such as footwear, is in fact much smaller. Similarly, the salaries paid by small firms in outlying regions, where many such firms often exist, are below those paid by large city-based corporations; but other costs, such as housing, for example, are also lower. In many small businesses, employees are authorized to use surplus materials, and even have access to equipment for their own use on weekends. Serious research is needed to go beyond simplistic generalizations and address the specific aspects of small businesses, as has been mentioned several times in preceding chapters. It must be remembered that all studies, as we shall see in section 4.7, seem to point to greater employee satisfaction in small businesses as compared to large corporations. This should be taken into account in drawing up a more appropriate set of questions concerning the considerable gap in compensation existing between small and large firms.

4.5   Personnel appraisal

It has often been assumed that the current practices of small business owner-managers do not include personnel appraisal. Research results tend to show that its application is, in fact, dependent on business size (Thériault and Le Louarn, 1984) and union status, as is the increased use of forms. Appraisal is generally carried out on an informal basis, mainly through observation of employees.

One-third of small businesses have written personnel appraisal policies, one-third have unwritten policies, and 28% have none at all (Benoit and Rousseau, 1993). Formal assessment procedures are found in only 30% to 50% of small businesses, and at least 25% rely solely on observations, although the data varies widely from sector to sector. Almost 50% of small businesses carry out periodic appraisals of performance, in a more formal manner (in writing) in only 20% to 25% of cases (Amba-Rao and Pendse, 1985). However, personnel monitoring and control seem to be carried out on a more systematic basis to improve worker motivation and improve management efficiency (Roger, 1985).

However, 71% of small US businesses have an appraisal system, and the national average can go as high as 95% (McEvoy, 1984). In the small family businesses studied by Astrachan and Kolenko (1994), 59% of respondents indicated that they had a formal, regular personnel appraisal procedure (for both family and non-family employees). This underlines, once again, the fundamentally heterogeneous nature of small businesses; several empirical studies provide data that differ greatly from the main trends observed in other sectors.

Appraisal objectives and content. Often confused, the objectives and content of appraisals are found in various forms in different businesses. Although the main goal of personnel appraisal is to provide data on the productivity of each employee in order to improve efficiency and increase the performance of the firm as a whole, it is more often than not used for a variety of purposes: selection, probation, compensation, training, development and discipline (Roger, 1985). In small businesses, appraisal is carried out in specific situations (production, discipline), and even in medium-sized businesses, it appears to be fairly informal, with a content centering on punctuality, absenteeism, discipline, compliance with orders, work quantity and quality, etc. In certain cases, managers and some other classes of employees (office and technical staff) are assessed formally; in a few rare cases, appraisal targets employee and communication development, as is most often the case in large corporations.

Assessors and responsibility for appraisal. In small and medium-sized businesses, responsibility for appraisal is seldom assigned to the director of personnel, but is generally undertaken by the owner-manager or supervisors. As businesses develop beyond the 25-employee mark, the responsibility passes from the owner-manager to the foreman or chief supervisor, as is the case in 74% of medium-sized businesses. Recently, the unanimous selection of supervisors as the automatic choice for assessor in all sizes of businesses (98% to 100%), and the importance of employees as assessors (25% in small and medium-sized businesses), have been pointed out (Thériault and Le Louarn, 1984; Roger, 1985). On the other hand, certain firms place greater faith in the personnel manager, who shares 25% of appraisal-related tasks with the owner-manager, although the latter retains almost 50% of the responsibility for appraisal (Mahé et al., 1985; Little, 1986).

Frequency of appraisal. The interval at which appraisals are carried out is somewhere between six months and one year. Overall, the larger the business, the longer the interval, which stretches to 10 to 12 months; in small businesses, it would appear to depend on individual preferences, underlining the greater informality of the appraisal process (Thériault and Le Louarn, 1984). The most popular intervals are one year (around 45%), six months (25% to 30%) and three months (10% to 12%). It should be noted that in a majority of "large" small businesses, appraisals are carried out yearly, and intervals of less than six months are rare (12% as compared with 28% in "small" small businesses) (Hornsby and Kuratko, 1990).

Appraisal methods and procedures. A certain similarity exists between the appraisal criteria used in small businesses and those used in larger firms, except for the subjective criteria (maturity, integrity, emotional stability, ambition, career interests) which seem to be used more often in firms with less than 249 employees, and the criteria reflecting a more formal approach to HRM, typical of large organizations (planning, organization, analytic and management skills, delegation, behaviour, punctuality). The other criteria used (objectives, knowledge, work quantity and quality, etc.) do not seem to depend on business size (Thériault and Le Louarn, 1984).

A wide variety of appraisal techniques are available, although small businesses tend to use four or five methods only, varying substantially according to business size. As shown in Table 11.11, the techniques used, from the most to the least common, are goal setting, narrative essays, critical incidents, ranking, and lastly rating scales and trait measurement, the other appraisal methods being observed only in large and very large corporations (Thériault and Le Louarn, 1984; Hornsby and Kuratko, 1990).

The lack of formal methods, or the lack of any kind of appraisal at all, can be traced to the tendency to discuss employees' performance openly with the employees themselves, an approach that appears to be well-established in small businesses (71%) and that decreases with size. Since, in smaller firms, individuals are closer to one another (in all the meanings of the word), appraisals are carried out through sometimes frequent informal discussions, and sometimes group discussions. In addition, appraisal methods vary according to the sector of activity.

362

Table 11.11
Personnel appraisal methods used in small businesses
(major trends observed)

All methods	Relative effectiveness	Moderately effective / Very effective	50 - 65 % / 30 %	
Most common in small businesses	Rating scales	•	35 - 65 %	↖
	Goal setting	4.03	30 - 65 %	↖
	Ranking	3.90	35 - 60 %	↖
	Narrative essays	3.90	20 - 65 %	↖
	Critical incidents	•	15 - 45 %	↗
	Trait measurement	•	25 - 35 %	↖
Least common in small businesses	Weighted scales		15 - 20 %	↖
	Compulsory choice		7 - 18 %	
	Various ranking techniques; paired comparison; seminars; forced distribution; others		(less than 10 %)	

363

Appraisal information and training. Information and training relating to personnel appraisals are not seen as important activities in HRM, depending on the frequency of programs and on program content. Such activities contain an element of difficulty that makes them less attractive to personnel managers; it is hard to make judgments about the manner in which other people carry out their tasks as trainers and assessors. In addition, training for assessors hardly exists at all in small businesses, and results vary widely according to business size. Where they exist, the preparation and implementation of appraisal training programs are almost exclusively the responsibility of the owner-manager of the firm concerned (62% to 69%), although they can be gradually delegated to inside and outside consultants (Thériault and Le Louarn, 1984).

Effectiveness of personnel appraisals. Only the few small businesses that possess a formal appraisal system actually manage their systems, and then only superficially; the effectiveness of the appraisal is verified mainly through informal discussions with the people concerned, and a majority of small businesses state that they are, in general, satisfied with the appraisal procedures (Thériault and Le Louarn, 1984). Most of the small businesses studied consider their appraisal procedures to be one of their most effective HRM practices, with effectiveness rates varying between 3.50 and 4.25 for various appraisal activities.

4.6   Training and development

The training and development of human resources constitute a fundamental HRM activity. Although in many cases such practices remain relatively informal, most businesses provide employees with the basic training needed to accomplish their tasks. Many small businesses rely on on-the-job training, and indeed even large corporations do not use formal, structured methods to the exclusion of all others. In North America, the link between business size and the implementation of policies is unclear, but the use of formal practices seems to be widespread in all business categories, although in small firms, workers have less access to training than in medium-sized or large firms.

1. Less than one-third of small businesses have a written training policy (Benoit and Rousseau, 1993), compared to 70% of firms with over 200 employees. In addition, a majority of the small businesses surveyed have no training procedures at all, and almost 50% have no procedures for human resource development.
2. Less than one quarter of small businesses have a human resource training and development plan, and the same number carry out planning in an intuitive manner.

3. It would appear that the new Quebec legislation requiring all businesses to devote at least 1% of their payroll to training, or to pay the equivalent amount into a training fund, will encourage firms to increase the resources they devote to this fundamental aspect of the fight to face international competition.

Training seems to be a matter of little concern for owner-managers (Lee, 1972; Ram, 1991), an observation contradicted by Garnier et al. (1991) who stress their interest in training programs and the results they produce. Neiswander et al. (1987) point out that only 17.6% of owner-managers attempt to improve the skill levels of their employees during the first years of their firms' existence. The relative future importance assigned by owner-managers and personnel managers in small businesses to training places it in fifth place, with a relatively low weighted score (Hornsby and Kuratko, 1990). On the other hand, Deshpande and Golhar (1994) underline the paramount importance of training for new employees, and their findings are in strong contrast to earlier observations, especially for small businesses (2: 3.72) and large corporations (4: 3.67)[6].

Since the early 1970s, almost all French businesses with 50 employees or more have implemented on-going training for all employees. The threshold was later reduced by ten employees, but seems to be relatively ineffective where small businesses are concerned since 20% provide no on-going training and 50% provide as little as possible while attempting to use up the related budget, an only slightly better solution. Most French firms have a training plan, a trend that increases with business size (Paumier and Gouadain, 1984), but professional training is generally merged with on-going training (Mahé et al., 1985).

Needs analysis, objectives and recipients of training and development. The first stage in the training process is generally the cornerstone of the training and development program. However, small businesses appear to neglect planning entirely, and often neglect to analyze their actual training needs, besides failing to define precise, verifiable objectives. However, several studies have shown that a real need for HRM training for new entrepreneurs exists (McEvoy, 1984; Malaise and De Keyser, 1988).

In several countries, associations of employers reduce the difficulties of recruiting qualified workers for small businesses by setting up vocational training programs, sometimes in collaboration with union organizations. However, owner-managers do not always understand the necessity for such programs, and complain about the lack of coordination

---

6   See note 3.

between the numerous government-sponsored courses and programs and the real needs of small businesses. Since training is governed by legislation in France, there is a strong interest in matters relating to needs analysis, the determination of objectives and the selection of trainees. An analysis of the transmission of information relating to training possibilities reports that it does not seem, overall, to be designed with small businesses in mind. Although widely available, it requires the assignment of personnel to collate mountains of paperwork, and does not reflect the concerns of management. Lastly, small firms receive fewer visits from training organizations, because they are considered to be less profitable targets than large corporations.

Rosanvallon (1990) reports a clear improvement in the ways in which knowledge is transmitted and acquired through internal placement schemes, whereas Hézard (1988) states that the diffusion of training objectives and activities is mainly the responsibility of Chambers of Commerce and Industry and, to a lesser extent, professional organizations. However, this deployment of efforts has only a moderate influence, since the influence exerted by training on employment is limited to a better adaptation of workers to their workstations or functions, in other words to an improvement in production rates.

Responsibility for training and development, and types of trainers. The assignment of responsibility for training depends mainly on the owner-manager, who often delegates the implementation of programs to a supervisor or outside organization (especially in France). In the North American context, there is only a weak link between responsibility for preparing on-the-job training and the size of the business: in most cases, trainers, or supervisors to a lesser extent, plan and develop their own training sessions within the business. The activities are delegated to an assistant (a manager or an administrative assistant) in 53% of cases, whereas owner-managers take responsibility in 34% of small businesses. These percentages vary considerably according to sectors of activity, especially as concerns the low rate of participation of personnel managers in construction firms (Little, 1986). Lastly, responsibility for on-going personnel training, as perceived by the company director, is assumed almost equally by employers and employees, since governments and unions are both seen as secondary in this contest (Benoit and Rousseau, 1993).

In France, responsibility for training and the types of trainers differ considerably from North American examples, especially because of legal constraints. Collaboration between employers and employees is far more developed, and outside players can often be observed; the larger the business, the more the determination of needs is carried out by heads of

366

departments, the director general or sometimes the director of personnel, and even, in some cases, by the training department or its coordinator. Lastly, outside training organizations, in France, represent a market that is currently undergoing change, mainly because of a reinforcement of traditional organizations, the wide range of public programs for employment and training assistance, and the strong development of private training-related assistance and counselling directed towards small businesses. Rosanvallon (1990) points to the development of made-to-measure courses designed specifically for small businesses, in contrast to "off the shelf" programs, and the growing overlapping and interpenetration of these aspects.

Methods and techniques. A wide array of training methods and techniques exist, but small businesses, both in France and North America, tend to rely on a limited number of approaches. In general, almost all small businesses carry out on-the-job training, and some also apply coaching by a coworker, group sessions, and outside training (Table 11.12). In all cases, the level of formality of these practices remains extremely low, even in small French businesses, since training is often organized on a one-off basis with no clear objectives and no prior analysis of needs.

Table 11.12
Training methods and techniques used in small businesses
(major trends observed)

	(on average)		(major study)
Internal:			
On-the-job	4,57	North America	30 - 75%
		France	96 - 100% informally
Coaching	4,17	North America	70 - 80%
Apprenticeship	3,36	North America	25 - 40%
Computer-aided instruction	2,55	North America	15 - 25%
In-house training		France	little used but increasing
Internal programmes		France	little used in small businesses
External:			
Lectures and seminars	3,44	North America	50 - 75%
		France	less than 15%
Educational institutions	•	North America	less than 5%
Equipment suppliers	•	France	30%
Government programmes	•	North America	less than 15%
Technical and professional organizations	•	North America	less than 5%
Conventions and symposiums	•	North America	20%
Private consultants	•	France	frequent for managers
External training	•		less than 5%

In the US and Quebec, all studies show a clear tendency for small businesses to rely on on-the-job training, with a direct link between business size and the use of various kinds of training. A low level of formality seems to have long been the rule, since in 1951, Baker had already reported it in a majority of small firms. McEvoy (1984) has collected even clearer data: 84% of respondents provided only on-the-job training, and only a few had formal internal or external training programs. Other studies have shown that 45% of the businesses surveyed provide internal training. Hoffman (1986) adds that personnel development should be based only on the qualifications and skills of individuals, and not on a system based on essentially subjective and biased criteria, as observed in certain small businesses.

Banks et al. (1987) present a more varied picture: they observed the existence of seven similar training methods, of differing scope and duration according to business size. Small firms could count on employers' associations, college courses lasting less than five days and in-house programs, whereas large corporations used the same techniques, but also college-level courses, training given within the firm by outside counsellors and professional technical staff within the appropriate sector of activity, and college courses lasting more than five days. Large corporations thus called on the full range of training methods.

Data collected in France does not show the same trends; training is mainly technical, with a strong reliance on on-the-job training, followed by training provided by suppliers, outside organizations and players, training courses, etc. Can this be traced to national standards, or to social andcultural preferences that favour values other than those observed in North American organizations? It must be remembered that small businesses traditionally offer on-the-job training, but without necessarily considering it to be an official training activity. Most of the data collected does not take on-the-job training, often the only kind provided in small businesses, into account. There are also major discrepancies between the formal elements that are declared and negotiated and actual expenditure (Rosanvallon, 1990).

Training topics. Unfortunately, very little information is available for an examination of the topics dealt with in training sessions in small businesses. The data as it stands provides an incomplete picture of reality, which seems to vary greatly depending on the country and culture concerned. Human relationships (communication, leadership) and general personnel management emerge as the most popular topics in the area of HRM training. However, sales, marketing and accounting are by far the most pressing concerns for entrepreneurs and, compared to other aspects of management, HRM comes at the bottom of the list. In the

North American context, the studies by Banks et al. (1987) and Deshpande and Golhar (1994) show no significant differences between small and large firms as regards the training needs stated by executive officers from all business sizes, whether group cohesion (9 and 7: 3.00 and 3.25) or the acquisition of quantitative skills (10 and 9; 2.85 and 2.80)[7].

In France, the most popular topics seem to be technical training (in connection with a profession or trade) and, to a lesser extent, sales, accounting, computer science and general culture (languages, mathematics, etc.). Certain management functions often seem to be reserved for outside consultants, such as marketing, finance and legal questions, perhaps because of the complexity of the commercial and regulatory environments in which French businesses function. Paradas (1993) corroborates these observations, stressing the fact that the main types of training taken by small business personnel are (by decreasing popularity) (1) the optimization of professional skills; (2) coherent professional training with no direct link to the position held; and (3), languages, general culture and, more rarely, complementary studies.

Evaluation, effectiveness and cost. With the exception of the work of Garnier et al. (1991), the evaluation of the results, effectiveness and costs of training activities have received less attention in North America than in France, where studies have been conducted to assess national regulations and programs. Even twenty years after the introduction of legislation, however, an important discrepancy between the demand for evaluation and the supply of methods subsists (Paradas, 1993). Any analysis of the positive results of training remains highly subjective and, even if the per capita costs are higher in small businesses they are little known (Benoît and Rousseau, 1993), since small businesses deliberately seek out the least costly activities. Most results assessment consists of simple observations or qualitative measures, occasionally quantitative measures, and rarely financial measures. The process remains largely informal, with a minimum of procedure and a few isolated observations in very small businesses where the manager is closer to the staff (Paradas, 1993). The small firms assign far less importance to training (30% and 42% less), whereas firms in the secondary sector carry out more training activities and retain their lead in the field. In medium-sized businesses, appraisal becomes more formal and resembles personnel appraisals with its quantitative and qualitative modes, forms and structured meetings. However, in small businesses it is hard to distinguish between evaluation of individuals (performance) and evaluation of training results. Hornsby

---

7   See note 3.

and Kuratko (1990) have shown, empirically, the effectiveness of on-the-job training (4.48 to 4.65) and coaching (4.09 to 4.25).

In general, training does not have a high impact in small North American businesses, but apparently has a considerable influence on the management and workforce qualification levels of small businesses in France, where inherent constraints of size and the omnipresence of owner-managers constitute important variables in the implementation and effectiveness of training activities. Training, in fact, seems to be the HRM practice the most affected by the overall set of contingency factors with an impact on small businesses (Jackson et al., 1989), since it is influenced by many internal and external factors. This situation means that small businesses that apply on-going and integrated training policies are apparently the most successful, and also the most active in other areas, whereas those that have an intermittent policy which are both less successful and less active (Paradas, 1993).

Difficulties related to training and human resource development. The managers of a business, whether it develops in a strongly regulated environment (France) or a more liberal one (Quebec, US), see training as a problem because they are torn between their objective of profitability and their need to maintain, and increase, their productivity and competitiveness. Concerns relating to training difficulties in small businesses are a recent development in North America, and have received little attention. The results reflect the lack of human and financial resources available for training, not to mention tradition and resistance to change which are deeply entrenched in the mentality of the owner-manager. The restricted range of training modes in small businesses can be linked to a lack of information about programs, in turn based on the choice of training providers and the habits and traditions of small businesses which tend to rely on the same provider and restrict themselves to the methods offered. In addition, it is possible that the training methods little used by small businesses are simply contrary to their selection criteria (subject, time, cost) (Banks et al., 1987).

In Quebec, Larrivée and d'Amboise (1989) have identified several constraints affecting personnel training in particular, including low availability of financial resources and the transfer of trained employees to larger firms. Sixty-five percent of small businesses admit to finding it difficult to organize training, because of lack of time or lack of the personnel needed to plan and organize activities, because of fluctuations in production or the difficulty of replacing workers undergoing training, or because of the excessive cost for firms with only a few employees in each type of position. Small businesses organize fewer training activities than medium-sized firms, which are more concerned with the issue but also experience the most problems in terms of organization (Benoit and Rousseau, 1993).

Measures stimulating training and development in small businesses. In view of the number of difficulties experienced in implementing training activities in small businesses, several authors have made recommendations or compiled empirical results bringing together successful solutions (Paradas, 1993). Fiscal incentives and government assistance seem to be the most popular with small businesses, closely followed by technical assistance and programs offered by organizations working in the field. Nevertheless, much remains to be done if entrepreneurs are to be persuaded to provide training. Almost no North American data has been compiled on this subject, except by Larrivée and d'Amboise (1989) who recommend school-based and factory-based training better adapted to the needs of small businesses and better planning for production operations. The objective of adapting training activities to the actual needs of small businesses means that educational technologies must also be adapted to the needs of the workforce (training and re-training). Managers must also be persuaded to become involved to the same extent as the education community, because the costs of deficient training can cancel out the benefits of higher production levels. Lastly, Malaise and De Keyser (1988) mention the need to take action to help and support businesses by making new entrepreneurs more aware of the issues, setting up advisory and specialist training organizations focusing on the creators of small businesses, training owner-managers in the main points of management, monitoring new small businesses during their start-up and growth phases, and providing information on access to public and private assistance.

4.7 Organization and participation

Few authors have, as yet, made an overall examination of work organization, working conditions and human resources communication and information practices in small businesses, and none has drawn a specific link between these questions and the contemporary issue of participatory management. The trend towards active employee participation is, in fact, a way of filling the void left by previous work organization methods (the scientific and technical approaches) which, by ignoring human factors, triggered a return to management methods providing greater employee gratification. The lack of concern in the "old" structures for human aspects has led to the emergence of psychosocial and socio-technical approaches which, in less than twenty years, have evolved into a set of participatory theories and methods often designed to re-establish balanced two-way dialogue. The link between traditional work organization and present-day participatory management is effected through the implementation of an information exchange network combined with multi-skilled, flexible work teams, and production methods based on the concept of the individual unit rather than the series (division of labour).

Work organization and working conditions. The jobs created by small businesses, in all countries, tend to be especially vulnerable because of the high mortality rate among small firms (although this rate can be deceptive, as discussed in Chapter 1). The pessimistic view of small business jobs is based on their vulnerability, making them highly precarious. However, this drawback to the jobs provided by small businesses is contradicted by the favourable descriptions of small firms as organizations in which working relationships are friendlier and less impersonal (Laroche, 1989).

Work organization is practically an independent discipline that covers a variety of approaches, methods and techniques that help to optimize productivity. The practices are generally less formal in small businesses where written procedures and policies are less common. However, the situation varies greatly from one business to another, with no significant links to business size, sector or location. There are also substantial differences connected with union status, and small businesses in which a collective agreement is in force are required to implement and apply certain more formal elements. This is not surprising in light of the fact that the first claims made by organized labour, in the mid-19th century, were to reduce arbitrary and abusive employer practices in the areas of work organization and working conditions. The situation also varies widely from country to country depending on the regulations adopted by their respective governments.

In France, these matters are subject to a number of standards and formal controls; the improvement of working conditions and worker information and participation are bound by a certain number of social, fiscal and organizational thresholds, although such legal obligations are often not complied with in medium-sized businesses. In Britain, small businesses typically have no control systems because of the informal and personal relationships that are generally of a higher quality and are more likely to lead to consensus than in large corporations.

Among the Mediterranean countries, Italy and Spain appear to favour an institutionalized form of laxity as regards legal and regulatory standards. Italian work legislation is restricted by a criterion of size that makes it inapplicable to businesses with less than 15 employees. The main rights of workers, and labour standards, are thus not complied with in a majority of very small businesses and trade concerns. Enterprise is seen as an extension of family life, out of bounds to the State.

Small Spanish businesses, at least those outside Catalonia, rely to a large extent on temporary or part-time labour, and black-market labour appears to be quite common. With regard to work organization and job security, the owner-directors of small businesses normally retain direct, personal control over their employees and offer little in the way of job security and promotion prospects, although large variations exists from sector to sector and region to region.

In addition, throughout industrialized countries, many large corporations have reduced their workforce in recent years, in particular following the introduction of computer technologies. In large corporations in which the workforce has increased, the new employees are mainly professional staff, and workers have been the hardest hit by job losses. These results show clearly that the negative impact of computer technologies has been felt less by the human resources of small businesses, where less job losses have occurred than in medium-sized and large firms, with wide variations according to job categories (Laroche, 1989).

Information, communication and participatory management. The first initiatives in the area of worker participation concerned the application of conditions of employment and reasonable working standards followed, in the 1950s, by the introduction of information and suggestion methods, and in the 1960s and 1970s, the first forms of bilateral communication and various attempts at participatory management. Since the beginning of the "energy crisis" (1973-75) an increase in participatory-type concerns has been observed, all based on healthy bilateral communication and an approach to work organization that is human, rather than machine, oriented. Against this background, strongly influenced by Japanese traditions in the areas of employment and production, "modern" HRM draws its inspiration from small work units to organize its practices along more personal, information-oriented, participatory and, for many workers, satisfying lines.

In small businesses, little research appears to have been carried out, whether in North America (Latona, 1979) or Europe (Nebenhaus, 1990; Bachelet, 1995), in the field of communication, information and participation. In fact, general trends rarely go beyond communication and suggestion systems, with a handful of descriptions of worker participation (Table 11.13). Entrepreneurs rely very little on participatory management for several reasons: some believe that the method applies only to large corporations which, alone, can assimilate it; others perceive it as requiring the services of an army of specialists that only a large corporation can support; and yet others see no need for it in their small business. Several dispersed efforts have been made, but mainly without any clear idea of the prior conditions needed and the results to be obtained, and without undertaking any major change in the organizational structure or in the behaviour of managers. The most frequent approach is that of informal communication with personnel, generally in the workplace or during breaks, followed closely by occasional meetings, organized social activities, the gathering of suggestions and full-scale meetings (Benoit and Rousseau, 1993).

Employer-employee relationships seem to be far more distant than shown by the results of earlier studies, partly because of a substantially higher staff turnover rate. This dysfunction could also be an indication of a difficult organizational climate, especially when employees have no channel for communicating as a group with the employer to air grievances. Incidentally, small business owner-managers often have a patronizing attitude towards labour relations and are unwilling to make any effort to formalize the communication and consultation process within their business (Callus et al., 1991). Few small businesses (30%) have regular formal communication mechanisms for individuals, and group communications are restricted to group meetings because of the narrow scope of the bilateral relationship (Gunnigle and Brady, 1984).

The situation in France provides a good illustration of the particularities of participatory informational processes in small businesses (Nebenhaus, 1990). Formalities are limited, except in meetings and employer-employee committees which sometimes take up a considerable portion of delegates' work time. Sophisticated participation models, such as quality circles, do not seem particularly popular, but information is circulated freely in most small businesses through natural or legally-required channels. Vertical employer-employee relationships are generally direct, with no or a reduced level of intermediate level of supervisors and middle managers. Internal communication seems to be of little concern to small business owner-managers, who do not consider it to be a factor in the performance and profitability of their business (Bachelet, 1995). Communications with staff seem to be generally informal and limited, since staff are involved in discussions using the consulting process to achieve goals of productivity and quality. Information circulates through a greater number of channels when there is a personnel manager, and there are more regular meetings on fixed dates; the main channels of communication are notice-boards, regular meetings and suggestion-making. Once again, the actual level of staff participation seems to be directly linked to business size (Mahé et al., 1985).

Table 11.13

Communication and participation methods used in small businesses
(major trends observed)

Category	Method	Percentage	Average
Informal methods	Direct contact with staff	90 - 100%	
	Rumours	25 - 30%	
	Direct gathering of opinions	30%	
Meetings	No meetings	55 - 60%	average: 57%
	Operational meetings	35 - 85%	average: 60%
	General meetings	15 - 75%	average: 46%
	As needed	40 - 50%	average: 45%
Documents	Notice boards	65 - 85%	average: 25%
	Bulletin, leaflet, in-house newsletter	10 - 55%	
	Circular	30 - 45%	
	Internal communications	35%	
	External communications	10%	... + in LB
	Brochures	10%	
	Welcome leaflet	7%	
	Audio-visual	40%	
	Electronic media	5 - 10%	
Suggestions	Ideas box, etc.	15 - 70%	average: 37%
Participation	Policy-making	45 - 85%	
	Organized social activities	70%	
	Cash bonus at meetings	70%	
	Business project	60%	
	Quality circles	10 - 60%	average: 32%
	Groups (self-expression, work, independent, etc.)	15 - 50%	average: 27%

These observations are contradicted directly in a study by Deshpande and Golhar (1994) which assigns first place to the wish of every employer to maintain an open line of communication with personnel, especially in small businesses (4.19), as compared to large corporations (3.90). Exchanges also extend to the implementation of projects to encourage staff participation, ranked sixth by businesses of all sizes (3.41 and 3.43). This evolution can also be seen in the importance assigned to collective responsibility, which shares eighth place and is more in evidence in small businesses (3.24) than in large corporations (2.18). Lastly, position rotations are ranked 12th and 11th, and are thus less prevalent in small businesses (2.65) than in large corporations (2.57). In short, this recent study shows unequivocally that, at least as far as North America is concerned, a substantial change in management methods has taken place to include closer collaboration between employers and employees, and that the trend is clearest in small businesses.

4.8   Workplace health and safety

Workplace health and safety (WHS) is a structured set of attitudes, activities and individual and collective programs involving the creation and maintenance of preventive and corrective measures in the workplace, in order to reduce accidents and physiological, physical or psychological injury among workers. WHS has, since the inception of HRM, constituted a major concern in most industrialized countries. The governments of almost all Western nations have legislated in this area to provide a minimum level of protection for individuals in the workplace. During the period when national programs were being implemented, WHS was one of the main priorities of union organizations and employers who took an interest in the well-being of their workforce. However, the level of interest seems to have declined in the last ten years whether in France, Quebec or the US.

It is clear that a high level of formality is imposed by government regulations, such as compulsory collective agreement clauses, preventive and WHS programs, human resource training, inspection mechanisms, the drafting of recommendations and the subsequent application of corrective measures, not to mention all the representative bodies required by government organizations (Scherer et al., 1993). All are elements that typical entrepreneurs see as a flagrant violation of their management prerogatives, a bureaucratic invasion of their flexible, user-friendly structures and, in extreme cases, as the loss of their autonomous, independent status. The relative importance of some practices is shown in Table 11.14.

Table 11.14
Workplace health and safety practices in small businesses
(major trends observed)

Workplace health and safety practices	Adequate rest facilities	70 - 80 %	average: 76 %	↗
	Healthy working conditions	55 - 80 %	average: 65 %	↗
	First aid available	45 - 90 %	average: 63 %	↗
	Fire prevention program	20 - 40 %	average: 27 %	↗
	Free safety clothing and equipment	10 - 50 %	average: 26 %	↗
	Accident prevention program	15 - 40 %	average: 23 %	↗
	Catering services	less than 25 %	average: 10 %	
	Periodic medical examinations	less than 20 %	average: 10 %	

Few businesses have formal programs or written prevention plans, although the latter are common when required by law. Most small firms have only one written document: the accident report, which is compulsory in all plans, and much more common as size and union presence increases. Berthelette and Planché (1995), in evaluative research examining the safety programs existing in 114 small businesses (plastics and rubber), observed that WHS information is usually transmitted verbally, and less than one-third of small firms actually distribute documents on the subject. These firms identify the risks in two ways: first, by observing work activities, and second, by consulting the workers. Moreover, the completeness of investigation subjects and the diversity of WHS information tools seems to increase with organization size, resulting in a substantial decrease in accident rates.

Owner-managers are responsible for WHS in over 40% of businesses, and the task is delegated to the head of HRM in a little over one quarter of businesses; the figures vary according to business size. In fact, the work of Berthelette and Planché (1995) reveals that 80% of the small firms analyzed centralized their WHS decisions at senior management level, entrusting all such decisions to a senior executive. They also pointed out that the small firms which use a middle manager or foreman seem to have lower accident rates than those which delegate to senior managers or employees. Thus, the most effective programs seem to result from decentralization of the prevention structure.

Berthelette and Planché (1995), more or less confirming the trends shown in Table 11.14, found that most of the firms studied had a WHS committee, even though 58% had less than 21 employees and three-quarters were not unionized. However, only 53% of the committees had decision-making powers, 47% had advisory powers, and only 17% of the small firms consulted had a prevention representative. The existence of a committee seemed to have an impact on the frequency - or disclosure? - of accidents in small firms, reducing the link between accident rates and organization size. In the same study, more than 50% of incidents were investigated, and accidents involving downtime tended to be investigated in more depth (74%). It is also interesting to note that 85% of the workers involved in the incidents carried out unchanging or repetitive tasks, and in 43% of cases the work rate was dictated by the machinery. The small firms in the study also seemed to favour interventions aimed at controlling worker behaviour, rather than introducing source eliminatory measures or preventive maintenance.

Unfortunately, most of the work on WHS in small firms shows that small businesses are often in a difficult situation, since cost, as a result of their limited resources, prevents them from complying with the obligations imposed by law. Special progressive and better-adapted provisions for training, prevention and management of WHS activities should be implemented (Malaise and De Keyser, 1988; Lasher and Grashof, 1993; Scherer et al., 1993).

Employee Support Programs
A number of medium-sized and larger firms, of all sizes and in all sectors, have introduced or are planning to introduce support programs for employees with personal problems caused by their working or outside environments (Audet et al., 1987). Nearly a quarter of the small firms studied by Amba-Rao and Pendse (1985) offered individual counselling services to all their employees. The situation seems to have improved significantly in the 1990s, especially by the provision of private outside services better-suited to small firms. Since the problems of stress, alcohol and substance abuse in the workplace are now of concern to a growing number of firms, solutions and measures better-suited to the small business context have become essential (Lasher and Grashof, 1993).

5. Contingency HRM analysis in small businesses

Human resource management can be seen as an open system interacting with the internal and external environment, and, like any management system, it is more or less strongly influenced by the set of factors that constitute those environments (Mahé de Boislandelle, 1994). A wide range of degrees of application of HRM practices can be observed in small businesses, depending on country, size, sector, entrepreneurial vision, economic situation, and so on. The differences are hard to analyze on a discriminatory basis, since the abundance of contingent variables imposes constraints on researchers that must be respected if unfounded or erroneous findings are to be avoided. Following previous worked devoted specifically (Mahé de Boislandelle, 1988) or not (Jackson et al., 1989) to small businesses, our intention here is use contingency theory to create a model designed, mainly, to integrate and articulate the various factors mentioned above that are likely to have a significant influence on HRM in small businesses. However, before describing the model in more detail, it is important to present an overview of the theoretical concepts and foundations underlying the concept of contingency and HRM in small businesses.

5.1 Conceptual foundations for a contingency model

Very few studies of HRM in small businesses have dealt with this question from a conceptual standpoint, which constitutes a major omission, even in a pre-paradigmatic discipline. It seems appropriate to fall back on the concept of formalization to understand and, perhaps, measure the evolution of various dimensions of HRM in the small business context. Several authors have observed a link between business size and the level of formalization of management practices, which appears to increase (in a non-linear relation) according to business size, with close ties to various internal and external variables, including the vision of the entrepreneur/owner-manager. We shall first examine the foundations for each concept.

Contingency. The contingency theory, as stated by Lawrence and Lorsch (1967), stipulates that no absolutes exist in management science, that a degree of relativity must be respected in the use of existing theories, and that, as a result, no one practice or method is applicable in all contexts. In schematic form, this model for the representation of an organization (internal factors) and its environment (external factors) is said to be "contingency-based" because it takes into account a multitude of factors that may have an effect on the organization and on its activities and functions, and other parameters. The specific characteristic of a contingency model is the ability to express the probability of an internal or external element having a direct or indirect influence on one or more components of the organization.

Formalization. Formalization is the degree to which policies, standards, rules, forms and specifications that have been established in an organization tend to be formal, rather than informal. A formalization process is generally initiated by managers and leads to the drawing up and implementation of a series of uniform rules and procedures to attain or maintain organizational objectives (Garand, 1993). This concept is very similar to the development concept discussed by various authors who have examined the evolution of HRM, and has gone through several different stages over the last one hundred years. This type of analysis has been carried out in several countries, in particular by Besseyre des Horts (1987) in France and by Bélanger (1990) in Quebec. A striking number of common trends can be observed in these studies.

First, HRM has become more complex. In its early days it addressed mainly basic questions such as staffing and compensation, and gradually integrated more diversified, extended and advanced practices such as career management and equality of access for various groups traditionally under-represented in the organization. Second, the role played by HRM as a service provided to first-level managers has gradually evolved as it has been included in other higher-level management functions, and is now integrated into the decision-making process. With the growth of small businesses, especially in terms of number of employees, the activities of the human resources function have become more structured and more sophisticated (often imperceptibly) until a genuine HRM service directed by a specialist emerges and finally becomes an integral part of the firm's strategic management process removed from the administrative aspects of mere personnel management (Fabi and Garand, 1989). Third, this evolution has not occurred at the same speed in all businesses, and some have remained at an embryonic stage of development.

Entrepreneurial vision. Planning and the perception of reality in an entrepreneurial approach seem to be guided by the vision of the entrepreneur. This vision is based on a unified overall understanding of, and reflection on, the market and market opportunities and resources, which generates a realistic, achievable dream (Filion, 1991). In a small business, the vision of the entrepreneur conditions the nature, complexity, diversity and degree of formalization of HRM within the business (Garand, 1993). Depending on individuals, the vision extends over a bidimensional continuum between operational and strategic poles. Between the two poles, an indefinite number of options are created by the flux between the two tendencies, leading to the emergence of various types of entrepreneurs as discussed in Chapter 5. This notion is clearly reflected in entrepreneurial activity during day-to-day actions that synergize with factors such as the goals of the enterprise.

Entrepreneurs thus tend to direct their personnel themselves for as long as possible, and worker loyalty depends on the entrepreneur's vision and choice of management practices, especially as they concern HRM. This approach evolves gradually towards a more defined structure comparable to that found in most organizations, but the rate and type of evolution depend largely on the entrepreneurial vision (Garand and Fabi, 1992). Although its influence tends to decrease as business size increases, the entrepreneurial vision remains fundamental and the early emergence of a human resources division appears to be closely linked to it. In businesses in which the owner-manager expressly favours human resource development in order to improve the working environment, productivity and profitability of the organization, a diversified, well-adapted range of HRM practices is frequently found. A "high vision" entrepreneur (GAP) acts as the initiator of and catalyst for the practices developed and implemented within a small business, by making collaborators aware of the fundamental need to manage human resources properly for both human and corporate reasons. On the other hand, a "low vision" entrepreneur does not define HRM as an organizational priority, preferring sales or a particular market niche, the opening of franchises in strategic locations or some other commercial element of the entrepreneurial vision. The human resource function, in such cases, is given a reduced role involving personnel administration activities: recruiting, compensation, administrative record-keeping and dismissals.

5.2   A contingency model for HRM in small businesses

It is an undisputed fact that all businesses operate in a contingency-related context in which the strategic elements linked to the development of the organization are placed in the foreground. This situation is accentuated for small businesses by the close proximity in which people work and the sensitivity of small environments to the constraints of the outside environment. In analyzing HRM in small businesses, almost all the empirical studies selected mention, explicitly or implicitly, the impact of one or more contingency factors that affect HRM practices as regards their presence within small businesses, their level of formalization and the implementation of their activities. Given the importance of these issues, we have carried out a systematic compilation of the contingency factors mentioned; their description and analysis constitutes one of the main results of our research, together with the development of a contingency-based model to illustrate the potential impact of internal and external factors on the nature, diversity and complexity of HRM practices.

The model (shown in Figure 11.1) incorporates, at its centre, the HRM practices listed in Table 11.1. Under the multi-dimensional influence of internal and external factors, the activities develop according to a level of formalization that can be assessed using a set of indicators located around the central block. The external factors include all the social and commercial factors, whereas the internal factors include the human and organizational factors. Each group of factors is divided up into principal factors according to the main trends observed in the handful of models previously published in this area and the results obtained in our compilations[8]. These contingency factors can be seen as the independent variables of the model, and form a conceptual basis for various empirical verifications to establish the links with the formalization indicators under the human resources function. The contingency factors probably, in fact, condition the whole set of "dependent variables", in other words the existence, development, level of formalization and extent of HRM practices.

We will now turn to a short examination of the interactions between the many contingency factors.

Internal factors. As a dynamic system, HRM appears to be fundamentally influenced by its internal environment, which can be subdivided into two groups of factors: human factors and organizational factors. The impact of these factors on HRM is shown in the model by the double direction of the right-angled arrows which emphasize the dynamic nature of the links between the various groups of internal factors and the dependent variables in the centre of the model. However, the practices themselves also have an indirect, even diffuse impact, illustrated by the outline arrows, on most of the internal factors by an increased effect, for example, on the vision of the actors, the personnel structure, the employer-employee relationship or the strategic decisions.

On the other hand, the level of HRM formalization will not have a major impact on the area of activity of the business, its production system or its type of strategy. The existence of a diffuse link, illustrated by the outline arrow linking the indicators to the "owner-manager", should be emphasized, since the latter conditions HRM within the business, although the impact of the level of HRM formalization on the entrepreneur seems to be indirect or, at least, spread over time.

---

8   More details are given in Garand (1993).

External factors. The external factors can be divided into two categories: commercial factors and social factors. The single direction of the black arrows illustrates that they have considerable influence not only on HRM but also on the business as a whole. On the other hand, we believe that the business, in general, has little impact on outside factors because of its size and limited resources. Small businesses can only influence their external environment through lobby groups that do their best to represent the wide range of interests of entrepreneurs, such as the Canadian Federation of Independent Business (CFIB), the *Confédération générale des PME* (Confederation of small and medium sized businesses) in France, and the National Federation of Independent Business (NFIB) in the US. Finally, the long dotted feedback line between the two groups of external factors illustrates the reciprocal nature of the on-going exchange between the commercial and social factors, closely linked in all contemporary economic, political and social systems.

5.3   Implementation of the model

The main advantage of the model is that it incorporates the set of variables that have a clear influence on the mechanisms governing the introduction and formalization of HRM practices in small businesses. Given the current state of knowledge, the model is obviously heuristic and requires more rigorous and sophisticated conceptual criticism and empirical verification. The empirical examination will require the preparation of a series of indicators that will sometimes be difficult to bring into operation, but the exercise will remain an important objective for researchers wishing to examine the question empirically in greater depth.

384

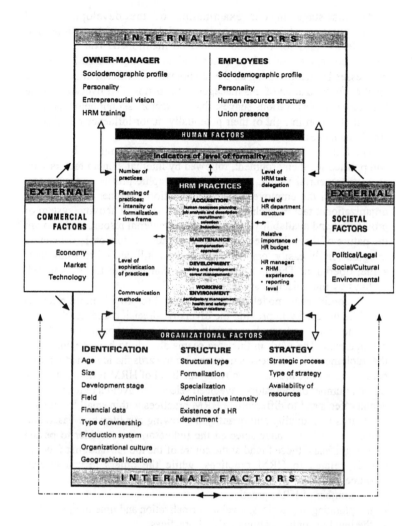

Figure 11.1
Contingency Model

At this stage in our examination of the development and implementation of the contingency model, some observations and possible avenues for research should be mentioned. The model can clearly contribute towards a better understanding of HRM in small businesses by incorporating all the factors with significant impact on the level of formalization of this management function. Our overview of the literature and observations suggest that the factors set out below deserve special attention in light of their potentially major influence on HRM in small businesses.

The first are the external factors such as the economic, technological and politico-legal environment, followed by internal, human factors such as entrepreneurial vision, the socio-demographic profile of the owner-manager and the employees, and unionization, together with internal, organizational factors such as business size, sector of activity, system of production and availability of financial and material resources. Although the nature of the influence of a number of these factors on HRM can be imagined fairly easily, empirical research is still needed to study their actual operation. This is a research area that has yet to be explored, perhaps by multidisciplinary teams.

The contingency model could also be used to provide more rigorous HRM diagnoses by improving the diversity, precision and flexibility of evaluation tools and could, eventually, lead to more appropriate styles of management. The work in this area seems already to have begun, since the implementation process is now turning towards the identification of a certain number of indicators showing the level of HRM formalization. A limited number of indicators have been selected to avoid a redundancy of actual effects and to differentiate HRM practices within small businesses as regards both quality and quantity. Following our literature-based and inductive work, we have selected the indicators we consider to be the most significant, those found at the centre of the model. The first four are mainly related to HRM practices, while the others reflect human resource structures within small businesses:
- the number of HRM practices;
- the planning of practices: level of formalization and time frame;
- the level of sophistication of HRM practices;
- the modes of communication used in the small business;
- the level of HRM task delegation;
- the structural type of the human resource service;
- the relative size of the human resource budget;
- the HRM experience and hierarchical level of the person responsible for human resources.

The complete set of indicators is not, however, confined to the above elements, which only represent some of the criteria which could be used to evaluate the level of formalization, the effectiveness and the quality of HRM practices within an organization[9]. Such a list can never claim to be exhaustive, but this first attempt to implement the concepts involved is intended to form a basis for future empirical research. On an experimental basis, we can suggest that such tools could be used to measure the dependent variable, namely the level of formalization of HRM in the small business context. The next step is to carry out the necessary work, possibly in collaboration with experts in other fields, to bring some of the independent variables, the contingency factors, up to an operational level comparable to that of the indicators relating to HRM. Only once this has been done will it be possible to increase the level of knowledge quite significantly and, as a consequence, the quality of human resource management practices in the specific context of small businesses.

6. Conclusion

The main objective of this critical overview of specialized literature was to answer the following questions:

- Which HRM practices are applied in small businesses, and to what extent?
- What are the main contingency factors having an impact on those practices and on their level of formalization?

In order to answer those questions satisfactorily, and to go beyond preconceived notions, opinions, perceptions and necessarily limited personal experiences, our diagnosis calls upon an analysis of international experience as found in empirical studies focusing on HRM practices in small businesses. To be included in our selection, a study had to meet certain criteria as to the academic status of the investigation, the composition of the sample and the use of at least one contingency factor in the interpretation of empirical findings. The analysis method was similar to content analysis, to the extent that the empirical data contained in the studies had already been classified into the significant units associated with HRM practices.

The results of this approach seem to support certain answers to the initial questions underlying the research. The HRM practices most often

---

9 An overview of these indicators is given in the proceedings of the CIFPME-Carthage convention, and the 94-04 GREPME research paper (Fabi, Garand and Pettersen, 1994).

applied in small businesses are recruitment, selection, compensation and administrative-type activities, together with discipline, which has not been discussed in this chapter since it is more of a labour relations issue. Other HRM practices are applied in small businesses discontinuously, depending on the objectives of the owner-manager, the internal and external constraints affecting the business and, in many cases, the presence of a union. Human resource planning, job analysis, personnel appraisal, training and all the activities linked to the work environment seem to be considerably more developed in unionized firms, and those of larger size.

Once this overview has been completed, other questions still remain or have been only partially answered. First, the diagnosis has to be explained more distinctly using a contingency-related approach to HRM practices. In operational terms,

- Which contingency factors can explain the current situation of HRM in small businesses?
- What is the nature and extent of their influence on HRM practices?

It is clear that the concept of contingency facilitates the understanding of the various levels of HRM formalization encountered in small businesses. The compilation and analysis of the contingency factors underlines the substantial impact of certain internal and external variables on the management process in small businesses, and suggests that some factors have a preponderant influence on the existence and formalization of HRM practices, especially:

- organization size;
- sector of activity;
- financial and material resources;
- organization strategies;
- socio-demographic profiles of the entrepreneur, managers and employees;
- entrepreneurial vision;
- union presence;
- production systems.

In general, the level of formalization of HRM practices can be seen to increase with business size, until a plateau is reached around the 400-600 employee mark. At this stage, most of the practices listed in Table 11.1 can be detected, under the supervision of a team of HRM professionals and in a more complex environment than that found in small and very small businesses. The formalization can be seen in the presence of certain elements that contribute to the development of a more complex overall organizational structure. As discussed in the previous section, several indicators allow the level of formalization of practices within a business to be assessed, regardless of the business size.

In order to make this conceptual approach more systematic, a contingency-related model was designed to incorporate and articulate the various contingency factors affecting HRM. An analysis of the empirical literature allows only a superficial, incomplete outline to be drawn. The resulting heuristic model is designed to improve knowledge using a number of contingency factors with a significant impact on formalization, which can then be assessed using the indicators proposed by the model. Needless to say, the model still requires conceptual criticism and improvement but, given the present state of knowledge, can serve as a conceptual basis for various empirical verifications using the contingency factors and formalization indicators for HRM practices.

Other limits also exist, and need to be taken into account in any appraisal of the results obtained. First, the overview of the existing literature cannot claim to be exhaustive. Although over 100 periodicals published in a dozen countries were consulted, the survey was limited to the empirical studies published in either French or English in Western countries. Second, it is possible that even within this limited sample, some of the enormous range of academic and professional publications distributed at the local and regional level were overlooked.

Another limit was imposed by the use of a method resembling content analysis, in which the relative importance of a given factor is associated with the frequency with which it appears in the literature. It is, however, possible that this frequency of appearance reflects the self-evident nature of the factor, rather than its actual importance as far as HRM practices are concerned. Although this drawback is, perhaps, less relevant in an overview of exclusively empirical studies, there are clearly inherent limits to an approach linking the relative importance of a factor to its frequency of appearance in empirical studies. Nevertheless, the approach remains useful in supplying an illustration of the contingency factors most frequently discussed by HRM researchers.

Third, the range of methodological approaches used in the empirical studies imposes one last limit on our survey. Summarizing empirical results obtained using a variety of methodological approaches remains a hazardous task, involving a high risk because of the generalization of the statistical data used. As a result, the preparation of some of the tables required the definition of median limits to exclude certain marginal results which nevertheless reflected the actual situation of HRM practices in certain small businesses.

These considerations lead us to formulate a series of recommendations to any researchers wishing to continue research into HRM practices in small businesses, in order to improve the methodological and conceptual quality of their findings. The adaptation of research to the real needs of small businesses in the human resources field (d'Amboise and Garand, 1995) should be based on a more complete information base, more closely reflecting actual small business practices, using directed empirical studies carried out in comparable and homogeneous sectors of activity and targeting businesses of similar size, without attempting to generalize results. In fact, the probability that any such findings will be insignificant remains high: the wide diversity of businesses studied may reduce the interpretative quality of the data dramatically. Another methodological precaution that should be taken is to use direct interviews rather than mailed questionnaires, a method particularly unsuited to the habitual characteristics of small business owner-managers. In the meantime, an exhaustive inventory of HRM practices in small businesses should allow the preparation of solutions and strategies to integrate the development of human resources in small businesses.

Another series of relevant questions concerns unexplored areas of HRM. Given the specific characteristics of their environment, should small businesses be encouraged to develop or adapt existing HRM practices? In keeping with such an approach, innovative adaptations of existing practices, or the definition of completely new practices better suited to the inherent constraints facing small businesses, could be suggested. The approach could thus move on from explaining the practices that currently exist to defining those that should exist. In parallel with the evolution of knowledge in the field of large corporations, solutions in keeping with new management paradigms could be envisaged (Bayad et al., 1995), just as the participatory management movement called the Taylorian paradigm of the scientific organization of work into question.

It therefore seems essential that future research should be directed towards a better understanding of the contingency model through empirical verification, which would allow the impact of various contingency factors on the formalization of HRM practices to be understood. For example, the links between certain socio-demographic characteristics of the owner-manager or the employees of a business (training, age, sex, professional experience) and the existence, development and sophistication of one or more HRM practices could be verified, for businesses of comparable size in the same sector of activity. The existence of possible links between the level of formalization of HRM practices and the sector of activity, financial and material resources, unionization and the system of production in a given business is another aspect that could be verified. Such empirical research would facilitate an evaluation of the true impact of an increased formalization of HRM practices on the structure, strategy and performance of small and medium-sized organizations.

One last avenue of research is also one of the most attractive: an evaluation of the potentially significant impacts of entrepreneurial vision on the existence and level of formalization of HRM practices in small businesses. Our analysis seems to show that more emphasis should be placed on the entrepreneurs themselves and on extending their vision to include the integration and delegation of HRM. Such a strategy often exists only as part of the entrepreneur's vision, and although it results in decisions and action within the organization, it remains informal and unconscious. Using this as a foundation, it is important, and even imperative, to develop and apply HRM practices that are compatible with entrepreneurial vision. In a large number of small businesses, the vision of the entrepreneur is very quickly reflected in concrete HRM policies and activities that are adapted to the realities of the organization and in harmony with all members of the business. These examples of "high vision" HRM deserve study and more public exposure; the body of more traditional entrepreneurs could draw inspiration from them and open the way for a renewed form of HRM in small businesses.

Lastly, a better understanding of the multiple phenomena associated with HRM requires that we adjust our aim now to take into account the visionary, personalized context in which entrepreneurs will evolve in the third millennium. In dealing with questions relating to HRM in small businesses, we have no choice but to consider the scarcity of resources which places tight limits on the implementation of formalized programs and systems in most small and medium-sized businesses. This re-examination is necessary if the discipline of HRM is to successfully follow the economic and social direction taken in the last twenty years by small businesses.

12 Conclusion

"I would much rather break the prison of a wall and of laws than my word... Sic est faciendum ut contra naturam universum nihil contendamus: ea tamen conservata, propriam sequamur. (We must act so as never to offend against the universal laws of nature; but once these laws are safeguarded, we must conform to our individual nature.)" Michel de Montaigne, "Essai".

1. Introduction

The different chapters of the book have shown that the creation of small businesses, and their particular type of dynamism in an economy still dominated to a large extent by big business, are extremely complex issues. To understand them properly, we must examine them from several standpoints at once. We need only look at the main points raised in each chapter to realize just how complex the questions really are. The basic elements of the variables discussed by the different authors can, however, be extracted to build a theory that will reflect the complexity of the situation and thus help us to understand the phenomenon. Such a theory may also be useful to predict the evolution of small business dynamism in the coming decades.

Just as recent research has called into question the traditional economic and managerial theories of corporate enterprise, as we saw in Chapter 5, so the previously-known aspects of small business behaviour must be qualified and restructured to arrive at a theory that better explains the unexpected renaissance of small business in the early 1970s, and the continued growth of the sector since that time.

It is obviously difficult to talk about *a* small business theory when small businesses themselves are so disparate. As we said in the Introduction, "small business" as an entity does not exist, because there are so many kinds of small businesses. First, we must make a distinction between small and medium-sized firms, with the latter exhibiting some behaviours that are similar in many ways to those of large corporations.

And even the small firm category includes sub-categories of very small and craft firms, which also have their own characteristics. This book is concerned above all with small firms having between two and 50 employees. This group, on average, represents more than 90% of all manufacturing firms in all industrialized countries. Even so, behaviours vary according to markets, type of production and, especially, the psychology and objectives of the entrepreneurs themselves.

In Chapter 2, we saw how the environment or territory played a major role in defining the characteristics of small firms, by providing resources and playing a medium- or long-term guidance role. In Chapter 3, we saw how the environment generally affects the initial location of the firm, and continues to influence subsequent locations. In Chapter 1, by comparing the performances of small firms by country, we showed that the environment and culture had an impact on dynamism leading to personalization of small business development, even though similar levels of dynamism existed in all countries. We also saw how small business dynamism could be explained in part by more segmented markets, better technology and worker aspirations more favourable to short production runs or decentralized production. In fact, the chapters in the first part of the book showed that small firms and then the entrepreneur exist only in osmosis with their environment, contributing to some extent towards the development of that environment and profiting in exchange from its resources, in particular its entrepreneurial resources.

However, the largest number of differences or potentialities affecting small business development were identified in the second part of the book, dealing with entrepreneur behaviour and with enterprise functions - although, as we have said, the functions themselves should be viewed as a single entity, and the fact that they are analyzed separately here is due to the difficulty of seizing all the complexity of small firms at once.

Chapter 4 study the difference between types of entrepreneur at the light of the history and the results of the recent research. It shows how the definition of entrepreneur is not clear and presents differents difficulties.

Chapter 5 examined the difficulty of identifying a single small business strategy when, even within the same firm, a strategy changes in response to the economic context, previous actions and the personal or family itinerary and objectives of the entrepreneur or owner-manager. In Chapter 6, we saw how small business marketing is also very different from corporate marketing, due to the type of environment, the direct links with the market and the behaviour of management.

Chapters 7 and 8 were concerned with production and new technologies. Here again, we cannot hope to understand operations management simply by studying type of equipment and organizational structure. In small firms, operations management is based on lower factor specialization, flexibility and an ever-changing combination of factors depending on circumstances and management objectives. The same applies to financing (Chapter 9), often obtained from several sources and incompatible with traditional effective portfolio analyses, although it often constitutes the first real constraint for small firms.

Chapters 10 and 11, on the other hand, consider two major variables that, with the psychological characteristics of entrepreneurs, best explain the different behaviours of small firms: control of internal and external information, and human resource management. In an increasingly turbulent environment, small business flexibility tends to be based on a good grasp of information and a flexible combination of employees. Flexibility, as we saw in Chapter 1, compensates for smaller economies of scale. We will come back later to information control as a major element of a new small business theory.

In short, then, these often very different elements explain the astonishing disparity or heterogeneity of the thousands or even millions of small firms that we mentioned at the beginning of the book. Our only option for identifying the components of small business is therefore contingency, although clearly this approach will not prevent us from identifying enough similarities to propose the elements of a new economic and management theory for small business.

2.   The Elements Of The Small Business System

The new theory is bound to differ from traditional economic and management theories applicable to big business, given that small production units are fundamentally different from large corporations, in terms of both management and organization of the various production functions and the relations with their environment. Once again, the primary differences between small and large firms lie in the areas of company management, type of organization, relations with the environment or community, and their general behaviour in light of these elements.

First, as we have said on several occasions, entrepreneurs or owner-managers[1] form the heart of small businesses. Their dynamism or prudence is the primary cause of the actions or reactions of their business. A GAP entrepreneur will create a growing firm, and a PIG entrepreneur will adopt slow growth strategies or opt for continual consolidation in the face of environmental disturbances. In order to

---

1   The entrepreneur in the sense of innovator and implementor of the innovation according to Schumpeter, or the owner-manager or "manager", as discussed in Chapter 4. We will come back to this later.

understand what small business is, we must therefore delve into the "black box" of management - an approach that nevertheless continues to be scorned by most neo-classical economists who, following Frederic Machlup (1967) and in the name of the purity of economic science, refuse to consider the behavioural or psychological aspects that govern economic agents. In any case, according to these economists, the inexorable laws of economic reason "force" behaviours, however vague they may be. And yet, we know that these so-called "agents" are in fact "players" who not only act under environmental constraints, but also develop different competitive strategies, both economic (in the interests of their firms) and social or political (according to their own personal and family interests), so as to influence and even "organize" the environment.

Next, the organization - that is, the combination of personnel (executives and employees) and materials or equipment that conditions production. The personnel, especially the people working with and influencing the owner-manager, are also subject to all kinds of external influences that promote or restrict the firm's development. For example, rumours, economic trends and "the business atmosphere", as described by the great economist Alfred Marshall at the beginning of the century[2] have a considerable effect on dynamics and the waiting or withdrawal stances adopted by small businesses. The organization receives and transmits all sorts of information - economic and social - to management. An example of this is the behaviour of salespeople and their impact on decisions when they return from sales trips, as we saw in Chapter 6. But all employees, depending on their enthusiasm or lack of it, the economic context and even management's behaviour towards them, can transform winning attitudes into positions of withdrawal or flight. In such a case, the environment often has a magnifying or reducing effect on behaviours.

The personnel also live in a community, and are influenced by social and economic policies and the dynamics, rules, taboos and prospects of a region. This is true even for organizations as supposedly rational as national stock markets, which should in theory be oases of pure economic realism, but which in fact function on the basis of rumours and the humour of a handful of major financiers, as Kenneth Galbraith pointed out in his study of the 1930 crisis (Bernstein, 1995). But it is also true of the regions sometimes described as "economic miracles",

---

2 The importance of the "industrial atmosphere" discussed by Marshall has been rediscovered recently by industrial economists, in particular during research on Italy's industrial districts. See Dominique Foray (1990).

whose particular dynamism cannot be explained simply by economic considerations[3]. However, the environment or community is also a source of information for entrepreneurs, supporting their strategies or alerting them to major or minor changes affecting the future of their firms. As we saw in Chapter 2 and Chapter 7, the environment or community is the site of first-level information networks, and also - sometimes - the source of information leading alert entrepreneurs into more complex networks.

It is difficult to understand the meaning of environmental influence. For example, the recent severe economic recession in North America (1991-1992) produced some fairly dynamic behaviour in the sense of equipment modernization by many small firms, as we saw in Chapter 7, when in fact we might have expected waiting or withdrawal strategies or rationalization by downsizing, as is all too often the case in large corporations. The community also plays another major role by influencing management's objectives. In fact, it becomes a subject of action for the entrepreneur's social and political itinerary. The entrepreneur may have ambitions, such as playing a political role in the local town. This may explain some of his or her behaviour in terms of employment, which is aimed at achieving visibility. In short, small firms exist in a kind of osmosis with their communities, while at the same time stimulating or acting as one of the forces of change. Not that the community explains everything - including the limits of or potential for entrepreneurship, as some theorists have tried to show by explaining the existence of peoples or cultures less propitious for entrepreneurs[4]. However, as studies by GREMI have shown (Maillat, Quévit and Senn, 1993), the dynamics of the economic community depend on business dynamics and, in exchange, stimulate business growth.

---

3   For example, in Beauce (Quebec), Mario Carrier (1992) showed that there was a tacit agreement between firms that they should not poach good employees from each other by offering better pay. This is what enabled the region to offer better prices on foreign markets and thus maintain employment levels. However, this rule also had an advantage for the workers themselves, since it meant that the firms would re-hire people laid off by firms in difficulties, thus enhancing employment security. Such informal standards or rules can be observed, for example, in most industrial districts (Beccatini, 1987).

4   See Taylor (1965) and, against this theory that has never been proved, J.M. Toulouse (1979).

396

3.   The levels of approach

These various elements are not static. They evolve quickly or slowly, in relation to one another. To understand this process of evolution and reorganization, we can look at the different types of exchanges supported by the economy in which the firms evolve: physical exchanges, capital exchanges, information exchanges and psycho-sociological exchanges.

3.1   Physical exchange

Physical exchange is the most ordinary and the easiest to grasp. The phenomenon has been studied for many years, and forms the basis of the early general analysis work of classical economists such as François Quesnay, Jean-Baptiste Say and Adam Smith. It explains how small firms, like large corporations, function by exchanging goods and services between themselves and with consumers.

Through physical exchange, small firms apply the principles of economic values, i.e. the *use value* (goods and services are required to satisfy needs), the *exchange value* (giving an added value to goods consequently "placed on the market"), and *signification value*, which explains the change (fashion, accumulation) even if the goods are not used, as certain sociologists (for example, Jean Baudrillard, 1972) and certain economists (for example, Igor Scitovski, 1978) have pointed out, and as the marketing specialists know (Chapter 6).

3.2   Capital exchange

Underlying physical exchange is the exchange of capital or monetary value which supports the commitment of production factors (labour, material or equipment and management capacity) and facilitates their organization. The separation between physical exchange and capital exchange was used by Richard Cantillon to distinguish entrepreneurs from managers. We know that the separation was a fact, especially in 18th century France as studied by Cantillon, when the nobility preferred to lend money to the bourgeois (living in *bourgs* or cities, rather than in country castles) to obtain a profit from their capital. This is why the words "entrepreneur" (according to Vérin, 1982, the word comes from the phrase "*prendre-entre*", meaning to invest in a city, market or business) and "manager" (from "*ménager*", meaning to manage a household) are of French origin, despite Cantillon's Scottish roots.

The great historian Fernand Braudel[5] has shown, in contradiction of Max Weber's theory of Protestant ethics, that the accumulation of capital, for example in the stock markets, was one of the major reasons why capitalism originated in England. Otherwise, the industrial revolution would have taken place in China or India, because of the large number of discoveries, or in the Arab countries, which controlled many international markets[6], or in Switzerland, where Puritanism was still flourishing.

The development of capital combines with the spirit of enterprise to bring about rapid modernization of production factors in all forms of business. Many developing countries cannot initiate the process because of a lack of capital, even though they have flourishing parallel or unofficial economies composed of thousands of small entrepreneurs who often combine production and distribution in a single economic network[7].

---

5   Other causes include the quasi-stability of the currency for nearly 25 years, thus reducing a major uncertainty, the creation of a true national market, the presence of an abundant, industrious workforce and the exploitation of colonies. See in particular Braudel's short book entitled La dynamique du capitalisme (1985), which is drawn in part from his monumental work Civilisation matérielle, économie et capitalisme, XVe - XVIIe siècle (1979). See also I. Wallerstein (1983).

6   The Indians invented algebra and geometry (this is summarized particularly well in the 8th century Treaty of Bragmegupta); for example, Euler's theorem was known in India ten centuries before Swiss mathematician Euler himself rediscovered it in the 18th century. The Chinese knew all about xylographic printing and engraving, the art of making porcelain, paper, silk fabric, mechanical seed sowing equipment, bore holes, suspension bridges, the public fire service, the use of a compass, gas lighting, etc., as far back as Antiquity, when Europe was still in the Bronze Age. The Arabs had measured the solar year quite precisely (365 days, 5 hours, 48 minutes) by the 9th century; they knew the circumference of the Earth and the latitudes and longitudes of the major cities of the world in the 12th century, after travelling throughout the known Eastern and Western worlds. In the 13th century, Mohammed-Ben-Mahmud (Kazwyny) explained earthquakes and laid the foundations for the theory of continental drift. And it was thanks to Ali-Houssain (Avicenne), in the 10th century, and Ibn-Roschd (Averroes) in the 12th century, at the University of Cordoba in Spain, that Europe learnt about Greek philosophy and the Greek discoveries in medicine, natural history and so on. See L. Figuier (1867).

7   On the problems of entrepreneurship and small business, for example in Africa, see the special edition of the Revue Internationale PME: Vol. 5, No. 3-4, 1992.

In Chapter 10, we reviewed the importance of controlling internal and external information for effective business management, a factor that was also mentioned in Chapter 7 as an element in better organizational management, the renewal of materials or equipment and the production of innovation in a rapidly-changing environment.

In fact, control of information allows large corporations to control their environment, up to a point or, in the case of smaller firms, to organize it. As we saw in Chapter 1, the quest for large size, when economic efficiency due to economies of scale does not justify growth above a certain point, can be explained to a large extent by aversion to risk. A good way of limiting risk is to control or act on information. Examples are the control of innovation by monopolies, the control of markets by cartels, the control of markets by massive advertising, financial control through manipulation of finances on the world market, and especially political control or action to influence governments. Controlling information means power, and helps to lessen the uncertainty inherent in the economy. Too much uncertainty limits investment because it increases risk.

Information can be divided into several different types. For example, Henri Laborit talks about circulating information and structuring information. The former is routine, repetitive and economically uninteresting. The latter, also known as "rich information" , leads to adaptations or changes in the system receiving it and thus produces "non-programmed" decisions favourable to change, as Simon (1979) explains. When we talk of structural evolution between small firms and large corporations, we are talking about structuring or rich information, since it is the source of small business innovation, flexibility and dynamism.

Various kinds of structuring information exist within the economy. Amendola and Gaffard (1988) identified collective information, i.e. information that cannot be appropriated by a single company or group, and private information. The latter can also be subdivided into new or created information, i.e. information *controlled* by a small group or a single company, and *shared* information, i.e. information shared between the members of a group or business club (according to Buchanan's definition).

Most economic information is collective information. It is public property, available to everyone, and cannot be controlled or hidden by a few. It includes, for example, scientific and technological information of the type found in textbooks, taught in classes and discussed in specialized publications, to which access is relatively *free*. Examples of this type of information, concerning the general state of progress of science and technology, include the types of technology available on the market and sold by suppliers, standards for its use, any additional resources required to use it, and the services available to facilitate its use. The information may be more or less complex, depending on the quality of the equipment suppliers, and the level of scientific culture and development of the teaching or research institutions and the transfer organizations in the economy. Free information is part of the "body of knowledge and know-how" described by Zurcovitch (1985) and Julien and Marchesnay (1996). It has a certain opportunity cost, because of the time and other limited resources needed to compare and sort through the mass of highly disparate information in order to extract what may be interesting for firms in the short or long term. It is one of the vital elements of business strategy, enabling firms to adapt to change.

One of the major roles of the national economic and technological information production and transfer system is to generate or seek out collective information, to facilitate its transfer and to provide additional resources to firms (thus ensuring its dissemination and "transportability"[8]).

Private information is usually "recent" or "leading edge". It is this type of information that enables a particular firm to stand out. When applied at the level of product, management, production or distribution, it also explains differences in enterprise competitiveness. Private information is, to a large extent, *controlled* by the company or private research centre that created it. It thus emerges from innovation and, consequently, R&D. It is often surrounded by secrecy, and may be governed by R&D contracts, patents and licences, and protected by legislation. It gives rise to very few exchanges on the market[9]. In any case, exchanges of this type of information involve major expenditures that increase in proportion to the expected income from its deployment. Such exchanges may also take place within the enterprise system, for example between subsidiaries, with partners in other countries and on

---

8   In fact, transfer does not equal exchange. Exchange concerns not only the container, but also the content and the conditions and means of transfer, as G. Stigler pointed out in 1939.

9   As T. Durand (1989) explained, the information supply of most interest economically speaking, such as high technology information, is often monopolistic and latent, because it is rarely formalized. This type of information nevertheless ends up on the market after a certain time, usually after having given up most of its "rent" and after being replaced by even more recent information.

other markets not covered by the firm that created it, for various types of consideration. This is the most important source of what Frank Knight called the quasi-rent on a competitive market and even on the oligopolistic or monopolistic market that it is capable of creating; in other words, the profit earned from the differentiation obtained as a result of the information, which disappears when the information is passed onto the market. It is therefore the most interesting type of economic information, because it is new and rare[10].

Private information may be *shared* within various kinds of restricted business groups such as cartels, between order providers and subcontractors, within industrial districts or local production systems, in vertical quasi-integrated systems in network businesses (see Chapter 2), and also in business incubators or technology parks, especially where it is produced by public or semi-public research centres with links to these particular forms of restricted organizations[11]. In such *private-type groups*, information is supplied in exchange for other information or other services, and thus evolves on the fringes of the market space, as Yves Morvan (1991) pointed out. The sharing of information is aimed precisely at minimizing its cost while creating a particular kind of synergy between the members of the "club", allowing them to gain more from the exchange of economic information. In "quasi-private" networks such as these, shared information may be incomplete. At the very least, it is often "entailed" or given in exchange for a consideration, thus creating obligations that generate a certain level of solidarity between members and prevent the information from being passed on to competitors outside the group (Julien, 1991). It generates a rent shared more or less equally among the group members, which increases in proportion to what non-members have to pay to obtain it. In *quasi-public groups* where public transfer centres intervene (for example the technical and technological information research centres in France, known by their French acronym CRITT, or the specialized research centres attached to technical universities in U.S.A.), information is available more easily to businesses, although it generates interpretation and adaptation costs because the businesses concerned are not direct members of the group.

Shared information is transmitted directly between firms by subcontracting, through internal or external research centres with which

---

10   It is also the information that confers the greatest power, a larger rent, and for this reason it is also "political" in the sense of Ouchi (1980).

11   Even where the research centres are public, agreements between the centres and outside companies may contain exclusivity clauses.

firms do business, or by other mechanisms such as specialized educational institutions or the consulting services controlled or created by partner firms, etc. Thus, shared information lies midway between public information and controlled information.

The transaction cost theory is concerned mainly with information costs. However, this theory alone is not sufficient to explain the behaviours of firms seeking information, since, for example, the various forms of economic relations for small businesses, such as subcontracting or group participation, require the calculation not just of optimality, but of economic, political and social opportunities and objectives, as we saw earlier in the discussion of the role of the entrepreneur. As Richardson (1972) has shown, transactions are concerned with broader concepts arising as much from economic behaviours as from relationships of trust based on the habits and varying long-term objectives or socio-psychological changes, or from psycho-sociological relationships operating outside the market.

3.4   Socio-psychological exchanges

To understand small firms, it is vital to consider the concepts relating to socio-psychological exchanges in their environment. As we have shown on several occasions, for example in the case of location, control of certain production factors and the search for information, the roles of the environment and thus the psycho-sociological relationships are of significant importance in the development of small businesses.

James Coleman (1988) spoke of the social capital on which exchanges are based, including exchanges outside the market and in the black economy[12]. He explained that exchanges are rarely purely economic in nature, and take account of the habits and learning acquired from previous relationships[13]. In our case, we talked of transaction space (Marchesnay and Julien, 1990) as a place for political and social and well as economic and technological exchanges. The political and sociological environment serves as a framework for more complex economic exchanges. Marc-Urbain Proulx (1992) showed this in his longitudinal study of a small isolated region by analyzing the intermingling of various types of transactions between small entrepreneurs.

---

12 Exchanges in the black economy, often confused with exchanges in the so-called informal economy (Julien and Solé Parellada, 1991).

13 For example, if all transactions were purely rational, there would be no reason for children to take over from their parents in many firms.

A number of studies have shown the importance of these relationships of trust in the development of the enterprise (Sabel, 1992). For example, in the case of supplies, firms can use purely economic calculations and change suppliers regularly to obtain the best prices. In the long term, however, when markets are difficult, they will often lose out as a result. The whole principle of business networks around the major European and Japanese firms, and the idea of partnership, as seen in the case of Bombardier Sea-Doo/Ski-Doo in Quebec, are based on the benefits of such socio-economic relationships.

In short, small firms exist within a complex system of economic, financial, information and socio-psychological exchanges. By considering these different levels of exchanges, we will be in a better position to construct a theory that reflects the true nature of small businesses and their behaviour on the market.

4. Towards a theory of small business based on instability or contingency

As we have said several times, small firms are highly disparate. Their behaviours are strongly influenced by the psychology of the management team. They operate in close relationships with their environment and market, affecting and being affected by them. We thus cannot avoid the contingency approach, as explained by Lawrence and Lorsch (1967)[14], despite the problems that this causes. On the other hand, given the behaviours of small firms in turbulent local and national economies, we can go beyond basic contingency to identify generalizations likely to lead to an analytical or predictable theory to justify the small business renaissance in Western economies.

In fact, what we need to do is to invent a new economic theory that takes account of the systematic creation and development of small firms, and the subsequent disappearance of many of them - in other words, a theory of instability. This is in direct contrast to traditional economic theory, based on the systematic tendency towards equilibrium, whether partial or in continual readjustment.

---

14 As these authors said, an organization subjected to an uncertain environment should function using a decentralized, fairly informal logic, based on versatile, autonomous staff and management focused more on experiment and feedback than on planning (see p.53 of their book). These features are particularly evident in small firms, as we observed at the beginning of the book.

To do this, we must come back to the different types of exchanges and the elements discussed above. In particular, to create such a theory, we must look first and foremost at the main player in small firms: the entrepreneur who defines the firm's behaviours and development. We have to consider the entrepreneur's ability not only to grasp opportunities in unstable environments, but actually to create instability through ongoing interference in production or distribution[15].

The new theory must recognize what entrepreneurs are: i.e. psycho-sociological players who act first and foremost in their own interest, and who "undertake" by trying to control all the variables at once. The "undertaking" (or enterprise) is an adventure for them. If it succeeds, it will be tangible proof of a challenge won. If it fails, it will reflect their own personal failure[16]. The adventure will be a success if the entrepreneur is able to organize the right resources to respond to the opportunity detected in the target market's instability, and if luck is on his or her side[17]. Entrepreneurs tend to use strategies based on intuition and *a posteriori* calculation, combining the short term of praxis with a longer-term vision (Filion, 1989)[18]. Later, if they remain entrepreneurial, they will always keep something in reserve for unexpected events, to continue their adventure in the face of permanent instability[19].

---

15 William Baumol (1968) stated that the trend in economic theory (despite vague references at the beginning of manuals or the analyses discussed in Chapter 1) not to take any real account of the entrepreneur was the equivalent of excluding the Prince of Denmark as a relevant part of Hamlet.

16 But an initial experience may lead to a second, and sometimes a third. We know that about 20% of new venture creations are performed by entrepreneurs who have failed at least once.

17 Luck is also necessary. Entrepreneurs can have the best possible idea, prepare well for enterprise creation and launch the business just as the economy takes a downturn. As we will see later, entrepreneurs do not have all the information they need to launch businesses, and reality often goes against their forecasts ... and their enthusiasm.

18 Contrary to the theory, even the theory of "limited rationality", there is a lot more non-rationality than rationality in an "undertaking", since uncertainty is often great, as Camagni (1991) pointed out.

19 It is possible that many large "entrepreneurial" firms function partly as small firms at upper managerial levels. For example, everyday production is based on generally formal strategic planning, but senior management reserves the right to make the decision based also on its intuition of the "adventura" (uncertainty and risk, but also the game - the "ludus" of Alain Cotta, 1980) and the "fortuna" (chance, but also possible fortune: Vérin, 1982), beyond market organization, in the

Successful entrepreneurs are like Bourdieu's football player, who, alongside his surplus "habitus", composed of "skills" acquired by experience, is able to invent constantly, adapting to an infinite variety of situations that are never perfectly identical (Bourdieu, 1987 : 79).

For entrepreneurs, the goal is not profit - profit is seen as a necessary constraint for the survival and development of the firm and to allow it to reach its goals. Maximization of profit in economic theory is therefore a false perception.

However, in the long term, aversion to risk ends up conditioning goals and incites entrepreneurs to seek better-controlled or more stable environments. However, this does not necessarily lead to a balanced or almost-balanced economic situation. There will always be entrepreneurs to disturb the equilibrium and take advantage of the new niches and opportunities present in a changing environment, while at the same time supporting or promoting the change. Entrepreneurs are therefore "producers and profiters" of instability, operating in a system that is both closed and open (with entry barriers), composed of information that is controlled and quickly outdated, and continuing to seek their own psycho-sociological interests within economic constraints.

The traditional theory of equilibrium (or quasi-equilibrium) unfortunately continues to condition current theory - classical, neo-classical and Keynesian - despite past (Kaldor, 1972) or more recent (Smith, 1985) criticism. This theory, always based on the unlimited availability of information, even if expensive, continues to explain the behaviour of agents in traditional theory, even though readily-available information is of little interest or has little effect on the economy. It is controlled or shared information that affects the economy and explains venture creation. In fact, entrepreneurs do everything they can to create or obtain information before anyone else (especially through innovation of all kinds), and to manipulate it for as long as possible, as we saw earlier and as Alex Jacquemin (1987) observed. They only hand it over to the market - often in a biased form - when it can be replaced by other, newer information[20]. On the other hand, managers offer to share part of

---

zone of instability that allows the game, justifying much of their commitment.

20 Lorino (1989) explains that, internally, "every enterprise man ... holds a quantity of information that he transmits only partially, because he cannot (because of lack of time or lack of ability to formalize it) or does not want to transmit all of it" (our translation). In other words, every member of the organization protects his or her interests in various ways. Outside, Foray (1990) added that little information is available because resources tend to be increasingly

their information (which is itself only partial) in a coalition, on condition that it will not be released.

In contrast to the theory, not only is it the job of the competition or the coalition to provide as little information as possible to the market, and to use all kinds of manoeuvres to achieve this (even if the market forces it to hand over some information - often biased - through the price mechanism), but also the entire strategy of the players is to try to protect their information, or to issue it irregularly or intermittently with as much noise as possible to confuse the competitors (except network members). The result is obviously instability on a market that functions on the basis of estimates, imprecise anticipation or "reasoned intuition", and on the ongoing production of new information with the arrival of new entrepreneurs and innovation, which leads to continual adjustment or adaptation.

However, the reality of small business markets is rather more complex than this picture suggests. The behaviour of entrepreneurs means that, while certain forces promote the quest for equilibrium between supply and demand, others do quite the reverse. In particular, entrepreneurs seek systematically to escape from this logic by changing the market through product, process or location innovations, so as to obtain an advantage as quickly as possible. There would be a trend towards equilibrium if markets were stable, but they are not. They change continually as a result of the arrival of new entrepreneurs and innovations by existing entrepreneurs. The relationship between supply and demand changes continually, preventing any form of equilibrium. Thus, the very logic of the theory of equilibrium or quasi-equilibrium is debatable. What seems to exist instead is a set of relationships that swing continually from explosion to implosion, and the trend towards equilibrium is no more valid than the trend towards non-equilibrium[21]. This is shown in diagram form in Diagram 12.1, with a period in which supply seeks to link up with demand, followed by a period in which it moves as far away as possible, and then by another period directed towards equilibrium, and so on, resulting in continual instability.

Instability is caused by, and affects, the behaviour of the entrepreneurs in their firms and leads them to seek the flexibility mentioned previously. Instability explains many of the situations

---

specific. In other words, in a dynamic market the "Walras Town Crier" is often absent or ineffective.

21 For an example of the application of this concept, see Raffa and Zollo (1994).

observed in the various enterprise functions. For example, in marketing, as we saw in Chapter 6, small firms prefer informality in their relations with their present or future markets. In production, they use the most flexible technologies possible, or technologies that work alongside simpler equipment (Chapter 7). Moreover, while they use new and fashionable production forms, such as tight flow and total quality systems, they adjust them to suit their own requirements and the context (Chapter 8). In finance, they tend to prefer independence, unless they have a GAP attitude that allows them to compensate or are less tied to external financing (Chapter 9). Their information systems also tend to be highly flexible, combining formal measures with more intuitive features (Chapter 10). The greatest level of informality, if we compare small businesses with large corporations, lies at the level of human resources, and this tends to favour the kind of flexibility that cannot be achieved by large firms (Chapter 11). So, while we need to look at small businesses from a contingency standpoint because of their extreme disparity, we can nevertheless identify common behaviour in their flexibility when faced with system instability.

Diagram 12.1
Evolution in supply and demand on an unstable market in constant fluctuation

Price

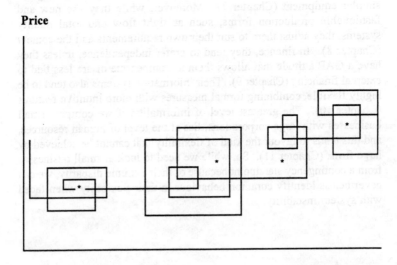

Quantity

Key: *: point of equilibrium

As Kirzner (1982) pointed out, and as we also observed (Julien, 1989), entrepreneurs and small firms are basically the phenomena of disequilibrium and instability. As in the fable of the oak and the reed, instability is a way of satisfying the needs of a rapidly-changing economy, and actually stimulates change. Large corporations are much more suited to an environment that changes slowly. The current dynamism of small firms can be explained in part by their greater capacity to survive and develop in unstable and turbulent environments.

Within instability, the intuitive strategy mentioned in Chapter 5 comes into play, including the "habitus" behaviours described by Bourdieu. Intuition leads to differentiation and generates rent or profit, and product or location differentiation enables the firm to satisfy the needs of segmented markets, as we saw in Chapter 1. However, process differentiation (especially in terms of the organization) also helps the firm develop a very specific relationship with its market, as we saw in Chapter 6.

Differentiation is also important at the level of information. Information is transmitted through a variety of networks in the "communication act" described by Habermas (1981), which explains small business interpenetration with the environment. This creates environmental dynamism, as we saw in Chapters 2 and 7. Within this vision, physical, financial, information and socio-psychological exchanges play a major role because they are interdependent or complementary. Physical exchanges are subject to financial contributions often obtained from the entrepreneur's community. The environment provides information or points to channels from which such contributions can be obtained. These exchanges are based on "controlled" relationships of trust which create consistency throughout the system. However, the system also evolves constantly, because it is fed systematically with information that forces it to adjust and innovate. In turn, the adjustments and innovations help the system evolve within a process of perpetual renewal and systemic instability.

Economic theory still has great difficulty in understanding this, because not only was it formulated at a time when researchers were looking for laws of natural order and equilibrium (and thus the premises of the theory are still firmly entrenched in this vision), but also because the resulting logic that was used to develop the theory is extremely difficult to criticize without calling the whole theoretical construction into question.

However, economic theory has nevertheless made some progress, first by reflecting on the problem of size (negatively at first, against small size) and then by incorporating the notions of space (with regional and local economies, and networks). However, it has yet to consider the role of the behaviour of the players and the notion of real time in industrial economy.

This will have to be done, sooner or later. At the very least, a better knowledge of small firms and their behaviour in the economy will help us in our quest to invent a new economy. After all, was Adam Smith's classical economy not created at a time when virtually the all existing firms were small?

"What I give to this person, as he is, I give purely and irrevocably, as though giving to a child the little good I have done, and it is no longer at my disposal; he can know many things that I no longer know, and have from me what I no longer remember, and I, like a stranger, would have to borrow from him if I were in need."

Montaigne, "Essai".

409

References

Introduction

Arena, R. et al. (1985), "Artisanat de production industrielle et évolution économique régionale", COREM-ERFI, Montpellier.

Barnard, C. (1949), "The entrepreneur and formal organization", in *Change and the Entrepreneur*, Cambridge, Harvard University Press.

Barry, S. (1978), "Organization design in the smaller enterprise", in D.T. Bryault and R.J. Niehaus, *Manpower, Planning and Organization*, New York, Plenum Press.

Basire, M. (1976), "La théorie des cinq niveaux", *Direction et gestion*, Nos. 2/3/4.

Baumol, W.J. (1968), "Entrepreneurship in economic theory", *American Economic Review*, Vol. 58, No. 2, May, pp. 64-71.

Bolton, J.E. (1971), *Report of the Committee on Inquiry on Small Firms*, London, Official Publisher.

Boswell, J. (1973), *The Rise and Decline of Small Firms*, London, George Allen and Unwin.

Candau, P. (1981), "Pour une taxonomie de l'hypofirme", *Revue d'économie industrielle*, No. 16.

Carland, J., F. Hoy, W. Boulton, and J.A. Carland (1984), "Differentiating entrepreneurs form small business owners: a conceptualization", *Academy of Management Review*, Vol. 9, pp. 354-359.

CEC (1976), "Definition de la petite et moyenne entreprise et de l'artisanat", Brussels, European Community, 413/111/76-f.

Chicha, J. and P.A. Julien (1979), "Les stratégies des PME et leur adaptation aux changements", GREPME Research Paper No. 79-06, UQTR.

Churchill, B.C. (1955), "Age and expectancy of business firms", *Survey of Current Business*, December, pp. 3-25.

Churchill, N. and V. Lewis. (1983), "Les cinq stades de l'évolution d'une PME", *Harvard-Expansion*, Autumn, pp. 51-63.

Cole, A.H. (1942), "Entrepreneurship as an area of research", *Journal of Economic History Supplement*, No. 2, pp. 118-126.

410

Cooper A. and C. Dunkelberg (1982), "Entrepreneurial typologies: an empirical study", in K. Vesper (ed.), *Frontiers of Entrepreneurial Research*, University of Washington.

Cooper, A.C. (1964), "R&D is more efficient in small companies", *Harvard Business Review*, May-June, pp. 75-83.

Cooper, A.C. (1979), "Strategic management: new venture and small business", in D.E. Schendell and C.W. Hofer (eds.), *Strategic Management: a New View of Business Policy and Planning*, Boston.

Dandridge, T.C. (1979), "Children are not "little grown-ups": small business needs its own organization theory", *Journal of Small Business Management*, Vol. 17, No. 2, pp. 53-57.

Deeks, J. (1973), "The small firm - asset or liability?", *Journal of Management Studies*, Vol. 10, No. 1, pp. 25-47.

Desjardins, C. (1975), *La PME au Québec. Situations et problèmes*, Ministère de l'Industrie et du Commerce du Québec.

Echene, D. (1974), "De la moyenne à la grande entreprise", *Direction et Gestion*, No. 4, pp. 7-17.

Evans, G.H. (1949), "The entrepreneur and economic theory: a historical and analytical approach", *American Economic Review. Paper and Proceeding*, Vol. 39, pp. 336-348.

Eymard-Duvernay, M. and M. Delattre (1983), "Le progrès des PME dans la crise: signe d'un relachement du tissu industriel", *Critique de l'économie politique*, Nos. 26-27, January-June, pp. 119-132.

Filey, A. and R. Aldag (1978), "Characteristics and measurement of an organizational typology", *Academy of Management Journal*, December.

Gélinier, O. and A. Gaultier (1974), *L'avenir des entreprises personnelles et familiales*, Paris, Éditions Hommes et Techniques.

Gervais, M. (1978), "Pour une théorie de l'organisation PME", *Revue Française de Gestion*, March-April, pp. 37-49.

Greiner, L. (1972), "Evolution and revolution of organization growth", *Harvard Business Review*, Vol. 50, No. 4, pp. 37-46.

Gross, H. (1958), *Petites entreprises et grands marchés*, Paris, Éditions d'Organisation.

Harrison, B. (1994), *Lean and Mean*, New York, Bask Books.

Hollander, E.D. et al. (1967), *The Future of Small Business*, New York, Praeger.

Horovitz, J. and M.C. Demillère (1978), "La vraie nature de la PME française", *Revue Française de Gestion*, March-April, pp. 27-36.

Hosmer, L., A. Cooper and K. Vesper (1977), *The Entrepreneurial Function*, Englewood Cliffs, Prentice Hall.

Hupper, R. (1981), "Stratégies de développement des PMI françaises", *Revue d'économie industrielle*, No. 17.

Ibnabdeljalil, N. (1980), "Contribution à une analyse financière et typologique des PME industrielle", Doctoral thesis, Université de Rennes, quoted in R. Arena, et al., *Traité d'économie industrielle*, Paris, Economica, 1988.

Jaeger, C. (1982), *Artisanat et capitalisme*, Paris, Payot.

Joyal, A. (1988), "Les PME alternatives", in P.A. Julien, J. Chicha and A. Joyal, op. cit., pp. 279-286.

Julien, P.A. and J. Chicha (1982), "Vers une typologie multicritères des PME manufacturières", GREPME Research Paper No. 82-06.

Julien, P.A., J. Chicha and A. Joyal (eds.) (1988), *La PME dans un monde en mutation*, Québec, Les Presses de l'Université du Québec.

Julien, P.A. and M. Marchesnay (eds.) (1988), *La petite entreprise*, Paris, Vuibert.

Kaplan, A.D.H. (1948), *Small Business: Its Space and Problems*, New York, McGraw-Hill.

Kilby, P. (ed.) (1971), *Hunting the Heffalump: Entrepreneurship and Economic Development*, New York, The Free Press.

Kroeger, C. (1974), "Managerial development of the small firm", *California Management Review*, Vol. 17, No. 1, pp. 41-46.

Laurent, P. (1989), "L'entrepreneur dans la pensée économique", *Revue Internationale PME*, Vol. 2, No. 1, pp. 57-71.

Liles, P. (1974), *New Business Ventures and the Entrepreneur*, Homewood, R.D. Irwin.

Lorrain, J. and L. Dusseault (1988), "Les entrepreneurs artisans et opportunistes: une comparaison de leurs comportements de gestion", *Revue Internationale PME*, Vol. 1, No. 2, pp. 157-177.

Mader, F. (1979), "Un échantillon d'entreprises en difficultés", Journée de la centrale de bilan, quoted by R. Arena et al., op. cit.

Marchini, I. (1988), "Piccole Imprese e piccole imprese emergenti", *Piccola Impresa*, No. 1, pp. 11-32.

McGuire, J.M. (1976), "The small enterprise in economics and organization theory", *Journal of Contemporary Business*, Vol. 5, No. 2, pp. 115-138.

Miller, D. and P.H. Friesen (1982), "Innovation in conservative and entrepreneurial firms: two models of strategic momentum", *Strategic Management Journal*, Vol. 3, No. 1, pp. 10-25.

Mueler, D.C. (1972), "A life cycle theory of firms", *Journal of Industrial Economics*, June.

412

Newton, K. (1978), "Is small really so beautiful? Is big really so ugly", Studies in Public Policy, No. 13, Centre for the Study of Public Policy, Glasgow.

Nguyen, T.H. and A. Belhumeur (1985), "À propos de l'interchangéabilité des mesures de taille d'entreprise", *Revue d'économie industrielle*, No. 33.

OECD (1964), *Rapport sur les politiques économiques des Etats en faveur des PME*, Paris, OECD.

OECD (1971), *Problèmes et politiques relatifs aux petites et moyennes entreprises*, Paris, OECD.

Paulson, S. (1980), "Organizational size, technology structure: replication of a study of social services agencies among small retail firms", *Academy of Management Journal*, June.

Pelletier, G.R. (1990), "L'entrepreneur dans la pensée économique: l'originalité méconnue de Turgot", *L'Actualité Économique*, Vol. 66, No. 2, June, pp. 187-193.

Penrose, E. (1952), "Biological analogies in the theory of the firm", *American Economic Review*, No. 42.

Penrose, E. (1959), *The Theory of the Growth of the Firm*, Oxford, Basil Blackwell.

Potier, M. (1986), "Quel espace économique pour les PME" in P.A. Julien, J. Chicha and A. Joyal (1988), op. cit., pp. 363-382.

Preston, L. (1977), "The world of small business: a suggested typology", *American Journal of Small Business*, April.

Quélennec, M. (1986), "Les statistiques d'entreprises: réalités observées et méthodes d'observations", l'INSEE Collection, Series No.101.

Rizzoni, A. (1988), "Innovazione tecnologica et piccola impresa: un approcio tipologico", *Piccola Impresa*, No. 1, pp. 67-89.

Robitaille, L. and M. Marchesnay (1988), "Le financement de la petite entreprise", Chapter X in P.A. Julien and M. Marchesnay (1988), op. cit., pp. 181-194.

Sengenberger, W., G.W. Loveman, and M.J. Piore (1990), *The Re-emergence of Small Enterprises*, Geneva, IIES.

Smith, N. and B. Miner (1983), "Type of entrepreneur, type of firm and managerial motivation: implication for organizational life cycle theory", *Strategic Management Journal*, Vol. 4, pp. 325-340.

Stanworth, M. and J. Curran (1976), "Growth and the small firm: an alternative view", *Journal of Management Studies*, May.

Steindl, J. (1947), *Small and Big Business: Economic Problems of the Size of Firms*, Oxford, Basil Blackwell.

413

Steiner, G.A. (1967), "Approaches to long-range planning for small business", *California Management Review*, Vol. 10, No. 1, pp. 3-16.

Steinneetz, L. (1969), "Critical stages of small business", *Business Horizons*, February.

Susbauer, J. (1979), "Strategic management and organization types: commentary", in D.E. Schendell and C.W. Hofer (eds.), *Strategic Management*, Englewood Cliffs, Prentice Hall.

Thain, D. (1969), "Stages of corporate development", *Business Quarterly*, Winter.

Toulouse. J.M. (1979), *L'entrepreneurship au Québec*, Montreal, Fides.

Vargas, G. (1984), "Les crises de croissance de la PMI-PME", *Revue française de gestion*, January-February.

Vesper, K. (1979), "Strategic management and organization types: commentary", in D.E. Schendell and C.W. Hofer (eds.), op. cit.

Waite, D. (1973), "The economic significance of small firms", *Journal of Industrial Economics*, Vol. XXI, No. 2, April, pp. 155-166.

Webster, F. (1976), "A model for new venture initiation", *Academy of Management Review*, Vol. 1, No. 1.

Chapter 1

Acs, J.Z. and D.B. Audretsch (1988), "Innovation in large and small firms: an empirical analysis", *American Economic Review*, September, pp. 678-690.

Amar, M. (1987), "Dans l'industrie, les PME résistent mieux que les grandes", *Économie et statistique*, No. 197, March, pp. 310-315.

Aoki, M. (1981), "Horizontal versus vertical information structure of the firm", *American Economic Review*, Vol. 5.

Archibugi, D. and S. Cesaretto (1989), "Piccole imprese e cambriatorento technologico. Modelli teorici e resultate dall'indagina CNR-ISTAT sull'innovazione tecnologica nel settore manufatturiero italiano", *Piccola Impresa*, Vol. 2, pp. 45-73.

Armington, C. and M. Odle (1982), "Small business: how many jobs?", *The Brookings Review*, Winter.

Ass. CAO/FAO (1989), "Tendances et degré de pénétration. L'automatisation et l'informatisation de la production", Quebec, CRIQ.

Audrestch, D.B. (1990), "The role of small- and medium-sized enterprises in R & D, innovation and diffusion of technology", paper given at the high-level small business seminar, Paris, OECD, July 2 and 3.

Baudrillard, J. (1976), *La société de consommation*, Paris, Gallimard.

Beccatini, G. (1989), "Riflessioni sul distretto industriale marshalliano come concetto socio-economica", *Stato e Mercato*, 1.

Bellandi, M. (1989), "Capacita innovativa diffusa e systemi locali di imprese", in G. Beccatini (ed.), *Modelli locali di sviluppo*, Bologne, Il Mulino.

Bernard, J. and A. Torre (1994), "La dynamique de l'innovation et de R-D des PMI françaises", *Revue Internationale PME*, Vol. 7, No. 3-4, pp. 19-41.

Bigras, Y. and D. Pettigrew (1991), "Impact de la déréglementation du camionnage dans une région du Québec", Paper given at the 26th Annual Conference of the Canadian Transportation Research Forum, Quebec, 28-31 May.

Boyer, R. (ed.) (1986), *Capitalismes: fin de siècle*, Paris, Presses universitaires de France.

Brockhaus, R.H. (1980), "Risk taking propensity of entrepreneurs", *Academy of Management*, Vol. 23, No. 3, pp. 509-520.

Bucaille, A. and B. Costa de Beauregard (1987), *PMI: enjeux régionaux et internationaux*, Paris, Economica.

Camagni, R.P. (1980), "Local "milieu", incertainty and innovation networks: toward a new dynamic theory of economic space", in Camagni, R.P. (ed.), *Innovation Networks. The Spatial Perspective*, London, Frances Pinter.

Carlsson, B. (1984), "The development and use of machine tools in historical perspective", *Journal of Economic Behavior and Organisation*, 5, pp. 91-114.

Carlsson, B. (1989), "The evolution of manufacturing technology and its impact on industrial structure: an international study", *Small Business Economics*, Vol. 1, No. 1, pp. 21-37.

Chicha, J. (1981), "Impact de certaines politiques horizontales sur les stratégies des PME", GREPME Research Papers, 81-11.

Contini, B. (1992), "Turbulence et caractéristiques de croissance au sein de l'industrie italienne", Paper given at the Conference on Small Business and Globalization, Montreal, BFI et OECD, May 24-27.

Contini, B. and R. Revelli (1987), "The process of job destruction and job creation in the Italian economy", *Labour*, Vol. 1, No. 3.

Cooper, A.C. et al. (1988), "Survival and failure: a longitudinal study", *Frontiers of Entrepreneurship Research*, Wellesley, Babson College.

Crosnier, P., J.P. François and T. Lehoucq (1991), *Les chiffres-clés. Les PMI* Paris, Ministère de l'Industrie et du Commerce extérieur (SESSI) and Dunod.

Cross, M. (1987), *New Firm Formation and Regional Development*, Guilford, Gower Inc.

Didier, M. (1982), "Crise et concentration du système productif", *Economie et statistique*, No. 144, pp. 3-13.

Duché, G. and S. Savey (1986), "Le rôle de la PME dans la mutation du mode de production capitaliste", in Julien, P.A., Chicha, J. and Joyal, A., *La PME dans un monde en mutation*, Québec, Presses de l'Université du Québec.

Enrietti, A. (1990), "Les rapports de pouvoir et de collaboration: filière, quasi-intégration verticale et réseaux", GREPME Research Paper, No. 90-15.

Evans, D.S. (1987), "Tests of alternative theories of firm growth", *Journal of Political Economy*, Vol. 95, No. 4, August 1987.

Evans, D.S. and L. Leignton (1989), "The determinants of change in U.S. self-employment", *Small Business Economics*, Vol. 1, No. 2.

Foray, D. (1990), "The secrets of industry are in the air", Paper given at the HEC-Montreal Conference on Innovators' Networks, May 1-3.

Gallagher, C.C. and J. Doyle (1986), "Job generation research: a reply to Storey and Johnson", *International Small Business Journal*, Vol. 4, No. 4, pp. 47-54.

Gold, B. (1981), "Changing perspective on size, scale and return: an interpretative study", *Journal of Economic Literature*, March.

Gould, J.P. (1969), "Adjustment costs in the theory of investment of the firm", *Review of Economic Studies*, 36.

Grabher, G. (1989), "Regional innovation by networking: The case of lower Austria", *Entrepreneurship and Regional Development*, Vol. 1, No. 2, pp. 141-142.

Guesnier, B. (1986), "Création d'emplois dans les petites et moyennes entreprises: la France", I.E.R., Université de Poitiers, Working Paper, July.

Hanaut, A. and A. Torre (1985), "L'évolution de la strategie d'externalisation des services par les entreprises industrielles", Nice, LATAPSES, March.

Hirst, P. and J. Zeitlin (1989), "Flexible specialisation and the competitive failure of UK manufacturing", *Political Quarterly*, April-June.

Hull, C.J. (1986), "Job generation in the Federal Republic of Germany: a review", W.P. Berlin, Wissenschaftszentrum, Labour market policy, Research Unit (quoted by Loveman et al.).

Ijiri, Y. and H.A. Simon (1977), *Skew distributions and the size of business firms*, Amsterdam, North Holland.

Julien, P.A. (1989), "The entrepreneur and economic theory", *International Small Business Journal*, Vol. 7, No. 3, pp. 30-38.

Julien, P.A. (1993), "Small business as a matter of research", *Small Business Economics*, Vol. 5, No. 2, pp. 157-166.

Julien, P.A. et al. (1995), "La veille technologique dans les PME manufacturières québécoises", Paper given at the 5th Strategic Management Conference, Paris, May 3-5.

Julien, P.A., J.B. Carrière and L. Hébert (1988), "Les facteurs de diffusion et de pénétration des nouvelles technologies dans les PME manufacturières québécoises", *Revue Internationale PME*, Vol. 1, No. 2, pp. 193-223.

Julien, P.A. and C. Lafrance (1983), "Toward the formalization of 'Small is Beautiful'. Societal effectiveness versus economic efficiency", *Futures*, June, pp. 211-221.

Julien, P.A. and M. Marchesnay (1990), "Sur le dynamisme des petites entreprises dans les pays industrialisés. Vers un nouvel équilibre entre les petites et les grandes entreprises", *Piccola Impresa*, 3, June.

Julien, P.A. and M. Morin (1995), *Mondialisation de l'économie et PME québécoises*, Québec, Presses de l'Université du Québec.

Julien, P.A. and F. Sole Parellada (1987), "Appropriation de l'information, intercommunication et développement régional", Paper given at the XIX conference of the Canadian Regional Science Association, June 3-5, Montreal.

Kickert, W.J.M. (1985), "The magic word flexibility", *International Studies in Management and Organization*, Vol. 14, No. 4, pp. 6-31.

Kirzner, I.M. (1980), *The prime movers of prospers: the entrepreneur in capitalism and socialism*, London, Institute of Economic Affairs.

Lawrence, P.R. and J.W. Lorsch (1973), *Adapter les structures de l'entreprise. Intégration ou différenciation*, Paris, Les Éditions d'Organisation.

Leonard, J.S. (1986), "On the size distribution of employment and establishment", W.P. No. 1951, Cambridge, National Bureau of Economic Research, June.

Leroux, F. (1982), "Sensibilité de la mesure de taille et déterminants de la taille minimale et de la taille moyenne d'efficacité des usines canadiennes", *Revue d'économie industrielle*, Vol. 12, pp. 47-66.

Lindmark, L. (1982), "Small firm in a new context in Sweden", Research Paper No. 42, University of Umëa.

Lindmark, L., P. Davidsson and C. Olofsson (1992), "La volativité des entreprises en Suède", Paper given at the Conference on Small Business and Globalization, Montreal, BFI et OECD, May 24-27.

Loveman, G. (1989), "Changes in the organization of production and the skill composition of the employment", Doctoral Thesis, Cambridge, MIT, September.

Loveman, G., W. Sengenberger and M.J. Piore (eds.) (1990), *The re-emergence of small enterprise: Industrial restructuring in industrialized countries*, IIES, International Labour Office, Geneva.

Lucas, R.E. (1978), "On the size distribution of business firms", *The Bell Journal of Economics*, Vol. 9, Autumn, pp. 508-523.

Maillat, D. and J.C. Perrin (eds.) (1990), *Entreprises innovatrices et réseaux locaux*, Paris, Economica.

Marchesnay, M. (1969), "Analyse dynamique et théorie de la firme", State Doctoral thesis, Paris.

Marchesnay, M. and P.A. Julien (1990), "Small business: as a transaction space", *Entrepreneurship et Regional Development*, 2.3, pp. 267-277.

Marchlup, F. (1967), "Theory of the firm: marginalist, behavioural, managerial", *American Economic Review*, Vol. 57, No. 1, pp. 1-33.

Marshall, A. (1919), *Industry and Trade*, London, MacMillan.

MFRT (German Federal Ministry of Research and Technology) (1989), "Promotion of research and development in small and medium-sized enterprises", Bonn, June, 104 p.

Mills, D.E. and L. Schumann (1985), "Industry structure with fluctuating demand", *American Economic Review*, Vol. 75, No. 4, pp. 758-767.

Mintzberg, H. (1990), *Mintzberg on Management. Inside our Strange World of Organization*, New York, Free Press.

OECD (1985), "Employment in small and large firms: where have the jobs come from?", *Employment Outlook*, Paris, September.

OECD (1993), *Small and Medium-Sized Enterprises: Technology and Competitiveness*, Paris.

Ouchi, W. (1980), "Markets, bureaucracies and clans", *Administrative Science Quarterly*, Vol. 25, pp. 129-141.

Oy, W.Y. (1993), "Heterogeneous firms and the organization of production", *Economic Inquiry*, Vol. 23, April, pp. 147-171.

Penrose, E. (1959), *The Theory of the Growth of the Firm*, Oxford, Basil Blackwell.

Petrella, R. (1989), "La mondialisation de la technologie et de l'économie: une hypothèse", *Futurible*, No. 135, pp. 3-26.

Phillips, B.D. (1985), "The effects of industry deregulation on the small business sector", *Business Economics*, Vol. 20, pp. 28-37.

Phillips, B.D. and B.A. Kirchoff (1989), "Formation, growth and survival: small firm dynamics in the U.S. economy", *Small Business Economics*, Vol. 1, No. 1, pp. 65-74.

Reix, R. (1979), *La flexibilité de l'entreprise*, Paris, Cujas.

Reynolds, P.D. and B. Miller (1989), "New firm survival: analysis of a panel's fourth year", *Frontiers of Entrepreneurship Research*, Wellesley, MA, Babson College.

Richardson, P. (1972), "The Organization of Industry", *Economic Journal*, Vol. 82.

Rothwell, R. (1984), "The role of small firms in the emergence of new technologies", *Omega*, Vol. 12, No. 1, pp. 19-30.

Schumpeter, J. (1972), *Capitalism, Socialism and Democracy*, New York, Harper and Row.

Scitovsky, I. (1976), *The Joyless Economy*, New York, Oxford University Press.

Scott, J.A. (1988), "Flexible production systems and regional development: the rise of new industrial spaces in North America and Western Europe", *International Journal of Urban and Regional Research*, Vol. 12, No. 2, pp. 171-186.

Sforzi, C. (1989), "The quantitative importance of marshallian industrial districts in the Italian economy", Paper given at the international conference on industrial districts and inter-firm cooperation, April 12-14, University of Florence.

Stigler, G. (1939), "Production and distribution in the short run", *Journal of Political Economy*, Vol. 47, No. 2, June.

Storey, D.J. and S. Johnson (1986), "Job generation in Britain: a review of recent studies", *International Small Business Journal*, Vol. 4, No. 4, Summer, pp. 29-47.

Thibodeau, J.C. and P.A. Julien (1986), "Les PME manufacturières dans la tourmente économique, de 1975 à 1982", *Revue d'économie industrielle*, 36, 2nd quarter, pp. 14-25.

Thibodeau, J.C., M. Martineau and P. Rioux (1995), "Essaimage des nouvelles technologies en région périphérique", Paper given at the XIX conference of the Canadian Regional Science Association, June 3-5, Montreal.

Van der Horst, R. (1992), "The volatility of the small business sector in the Netherlands", Paper given at the conference on small business and economic globalization, Montreal, BFI and OECD, May 24-27.

Veblen, T. (1899), *The Theory of the Leisure Class*, New York, Macmillan.

Wallenstein, A. (1985), Historical Capitalism, New York, McGraw Hill.

Chapter 2

Aldrich, H. and C. Zimmer (1986), "Entrepreneurship through Social Networks", in D.L. Sexton and R.W. Smilor (eds.), *The Art and Science of Entrepreneurship*, Cambridge, MA, Ballinger.

Arocena, J. (1986), *Le développement par l'initiative locale*, Paris, L'Harmattan.

Birley, S. (1985), "The Role of Networks in the Entrepreneurial Process", in J.A. Hornaday, E.B. Shills, J.A. Timmons and K.H. Vesper (eds.), *Frontiers of Entrepreneurship Research*, Wellesley, MA, Babson College.

Blakeley, E.J. (1994), *Local Planning and Economic Development*, 2nd Edition, Los Angeles, SAGE.

Boure, R. and J. Menville (1990), "Sur et sous le 'Local'", *Les Cahiers du LERASS*, No. 20, LERASS-IUT, Toulouse.

CADC Mékinac-Des Chenaux (1989), *Stratégie de développement économique et social*, Saint-Célestin.

Carsrud, A.L., C.M. Gaglio and K.V. Olhm (1986), "Entrepreneurs-mentors networks and successful new venture development: an exploratory study", in R. Ronstadt, J.A. Hornaday, R.Peterson and K.H. Vesper (eds.), *Frontiers of Entrepreneurship Research*, Wellesley, MA, Babson College.

Chassagne, M.E. (1988), *Le projet rural*, Paris, L'Harmattan.

Chassagne, M.E. (1988), *Les initiatives locales de création d'emplois en milieu rural*, SME/ILE/88.01, OCDE.

Cochrane, A. (1987), *Developing Local Economic Strategies*, Milton Keynes, Open University Press.

Conseil économique du Canada (1989a), *La relance locale: pour une approche communautaire du développement économique*, Ottawa.

Conseil économique du Canada (1990), "Le développement local", *Au courant*, March.

Dionne, H. (1989), "Le développement local villageois comme projet de société", *Le local en mouvement*, GRIR, Université du Québec à Chicoutimi.

Derycke, P.H. (1993), "Le 'local' dans l'analyse économique", in *À la recherche du "local"* under the direction of A. Mabileau, Paris, L'Harmattan.

420

Douglas, D. (1989), Community Economic Development In Rural Canada: A Critical Review, *Plan Canada*, Vol. 29, No. 2.

Douglas, D. (1994), *Community Economic in Canada*, Vol. 1, Toronto, MacGraw-Hill.

Dykerman, F.W. (1989), "Local Rural Planning and Development in Atlantic Canada: Perspectives and Direction", *Plan Canada* Vol. 29, No. 2.

Filion, L.J. (1991), *Vision et relations: clefs du succès de l'entrepreneur*, Montréal, Les éditions de l'entrepreneur.

Greffe, X. (1988), *Décentraliser pour l'emploi*, Paris, Seuil.

GRIR (1990), "Un pays à construire", *Réseau*, March.

Jean, B. (1989), "Le développement local à sa place: la problématique du développement local", *Revue canadienne de sciences régionales*, Vol. 12, No. 1.

Johanisson, J. (1987), "Organizing The Network Metaphor", in *International Studies Of Management and Organization*, Vol. XII, No. 1.

Joyal, A. (1987), "Réflexions sur le concept du développement local", *Revue d'économie régionale et urbaine*, No. 7.

Joyal, A. (1991), "Facteurs de succès et d'échecs des entreprises alternatives", in *Petites entreprises et développement local*, under the direction of C. Fourcade, Éditions Eska, Paris.

Joyal, A. (1994a), Community Economic Development: The Montreal examples, in *Community Economic Development in Canada*, Vol II, op. cit.

Joyal, A. (1994a), Les prés du développement économique local en France: aussi verts ou plus verts que ceux du Québec, in *Développement économique: clé de l'autonomie locale*, under the direction of M.U. Proulx, Montréal, Les Éditions Transcontinentales inc.

Julien, P.A. and M. Marchesnay (1990), "Small business as space of transactions", *Journal of Entrepreneurship and Regional Development*, Vol. 2, No. 2, pp. 267-277.

Lacour, C. (1986), "Le développement local est mort, vive le développement local!", *Correspondance Municipale*, Dec.

Lamontagne, F. (1989), "Le développement des régions canadiennes: la nécessité d'une approche alternative", *Revue Canadienne de Santé Mentale*, Vol. 8, No. 2.

Lecoq, B. (1989), *Réseaux et système productif régional: contenu portée et fondements théoriques du concept de réseau*, C.R.E.R., Dossier No. 23, Université de Neuchâtel.

Le local en action (1989), actes d'un colloque international, Paris, Les Éditions de l'Épargne.

Lotz, J. (1990), *Community Enterprise In Scotland*, rapport polycopié remis au Conseil de recherche en sciences sociales du Canada, April.

MacFarlane, R. (1990), "C-BED, l'expérience britannique", *Revue d'économie sociale*, June.

MacLeod, G. (1989), "Le développement communautaire: quelques expériences canadiennes", in *L'autre économie: une économie alternative?*, under the direction of B. Lévesque, A. Joyal and O. Chouinard, Québec, Presses de l'Université du Québec.

Maillat, D. (1992), "Milieux et dynamique territoriale de l'innovation", *Revue canadienne de sciences régionales*, Vol. XV, No. 2.

Maillat, D. (1994), Comportements spatiaux et milieux innovateurs, in *Encyclopédie d'économie spatiale, concepts, comportements, organisations*, under the direction of J.P. Auray, A. Bailly, J.P. Derycke, J.M. Huriot, Paris, Economica.

Maillat, D., O. Crevoisier and J.Y. Vasserot (1992), L'Innovation et disrict industriel in *Entreprises innovatrices et développement territorial*, under the direction of D. Maillat and J.-C. Perrin, Neuchâtel, EDES.

Mengin, J. (1989), L'évaluation qualitative appliquée au développement local, *Recherches sociales*, No 111, July-September.

Mifsud, P. (1991), "Les petites entreprises", in *Petite entreprise et développement local*, op. cit.

MIS Report (1985), "Local Development Corporation: A Tool For Economic Development", *ICMA*, Vol. 17, No. 6, June.

Neuschwander, C. (1991), *L'acteur et le changement: essai sur les réseaux*, Paris, Seuil.

Newman, L.H. et al. (1986), *Community Economic Development: An Approach for Urban-based Economies*, Winnipeg, Institute for Urban Studies.

OCDE (1987), *Le développement économique et de l'emploi au niveau local*, Note du Secrétariat, SME/ILE, April.

OCDE (1988), *Création d'emplois en milieu rural, Emplois et Innovation*, October.

OCDE (1989a), *La planification stratégique axée sur la collectivité: une approche au développement économique et à la mise en valeur du potentiel local dans les régions rurales du Canada*, SME/ILE 89.12.

OCDE (1989b), *Les mécanismes de la création d'emplois: l'exemple américain*, Paris.

OCDE (1990), *Programme ILE*, Note du Secrétariat.

Pecqueur, B. (1989), *Le développement local*, Paris, Syros/Alternatives.

Pecqueur, B. (1989), "Un réseau ne se crée pas par décret", in *Villes intermédiaires pour l'Europe*, under the direction of M. Gault, Paris, Syros/Alternatives.

Perrin, J.C. (1990), "Organisation industrielle: la composante territoriale", *Revue d'économie industrielle*, No. 21.

Perry, S. (1987), *Communities On The Way: Rebuilding Local Economies in the United States and Canada*, State University of New York Press.

Perry, S. (1989), "Le développement régional par l'engagement communautaire", *Cahier du Conseil économique du Canada*, No. 17.

Plassard, F. (1988), *Le projet de dévelopement local dans la mutation économique et culturelle des sociétés industrialisées*, Epsilon/ALDEA.

Prévost, P. (1993), *Entrepreneurship et développement local: quand la population se prend en main*, Les Éditions Transcontinentales, GRIR, Université du Québec à Chicoutimi.

Proulx, P.P. (1990), *Éléments d'une théorie globale du développement des villes internationales: le contexte, le milieu, les réseaux, le couplage local-régional-international et les politiques*, Research Notebook, Département des Sciences Économiques, Université de Montréal.

Quévit, M. (1986), *Le pari de l'industrialisation rurale*, Genève, Éditions régionales européennes S.A.

Rousseau, M. P. (1989), *Le management des économies locales*, Paris, Eyrolles.

SADC de la Vallée de la Bastiscan (1994), *Plan stratégique*, Saint-Stanislas.

Shapero, A. (1984), "Entrepreneurship in Economic Development", in *Shaping the Local Economy*, ICMA.

Sinclair, P.E. (1989), "The GNPDC: An Organizational Framework for Revitalization", *Local Development Paper*, No. 6, Economic Council of Canada.

Sorbets, C. (1990), "Le local au miroir de la communication", Conference entitled *La communication dans l'espace régional et local*, Maison des sciences de l'Homme, Bordeaux, March 23-24.

Szarka, J. (1990), "Networking and Small Firms", *International Small Business Journal*, Vol. 8, No. 2.

Tremblay, D.G. and J.M. Fontan (1994), *Le développement économique local*, Télé-Université, Québec.

Vachon, B. (1993), *Le développement local: théorie et pratique*, Boucherville, Gaëtan Morin Ed.

Watt, J. (1988), *Community Enterprise in the Highlands and Islands*, International Conference on Rural Entrepreneurship, Silsoe College.

Chapter 3

Acs, Z.J. and D.B. Audretsch (eds.) (1990), *The Economics of Small Firms. A European Challenge*, Dordrecht, Kluwer Academic Publishers, 226 p.

Ansoff, H.I. (1988), *The New Corporate Strategy*, New York, John Wiley and Sons, 258 p.

Applebaum, W. (1968), *Guide to Store Location Reseach*, Reading, Supermarket Institute Inc.

Applebaum, W. and H.L. Green (1974), *Determining Store Trade Areas*, New York, McGraw-Hill.

Bailly, A.S. (1984), "Images de l'espace et pratiques commerciales: l'apport de la géographie de la perception", in *Annales de géographie*, No. 518, pp. 423-431.

Beauregard, L. (1987), "Les services aux entreprises dans le centre-ville de Montréal. Une analyse géographique", *Notes et documents de géographie*, Université de Montréal, No. 87-02, 28 p.

Belley, A. and J. Lorrain (1990), *Guide de préparation du plan d'affaires*, Quebec, Association des cadres de l'éducation aux adultes des collèges du Québec, 18 p. and an appendix of 34 p.

Benko, G.B. (ed.) (1990), *La dynamique spatiale de l'économie contemporaine*, Paris, Éditions de l'Espace Européen, 396 p.

Berry, B.J.L. (1971), *Géographie des marchés et du commerce de détail*, Paris, Armand Colin, 254 p.

Berry, B.J.L., E.C. Conkling and M. Ray (1976), *The Geography of Economic Systems*, Englewood Cliffs, Prentice-Hall, 529 p.

Boyce, R.R. (2nd ed.) (1978), *The Bases of Economic Geography*, New York, Holt Reinehart and Winston, 433 p.

Brouillette, N. (1982), "Les liaisons interindustrielles de la région Mauricie-Bois-Francs (région 04)", *Cahiers de géographie du Québec*, Vol. 26, No. 67, pp. 65-87.

Brouillette, N. (1986), "Les liaisons de services des établissements manufacturiers de la région Mauricie-Bois-Francs (région 04)", in L. Deshaies and R. Pelletier, *Proceedings of the Canadian Conference of the Canadian Association of Geographers, 1985*, Trois-Rivières, ACG-85, pp. 85-203.

Chapman, K. (1987), *Industrial location. Principles and policies*, Don Mills, Oxford University Press, 320 p.

Claval, P. (1976), *Éléments de géographie économique*, Paris, Éditions M. Th. Génin, 361 p.

Colbert, F. and R. Côté (1990), *Localisation commerciale*, Boucherville, Gaëtan Morin Éditeur, 152 p.

Collaboration (1989), *Les petites et moyennes entreprises*, Paris, Berger-Levrault, 281 p.

Collaboration (1989), *La sous-traitance industrielle. Nouveaux chantiers de développement régional*, Québec, OPDQ, 101 p.

Crozier, M. and E. Friedberg (1977), *L'acteur et le système*, Paris, Seuil, 504 p.

Davis, R.L. and D.S. Rogers (1984), *Store Location and Store Assessment Research*, New York, John Wiley and Sons.

de Koning, A.C.P. and J.A.H. Snijders (1991), *La politique pour les petites et moyennes entreprises dans les pays des communautés européennes, Inventaire et étude comparative*, Zoetermeer, Institut d'études économiques pour les petites et moyennes entreprises, 150 p.

Derycke, P. and G. Gilbert (1988), *Économie publique locale*, Paris, Economica, 308 p.

Desjardins, C. (1974), *La PME au Québec: situations et problèmes*, Quebec, M.I.C., 69 p.

Eilon, S. (1971), *Distribution management: mathematical modelling and practical analysis*, London, Griffin.

Fenwick, I. (1978), *Techniques in Store Location Research: Review and Applications*, Corbridge, Retailing and Planning Associates.

Fielding, G.J. (1967), *Geography as Social Science*, New York, Harper & Row, 336 p.

Filey, A. (1978), "Characteristics and measurement of an organizational typology", in *Academy of Management Journal*, December.

Filion, L.J. (1990), "Visions et relations: éléments pour un métamodèle entrepreneurial", Exposé aux Séminaires Joseph-Chicha, December 6.

Gagnon, Savard, Carrier and Decoste (1990), *L'entreprise et son environnement*, Boucherville, Gaëtan Morin Éditeur, 381 p.

Gallayher, R.R. (1989), *Stonesong Press Your Small Business Made Simple*, New York, Doubleday, 158 p.

Gasse, Y. (1989a), "Les stades d'évolution d'une entreprise", *Le Québec industriel*, Vol. 44, No. 2.

Gasse, Y. (1989b), "Gérer la croissance", *Le Québec industriel*, Vol. 44, No. 7.

Giaoutzi, M., P. Nijkamp and D.J. Storey (eds.) (1988), *Small and Medium-Sized Enterprises and Regional Development*, London, Routledge, 314 p.

Gill, J. (1985), *Factors affecting the Survival and Growth of the Smaller Company*, Brookfield (Vermont), Gower Publishing Company, 227 p.

Gudgin, G. (1978), *Industrial Location Processes and Regional Employment Growth*, Westmead, Saxon House.

Gupta, K.L. (1989), *Industrialization and Employment in Developing Countries: A Comparative Study*, London, Routledge, 205 p.

Hagget, P. (1976), *L'analyse spatiale en géographie humaine*, Paris, Armand Colin, 390 p.

Julien, P.A. and M. Marchesnay (1988), *La petite entreprise, principes d'économie et de gestion*, Éditions G. Vermette, pp. 161-170.

Julien, P.A. and M. Marchesnay (1995), *L'entreprenariat*, Paris, Economica.

Kane, B.J. (1966), *A Systematic Guide to Supermarket Location Analysis*, New York, Fairchild Publications Inc.

Kirchhoff, B. (1992), "La vérité au sujet de la survivance des entrepreneurs: l'expérience américaine", Paper presented at the BFD-OCDE Conference entitled "Les PME et la globalisation économique", Montreal, May 24-27.

Laroche, G. (1988), *La PME au Québec: une manifestation de dynamisme économique*, Québec, MMSR, 66 p.

Lewis, J., J. Stanworth and A. Gibb (1984), *Success and Failure in Small Business*, Brookfield, Gower Publishing Company, 275 p.

Manzagol, C. (1974a), Quelques problèmes de méthode en géographie industrielle, 1. La mesure de la distribution géographique de l'industrie, *Revue de géographie de Montréal*, Vol. XXVIII, No. 1, pp. 85-93.

Manzagol, C. (1974b), Quelques problèmes de méthode en géographie industrielle, 2. Les analyses de localisation, *Revue de géographie de Montréal*, Vol. XXVIII, No. 3, pp. 291-299.

Manzagol, C. (1980), *Logique de l'espace industriel*, Paris, P.U.F., 248 p.

Merenne-Schoumaker, B. (1985), Spécialisation spatiale et dynamisme régional dans l'espace industriel wallon: considération méthodologiques, *Hommes et Terres du Nord*, No. 2, pp. 110-117.

M.I.C. (1987), *La PME au Québec: état de la situation*, Québec, MIC, 320 p.

Ministère de l'industrie, du commerce et de la technologie (1989), *Guide par étapes qui mène à la réussite: le marketing pour la petite entreprise de services*, Toronto, Ontario Government Library, 80 p. plus appendix.

Morel, B. and T. Fellmann (1989), *Les effets de polarisation sur la métropole marseillaise: mobilité économique, concurrence, complémentarité*, Marseille, EHESS, 268 p.

Morvan, Y. and M.J. Marchand (1994), *L'intervention des régions*, Paris, Montchrétien.

Neck, P.A. and R.E. Nelson (eds.) (1990), *Le développement des petites entreprises: politiques et programmes*, Geneva, International Labour Office, 256 p.

Nelson, R. (1958), *The Selection of Retail Location*, New York, F.W. Dodge Corp.

Nelson, R. E. (1990), *La promotion des petites entreprises*, Neck and Nelson, op. cit., pp. 1-13.

Norcliffe, G.B. (1975), *A Theory of Manufacturing Places*, in L. Collins and D.B. Walker (eds.), Locational Dynamics of Manufacturing Activity, London, John Wiley and Sons, pp. 19-57.

Oakey, R.P. (1981), *High Technology Industry and Industrial Location*, Aldershot, Gower Publishing.

Pettigrew, D. (1989), *La gestion des commerces de détail*, Montreal, McGraw-Hill.

Le Service des statistiques industrielles (1988), *L'état des P.M.I.*, Paris, Ministère de l'industrie et de l'aménagement du territoire, 154 p.

Shaffer, R. (1989), *Community Economics. Economic Structure and Change in Small Communities*, Ames, Iowa State University Press, 321 p.

Smith, D.M. (1971), *Industrial Location*, New York, John Wiley and Sons, 553 p.

Steinhoff, D. and J.F. Burgess (1989), *Small Business Management Fundamentals*, New York, McGraw-Hill, 492 p.

Steinneetz, L. (1969), "Critical Stages of Small", in *Business Horizons*, February.

Stöhr, W.B. (1990) (under the direction of), *Global Challenge and Local Response Initiatives for Economic Regeneration in Contemporary Europe*, London, Mansell Publishing Limited, 472 p.

Storey, D.J. (1982), *Entrepreneurship and the New Firm*, London, Croom Helm, 223 p.

Storey, D.J. (ed.) (1983), *The Small Firm. An International Survey*, London, Croom Helm, 274 p.

Storey, D.J. (ed.) (1985), *Small Firms in Regional Economic Development: Britain, Ireland and the United States*, London, Cambridge University Press, 234 p.

Thomas, I. (1982), "Estimation de la demande postale: l'exemple des bureaux de Namur (Belgique)", in *Recherches économiques de Louvain*, Vol. 48, special edition 3-4, pp. 337-350.

Törnqvist, G. (1968), "Flows of information and the location of economic activity", in *Geografiska Annaler*, Vol. 50B, pp. 99-107.

Wallace, I. (1972), "Towards the integration of industrial location and commodity. Flow studies", in *Geography*, No. 2, pp. 1209-1211.

Chapter 4

Amit, R., L. Glosten et al. (1993), "Challenges to Theory Development in Entrepreneurship Research", *Journal of Management Studies*, 30(5), pp. 815-834.

Bannock, G. (1981), *The Economics of Small Firms: Return from the Wilderness*, Oxford: Basil Blackwell.

Baumol, W. J. (1968), "Entrepreneurship in Economic Theory", *The American Economic Review*, 58, pp. 64-71.

Baumol, W. J. (1990), "Entrepreneurship: Productive, Unproductive, and Destructive", *Journal of Political Economy*, Vol. 98, No. 5, pp. 893-921.

Baumol, W. J. (1993), "Formal Entrepreneurship Theory in Economics: Existence and Bounds", *Journal of Business Venturing*, 3, pp. 197-210.

Béchard, J.P. (1996), *Comprendre le champ de l'entrepreneurship*, research paper 96-01-01, Maclean Hunter Chair of Entrepreneurship, HEC, the University of Montreal Business School.

Birch, D.L. (1983), *The Contribution of Small Enterprise to Growth and Employment*, Cambridge, Mass.

Birley, S. (1989), "The Role of Networks in the Entrepreneurial Process", *Journal of Business Venturing*, Vol. 1, pp. 107-117.

Blawatt, K. (1995), "Defining the Entrepreneurs: A Conceptual Model of Entrepreneurship", *Proceedings of the 12th Annual Conference of the CCSBE* (Canadian Council for Small Business and Entrepreneurship), Thunder Bay, Ontario, October, pp. 13-37.

Bolton, J. E. (1971), *Small Firms: Report of the Committee of Inquiry on Small Firms*, Chairman J.E. Bolton DSC. Presented to Parliament (Nov.), UK: HMSO (Her Majesty's Stationery Office) Cmnd 4811.

Brockhaus, R.H. Sr (1982), "The Psychology of the Entrepreneur", in Kent et al. (eds.) (1982), *Encyclopedia of Entrepreneurship*, Englewood Cliffs, N.J., Prentice Hall, pp. 39-57.

Broehl, W. G. Jr (1978), *The Village Entrepreneur: Change Agents in India's Rural Development*, Cambridge, Mass., Harvard University Press.

Buchanan, J.M. and A. Di Pierro (1980), "Cognition, Choice and Entrepreneurship", *Southern Economic Journal*, Vol. 46, pp. 693-701.

Bull, I. and G.E. Willard (1993), "Towards a Theory of Entrepreneurship", *Journal of Business Venturing*, Vol. 8, No. 3, pp. 183-196.

Bull, I., H. Thomas and G. Willard (eds.) (1995), *Entrepreneurship. Perspectives on Theory Building*, Oxford, Pergamon Press.

Burdeau, G. (1979), *Le libéralisme*, Paris, Éditions du Seuil.

Burns, P. and J.C. Dewhurst (eds.) (1989), *Small Business and Entrepreneurship*, London, MacMillan.

Bygrave, W. D. (1989a), "The Entrepreneurship Paradigm (I): A Philosophical Look at its Research Methodologies", *Entrepreneurship Theory & Practice*, Autumn, pp. 7-26.

Bygrave, W. D. (1989b), "The Entrepreneurship Paradigm (II): Chaos and Catastrophes Among Quantum Jumps?", *Entrepreneurship Theory and Practice*, Winter, pp. 7-30.

Bygrave, W. D. (1993), "Theory Building in the Entrepreneurship Paradigm", *Journal of Business Venturing*, Vol. 8, No. 3, pp. 255-280.

Cantillon, R. (1755), *Essai sur la nature du commerce en général*, London: Fetcher Gyler. Also edited in an English version, with other material, by Henry Higgs, C.B., London, MacMillan (1931).

Casson, M. (1982), *The Entrepreneur: An Economic Theory*, Oxford, Martin Robertson.

Chell, E. (1985), "The Entrepreneurial Personality: A Few Ghosts Laid to Rest?", *International Small Business Journal*, Vol. 3, No. 3, pp. 43-54.

Chicha, J. and P.A. Julien (1979), "Les stratégies des P.M.E. et leur adaptation au changement", Département d'administration et d'économique, Université du Québec à Trois-Rivières.

Clark, J.B. (1899), *The Distribution of Wealth: A Theory of Wages, Interest and Profits*, New York and London, MacMillan.

Cochran, T.C. (1968), "Entrepreneurship", in Sills, D.L. (ed.), *International Encyclopedia of the Social Sciences*, London and New York, The MacMillan Co. & The Free Press, Vol. 5, pp. 87-91.

Cole, A.H. (1959), *Business in its Social Setting*, Cambridge, Mass., Harvard University Press.

Collins, O.F., D.G. Moore and D.B. Unwalla (1964), *The Enterprising Man*, MSU Business Studies, Bureau of Business and Economic Research, Graduate School of Business Administration, Michigan State University, East Lansing, Michigan.

Collins, O. F. and D. G. Moore, (1970), *The Organization Makers: A Behavioral Study of Independent Entrepreneurs*, New York, Appleton-Century-Crofts (Meredith Corp.).

Cossette, P. (1994a), "Développement d'une méthode systématique d'aide à la mise au point de la vision stratégique chez le propriétaire-dirigeant de PME: une étude exploratoire", in Obrecht, J.J., *Les P.M.E./P.M.I. et leur contribution au développement régional et international*, Proceedings of the 39th World Conference of the ICSB, Strasbourg, pp. 73-82.

Cossette, P. (ed.) (1994b), *Cartes cognitives et organisations*, Québec, Presses de l'Université Laval, Paris, Éditions Eska.

Covin, J.G. and D.P. Slevin (1991), "A Conceptual Model of Entrepreneurship As Firm Behavior", *Entrepreneurship: Theory & Practice*, Vol. 16, No. 1, pp. 7-25.

Cunningham, J.B. and J.C. Lischeron (1991), "Defining Entrepreneurship", *Journal of Small Business Management*, Vol. 29, No. 1, pp. 45-67.

Deakins, D. (1996), *Entrepreneurship and Small Firms*, McGraw-Hill.

Déry, R. and J.M. Toulouse (1994), *La structuration sociale du champ de l'entrepreneurship: le cas du Journal of Business Venturing*, research paper No. 94-06-02, Maclean Hunter Chair of Entrepreneurship, HEC, the University of Montreal Business School.

Durand, D. and D. Shea (1974), "Entrepreneurial Activity as a Function of Achievement Motivation and Reinforcement Control", *The Journal of Psychology*, 88, pp. 57-63.

Durand, D.E. (1975), "Effects of Achievement Motivation and Skill Training on the Entrepreneurial Behaviour of Black Businessmen", *Organizational Behaviour and Human Performance*, 14, 1, pp. 76-90.

Du Toit, D.F. (1980), "Confessions of a Successful Entrepreneur", *Harvard Business Review*, November-December, pp. 44-48.

Ellis, W.H. (1983), *Canadian Entrepreneurs: Innovators or Manipulators*, paper presented at the 2nd international conference of the International Council for Small Business, Halifax, Nova Scotia, Canada, June 26 to 29. Also in Vesper, K.H. (1982),

430

Frontiers of Entrepreneurship Research, Wellesley, Mass., Babson Center for Entrepreneurial Studies, pp. 16-24.

Ely, R.T. and R.H. Hess (1893), *Outline of Economics*, New York, MacMillan.

Eysenk, H.J. (1967), "Personality Patterns in Various Groups of Businessmen", *Occupational Psychology*, Vol. 41, pp. 249-250.

Filion, L.J. (1987), *Entrepreneurship: bibliographie choisie et une revue de la documentation essentielle sur le sujet*. Research paper No. 87-03, Groupe de recherche en Économie et gestion des petites et moyennes organisations et de leur environnement (GREPME). Université du Québec à Trois-Rivières (UQTR).

Filion, L.J. (1988), *The Strategy of Successful Entrepreneurs in Small Business: Vision, Relationships and Anticipatory Learning*. Ph.D. Thesis, University of Lancaster, Great Britain (UMI 8919064) (Volume 1: 695 pp. Volume 2: 665 p.).

Filion, L.J. (1989a), "The Design of Your Entrepreneurial Learning System: Identify a Vision and Assess Your Relations System", Third Canadian Conference on Entrepreneurial Studies, University of Calgary, September 28-30, 1989. *Proceedings of the Third Canadian Conference on Entrepreneurial Studies*, pp. 77-90.

Filion, L.J. (1989b), "Le développement d'une vision: un outil stratégique à maîtriser". *Gestion: Revue internationale de gestion*, Vol. 14, No. 3, September, pp. 24-34.

Filion, L.J. (1990a), "Vision and Relations: Elements for an Entrepreneurial Metamodel". Tenth Annual Babson Entrepreneurship Research Conference, Babson College, MA., April 4-6, 1990. Published in Churchill, N.C. and Bygrave, W.C. (eds.) (1990), *Frontiers of Entrepreneurship Research 1990*. Proceedings of the Tenth Annual Babson College Entrepreneurship Research Conference, Babson Park, MA, Center for Entrepreneurial Studies, Babson College, pp. 57-71.

Filion, L.J. (1990b), *Les entrepreneurs parlent*, Montreal, Qc, Éditions de l'entrepreneur, 1990, 303 p.

Filion, L.J. (1991a), "Vision and Relations: Elements for an Entrepreneurial Metamodel", *International Small Business Journal*, Vol. 9, No. 2, Jan. 1991, pp. 26-40.

Filion, L.J. (1991b), *Vision et relations: clefs du succès de l'entrepreneur*, Montreal, Qc, Éditions de l'entrepreneur, 272 p.

Filion, L.J. (1992), *Review*: Stanworth, J. and Gray, C. (eds.) (1991), *Bolton Twenty Years On. The Small Firm in the 1990s*, London, Paul Chapman, Revue Internationale PME, Vol. 5, Nos. 3-4, p. 171-189.

Filion, L.J. (1993), Entrepreneur, organisation et apprentissage: nécessité de s'aménager un espace de soi, partie 1: l'entrepreneur et l'apprentissage, Revue *Organisation*, Vol. 2, No. 2, Summer, p. 59-69.

Filion, L.J. (1994), Entrepreneur, organisation et apprentissage: nécessité de s'aménager un espace de soi, partie 2: entrepreneur, organisation et entreprise, Revue *Organisation*, Vol. 3, No. 1, Winter, pp. 47-55.

Filion, L.J. (1996a), "Différences dans les systèmes de gestion des propriétaires-dirigeants, entrepreneurs et opérateurs de PME. *Canadian Journal of Administrative Sciences*, Vol. 13, No. 4, December, pp. 306-320.

Filion, L.J. (1996b), "A Marketing System for Micro-Enterprises", *UIC/AMA Research Symposium on Marketing and Entrepreneurship*, Stockholm, Sweden, June 14-15 1996, Vol. 2, pp. 150-166.

Fukuyama, F. (1992), *The End of History and the Last Man*, New York, The Free Press.

Fukuyama, F. (1994), *Trust: The Social Virtues and the Creation of Prosperity*, New York, The Free Press.

Gartner, W.B. (1985), "A Conceptual Framework of Describing the Phenomenon of New Venture Creation", *Academy of Management Review*, Vol. 10, No. 4, pp. 696-706.

Gartner, W.B. (1990), "What are we talking about when we talk about entrepreneurship?", *Journal of Business Venturing*, Vol. 5, No. 1, p. 15-29.

Gartner, W.B., J.W. Carland et al. (1988), "'Who Is an Entrepreneur?'" Is the Wrong Question", *American Journal of Small Business*, 12(4), pp. 11-39.

Gasse, Y. (1978), *Characteristics, Functions and Performance of Small Firms: Owner-managers in Two Industrial Environments* (2 volumes), Ph.D. thesis, Northwestern University, Evanston Ill., University Microfilm International, No. 79-3265.

Gasse, Y. (1982), "Elaboration on the Psychology of the Entrepreneur", in Kent et al., (1982) *Encyclopedia of Entrepreneurship*, Englewood Cliffs, N.J., Prentice Hall, pp. 57-66.

Gibb, A. and J. Ritchie (1981), "Influence on Entrepreneurship: A Study Over Time", in *Bolton Ten Years On*, Proceedings of the U.K. Small Business Research Conference held November 20 and 21 at the Polytechnic of Central London.

Glueck, W.F. (1977), *Management*, Hinsdale, I.L.L., The Dryden Press.

Gunder, F.A. (1969), "Sociology of Development and Underdevelopment of Sociology" in Howel, N. et al. *Catalyst.* Reference in Kent, C.A., Sexton, D.L. et al. (eds.) (1982) *Encyclopedia of Entrepreneurship*, Englewood Cliffs, N.J., Prentice Hall, p. 58.

Hayek, F.A. von (1937), "Economics and Knowledge", in *Economica*, New Series, 4 (13-16), pp. 33-54. (Presidential Address to the London Economic Club, November 10, 1936.) Reprinted in Hayek, F.A. von (1959), *Individualism and Economic Order*, London, Routledge and Kegan Paul, pp. 33-56.

Hayek, F.A. von (1959), "The Use of Knowledge in Society", *American Economic Review* (1945), 35, pp. 519-530. Also in *Individualism and Economic Order* (1959), London, Routledge and Kegan Paul, Chicago, University of Chicago Press (1948, 1957). Voir aussi "The Meaning of Competition", 1949, in *Individualism and Economic Order*, 1959, pp. 92-106.

Hébert, R. F. and A.N. Link (1982), *The Entrepreneur: Mainstream Views and Radical Critiques*, New York, Praeger.

Higgins, B. H. (1959), *Economic Development: Principles, Problems, and Policies*, New York, Norton.

Hofer, C.W. and W.D. Bygrave (1992), "Researching Entrepreneurship", *Entrepreneurship Theory & Practice*, Vol. 16, No. 3, pp. 91-100.

Hornaday, J.A. (1982), "Research About Living Entrepreneurs", in Kent, C.A., Sexton, D.L. et al. (eds.), *Encyclopedia of Entrepreneurship*, Englewood Cliffs, N.J., Prentice Hall, pp. 20-34.

Hoselitz, B.F. (1952), "Entrepreneurship and Economic Growth", *American Journal of Economic Sociology*, pp. 97-106.

Hoselitz, B.F. (ed.) (1968), *The Role of Small Industry in the Process of Economic Growth*, Japan by Miyohei Shinohara, India by Douglas Fisher, The Hague, Paris, Mouton.

Hull, D.L., J.J. Bosley and G.G. Udeel (1980), "Renewing the Hunt for the Heffalump: Identifying Potential Entrepreneurs by Personality Characteristics", *Journal of Small Business Management*, 18, 1, p. 11-18.

Hundall, P.S. (1971), "A Study of Entrepreneurial Motivation: Comparison of Fast - and Slow - Progressing Small Scale Industrial Entrepreneurs in Punjab, India", *Journal of Applied Psychology*, 55, 4, p. 317-323.

Ibrahim, A.B. (1994), "Strategy Types and Small Firm's Performance: An Empirical Investigation", *Journal of Small Business Strategy*, Vol.4 , No. 1.

Innis, H.A. (1930), *The Fur-Trade in Canada: An Introduction to Canadian Economic History*, Toronto, University of Toronto Press (see also the revised edition of 1956).

Innis, M.Q. (ed.) (1956), *Essays in Canadian Economic History* (Harold Adam Innis), Toronto, University of Toronto Press.

Julien, P.A. (1989), "The Entrepreneur and Economic Theory", *International Small Business Journal*, Vol.7, No. 3, pp. 29-38.

Julien, P.A. (1990), "Vers une typologie multicritère des PME", *Revue Internationale PME*, Vol. 3, No. 3-4, pp. 411-425.

Julien, P.A. and M. Marchesnay (1987), *La petite entreprise*, Paris, Vuibert.

Julien, P.A. and M. Marchesnay (1996), *L'entrepreneuriat*, Paris, Economica.

Kennedy, P. (1988), *The Rise and Fall of the Great Powers*, London, Unwin Hyman.

Kent, C.A., D.L. Sexton and K.H. Vesper (eds.) (1982), *Encyclopedia of Entrepreneurship*, Englewood Cliffs, N.J., Prentice Hall.

Kets de Vries, M.F.R. (1985), "The Dark Side of Entrepreneurship", *Harvard Business Review*, November-December, pp. 160-167.

Kihlstrom, R.E. and J.J. Laffont (1979), "A General Equilibrium Entrepreneurial Theory of Firm Formation Based on Risk Aversion", *Journal of Political Economy*, Vol.87, No. 4, pp. 719-748.

Kirchhoff, B.A. (1992), "Entrepreneurship's Contribution to Economics", *Entrepreneurship: Theory & Practice*, Vol.16, No. 2, pp. 93-112.

Kirchhoff, B.A. (1994), *Entrepreneurship and Dynamic Capitalism*, Westfort, Conn., Praeger.

Kirzner, I.M. (1976), *The Economic Point of View: An Essay in the History of Economic Thought*, 2nd edition, Kansas City, Sheed and Ward.

Kirzner, I. M. (1983), *Perception, Opportunity and Profit: Studies in the Theory of Entrepreneurship*, 1st edition 1979, Chicago, University of Chicago Press.

Knight, F.H. (1921), *Risk, Uncertainty and Profit*, New York, Houghton Mifflin. Also Chicago, University of Chicago Press (1971).

Kunkel, J.H. (1965), "Values and Behavior in Economic Development", *Economic Development and Cultural Change*, 13, 3, pp. 257-277.

Lafuente, A. and V. Salas (1989), "Types of Entrepreneurs and Firms: the Case of New Spanish Firms", *Strategic Management Journal*, 10, pp. 17-30.

Laufer, J.C. (1974), "Comment on devient entrepreneur", *Revue française de gestion*, Vol. 2, pp. 18-29.

Leff, N.H. (1978), "Industrial organization and entrepreneurship in the developing countries: The economic groups", *Economic Development and Cultural Change*, Vol.26, No. 4, pp. 661-675.

Leff, N.H. (1979), "Entrepreneurship and Economic Development: The Problem Revisited", *Journal of Economic Literature*, 17 (1-2), pp. 46-64.

Leibenstein, H. (1968), "Entrepreneurship and Development", *American Economic Review*, Vol. 38, No. 2, pp. 72-83.

Leibenstein, H. (1978), *General X-Efficiency Theory and Economic Development*, London, Oxford University Press.

Leibenstein, H. (1979), "The General X-Efficiency Paradigm and the Role of the Entrepreneur", in Rizzio, M.J. (ed.), *Time, Uncertainty And Disequilibrium*, Lexington, Mass., D.C. Heath, pp. 127-139.

Lorrain, J. and L. Dussault (1988a), "Relation Between Psychological Characteristics, Administrative Behaviors and Success of Founder Entrepreneurs at the Start-up Stage", in Kirchhoff, B.A., Long, W.A. et al. (eds.), *Frontiers of Entrepreneurship Research*, Babson, pp. 150-164.

Lorrain, J. and L. Dussault (1988b), "Les entrepreneurs artisans et opportunistes: une comparaison de leurs comportements de gestion", *Revue Internationale PME*, Vol. 1, No. 2, pp. 157-176.

Low, M. B. and I.C. MacMillan (1988), "Entrepreneurship: Past Research and Future Challenges", *Journal of Management*, Vol.14, No. 2, pp. 139-161.

Lynn, R. (1969), "Personality Characteristics of a Group of Entrepreneurs", *Occupational Psychology*, Vol. 43, pp. 151-152. See also Eysenk, H. J. (1967) and Jessup, G. and Jessup, H. (1971).

McClelland, D.C. (1961), *The Achieving Society*, Princeton, N.J., Van Nostrand (see also the new introduction to the book, New York, Irvington Publishers (1976)).

McClelland, D.C. (1971), "Entrepreneurship and Achievement Motivation: Approaches to the Science of Socio-economic Development" in Lengyel, P. (ed.), Paris, U.N.E.S.C.O.

McGuire, J. (1964), *Theories of Business Behavior*, Englewood Cliffs, N.J, Prentice Hall.

McGuire, J.W. (1976), "The Small Enterprise in Economics and Organization Theory", *Journal of Contemporary Business*, 5, 2, p. 115-138.

Marx, K. (1844), *Économie et philosophie*, in Marx, K., *Oeuvres Économie*, Vol. II, Paris, Gallimard, 1968, pp. 1-141.

Marx, K. (1848), *Le manifeste communiste*, in Marx, K., *Oeuvres Economie*, Vol. I, Paris, Gallimard, 1965, pp. 157-195.

Meredith, G.G., R.E. Nelson and P.A. Neck (1982), *The Practice of Entrepreneurship*, Geneva, International Labour Office.

Miles, R. E. and C. S. Snow (1978), *Organizational Strategy, Structure, and Process*, McGraw-Hill.

Mill, J.S. (1848), *Principles of Political Economy with Some of Their Applications to Social Philosophy*, in two volumes. 9th edition, London, Longmann, Green (1886).

Miller, G.A. (1962), *Psychology: The Science of Mental Life*, Harmondsworth, Middlesex, England, Penguin Books (1982).

Miner, J. B. (1990), "Entrepreneurs, High Growth Entrepreneurs and Managers: Contrasting and Overlapping Motivational Patterns", *Journal of Business Venturing*, Vol.5, pp. 221-234.

Miner, J. B., N.R. Smith and J.S. Bracker (1989), "Role of Entrepreneurial Task Motivation in the Growth of Technologically Innovative Firms", *Journal of Applied Psychology*, 74, 4, pp. 554-560.

Mulholland, R. (1994), *Approaches to Entrepreneurship Research*, in Mount, J. (ed.), *Proceedings of the 11th Annual Conference - Canadian Council for Small Business and Entrepreneurship*, Winnipeg, October 27-29, pp. 122-133.

Neck, P. (1971), "Report on Achievement Motivation Training Program Conducted in Uganda", in Kent, C.A., Sexton, D.L. et al. (eds.) (1982), *Encyclopedia of Entrepreneurship*, Englewood Cliffs, N.J., Prentice Hall, p. 42.

Newman, P.C. (1981), *The Acquisitors*, Toronto, McClelland and Stewart.

Oxenfeldt, A.R. (1943), *New Firms and Free Enterprise: Pre-war and Post-war Aspects*, Washington, D.C., American Council on Public Affairs.

Patel, V.G. (1975), *Venture Assistance Experiments in India*, Proceedings of the International Symposium on Entrepreneurship and New Venture Creation, Summer. Reference in Kent, C.A., Sexton, D.L. et al. (eds.) (1982), *Encyclopedia of Entrepreneurship*, Englewood Cliffs, N.J., Prentice Hall, p. 42.

Penrose, E.T. (1959), *The Theory of the Growth of the Firm*, Oxford, Basil Blackwell, New York, Wiley.

Peterson, R. (1977), *Small Businesses: Building a Balanced Economy*, Erin, Ontario, Press Porcepic.

Peterson, R. and K. Ainslie (ed.) (1988), *Understanding Entrepreneurship*, Dubuque, Iowa, Kendall/Hunt.

Pinchot, G. (1985), *Intrapreneuring*, New York, Harper D. Row.

Reynold, P. (1991), "Sociology and Entrepreneurship: Concepts and Contributions", *Entrepreneurship Theory and Practice*, Vol. 16, No. 2, pp. 47-70.

Rosa, P. and A. Bowes (1990), *Entrepreneurship: Some Lessons of Social Anthropology*, E.C.S.B. 4th Workshop on Research in Entrepreneurship, University of Cologne.

Rosenberg, N. and L.E. Birdzell Jr. (1986), *How the West Grew Rich*, New York, Basic Books.

Rotter, J.B. (1966), *Generalised Expectations for Internal Versus External Control of Reinforcement*, American Psychological Association (Psychological Monographies, generalities et appl. p. 80, No. 1, entirely No. 609).

Say, J.B. (1803), *Traité d'économie politique: ou, simple exposition de la manière dont se forment, se distribuent et se consomment les richesses*, Translation, Treatise on Political Economy: On The Production, Distribution and Consumption of Wealth, Kelley, New York, 1964 (1st edition, 1827).

Say, J.B. (1815), *De l'Angleterre et des Anglais*, Paris, Arthur Bertrand.

Say, J.B. (1816), England and the English People, 2nd edition (1816), by John Richter, London, Sherwood, Neely et Jones. Translation of preceding title (1815).

Say, J.B. (1839), *Petit volume contenant quelques aperçus des hommes et de la société*, 3rd edition completely revised from manuscripts left by the author, and published by Horace Say, his son, Paris, Chez Guillaumin, Libraire.

Scase, R. and R. Goffee (1980), *The Real World of the Small Business Owner*, London, Croom Helm.

Schloss, H.H. (1968), "The Concept of Entrepreneurship in Economic Development", *Journal of Economic Issues*, June, pp. 228-232.

Schollhammer, H. (1980), *Analysis and Assessment of Internal Corporate Entrepreneurship Strategies*, Los Angeles, C.A., Graduate School of Management, U.C.L.A.

Schrage, H. (1965), "The R&D Entrepreneur: Profile of Success", *Harvard Business Review*, November-December, pp. 56-69.

Schumpeter, J.A. (1928), "Der Unternehmer", in Ludwig Elster et al. (eds.) (1928), *Handworterbuch der Staatswissenschaften* (4th edition, Jena 1928, 483). Reference in Hartmann, H. (1959), "Managers and Entrepreneurs: A Useful Distinction", *Administrative Science Quarterly*, 3, 3, pp. 429-451.

Schumpeter, J.A. (1934), *The Theory of Economic Development*, published in German (1912), 1st edition in English, Cambridge, Mass., Harvard University Press 1934, also, Cambridge, Mass., Harvard Economic Studies, volume 46, London, Oxford University Press.

Schumpeter, J.A. (1954), *History of Economic Analysis*, edited by Elizabeth Boody Schumpeter, New York, Oxford University Press, also London, George Allen & Unwin (6th edition, 1967).

Sexton, D.L. and J.D. Kasarda (eds.) (1992), *The State of the Art of Entrepreneurship*, Boston, PWS-Kent Publishing.

Sexton, D.L. and R.W. Smilor (eds.) (1986), *The Art and Science of Entrepreneurship*, Cambridge, Ma., Ballinger.

Singh, N.P. (1970), "N/Ach, Risk-Taking and Anxiety as Related to Age, Years of Schooling, Job Experience and Family", *Psychologia*, 13, pp. 113-116.

Singh, N.P. and K. Singh (1972), "Risk-taking Among Agricultural and Business Entrepreneurs of Delhi", *Psychologia*, 15, pp. 175-180.

Smith, A. (1776), *An Enquiry Into the Nature and Cause of the Wealth of Nations*, London, Edwin Cannan. Also London, Methuen (1950), Irwin (1963). Re-edited in two volumes. See especially edition by James E. Thorold Rogers, Oxford, Clarendon Press (1869).

Smith, N.R. (1967), *The Entrepreneur and His Firm: The Relationship between Type of Man and Type of Company*, Bureau of Business Research, East Lansing, Michigan, Michigan State University Press.

Smith, N.R. and J.B. Miner (1983), "Type of Entrepreneur, Type of Firm, and Managerial Motivation: Implications for Organizational Life Cycle Theory", *Strategic Management Journal*, 4, pp. 325-340.

Sombart, W. (1928), *Le bourgeois - Contribution à l'histoire morale et intellectuelle de l'homme économique moderne*, Paris, Petite bibliothèque Payot.

Stanworth, J. and J. Curran (1973), *Management Motivation in the Smaller Business*, Epping, Essex, England, A Gower Press Special Study.

Stanworth, J. and C. Gray (eds.) (1991), *Bolton, 20 Years on. The Small Firm in the 1990's*, London, Chapman.

Stanworth, J., A. Westrip, D. Watkins and J. Lewis (1982), *Perspectives on a Decade of Small Business Research: Bolton Ten Years On*, Aldershot, Hampshire, England, Gower.

Stevenson, H.H. and C. Jarillo (1990), "A Paradigm of Entrepreneurship: Entrepreneurial Management", *Strategic Management Journal*, 11 (Summer), pp. 17-27.

Storey, D.J. (1982), *Entrepreneurship and the New Firm*, London and Canberra, Croom Helm.

Storey, D.J. (1994), *Understanding the Small Business Sector*, London and New York, Routledge.

Tawney, R. H. (1947), *Religion and the Rise of Capitalism*, New York, Penguin.

Timmons, J.A. (1971), "Black is Beautiful - Is it Bountiful?", *Harvard Business Review*, November-December, pp. 81-94.

Timmons, J.A. (1973), *Motivating Economic Achievement: A Five-Year Appraisal*, Proceedings, American Institute of Decision Sciences (Nov.), Boston. Reference in Timmons, J.A. (1978a), "Characteristics and Role Demands of Entrepreneurship", *American Journal of Small Business*, 3, 1, pp. 5-17.

Timmons, J.A. (1978), "Characteristics and Role Demands of Entrepreneurship", *American Journal of Small Business*, 3, 1, pp. 5-17.

Toulouse, J.M. (1979), *L'entrepreneurship au Québec*, Montreal, Les Presses HEC et Fides.

Toulouse, J.M. and G.A. Brenner (1992), *Activités d'affaires et groupes ethniques à Montréal*, Research Paper 92-09-02, Maclean Hunter Chair of Entrepreneurship, HEC, the University of Montreal Business School.

Toynbee, A. (1976), *Mankind and Mother Earth: A Narrative History of the World*, London, Oxford University Press.

Vachet, A.C. (1988), *L'idéologie libérale. L'individu et sa propriété*, Presses de l'université d'Ottawa.

Vérin, H. (1982), *Entrepreneurs, entreprises, histoire d'une idée*, Paris, Presses universitaires de France.

Vesper, K.H. (1980), *New Venture Strategies*, Englewood Cliffs, N.J., Prentice Hall.

Vesper, K.H. (ed.) (1985), *Entrepreneurship Education 1985*, Wellesley, Mass., Babson College, Center for Entrepreneurial Studies.

Vesper, K.H. (ed.) (1993), *Entrepreneurship Education 1993*, Los Angeles, CA, The Anderson School, University of California.

Weber, M. (1930), *The Protestant Ethic and the Spirit of Capitalism*, translated by Talcott Parsons, London, Allen and Unwin.

Welsch, H. P. (1992), *International Entrepreneurship and Small Business Bibliography*, Paul University, Chicago.

Woo, C.Y., A.C. Cooper and W.C. Dunkelberg (1991), "The Development and Interpretation of Entrepreneurial Typologies", *Journal of Business Venturing*, Vol. 6, No. 2, pp. 93-114.

Wortman, M. and W. Birkenholz (1991), "Entrepreneurship Research on a Global Basis: An Empirically Based Model", 36th Annual World Conference ICSB, Vienna, *Proceedings Volume 1*, pp. 67-77.

Chapter 5

Abell, D. (1980), *Defining the Business*, Englewood Cliffs, Prentice-Hall.

Andrews, K. (1987), *The Concept of Corporate Strategy*, Englewood Cliffs, Homewood, Irwin.

Andrews, P.W.S. (1964), *On Competition in Economic Theory*, New York, MacMillan.

Ansoff, I. (ed.) (1969), *Business Strategy*, Harmondsworth, Penguin.

Ansoff, I. (1984), *Implanting Strategy Management*, Englewood Cliffs, Prentice-Hall.

Ansoff, I. (1987), *The New Corporate Strategy*, New York, Wiley.

Baumol, W.J. (1968), "Entrepreneurship in economic theory", *American Economic Review*, Vol. 58, No. 2, pp. 64-71, cited by Julien, 1989.

Boston Consulting Group (1984), *Les mécanismes fondamentaux de la compétitivité*, Paris, Hommes et Techniques.

Boutillier, S. and D. Uzundis (1995), *L'entrepreneur*, Pocket collection "Finance appliquée", Paris, Economica.

Bower, J., C. Bartlett, C. Christensen, A. Pearson and K. Andrews (1991), *Business Policy*, Homewood, Irwin, 7th edition.

Bygrave and Hofer (1991), "Theorizing about entrepreneurship", *Entrepreneurship Theory and Practice*, Vol. 16, No. 1.

Carrance, F. (1988), "Splendeurs et misères des matrices stratégiques", *Annales des mines*, March.

Carrier, C. (1992), "L'intrapreneuriat en PME", Thesis, l'Université de Montpellier I, July.

Casson, M. (1991), *L'entrepreneur*, Paris, Economica.

Covin, J. and T. Covin (1990), "Competitive aggressiveness, environmental context, and small firm performance", *Entrepreneurship Theory and Practice*, Vol. 14, No. 4.

Crozier, M. and E. Friedberg (1977), *L'acteur et le système*, Paris, Seuil.

Demailly, A. and J.L. Le Moigne (1986), *Sciences de l'intelligence, sciences de l'artificiel*, Lyon, Réseau universitaire de P.U., Lyon.

Dubini, P. and H. Aldrich (1991), "Personal and extended networks are central to the entrepreneurial process", *Journal of Business Venturing*, Vol. 16, No. 5.

ERFI (1989), *Cas et solutions de stratégie en PME*, Paris, Chotard.

ERFI (1991), *Qu'est-ce que la gestion?*, Paris, Eyrolles.

Filion, L.J. (1989), *The strategy of successful entrepreneurs in small business*, Doctoral Thesis, University of Lancaster.

Filion, L.J. (1991), *Vision et relations*, Montreal, Editions de l'entrepreneur.

Fourcade, C. (1991), *Petite entreprise et développement local*, Paris, ESKA.

Friedlander, F. and H. Pickle (1968), "Components of effectiveness in small organisations", *Administrative Science Quarterly*, Vol. 13, No. 2, pp. 289-304.

Gaffard, J.L. (1990), *Économie industrielle et de l'innovation*, Paris, Dalloz.

Gasse, Y. (1982), "L'entrepreneur moderne: attributs et fonctions", *Gestion*, Vol. 7, No. 4.

Gibb, A. (1992), "Can academe achieve quality in small firm policy research?", *Entrepreneurship and Regional Development*, Vol. 4, No. 2.

Guichard, M. and R. Richard (1994), *La stratégie à pas contés*, Dijon, Enesa.

Guilhon, A. (1992), "Changement organisationnel et stratégie technologique dans les PME", *ERFI research and documents*, Montpellier.

Guilhon, B. and M. Marchesnay (eds.), "Économie industrielle et PME", Special edition of the *Revue d'économie industrielle*, No. 67 (1st quarter 1994).

Hampden-Turner, C. (1990), "Henri Mintzberg: a profile", *Business Strategy Review*, Vol. 1, No. 1.

Handler, W. (1991), "Key interpersonal relationships of next generation family members in family firms", *Journal of Small Business Management*, Vol. 29, No. 3, July, pp. 21-32.

Hofer, C. and D. Schendel (1978), *Strategy Formulation: Analytical Concepts*, Los Angeles, West Pub. Co.

Hofstede, G. (1987), "Relativité culturelle des pratiques et théories de l'organisation", *Revue française de Gestion*, Sept.-Oct., pp. 10-21.

Ibrahim, A.B. (1992), "Strategy formulation in small business: a conceptual framework", *Journal of Small Business and Entrepreneurship*, Vol. 9, No. 4.

Jensens, M. and W. Meckling (1986), "Theory of the firm: managerial behavior, agency costs and ownership structure", in L. Putterman (ed.), *The Economic Nature of the Firm*, Cambridge, University Press.

Johnson, G. and K. Scholes (1989), *Exploring Corporate Strategy*, Englewood Cliffs, Prentice-Hall.

Julien, P.A. (1989), "The entrepreneur and economic theory", *International Small Business Journal*, Vol. 7, No. 3, pp. 411-423.

Julien, P.A. (1990), "Vers une typologie multicritère des PME", *Revue Internationale PME*, Vol. 3, No. 3-4.

Julien, P.A. (1992), "Small Business as a research subject", *Small Business Economics*, Vol. 4, No. 3.

Julien, P.A., J. Chicha and A. Joyal (eds.) (1986), *La PME dans un monde en mutation*, Québec, Les Presses de l'Université du Québec.

Julien, P.A., R. Jacob, L. Raymond and C. Ramangalahy (1995), "La veille technologique dans les PME manufacturières", 5th International Conference on Strategic Management, Paris, May.

Julien, P.A. and M. Marchesnay (1990), "Sur le dynamisme des petites entreprises dans les pays industrialisés", *Piccola Impresa*, Vol. 1, No. 2, pp. 3-21.

Julien, P.A. and M. Marchesnay (1992), "Des procédures aux processus stratégique et PME", *Piccola Impresa*, Vol. 1, pp. 13-43.

Kepner-Tregoe (1990), *La vision stratégique en action*, Paris, Editions d'Organisation.

Koenig, G. (1990), *Management stratégique*, Paris, Nathan.

Laurent, P. (1989), "L'entrepreneur dans la pensée économique", *Revue Internationale PME*, Vol. 2, No. 1.

Longeneker, J., J. MacKinney and C. Moore (1989), "Ethics in Small Business", *Journal of Small Business Management*, Vol. 27, No. 1, January, pp. 27-31.

Lorrain, J., J.D. Perreault and L. Dussault (1992), "Marketing behavior of new entrepreneurs specific to the start-up crisis", *Journal of Small Business and Entrepreneurship*, Vol. 9, No. 2.

Mahé de Boislandelle, H. (1988), *Gestion des ressources humaines dans la PME*, Paris, Economica.

Marchesnay, M. (1982), "Is small so beautiful?", *Revue d'économie industrielle*, No. 19.

Marchesnay, M. (1986), *La stratégie*, Paris, Chotard.

Marchesnay, M. (1988), "La mercatique de la petite entreprise", *Revue Internationale PME*, Vol. 1, No. 3-4.

Marchesnay, M. (1991a), *Économie d'entreprise*, Paris, Eyrolles.

442

Marchesnay, M. (1991b), "Mintzberg on PME", *Revue Internationale PME*, Vol. 4, No. 1.

Marchesnay, M. (1991c), "Le transfert de technologie de la région vers les PME", *Économies et Sociétés*, Series F, No. 33.

Marchesnay, M. (1992), "La PME: une gestion spécifique?", Économie rurale, repris dans: Problèmes économiques, No. 2276.

Marchesnay, M. (1992), "Les bases de compétitivité de la petite entreprise face à la globalisation des marchés", Paper at the Conference of the OECD-Federal Development Bank, Montreal, May.

Marchesnay, M. and P.A. Julien (1990), "The small firm, as a transaction space", *Entrepreneurship and Regional Development*, Vol. 2, No. 3.

Marchesnay, M., R. Perez and R. Reix (1984), "Compétitivité, système de gestion et politique industrielle", in *Entreprise, gestion et compétitivité*, Paris, Economica.

Martinet, B. and J.R. Ribault (1989), *La veille technologique, concurrentielle et commerciale*, Paris, Editions d'Organisation.

Miles, R. and C. Snow (1978), *Organizational Strategy, Structure and Process*, New York, McGraw-Hill.

Mintzberg, H. (1990), *Le management*, Montreal, Arc, and Paris, Editions d'Organisation.

Mintzberg, H. (1990), "The design school: reconsidering the basic premises of strategic management", with response by Ansoff and Mintzberg in *Sloan Management Journal*, Vol. 11, No. 9, September.

Mintzberg, H. and J. Quinn (1991), *The Strategy Process*, Englewood Cliffs, Prentice-Hall International.

Naffziger, D.W., J.S. Hornsby and D.F. Kurakko (1994), "A proposed research model of entreprenarial motivation", *Entrepreneurship: Theory and Practice*, Vol. 18, No. 4, pp. 29-39.

Naro, G. (1990), "Les PME face à la gestion de leurs effectifs", *Revue Internationale PME*, Vol. 3, No. 1.

Porter, M. (1981), *Choix stratégiques et concurrence*, Paris, Economica.

Porter, M. (1991), "Towards a dynamic theory of strategy", *Sloan Management Journal*, special Winter edition.

Ricard, N. (1992), "Processus d'apprentissage et style de dirigeant de PME", ERFI-Montpellier research and documents.

Sandberg, W.R. (1992), "Strategic Management's Potential Contributions to a Theory of Entrepreneurship", *Entrepreneurship: Theory and Practice*, Vol. 16, No. 3, Spring, pp. 73-90.

Schendle, D. (1991), Presentation of a special edition of the *Sloan Management Journal*, on "Fundamental research issues in strategy and economics", Winter.

Serwinek, P.J. (1992), "Demographic and Related Differences in Ethical Views among Small Business", *Journal of Business Ethics*, Vol. 11, No. 7, July, pp. 555-563.

Smith, N., J.B. Miner and J. Bracker (1992), "Defining the inventor-entrepreneur in the context of established firms", *Journal of Business Venturing*.

Sweeney, G.P. (1982), *Les nouveaux entrepreneurs*, Paris, Editions d'Organisation.

Timmons, J. (1990), *New Venture Creation*, Homewood, Irwin, 3rd edition.

Varies autores (1989), "Le modèle italien: mythe ou réalité?", Special Issue, *Revue Internationale PME*, Vol. 2, No. 2-3.

Varies autores (1990-91), "Entreprise la vague éthique", Special Issue, *Project*, No. 224, Winter.

Varies autores (1993), "Stratégie: les PME aussi", Special Issue, *Revue d'économie Industrielle*, No. 95, Sept-Oct.

Williamson, O. (1975), *Markets and Hierarchies*, New York, Free Press.

Woo, C., A. Cooper and W. Dukenberg (1991), "The development and interpretation of entrepreneurial typologies", *Journal of Business Venturing*, Vol. 6, No. 2.

Chapter 6

Ayral, S. (1988), "Le comportement commercial du dirigeant de petite entreprise: le cas de T.P.E. 'High Tech'", Master's Thesis, Université de Montpellier, Équipe de recherche sur la firme et l'industrie.

Bertalanfy, L. Von (1961), *Les problèmes de la vie*, Paris, Gallimard.

Bertrand, Y. and P. Guillemet (1989), *Les Organisations, une approche systémique*, Télé-Université, Éditions Agence d'Arc, Chotard et associés éditeurs, 333 p.

Brisoux, J.E., J.D. Perreault and D. Paquet (1992), "Le processus décisionnel des PME en Marketing international", Proceedings of *ASAC*, Annual Conference in Quebec City, June 6-8.

Brisoux, J.E., J.D. Perreault and D. Paquet (1991), "Les stratégies d'exportation des PME québécoises", Pan-Canadian Conference "Mieux réussir", Trois-Rivières, May 29.

Brochu, C. (1991), "Les voies d'accès aux marchés extérieurs", Master's Thesis on Small Business Management, Université du Québec à Chicoutimi, 196 p.

Brown, R. (1986), *Marketing for the Small Firm*, Holt, Rinehart & Winston, 184 p.

Carson, D.J. (1990), "Some exploratory models for assessing small firms marketing performance (a qualitative approach)", *European Journal of Marketing*, Vol. 24, No. 11, pp. 5-51.

Carson, D.J. and S. Cromie (1990), "Marketing Planning in small enterprises: a model and some empirical evidence", *The Journal of Consumer Marketing*, Vol. 7, No. 3, Summer, pp. 5-18.

Cheron, E. and F. Cheyssial (1992), "La gestion du marketing direct dans les petites entreprises industrielles québécoises", *Revue Française du Marketing*, No. 139, 1992/4, pp. 39-50.

Cohen, W.A. and S.M. Stretch (1989), "Problems in Small Business Marketing as perceived by Owners", Proceedings of Research Symposium on the Marketing/Entrepreneurship Interface, Chicago, pp. 429-432.

Cort, S. (1987), "International Marketing opportunities for entrepreneurs through counterdistribution", Proceedings of Research Symposium on the Marketing/Entrepreneurship Interface, Chicago, pp. 205-214.

Darmon, R., M. Laroche and J. Pétrof (1986), *Le marketing, fondements et applications*, McGraw-Hill.

De Leersnyder, J.M. (1982), *Marketing International*, Paris, Dalloz.

Dennis, W.J. Jr. (1987), "Small retailer forecasts of next quarter sales: How accurate?", Proceedings of Research Symposium on the Marketing/Entrepreneurship Interface, Chicago, pp. 270-282.

Downing, G. (1971), *Basic marketing, a strategic systems approach*, Merrill Publishing Co., Chapter 4.

Ellis, D.S. and A. Jolibert (1991), "The Role of Marketing in the Survival of Small Industrial Firms in a Developing Region", Proceedings of Research Symposium on the Marketing/Entrepreneurship Interface, San Diego, pp. 303-332.

Gauzente, C. (1995), "L'Orientation marché: Bilan et Perspectives", Proceedings of the 9th International Conference of the Association Française du Marketing, Marseille, May 13-14.

Herrmann, J.L. (1993), "Le Marketing en PME: Point sur les recherches et repères pour la recherche", Proceedings of the 9th International Conference of the Association Française du Marketing, Marseille, May 13-14.

Hills, G.E. (1985), "Market analysis in the Business Plan: Venture capitalists' perceptions", *Journal of Small Business Management*, January, pp. 38-46.

Hills, G.E. (1987), "Marketing and Entrepreneurship Research Issues: Scholarly Justification", Proceedings of Research Symposium on the Marketing/Entrepreneurship Interface, Chicago, pp. 3-15.

Hills, G.E. and C.L. Narayana (1989), "Profile characteristics, success factors and marketing in highly successful firms", paper presented at the IX Babson Conference of Entrepreneurship Research, University of St-Louis.

Hunt, H.K. and R. LaForge (1990), "Promotion in New/Growing Enterprises: a discussion summary", Proceedings of Research Symposium on the Marketing/Entrepreneurship Interface, Chicago, pp. 346-350.

Iannarelli, C.L. (1987), "Marketing implementation strategies among owner managed small firms: A conceptual model of differences", Proceedings of Research Symposium on the Marketing/Entrepreneurship Interface, Chicago, pp. 101-106.

Jenkins, J. (1989), "The advertisement management practices of small retail enterprises: some Ontario findings", *Journal of Small Business and Entrepreneurship*, Vol. 6, No. 2, pp. 38-49.

Joyal, A., P.A. Julien and L. Deshaies (1995), "Une typologie des comportements stratégiques des PME exportatrices", Revue *Gestion*.

Kemp, P.R. (1989), "Marketing activities of Home based entrepreneurs", Proceedings of Research Symposium on the Marketing/Entrepreneurship Interface, Chicago, pp. 151-162.

Kinsey, J. (1987a), "The Marketing/Entrepreneurship interface in manufacturing firms in Scotland", Proceedings of Research Symposium on the Marketing/Entrepreneurship Interface, Chicago, pp. 232-243.

Kinsey, J. (1987b), "Marketing and the small manufacturing firm in Scotland: findings in a pilot survey", *Journal of Small Business Management*, Vol. 25, No. 2, pp. 18-25.

Kohli, A.K and B. Jaworski (1990), "Market orientation: The construct, research implications, and managerial implications", *Journal of Marketing*, Vol. 54, pp. 1-18.

Kraft, F.B. and P.W. Goodell (1989), "Marketing, Management, and environment problems of small business in relation to business age", Proceedings of Research Symposium on the Marketing/Entrepreneurship Interface, Chicago, pp. 90-104.

LaBarbera, P.A. and S.A. Rosenberg (1989), "Marketing research and small entrepreneurial enterprises", Proceedings of Research Symposium on the Marketing/Entrepreneurship Interface, Chicago, pp. 233-246.

LaForge, R., W. and S.J. Miller (1987), "The moderating effects of Company size on Business level Marketing strategies", Proceedings of Research Symposium on the Marketing/Entrepreneurship Interface, Chicago, pp. 54-64.

Lambin, J.J. (1994), *Le Marketing stratégique*, McGraw-Hill, 3rd edition.

Lorrain, J. and J.D. Perreault (1992), "The young entrepreneurs and their marketing problems", Research Symposium on the Marketing/Entrepreneurship Interface, Chicago, August 7-8.

Lorrain, J., J.D. Perreault and L. Dussault (1989), "Types of entrepreneurs and marketing behaviors: The case of newly born firms", Proceedings of Research Symposium on the Marketing/Entrepreneurship Interface, Chicago, August 5-6.

Lorrain, J., J.D. Perreault and L. Dussault (1990), "Marketing behaviors related to types of new entrepreneurs: a longitudinal study", presented at the American Marketing Association 1990 Winter Educator's Conference, Scottsdale, Arizona, February 24-27.

Lorrain, J., J.D. Perreault and L. Dussault (1991), "Types of entrepreneurs and marketing behaviors: The case of newly born firms", Piccola Impresa, No. 1, pp. 9-20.

Marchesnay, M. (1988), "La mercatique de la petite entreprise", *Revue Internationale PME*, Vol. 1, No. 3-4, pp. 259-276.

Meziou, F. (1991), "Areas of strength and weakness in the adoption of the marketing concept by small manufacturing firms", *Journal of Small Business Management*, October, pp. 72-78.

Morris, L.J. and L. Stenberg (1991), "Entrepreneurship research: Methodological issues in Marketing strategy studies", San Diego, pp. 185-201.

Narver, J.C. and S.F. Slater (1990), "The Effect of a Market orientation on business profitability", *Journal of Marketing*, October, pp. 20-35.

Perreault, J.D., D. Pettigrew and F. Munyabagisha (1990), "Means of control of the advertising effectiveness among the Québec advertising agencies", Atlantic Schools of Business Conference, Charlottetown, Ile-du-Prince-Édouard, November 1-3.

Ram, S. and S.J. Forbes (1990), "Marketing variables that affect entrepreneurial success: an empirical investigation", Proceedings of

Research Symposium on the Marketing/Entrepreneurship Interface, Chicago, pp. 99-103.

Reagan, C.C. and T.A. Gavin (1988), "The small accounting firm: managing the dynamics of the marketing function", *Journal of Professional Services Marketing*, Vol. 3, No. 3-4, pp. 305-314.

Schlegelmilch, B.B., K. Boyle and S. Therivel (1986), "Marketing research in medium-sized UK and US firms", *Industrial Marketing Management*, Vol. 15, pp. 177-182.

Smith, N.R. (1967), "The entrepreneur and his firm: the relationship between type of man and type of company", Bureau of Business and Economic Research, Michigan State University, East Lansing, Michigan.

Spitzer, D.M., G.E. Hills and P. Alpar (1989), "Marketing Planning and research among high technology entrepreneurs", Proceedings of Research Symposium on the Marketing/Entrepreneurship Interface, Chicago, pp. 411-424.

Stancill, J.M. (1981), "Realistic criteria for judging new ventures", *Harvard Business Review*, Nov.-Dec., pp. 60-72.

Stasch, S.F. and J.L. Ward (1987), "Some observations and research opportunities regarding Marketing of smaller businesses", Proceedings of Research Symposium on the Marketing/Entrepreneurship Interface, pp. 39-53.

Teach, R.D. (1990), "Entrepreneurship and Marketing: the Pricing and Distribution link to success", Proceedings of Research Symposium on the Marketing/Entrepreneurship Interface, Chicago, pp. 351-356.

Teach, R.D. and F.A. Tarpley (1989), "Entrepreneurs and marketing: The allocation of time among business activities", Proceedings of Research Symposium on the Marketing/Entrepreneurship Interface, Chicago, pp. 75-89.

Tesar, G. (1987), "An examination of planning strategies among small and medium-sized Firms", Proceedings of Research Symposium on the Marketing/Entrepreneurship Interface, Chicago, pp. 172-182.

Timmons, J.A., L. Smollen and A. Dingee Jr (1985), *New Venture Creation*, Homewood (Illinois), Richard D. Irwin Inc, pp. 3-6.

Tyebjee, T.T., A.V. Bruno and S.M. McIntyre (1983), "Growing ventures can anticipate Marketing stages", *Harvard Business Review*, Vol. 61, No. 1, pp. 62-65.

Weinrauch, J.D. et al. (1990), "An exploratory survey of low cost Marketing Strategies and techniques among selected small business owners: research opportunities and implications", Proceedings of

Research Symposium on the Marketing/Entrepreneurship Interface, Chicago, pp. 122-136.

Woodruff, R.B. and E. Cadotte (1991), "Analyzing Market Opportunities for New Ventures", Proceedings of Research Symposium on the Marketing/Entrepreneurship Interface, San Diego, pp. 214-226.

Chapter 7

Acs, Z. and D.B. Audretsch (1990), *Innovation and Small Firms*, Cambridge, MIT Press.

Agence nationale pour le développement de la productique appliquée à l'industrie (ADEPA) (1992), "État de l'automation dans les PMI manufacturières", Paris, Department of Industry, Mail, Telecommunications and Tourism.

Aktouf, O. (1989), *Le management: entre tradition et renouvellement*, Chicoutimi, Morin.

Alsène, E. (1988), "Le changement technologique en entreprise", *Technologie de l'Information et Société*, Vol. 1, No. 1, pp. 91-108.

Argyris, C. and D. Schön (1978), *Organizational Learning*, Reading, Addison Wesley.

Assoc. CAO/FAO (1989), "Tendances et degré de pénétration. L'automatisation et l'informatisation de la production", Quebec, CRIQ.

Audet, M. and L. Bélanger (1989), "Nouveaux modes de gestion et relations industrielles au Canada", *Relations industrielles*, Vol. 44, No. 1, pp. 62-96.

Bartunek, J.M. and M.K. Moch (1987), "First-order, second-order, and third-order change and organizational development interventions: a cognitive approach", *The Journal of Applied Behavioral Science*, Vol. 23, No. 4, pp. 483-550.

Beatty, C.A. and J.R. Gordon (1990), "Tactics for the implementation of advanced manufacturing technologies", *Working Paper* series No. NC 90-02, National Centre for Management Research and Development, School of Business Administration, The University of Western Ontario, 22 p.

Benoit, C. and M. Tremblay (1990), "La gestion des ressources humaines dans les PME au Québec: résultats préliminaires d'une étude empirique", *Revue Internationale PME*, Vol. 3, No. 2.

Bernard, J. and A. Torre (1984), "La dynamique d'innovation et de R-D des PMI françaises", *Revue Internationale PME*, Vol. 7, No. 3-4, pp. 19-41.

Bernstein, P. (1982), "Necessary elements for effective worker participation in decision-making", in F. Lindenfeld and J. Rothschild-Whitt: *Workplace democracy and social change*, Boston, Porter-Sargent, pp. 51-84.

Betcherman, G. and K. McMullen (1986), *La technologie en milieu de travail - Enquête sur l'automatisation au Canada*, Economic Council of Canada, Ottawa, Supplies and Services.

Betcherman, G., K. Newton and J. Godin (1990), *Une double révolution, technologie et gestion des ressources humaines*, Economic Council of Canada, Government of Canada Publishing.

Borzeix, A. and D. Linhart (1988), "La participation: un clair-obscur", *Sociologie du travail*, Vol. 1, p. 37-53.

Burrell, G. and G. Morgan (1979), *Sociological Paradigms and Organizational Analysis*, London, Heinemann.

Cantalone, R.J. and C. di Benedetto (1988), *Successful Industrial Product Innovation*, NewYork, Greenwood Press.

Clegg, C. and N. Kemp (1986), "Information technology", *Personnel*, Vol. 15, No. 1, pp. 8-15.

Cohn, S.F. and R.M. Turyn (1980), "The structure of the firm and the adoption of progress innovations", *IEEE. Transactions on Engineering Management*, Vol. EM-27, No. 4, p. 98-102.

Conseil de la science et de la technologie (1990), *L'adaptation de l'entreprise aux nouvelles technologies*, November, Gouvernement du Québec.

Cordova, E. (1982), "La participation des travailleurs aux décisions dans l'entreprise", *Revue Internationale du Travail*, Vol. 121, No. 2, pp. 139-156.

Cotton, J.L., D.A. Vollrath, K.L. Froggatt, M.L. Lengnick-Hall and K.R. Jennings (1988), "Employee participation: diverse forms and different outcomes", *Academy of Management Review*, Vol. 13, No. 1, pp. 8-22.

Covin, J.G. and D.P. Slevin (1989), "The strategic management of small firms in hostile and benign environments", *Strategic Management Journal*, Vol. 10, No. 1, pp. 75-87.

Crozier, M. (1989), *L'entreprise à l'écoute, apprendre le management post-industriel*, Paris, InterEditions.

D'Iribarne, A. (1983), "Technologies nouvelles, qualifications et Education: l'intérêt d'une approche sociétale", *Histoire, Économie et Société*, pp. 147-159.

D'Iribarne, A. (1986), "Renouvellement technologique, "PME" et création d'emplois: "recherches" et nécessité d'une compétitivité économique", France, document LEST, No. 86-7.

Dachler, H.P. and B. Wilpert (1978), "Conceptual dimensions and boundaries of participation in organization: a critical evaluation", *Administrative Science Quarterly*, Vol. 23, pp. 1-39.

Dejours, C. (1987), *Plaisir et souffrance dans le travail*, Paris, Entreprise Moderne d'Edition.

Desjardins, A. (1985), "Les changements technologiques, recueil de clauses-types", Québec, Centre de recherche et de statistiques sur le marché du travail.

Dumont, F. (1987), "Culture et valeurs dans les organisations" in A. Larocque et al., *Technologies nouvelles et aspects psychologiques*, Québec, Presses de l'Université du Québec, pp. 109-116.

Economic Council of Canada (1987), *Innovations, employment, adaptations*, Ottawa: Supplies and Services Canada.

Elden, M. (1983), "Democratization and participative research in developing local theory", *Journal of Occupational Behavior*, Vol. 4, No. 1.

Eraly, E. (1989), *La structuration de l'entreprise: la rationalité en action*, Bruxelles, Université Libre de Bruxelles.

Estimé, M.F., G. Drilhon and P.A. Julien (1993), *Small and Medium-Sized Enterprises Technology and Competitiveness*, Paris, OECD.

Filion, A. and C. Bernier (1987), "La sociologie face à l'étude des nouvelles technologies", in D. Tremblay, *Diffusion des nouvelles technologies*, Montréal, Saint-Martin, pp. 239-254.

G.R.E.M.I. (1986), "Technologies nouvelles et développement régional", Proceedings of A.S.R.L.F. convention, Paris, September 1-3.

Gagnon, Y.C. and M. Landry (1989a), "Les syndicats québécois face aux changements technologiques", *Gestion*, Vol. 14, No. 2, pp. 41-50.

Gagnon, Y.C. and M. Landry (1989b), "Les changements technologiques, une stratégie d'étude exploratoire", *Relations Industrielles*, Vol. 44, No. 2, pp. 421-447.

Gagnon, Y.C. and J. Nollet (1990), "Pour accroître les chances de succès dans l'implantation de systèmes d'information", *Gestion*, Vol. 15, No. 4, pp. 16-26.

Garsombke, T.W. and D.J. Garsombke (1989), "Strategic implications facing small manufacturers: The linkage between robotization and computerization", *Journal of Small Business Management*, Vol. 27, No. 4, pp. 34-45.

Gill, C. (1991), "Résultats d'une enquête récente sur la participation des travailleurs par rapport aux nouvelles technologies dans les douze

États membres de la Communauté européenne", *Technologie de l'Information et Société*, Vol. 3, No. 2-3, pp. 33-65.

Gold, B. (1983), "Strengthening managerial approaches to improving technological capabilities", *Strategic Management Journal*, No. 4, pp. 209-220.

Grisé, J. (1989), "L'informatisation du Québec. Profil de la demande", Québec, Les publications du Québec, 206 p.

Guesnier, B. (1984), "Développement local et micro-régional: priorités à l'information", *Revue canadienne d'économie régionale*.

Guilhon, A. (1994), "Le rôle de l'investissement intellectuel dans les stratégies d'implantation des nouvelles techniques dans les PME", *Revue Internationale PME*, Vol. 7, No. 3-4, pp. 147-173.

Guimond, S. and G. Bégin (1987), *Le choc de l'informatique, les répercussions psychosociales et le rôle des attitudes*, Québec, Presses de l'Université du Québec.

Gustavsen, B. (1985), "Workplace reform and democratic dialogue", *Economic and Industrial Democracy*, Vol. 6, pp. 461-479.

Howard, R. (1990), "Can small business help countries compete", *Harvard Business Review*, Nov.-Dec., pp. 88-103.

Jacob, R. (1990), "De la culture d'entreprise à la collaboration négociée", in Institut des Sciences du Travail (ed.), *Culture d'entreprise*, Louvain-La-Neuve, Université Catholique de Louvain, p. 137-148.

Jacob, R. and J. Ducharme (ed.) (1995), *Changement technologique et gestion des ressources humaines*, Boucherville, Gaëtan Morin.

Johannisson, B. (1989), "Network strategies: management technology for entrepreneurship and change", *International Small Business Journal*, Vol. 5, No. 1, pp. 19-30.

Julien, P.A. (1991), "Le rythme de pénétration des nouvelles technologies de production dans les PME", *Journal of Small Business and Entrepreneurship*, Vol. 8, No. 3, pp.21-32.

Julien, P.A. and J.B. Carrière (1994), "L'efficacité des PME et les nouvelles technologies", *Revue d'économie industrielle*, No. 67, pp. 120-135.

Julien, P.A., J.B. Carrière and L. Hébert (1988), "Les facteurs de diffusion et de pénétration des nouvelles technologies dans les PME manufacturières québécoises", *Revue Internationale PME*, Vol. 1, No. 2, pp. 193-223.

Julien, P.A., J.B. Carrière, L. Raymond and R. Lachance (1994), "La gestion du changement technologique dans la PME manufacturière au Québec", *Revue Internationale PME*, Vol. 7, No. 3-4, pp. 87-121.

452

Julien, P.A., R. Jacob, L. Raymond and C. Ramangalahy (1995), "La veille technologique dans les PME manufacturières", Research Report, Bombardier Chair, Université du Québec à Trois-Rivières, June.

Julien, P.A., A. Joyal and L. Deshaies (1994), "SMEs and international competition free trade agreement or globalization", *Journal of Small Business Management,* Vol. 32, No. 3, pp. 52-65.

Julien, P.A. and M. Morin (1995), *Mondialisation de l'économie et PME québécoises,* Québec, Presses de l'Université du Québec.

Julien, P.A. and L. Raymond (1994), "Factors of new technology adoption in the retail sector", *Entrepreneurship: Theory and Practice,* Vol. 18, No. 4, pp. 79-90.

Julien, P.A. and J.C. Thibodeau (1991), *Nouvelles technologies et économie,* Québec, Les Presses de l'Université du Québec.

Kling, R. (1980), "Social analyses of computing: theoretical perspectives in recent empirical research", *Computing Surveys,* No. 12, pp. 1-91.

Kling, R. and S. Lacono (1988), "L'informatisation du travail de bureau et l'organisation du travail", *Technologies de l'information et Société,* Vol. 1, No. 1, pp. 57-90.

Laborit, H. (1985), "Ordre et désordre dans les systèmes naturels" in A. Chanlat and M.Dufour, *La rupture entre l'entreprise et les hommes: le point de vue des sciences de la vie,* Montréal, Québec/Amérique, pp.119-140.

Lambooy, J.G. (1986), "Information and internationalization. Dynamics of the relations of small and medium sized enterprises in a network environment", in *Les PME innovatrices et leur environnement local et économique,* France, *Revue d'économie régionale et urbaine,* No. 5, pp. 719-731.

Landry, M., D. Pascot and D. Ridjanovic (1989), "Complexité, représentations et systèmes d'information", *Technologies de l'Information et Société,* Vol. 2, No. 2, pp. 7-23.

Lapointe, S. (1991), "L'adoption des nouvelles technologies dans le secteur du vêtement. Etude du processus informationnel", Paper given at the annual conference of ICSB-Canada, Trois-Rivières, 14-16 November.

Le Goff, J.P. (1987), Portée et limites des formations aux nouvelles technologies in J.L. Ferraud et al., *Quelle pédagogie pour les nouvelles technologies,* Paris, La Documentation Française, pp. 13-24.

Leavitt, B. and J.G. March (1988), Organizational learning, *Annual Review of Sociology,* Vol. 14, pp. 319-340.

Lefebvre, E., L.A. Lefebvre and D. Colin (1990), "Facteurs d'adoption des nouvelles technologies de production dans les PME manufacturières innovatrices", *Revue Internationale PME*, Vol. 3, No. 2.

Lefebvre, L.A., E. Lefebvre and J. Ducharme (1985), "Les entreprises québécoises et l'informatisation: situations et perspectives futures", *Gestion*, Vol. 10, No. 4, November, pp. 31-34.

Lesne, M. (1977), *Travail pédagogique et formation des adultes*, Paris, Presses Universitaires de France.

Lincoln, Y. (1985), *Organizational Theory and Inquiry: The Paradigm Revolution*, London, Sage.

Lobet-Maris, C. (1984), "Implantation bureautique et participation" in Institut des Sciences du Travail, *Comprendre et maîtriser la bureautique*, Université Catholique de Louvain, pp. 81-136.

Long, R.J. and M. Warner (1987), "Organizations, participation and recession", *Relations Industrielles*, Vol. 42, No. 1, pp. 65-90.

Loveridge, R. (1980), "What is participation: a review of the literature and some methodological problems", *British Journal of Industrial Relations*, pp. 297-317.

Majchrzak, A. and D.D. Davis (1990), "The human side of flexible factory automation: research and management practice" in S. Oskamp and S. Spacapan (eds.), *People's Reactions to Technology*, Newbury Park, Sage, pp. 33-66.

Marchesnay, M. and P.A. Julien (1990), "Small business as a transaction space", *Entrepreneurship and Regional Development*, Vol. 2.3, No. 1, pp. 267-277.

Martin, D. (1981), "Reflexions sur la participation", *Revue Française des Affaires Sociales*, Vol. 35, No. 2, pp. 55-104.

Martinet, B. and J.M. Ribeault (1989), *La veille technologique, concurrentielle et commerciale: sources, méthodologie et organisation*, Paris, Editions d'Organisation.

Maruyama, M. (1974), "Paradigmatology and its application to cross-disciplinary, cross-professional and cross-cultural communication", *Cybernetica*, No. 2, pp. 136-156 and No. 4, pp. 237-281.

Maruyama, M. (1980), "Information and communication in poly-epistemological systems", in K. Woodward, *The Myths of Information Technology and Post-Industrial Culture*, London, Routledge, pp. 28-40.

Meredith, J. (1987), "The strategic advantages of new manufacturing technologies for small firms", *Strategic Management Journal*, Vol. 8, pp. 249-258.

Meyer, O. and J.B. Goes (1987), "How organizations adopt and implement new technologies", *Academy of Management Proceedings*, pp. 175-179.

MFRT (German Federal Ministry of Research and Technology) (1989), "Promotion of research and development in small and medium-sized enterprises", Bonn, June, 104 p.

Ministère du travail (1991), "À l'heure de la formation, la situation des syndiqués au Québec", *Le Marché du Travail*, February, No. 6-10, pp. 85-91.

Morgan, G. (1986), *Images of Organization*, Newbury Park, Sage.

Morin, E. (1985), "Nouvelles technologies et société", in Actes de Colloque, *Nouvelles technologies et société*, Québec, Université Laval, Social Science Faculty, pp. 15-27.

*OECD (1991), *Human Resources and Advanced technologies of production*, Paris, OECD.

Orofiamma, R. (1987), "De nouvelles compétences pour de nouvelles situations de travail", in J.L. Ferrand et al., *Quelle pédagogie pour les nouvelles technologies*, Paris, La Documentation Française, pp. 99-122.

Pateman, C. (1970), *Participation and Democratic Theory*, London, Cambridge University Press.

Perrin, J.C. (1990), "Réseaux d'innovation: contribution à une typologie", H.E.C.-Montréal symposium on "Innovative Networks", May 1-3.

Pettersen, N. and R. Jacob (1992), *Comprendre le comportement de l'individu au travail, un schéma d'intégration*, Montréal, Editions Agence d'Arc.

Pichault, F. (1990), *Le conflit informatique, gérer les ressources humaines dans le changement technologique*, Brussels, De Boeck-Wesmael.

Planque, B. (1987), "PME innovatrices et potentiel d'information et de compétences", *Research notes*, No. 76, Centre d'économie régionale, Aix-en-Provence, February, 23 p.

Proulx, M.U. (1992), "Appartenance, utilités, fonctions: les milieux MRC du Québec", *Canadian Review on Regional Science*, Vol. 15, No. 2.

Proulx, S. (1984), L'informatisation: mutation technique ou changement de société?, *Sociologie et Sociétés*, Vol. 16, No. 1, pp. 3-13.

Raymond, L. (1985), "Une étude empirique des facteurs de succès d'un système d'information en contexte de PME", Ph.D. thesis, HEC Montréal.

Raymond, L., F. Bergeron, L. Gingras and S. Rivard (1990), "Problématique de l'informatisation des PME", *Technologies de l'information et société*, Vol. 3, No. 1, pp. 131-148.

Sainsaulieu, R. (1987), *Sociologie de l'organisation et de l'entreprise*, Paris, Presses de la fondation nationale des sciences politiques et Dalloz.

Sandberg, U. (1992), "Reasons for the success or failure of an automation project: an investigation of small and medium-sized Swedish manufacturing companies", *Integrated Manufacturing Systems*, Vol. 3, No. 1, pp. 21-26.

Sankar, Y. (1991), *Management of technological change*, New York, Wiley (series in engineering and technology management).

Savi, F. (1988), "Business services and industrial innovation in the Italian periphery", in G.J.R. Linge (ed.), *Peripherilisation and Industrial Change. Impacts on Nations, Regions, Firms and People*, London, Croom Helm.

Schroeder, D.M., C. Gopinath and S.W. Congden (1989), "New technology and the small manufacturer: panacea or plague", *Journal of Small Business Management*, Vol. 27, No. 3, pp. 1-10.

Séguin-Bernard, F. and J.F. Chanlat (1983), *L'analyse des organisations: une anthologie sociologique*, Montréal, Préfontaine.

Sethi et al.(1985), "Can technology be managed strategically?", *Long Range Planning*, Vol. 18, No. 4, pp. 89-99.

Solé Parrellada, F. (1990), "Technological efforts and the promotion of innovation", Université de Catalogne (Barcelone), *Working paper*.

Stankiewicz, F. (ed.) (1988), *Les stratégies d'entreprises face aux ressouces humaines*, Paris, Economica.

Strauss, G. (1982), "Workers' participation in management: an international perspective", *Research in Organizational Behavior*, No. 4, pp. 173-265.

Szarka, J. (1989), "Networking and small firms", *International Small Business Journal*, Vol. 8, No. 2, pp. 10-22.

Thibodeau, J.C. (1989), "Les services du secteur privé pour la diffusion et l'adoption de nouvelles technologies", Conseil de la Science et de la Technologie du Québec, Québec.

Tinacci-Mossello, M. and F. Dini (1989), "Innovation et communication sociale dans les districts industriels", *Revue Internationale PME*, Vol. 2, No. 2-3, pp. 229-253.

Vallée, G. (1986), *Les changements technologiques et le travail au Québec*, Commission consultative sur le travail, Québec, Les Publications du Québec.

Veltz, P. (1986), "Informatisation des industries manufacturières et intellectualisation de la production", *Sociologie du Travail*, No. 1, pp. 5-22.

White, W.F. (1987), "From human relations to organizational behavior: reflections on the changing scene", *Industrial and Labour Relations Review*, Vol. 40, No. 4, pp. 487-500.

Womack, J.P., J.T. Jones and D. Roos (1990), *The Machine That Changed The World*, New York, Macmillan.

Chapter 8

Alpar, P. and A. Reeves (1990), "Predictors of MS/OR Application in Small Businesses", *Interfaces*, Vol. 20, No. 2, pp. 2-11.

Anderson, J.C., R.G. Schroeder, S.E. Tupy and E.M. White (1982), "Material Requirements Planning Systems: The State of the Art", *Production and Inventory Management*, Fourth Quarter, pp. 51-66.

Ashcroft, S.H. (1989), "Applying the Principles of Optimized Production Technology in a Small Manufacturing Company", *Engineering Costs and Production Economics*, No. 17, pp. 79-88.

Canadian Centre for Labour and Productivity (1988), "La dynamique de l'amélioration de la productivité dans la PME manufacturière québécoise", Research report submitted by the Productivity Research and Intervention Group (GRIP) of the Canadian Centre for Labour and Productivity, Dec., 214 p.

Carpenter, T.H. (1984), "Computer-Integrated Manufacturing in a Small Business", *Tech Pap Soc Manuf Eng*, Pap MS84-752, 12p.

Courtois, A., M. Pillet and C. Martin (1989), "Gestion de production", *Les Éditions d'Organisation*.

Eisenhower, C.E. (1990), "Crise dans la production de classe mondiale au Canada", *Conférence annuelle de la SCGPS*, Montreal, May.

Goldratt, M. and J. Cox (1986), "Le But, l'Excellence en Production", *Afnor Gestion*.

Group of Case Studies presented by Company representatives (1991), "Making the MRP II Decision is Tough. But Worth the Effort", *Industrial Engineering*, March, pp. 52-63.

Hartley, K. (1991), "How to Plan and Organize an MRP II Project", *Industrial Engineering*, March, pp. 41-44.

Inman, R.A. and S. Mehra (1990), "The Transferability of Just-in-Time Concepts to American Small Businesses", *Interfaces*, Vol. 20, No. 2, March-April, pp. 30-37.

Interfaces, Vol. 20, No. 2, March-April, pp. 2-11.

Jain, A.K. (1991), "Beyond MRP II: the Enterprise Solution", *Industrial Engineering*, March, pp. 33-36.

Krause, P. and D.E. Keller (1988), "Bringing World-Class Manufacturing and Accounting to a Small Company", *Management Accounting*, November, pp. 28-33.

LaForge, R.L. and L.S. Vanessa (1986), "MRP practices in a random sample of manufacturing firms".

Manoochehri, G.H. (1988), "JIT for Small Manufacturers", *Journal of Small Business Management*, October, pp. 23-30.

Nollet, Kélada, Diorio (1986), "*La gestion des opérations et de la production*", Gaëtan Morin, éditeur.

Odon, J. (1984), "Computer Integrated Manufacturing in a Small Company 'A Case Study'", *Autofact Conf. Proc.*, pp. 13-28 to 13-32.

Production and Inventory Management (1983), Third Quarter, p. 129-136.

Raphaël, G.M. and J.D. Antonio (1992), "Industrial applications of Just-in-Time: lessons to be learned", *Production and Inventory Management Journal*, Third Quarter, pp. 25-29.

Rochette, R. (1991), "Gestion de la production assistée par ordinateur: une définition, les intervenants, les besoins", *Rapport sur la GPAO*, sponsored by CQIP, December.

Sadowski, R.P. (1990), "History of Computer Use in Manufacturing Shows Major Need Now is for Integration", *Reprint from IE*, March, 7 p.

Satish, M. (1990), "Applying MS/OR Techniques to Small Businesses", *Interfaces*, Vol. 20, No. 2, March-April, pp. 38-41.

Sharp, J.A., A.P. Muhlemann, D.H.R. Price, J.K. Andrews and M.J. Afferson (1990), "Defining production management core applications for smaller businesses", *Computers Industrial Engineering*, Vol. 18, No. 2, pp. 191-199.

Spearman, M.L., D.L. Woodruff and W.J. Hopp (1990), "Conwip: a pull alternative to kanban", *International Journal of Production Research*, Vol. 28, No. 5, pp. 879-894.

Wight, O.W. (1981), "*MRP II: Unlocking America's Productivity*", Oliver Wight Ltd.

Winston, R. Jr. and L. Heiko (1990), "Just-in-Time and Small Business Evolution", *Entrepreneurship Theory and Practice*, Summer, pp. 51-64.

Altman, E.I. (1968), "Financial ratios, discriminant analysis, and the prediction of corporate bankruptcy", *The Journal of Finance*, Vol. 23, pp. 589-609.

Ang, J. (1991), "Small business uniqueness and the theory of financial management", *The Journal of Small Business Finance*, Vol. 1, No. 1, pp. 1-13.

Ang, J. (1992), "On the theory of finance for privately held firms", *The Journal of Small Business Finance*, Vol. 1, No. 3, pp. 185-203.

Apilado, V.P. and J.K. Millington (1992), "Restrictive loan covenants and risk adjustment in small business lending", *Journal of Small Business Management*, pp. 38-48.

Baldwin, J., W. Chandler, C. Le and T. Papailiadis (1994), *Stratégies de réussite: Profil des petites et moyennes entreprises en croissance (PMEC) au Canada*, Statistics Canada, No. 61-523R F.

Barnea, A., R.A. Haugen and L.W. Senbet (1981), "Market imperfections, agency problems and capital structure: A review", *Financial Management*, September, pp. 7-22.

Barton, S.L. and C.H. Matthews (1989), "Small firm financing: Implications from a strategic management perspective", *Journal of Small Business Management*, January, pp. 1-7.

Beaver, W.H. (1966), "Financial ratios as predictors of failure", *Journal of Accounting Research*, Supplement, pp. 71-111.

Berryman, J. (1982), "Small business failure and bankruptcy: A survey of the literature", *European Small Business Journal*, Vol. 1, No. 4, pp. 47-59.

Bird, R. and D. Juttner (1975), "The financing of small business in manufacturing sector", Working paper No. 69, School of Economic and Financial Studies, Macquarie University, Sydney.

Calof, J. (1985), "Analysis of small business owners' financial preferences", *Journal of Small Business and Entrepreneurship*, Vol. 3, No. 3, pp. 39-44.

Chen, K. and T. Balke (1979), "Scale of operation, industry and financial ratios", *International Journal of Accounting*, Vol. 14, No. 2, pp. 17-28.

Churchill, N.C. and V.L. Lewis (1986), "Bank lending to new and growing enterprises", *Journal of Business Venturing*, Vol. 1, pp. 193-206.

Constand, R.L., J.S. Osteryoung and D.A. Nast (1991), "Asset-based financing and the determinants of capital structure in the small firm", in R. Yazdipour (ed.), *Advances in Small Business Finance*, Kluwer Academic Publishers, Boston, Massachusetts, pp. 29-45.

Cooley, P.L. and C.E. Edwards (1983), "Financial objectives of small firms", *American Journal of Small Business*, Vol. 8, No. 1, July-September, pp. 27-30.

Davidson, W. and D. Dutia (1991), "Debt, liquidity and profitability problems in small firms", *Entrepreneurship Theory and Practice*, Vol. 16, No. 1, pp. 53-63.

Dodge, H.R. and J.E. Robbins (1992), "An empirical investigation of the organizational life cycle model for small business development and survival", *Journal of Small Business Management*, January, pp. 27-36.

Dunstan, K., D. Dwyer, and S. Holmes (1992), "The small business funding debate: An empirical review", *International Research Symposium on Small Firm Finance*, Baylor University, Texas.

Elliott, J. (1972*), "Control, size, growth and financial performance in the firm", *Journal of Financial and Quantitative Analysis*, Vol. 7, pp. 1309-1320.

Fieldsend, S., N. Longford and S. McLeay (1987), "Industry effect and the proportionality assumption in ratio analysis: A variance component analysis", *Journal of Business Finance and Accounting*, Vol. 14, No. 4, pp. 497-517.

Gagnon, J.M. and B.M. Papillon (1984), *Risque financier, taux de rendement des entreprises canadiennes et intervention de l'État*, Economic Council of Canada, Ottawa.

Gaskill, L.R., H.E. Van Auken and R.A. Manning (1993), "A Factor Analytic Study of the Perceived Causes of Small Business Failure", *Journal of Small Business Management*, Vol. 31, No. 4, October, pp. 18-31.

Gupta, M. (1969*), "The effect of size and growth and industry on the financial structure of manufacturing companies", *The Journal of Finance*, Vol. 24, No. 3, pp. 517-529.

Hall, G. and B. Young (1991), "Factors associated with insolvency amongst small firms", *International Small Business Journal*, Vol. 9, No. 2, pp. 4-63.

Holmes, S. and P. Kent (1990*), "An empirical analysis of the financial structure of small and large Australian manufacturing enterprises", document presented at the 5th National Small Business Research Conference, Toowoomba, Queensland.

Holmes, S. and P. Kent (1991), "An empirical analysis of the financial structure of small and large Australian manufacturing enterprises", *The Journal of Small Business Finance*, Vol. 1, No. 2, pp. 141-154.

Hutchinson, P. and G. Ray (1986), "Surviving the financial stress of small enterprise growth", in J. Curran, J. Stanworth and D. Watkins (eds.), *The Survival of the Small Firm. Volume 1: The Economics of Survival and Entrepreneurship*, Aldershot, Gower Publishing.

Keasey, K. and R. Watson (1987), "Non-financial symptoms and the prediction of small company failure: A test of Argenti's hypotheses", *Journal of Business Finance and Accounting*, Vol. 14, No. 3, Autumn, pp. 335-354.

Keasey, K. and R. Watson (1991), "The state of the art of small firm failure prediction: achievements and prognosis", *International Small Business Journal*, Vol. 9, No. 4, pp. 11-29.

Larson, C.M. and R.C. Clute (1979), "The failure syndrome", *American Journal of Small Business*, Vol. 4, No. 2, October, pp. 35-43.

Levratto, N. (1992), "L'analyse du financement des P.M.E.: Une mise en relation du coût des ressources et de la notion de territoire financier", *Revue d'Économie Régionale et Urbaine*, No. 2, pp. 257-278.

McMahon, R.G.P., S. Holmes, P.J. Hutchinson and D.M. Forsaith (1993), *Small Enterprise Financial Management: Theory & Practice*, Sydney, Harcourt Brace.

McNamara, R.P., N.J. Cocks and D.F. Hamilton (1988), "Predicting Private Company Failure", *Accounting and Finance*, November, pp. 53-64.

Osteryoung, J., R.L. Constand and D. Nast (1992), "Financial ratios in large public and small private firms", *Journal of Small Business Management*, July, pp. 35-46.

Paranque, B. (1994), "Fonds propres, rentabilité et efficacité chez les PMI: Méthodes d'analyse et appréciation des situations financières", *Revue d'Économie Industrielle*, Vol. 67, No. 1, pp. 175-190.

Perry, C. and W. Pendleton (1983), *Successful small business management*, Pitman Publishing, Sydney.

Peterson, R. and J. Shulman (1987), "Capital structure of growing firms: a 12-country study on becoming bankable", *International Journal of Small Business*, Vol. 5, No. 4, pp. 10-22.

Pettit, R.R. and R.F. Singer (1985), "Small Business Finance: A Research Agenda", *Financial Management*, Autumn, pp. 47-60.

Remmers, L., A. Stonehill, R. Wright and T. Beekhuisen (1974), "Industry and size as debt ratio determinants in manufacturing internationally", Financial Management, Vol. 36, No. 3, pp. 879-888.

Renfrew, K. (1982*), "The adequacy of finance for small business in Australia" in W. Dunlop and W. Sheehan (eds.), *Small Business Research Series No. 11*, Institute of Industrial Economics, Newcastle, pp. 103-108.

Small Business Administration (SBA) (1984*), *Report by the President on small business*, Small Business Administration, Washington DC.

St-Pierre, J. and R. Beaudoin (1995), "L'évolution de la structure de financement après un premier appel public à l'épargne: une étude descriptive", *Revue Internationale PME*, Vol. 8, No. 3-4.

Suret, J.M. and L. Arnoux (1995), "Capitalisation des entreprises québécoises: Évolution et État de la situation", *Revue Internationale PME*, Vol. 8, No. 3-4.

Tamari, M. (1972*), "A postal survey questionnaire of small firms: an analysis of financial data", *Research Report No. 16*, Committee of Inquiry on Small Firms, Her Majesty's Stationery Office, London.

Tamari, M. (1980), "The financial structure of the small firm: an international comparison of corporate accounts in the U.S.A., France, U.K., Israel and Japan", *American Journal of Small Business*, Vol. 4, No. 4, April-June, pp. 20-34.

Walker, E.W. and J.W. Petty II (1978), "Financial differences between large and small firms", *Financial Management*, Winter, pp. 61-68.

Watson, J. and J. Everett (1993), "Defining small business failure", *International Small Business Journal*, Vol. 11, No. 3, pp. 35-48.

Wilson, H. (1979*), *The financing of small firms: Interim report of the committee to review the functioning of financial institutions*, CMND 7503, Her Majesty's Stationery Office, London.

Williams, A. (1987*), *The characteristics and performance of small business in Australia (1973 to 1985)*, Report prepared for the Federal Department of Industry, Technology and Commerce, University of Newcastle, NSW.

Chapter 10

Alpar, P. (1989), "The role of information systems in entrepreneurial firms", Working Paper No. 89-3, University of Illinois at Chicago, Center for Research on Information Management.

Barcet, A., J. Bonamy and A. Mayère (1984), "Informatique et PME: un dialogue en différé", *Économie et Humanisme*, Vol. 275, January-February, pp. 44-56.

Bergeron, F., C. Buteau and L. Raymond (1991), "Identification of strategic information systems opportunities: Applying and comparing two methodologies", *MIS Quarterly*, Vol. 15, No. 1, pp. 88-103.

Bergeron, F. and L. Raymond (1992a), "Planning of information systems to gain a competitive edge", *Journal of Small Business Management*, Vol. 30, No. 1, pp. 21-26.

Bergeron, F. and L. Raymond (1992b), "The advantages of electronic data interchange", *Data Base*, Vol. 23, No. 4, pp. 19-31.

Bergeron, F. and L. Raymond (1993), "Échange de documents informatisés dans la PME et la grande entreprise: une étude comparative", *Congrès International Francophone de la PME*, Carthage, Tunisia, pp. 78-91.

Bergeron, F., L. Raymond and R. Reix (1992), *Informatiser son entreprise*, Montréal, Gaëtan Morin Éditeur.

Blili, S. (1989), "De la démarche d'informatisation comme déterminant de la satisfaction informationnelle", *Revue Internationale PME*, Vol. 2, No. 1, pp. 39-56.

Blili, S. and L. Raymond (1988), "Facteurs d'efficacité du processus d'informatisation dans les PME", *Journal of Small Business and Entrepreneurship*, Vol. 6, No. 2, pp. 10-22.

Blili, S. and L. Raymond (1993), "Information technology: Threats and opportunities for SMES", *International Journal of Information Management*, Vol. 13, No. 6, pp. 439-448.

Blili, S., L. Raymond and S. Rivard (1996), "Definition and measurement of end-user computing sophistication", *Journal of End User Computing*, Vol. 8, No. 2, pp. 15-24.

Blili, S. and S. Rivard (1990), "Technologies de l'information et stratégies d'entreprise: les prémisses d'une mutation", *Technologies de l'Information et Société*, Vol. 2, No. 2, pp. 25-48.

Boland, R.S. and R.A. Hirscheim (1987), *Critical issues in information systems research*, New York, John Wiley and Sons.

Bradbard, D.A., D.R. Norris and P.H. Kahai (1990), "Computer security in small business", *Journal of Small Business Management*, Vol. 28, No. 1, pp. 9-19.

Brancheau, L.J., D.R. Vogel and J.C. Wetherbe (1985), "An investigation of the information center from the user perspective", *Data Base*, Vol. 17, No. 1, pp. 4-18.

Chen, K.C. (1989), "Developing decision support systems for small business management: A case study", *Journal of Small Business Management*, Vol. 27, No. 3, pp. 11-22.

Child, J. (1972), "Organizational structure, environment and performance: The role of strategic choice", *Sociology*, Vol. 6, No. 1, pp. 1-22.

Cooley, P.L., D.T. Walz and D.B. Walz (1987), "A research agenda for computers and small business", *American Journal of Small Business*, Vol. 10, No. 4, pp. 31-42.

Cragg, P. and M. King (1992), "Information technology sophistication and financial performance of small engineering firms", *European Journal of Information Systems*, Vol. 1, No. 6, pp. 417-426.

Cron, W.L. and M.G. Sobol (1983), "The relationship between computerization and performance: A strategy for maximizing the economic benefits of computerization", *Information & Management*, Vol. 6, No. 3, pp. 171-181.

DeLone, W.H. (1981), "Firm size and the characteristics of computer use", *MIS Quarterly*, Vol. 5, No. 4, pp. 65-77.

DeLone, W.H. (1988), "Determinants of success for computer usage in small business", *MIS Quarterly*, Vol. 12, No. 1, pp. 51-62.

DeLone, W.H. and T.A. Gray (1991), "Small Business and Information Technology in the 21st Century", Working Paper, American University, Kogod College of Business Administration.

Dewar, R. and J. Hage (1978), "Size, technology and structure differentiation: Toward a theoretical synthesis", *Administrative Science Quarterly*, Vol. 23, No. 1, pp. 111-134.

Downey, H.K. and J.W. Slocum (1975), "Uncertainty: Measures, research and sources of variation", *Administrative Science Quarterly*, Vol. 18, pp. 562-577.

Dupuy, Y. (1987), "Vers de nouveaux systèmes d'information pour le chef de petite entreprise?", Research publication 87-2, I.A.E. de Montpellier, Centre de recherche en gestion des organisations.

Ein-Dor, P. and E. Segev (1978), "Organizational context and the success of management information systems", *Management Science*, Vol. 24, No. 10, pp. 1067-1077.

Ein-Dor, P. and E. Segev (1982), "Organizational context and MIS structure: Some empirical evidence", *MIS Quarterly*, Vol. 6, No. 3, pp. 55-68.

Fallery, B. (1983), "Un système d'information pour les PME", *Revue Française de Gestion*, No. 43, pp. 70-76.

Fuller, E. (1987), "Artificial intelligence and small firms management: Theory and practice", *Proceedings of the Small Business Research and Policy Conference*, Cardiff, Cranfield Institute of Technology.

Gable, G.G. (1990), "Consultant engagement for first time computerization: Measuring engagement success", *Proceedings of the Annual Conference of the ASAC*, Vol. 11, Part 4, pp. 70-81.

Galbraith, J.R. (1973), *Designing Complex Organizations*, Reading, Mass., Addison-Wesley.

Gingras, L., N. Magnenat-Thalmann and L. Raymond (1986), *Systèmes d'information organisationnels*, Chicoutimi, Gaétan Morin Éditeur.

Gingras, L., J. Rouette and G. d'Amboise (1985), "Information systems consultants and the small business manager", Document RIO-04, Québec, Université Laval, Faculté des sciences de l'administration.

Gremillion, L.L. (1984), "Organizational size and information system use", *Journal of Management Information Systems*, Vol. 1, No. 2, Autumn, pp. 4-17.

Griese, J. and R. Kurpiecz (1985), "Investigating the buying process for the introduction of data processing in small and medium-sized firms", *Information & Management*, Vol. 8, No. 1, pp. 45-51.

Hayen, R.L. (1982), "Applying decision support systems to small business financial planning", *Journal of Small Business Management*, Vol. 20, No. 3, pp. 35-46.

Ives, B., S. Hamilton and G.B. Davis (1988), "A framework for research in computer-based management information systems", *Management Science*, Vol. 26, No. 9, pp. 910-934.

Julien, P.A. and M. Marchesnay (1992), "Des procédures aux processus stratégiques dans la PME", *Piccola Impresa*, No. 1, pp. 13-43.

Julien, P.A. and L. Raymond (1994), "Factors of new technology adoption in the retail sector", *Entrepreneurship - Theory and Practice*, Vol. 18, No. 4, pp. 79-90.

Julien, P.A. and L. Raymond (1994), "L'entreprise partagée: Contraintes et opportunités", Proceedings of the *2nd Annual Technology and Innovation Management NETwork Meeting*, The Canadian Association for the Management of Technology, Toronto, pp. 55-74.

Kagan, A., K.R. Nusgart and K. Lau (1990), "Information system usage within small business firms", *Entrepreneurship theory and practice*, Spring, pp. 25-38.

Katz, D. and R. Kahn (1966), *The social psychology of organizations*, New York, John Wiley and Sons.

Kole, M.A. (1983), "A non-developmental MIS strategy for small organizations", *Systems, Objectives, Solutions*, Vol. 3, No. 1, pp. 31-39.

Lees, J.D. and D.D. Lees (1987), "Realities of small business information system implementation", *Journal of Systems Management*, Vol. 38, No. 1, pp. 6-13.

Lesca, H. and L. Raymond (1993), "Expérimentation d'un système-expert pour l'évaluation de la veille stratégique dans les PME", *Revue Internationale PME*, Vol. 6, No. 1, pp. 49-65.

Magnier, J.P. and J. Ruiz (1993), "Compétitivité des PME et maîtrise du système d'information", *Congrès International Francophone de la PME*, Carthage, Tunisie, pp. 405-420.

Mahmood, E. and N. Malhotra (1986), "The decision-making process of small business for microcomputers and software selection and usage", *INFOR - Information Systems and Operational Research*, Vol. 24, No. 2, pp. 116-133.

Malone, S.C. (1985), "Computerizing small business information systems", *Journal of Small Business Management*, Vol. 23, No. 2, pp. 10-16.

March, J.G. and H. Simon (1958), *Organizations*, New York, John Wiley and Sons.

Martin, C.J. (1989), "Information management in the smaller business: The role of the top manager", *International Journal of Information Management*, Vol. 9, pp. 187-197.

Martin, W.S., W.T. Jones, E. McWilliams and M.V. Nabors (1991), "Developing artificial intelligence applications: A small business development center case study", *Journal of Small Business Management*, Vol. 29, No. 4, pp. 28-32.

Massey, T.K. (1986), "Computers in small business: A case of under-utilization", *American Journal of Small Business*, Vol. 10, No. 3, pp. 51-60.

Massotte, A.M. (1994), "World-Wide-Web: un outil de communication hyper-média dans le cadre du réseau Internet", *Actes du Colloque International de Management des Réseaux d'Entreprises*, Ajaccio, p. 524-538.

McGuire, J.W. (1976), "The small enterprise in economics and organization theory", *Journal of Contemporary Business*, Vol. 5, No. 2, pp. 115-138.

Moch, M.K. and E.V. Morse (1975), "Size, centralization and organizational adoption of innovation", *American Sociological Review*, Vol. 42, No. 4, August, pp. 716-725.

Montazemi, A.R. (1987), "An analysis of information technology assessment and adoption in small business environments", *INFOR - Information Systems and Operational Research*, Vol. 25, No. 4, pp. 327-340.

Montazemi, A.R. (1988), "Factors affecting information satisfaction in the context of the small business environment", *MIS Quarterly*, Vol. 12, No. 2, June, pp. 239-256.

Morgan, J.G. (1989), *Images de l'organisation*, Québec, Les Presses de l'Université Laval.

Morin, E. (1977), *La nature de la nature*, Paris, Éditions du Seuil.

Nickell, G.S. and P. C. Seado (1986), "The impact of computer attitudes and experience on small business computer use", *American Journal of Small Business*, Vol. 10, No. 1, pp. 51-60.

Nolan, R.L. Jr. (1979), "Managing the crises in data processing", *Harvard Business Review*, Vol. 57, No. 2, pp. 115-126.

O'Shea, T.J. (1989), "Low-cost approaches to executive information systems", Journal of Information Systems Management, Vol. 6, No. 2, pp. 34-41.

Raymond, L. (1983), "Decision-aid for the selection of a small business computer", *Journal of Systems Management*, Vol. 34, No. 9, pp. 19-21.

Raymond, L. (1984a), "Information systems and the specificity of small business", *Journal of Small Business-Canada*, Vol. 2, No. 2, pp. 36-42.

Raymond, L. (1984b), "Personal and attitudinal correlates of MIS success in small business", *Journal of Business Administration*, Vol. 15, No. 1-2, pp. 159-173.

Raymond, L. (1985), "Organizational characteristics and the success of MIS in the context of small business", *MIS Quarterly*, Vol. 9, No. 1, pp. 37-52.

Raymond, L. (1987a), "The presence of end-user computing in small business: an exploratory investigation of its distinguishing organizational and information system context", *INFOR - Information Systems and Operational Research*, Vol. 25, No. 3, pp. 198-213.

Raymond, L. (1987b), *Validité des systèmes d'information dans les PME: Analyse et perspectives*, Québec, Les Presses de l'Université Laval.

Raymond, L. (1988a), "La sophistication des systèmes d'information en contexte de PME: une approche par le portefeuille d'applications", *Canadian Journal of Administrative Sciences*, Vol. 5, No. 2, pp. 32-39.

Raymond, L. (1988b), "L'impact des tâches critiques du gestionnaire de PME sur le succès d'un système d'information organisationnel", *Revue Internationale PME*, Vol. 1, No. 1, pp. 77-95.

Raymond, L. (1988c), "The impact of computer training on the attitudes and usage behavior of small business managers", *Journal of Small Business Management*, Vol. 26, No. 3, pp. 8-13.

Raymond, L. (1989), "Management information systems: Problems and opportunities for small business", *International Small Business Journal*, Vol. 4, No. 4, pp. 44-53.

Raymond, L. (1990a), "End-user computing in the small business context: Foundations and directions for research", *Data Base*, Vol. 20, No. 4, pp. 20-28.

Raymond, L. (1990b), "Organizational context and information systems success: A contingency approach", *Journal of Management Information Systems*, Vol. 6, No. 4, pp. 5-20.

Raymond, L. and F. Bergeron (1992), "Personal DSS success in small enterprises", *Information & Management*, Vol. 22, pp. 301-308.

Raymond, L. and F. Bergeron (1996), "EDI success in small and medium-sized enterprises: a field study", *Journal of Organizational Computing and Electronic Commerce*, Vol. 6, No. 2, pp. 161-172.

Raymond, L., F. Bergeron, L. Gingras and S. Rivard (1988), "La qualité des applications de la micro-informatique: Les utilisateurs sont-ils de bons concepteurs?", *Gestion - Revue Internationale de Gestion*, Vol. 13, No. 4, pp. 34-40.

Raymond, L., F. Bergeron, L. Gingras and S. Rivard (1990), "Problématique de l'informatisation des PME", *Technologies de l'Information et Société*, Vol. 3, No. 1, pp. 131-148.

Raymond, L., S. Blili and F. Bergeron (1994), "Les facteurs de succès de l'EDI dans les PME: une étude empirique", *Actes du Colloque International de Management des Réseaux d'Entreprises*, Ajaccio, pp. 412-422.

Raymond, L., P.A. Julien, J.B. Carrière and R. Lachance (1996), "Managing technological change in manufacturing SMEs: a multiple case analysis", *International Journal of Technology Management*, Vol. 11, No.3 - 4, pp. 270-285.

Raymond, L. and J. Lorrain (1991), "Organizational and entrepreneurial correlates of computer use at the start-up stage", *Piccola Impresa/Small Business*, Vol. 4, No. 2, pp. 119-137.

Raymond, L. and N. Magnenat-Thalmann (1982), "Information systems in small business: Are they used in managerial decisions?", *American Journal of Small Business*, Vol. 6, No. 4, pp. 20-26.

Raymond, L. and G. Paré (1992), "Measurement of information technology sophistication in small manufacturing businesses", *Information Resources Management Journal*, Vol. 5, No. 2, pp. 1-13.

Raymond, L., G. Paré and F. Bergeron (1993), "Information technology and organizational structure revisited: Implications for performance", *Proceedings of the 14th International Conference on Information Systems*, Orlando, Florida, pp. 129-143.

Raymond, L., S. Rivard and F. Bergeron (1988), *L'informatisation dans les PME - Douze cas types*, Québec, Les Presses de l'Université Laval.

Raymond, L., S. Uwizeyemungu, S. Blili and S. Rivard (1994), "La sophistication des technologies de l'information dans les PME des pays en voie de développement", *Proceedings of the 39th World Conference of the International Council for Small Business*, Strasbourg, pp. 305-316.

Reix, R., F. Bergeron and L. Raymond (1990), *L'entreprise et son informatique*, Paris, Les Éditions Foucher.

Rivard, S. and S.L. Huff (1988), "Factors of success for end-user computing", *Communications of the ACM*, Vol. 31, No. 5, pp. 552-561.

Rumberger, R.W. and H.M. Levin (1986), "Computers in small business", Research report, Washington, D.C., Institute for Enterprise Advancement, National Federation of Independent Business.

Simon, H. (1969), *The science of the artificial*, Cambridge, Mass., MIT Press.

Sumner, M. and R. Klepper (1987), "Information systems strategy and end-user application development", *Data Base*, Vol. 18, No. 4, pp. 19-30.

Thompson, J.D. (1967), *Organizations in action*, New York, McGraw-Hill.

Treadgold, A. (1989), "Information technology and the independent retail business", *International Small Business Journal*, Vol. 7, No. 3, pp. 10-28.

Tushman, M.L. and D. Nadler (1979), "Information processing as an integrating concept in organizational design", *Academy of Management Review*, Vol. 3, No. 3, pp. 613-624.

Weber, H. and E. Tiemeyer (1981), "Teaching information systems to small business management", *Information & Management*, Vol. 4, No. 6, pp. 297-303.

Weil, P. and M. Broadbent (1990), "The use of strategic information technology by entrepreneurial firms", *Proceedings of the 11th International Conference on Information Systems*, Copenhagen, pp. 205-214.

Welsh, J.A. and J.F. White (1981), "A small business is not a little big business", *Harvard Business Review*, Vol. 59, No. 4, pp. 18-32.

Chapter 11

Amba-Rao, S.C. and D. Pendse (1985), "Human resource compensation and maintenance practices", *American Journal of Small Business*, Vol. 10, No. 2, pp. 19-29.

Astrachan, J.H. and T.A. Kolenko (1994), "A neglected factor explaining family business success: Human resource practices", *Family Business Review*, Vol. 7, No. 3, pp. 251-262.

Auer, P. and H. Fehr-Duda (1989), *Industrial relations in small and medium-sized enterprises – Final Report*, Enterprise Policy Document, Official Publications of the European Community.

Bachelet, C. (1995), "GRH et communication interne: quelle place dans les préoccupations des dirigeants de PMI", *Gestion 2000*, Vol. 11, No. 1, pp. 181-202.

Bacon, J. (1970), *Executive compensation plans in the smaller company*, Report No. 15, Managing the Moderate-sized Company Series, National Industrial Conference Board, New York, 27 p.

Bacon, N., P. Achers, J. Storey and D. Coates (1996), "It's a small world: Managing human resources in small businesses", *International Journal of Human Resource Management*, Vol. 7, No. 1, February, pp. 82-100.

Bagby, D.R. (1987), "Employee benefits in small firms", in R.G. Wyckham, L.N. Meredith and G.R. Bushe (eds.), *The spirit of entrepreneurship*, Proceedings of the 32nd Annual World Conference of the International Council for Small Business (ICSB), Vancouver, pp. 278-286.

Baker, A.W. (1955), *Personnel management in small plants: A study of small manufacturing establishments in Ohio*, Bureau of Business Research, College of Commerce and Administration, The Ohio State University, Colombus, 288 p.

Banks, M.C., A.L. Bures and D.L. Champion (1987), "Decision making factors in small business: Training and development", *Journal of Small Business Management*, Vol. 25, No. 1, pp. 19-25.

Barron, J.M., D.A. Black and M.A. Loewenstein (1987), "Employer size: The implications for search, training, capital investment, starting wages, and wage growth", *Journal of Labor Economics*, Vol. 5, No. 1, pp. 76-89.

Bartram, D., P.A. Lindley, L. Marshall and J. Foster (1995), "The recruitment and selection of young people by small businesses", *Journal of Occupational and Organizational Psychology*, Vol. 68, No. 4, December, pp. 339-358.

Bayad, M. and J.L. Herrmann (1991), "Gestion des effectifs et caractéristiques des petites et moyennes entreprises industrielles: vers quelles relations?", *Revue Internationale PME*, Vol. 4, No. 2, pp. 5-41.

Bayad, M., H. Mahé de Boislandelle, D. Nebenhaus and P. Sarnin (1995), "Paradoxe et spécificités des problématiques de GRH en PME", *Gestion 2000*, Vol. 11, No. 1, pp. 95-108.

Bayad, M. and D. Nebenhaus (1993), "Les préoccupations de GRH des dirigeants de PME et leur profil", in G. Trepo et al. (ed.), *Universalité et contingence de la GRH*, Actes du 4° Congrès de l'AGRH, Jouy-en-Josas, pp. 524-533.

Bélanger, J. and J. Mercier (1994), "Le plafonnement de la densité syndicale au Québec et au Canada", in R. Blouin et al., op. cit., pp. 103-128.

Bélanger, L. (1990), "Évolution historique de la gestion des ressources humaines", in R. Blouin (ed.), *Vingt-cinq ans de pratique en relations industrielles au Québec*, Éd. Yvon Blais, Cowansville, pp. 651-665.

Benoit, C. and M.D. Rousseau (1993), *La gestion des ressources humaines dans les PME au Québec: perception des dirigeants*, prepared for the Ministère de la Main-d'œuvre, de la Sécurité du revenu et de la Formation professionnelle, Direction de la recherche, Publications du Québec, 315 p.

Berthelette, D. and F. Planché (1995), *Évaluation des programmes de sécurité du travail dans des petites et moyennes entreprises*, "Études et recherches" Report No. R-107, Institut de recherche en santé et en sécurité du travail du Québec (IRSST), July, 56p.

Besseyre des Horts, C.H. (1988), *Vers une gestion stratégique des ressources humaines*, Éditions d'Organisation, Paris, 224 p.

Callus, R., A. Morehead, M. Cully and J. Buchanan (1991), *Industrial relations at work*, AGPS, Canberra, Australia, in P. Marginson (1991), "Beyond size and sector: A view from overseas", *Journal of Industrial Relations*, Australia, Vol. 33, No. 4, pp. 586-600.

Carrington, W.J. and K.R. Troske (1995), "Gender segretation in small firms", *The Journal of Human Resources I*, Vol. 30, No. 3, pp. 503-534.

Christiansen, R.O. (1980), "Impact of employee stock ownership plans on employee morale", *American Journal of Small Business*, Vol. 5, No. 1, pp. 22-31.

Curran, J., J. Kitching, B. Abbott and V. Mills (1993), *Employment and Employment Relations in the Small Service Sector Enterprise - A*

Report, ESRC, Centre for Research on Small Service Sector Enterprises, Kingston University.

D'Amboise, G. and A. Parent (1989), *Les problèmes des petites entreprises: ce que révèlent des études nord-américaines*, Working Paper, Faculté des sciences de l'administration, Université Laval, Sainte-Foy, 89-07.

D'Amboise, G. and D.J. Garand (1993), *Identification des difficultés et besoins des PME en matière de GRH*, unpublished report for the Société québécoise de développement de la main-d'œuvre (SQDM), Montréal, October, 125 p.

D'Amboise G. and D.J. Garand (1995), "Identification des difficultés et besoins des PME en matière de gestion des ressources humaines", *Gestion 2000*, Vol. 11, No. 1, pp. 109-132.

Deshpande, S.P. and D.Y. Golhar (1994), "HRM practices in large and small manufacturing firms: A comparative study", *Journal of Small Business Management*, Vol. 32, No. 2, pp. 49-56.

Dini, M. and M. Guerguil (1994), "Small firms, new technologies and human resources requirements in Chile", *International Journal of Technology Management*, Special issue on Technology, Human Resources and Growth, Vol. 9, pp. 440-463.

Duberley, J.P. and P. Walley (1995), "Assessing the adoption of HRM by small and medium-sized manufacturing organizations", *International Journal of Human Resource Management*, Vol. 6, No. 4, December, pp. 891-909.

Evans, D.S. and L.S. Leighton (1989), "Why do smaller firms pay less?", *Journal of Human Resources*, XXIV, 2, pp. 299-318.

Fabi, B. (1991), "Les facteurs de contingence des cercles de qualité: une synthèse de la documentation empirique", *Canadian Administrative Science Review*, Vol. 8, No. 3, pp. 161-174.

Fabi, B. and D.J. Garand (1989), Notes de lecture, "À propos de l'ouvrage d'Henri Mahé de Boislandelle: Gestion des ressources humaines dans les PME", Paris, Economica, *Revue Internationale PME*, Vol. 2, No. 1, pp. 99-108.

Fabi, B. and D.J. Garand (1994), "L'acquisition des ressources humaines en PME", *Revue Internationale PME*, Vol. 6, No. 3-4, pp. 91-129.

Fabi, B., D.J. Garand and N. Pettersen (1994), "La GRH en contexte de PME: proposition d'un modèle de contingence", Research Paper 94-04, Groupe de recherche en économie et gestion de PME (GREPME), Département d'administration et d'économique, Université du Québec à Trois-Rivières, 24 p.

Fay, C.H. and S.D. Maurer (1986), "Developing compensation programs for the small business", in H. Buckman Stephenson (ed.), *The impact of the eighties on small business: Trends and issues*, Proceedings of the 10th Annual Conference of the Small Business Institute Directors' Association (SBIDA), Washington, pp. 267-274.

Fenton, J.W. Jr. and K.W. Lawrimore (1992), "Employment reference checking, firm size, and defamation liability", *Journal of Small Business Management*, Vol. 30, No. 4, pp. 88-95.

Filion, L.J. (1991), *Vision et relations: clefs du succès de l'entrepreneur*, Éd. de l'entrepreneur, Montreal, 272 p.

Garand, D.J. (1993), *Les pratiques de gestion des ressources humaines (GRH) en petites et moyennes entreprises (PME): une synthèse conceptuelle et empirique*, Research report, Groupe de recherche en économie et gestion des PME (GREPME), Département d'administration et d'économique, Université du Québec à Trois-Rivières, 386 p.

Garand, D.J. and B. Fabi (1992), "État de la recherche. Les pratiques de gestion des ressources humaines (GRH) en PME", *Revue Organisation*, Vol. 2, No. 1, pp. 61-99.

Garand, D.J. and B. Fabi (1994), "La conservation des ressources humaines en PME", *Revue Internationale PME*, Vol. 7, No. 1, pp. 85-126.

Garnier, B., Y. Gasse and A. Parent (1991), "Évaluation des retombées d'un programme de formation en gestion de dirigeants de PME", *Relations Industrielles*, Vol. 46, No. 2, pp. 357-377.

Gunnigle, P. and T. Brady (1984), "The management of industrial relations in the small firm", *Employee Relations*, Vol. 6, No. 5, pp. 21-24.

Halatin, T., J. Roy and B. Middlebrook (1985), "The application form in the small business: Design and legal considerations", in J.E. Brothers (ed.), *The challenge of small business management assistance unification*, Proceedings of the 9th Annual Conference of the SBIDA, San Diego, pp. 280-283.

Hess, D. (1987), *La gestion préventive de l'emploi en PMI*, Les cahiers de la recherche, Méthodes-études, I.A.E. de Lille, No. 87/11, 26 p.

Hézard, L. (1988), "Les besoins de formation dans les commerces de détail de moins de 10 salariés", *Actualité de la Formation Permanente*, Vol. 92, pp. 55-61.

Hoffman, K. (1986), "Opinions of small Kansas business owners/operators concerning hiring, training, and advancement of male/female non-traditional workers in Kansas", in Stephenson (ed.), op. cit., pp. 261-266.

Hornsby, J.S. and D.F. Kuratko (1990), "Human resource management in small business: Critical issues for the 1990's", *Journal of Small Business Management*, Vol. 28, No. 3, pp. 9-18.

Hoy, F. and B.C. Vaught (1980), "The rural entrepreneur—A study in frustration", *Journal of Small Business Management*, Vol. 18, No. 1, pp. 19-24.

Jackson, S.E., R.S. Schuler and J.C. Rivero (1989), "Organizational characteristics as predictors of personnel practices", *Personnel Psychology*, Vol. 42, No. 4, pp. 727-786.

Jones, J.J. Jr. and T.A. De Cotiis (1969), "Job analysis: National survey findings", *Personnel Journal*, Vol. 48, No. 10, pp. 805-809.

Laroche, G. (1989), *Petites et moyennes entreprises au Québec: organisation économique, croissance de l'emploi et qualité de vie au travail*, Research Series No. 91, Institut International d'Études Sociales, Geneva, 84 p.

Larouche, V. (1994), "La mobilisation des ressources humaines— orientations récentes", in R. Blouin et al., op. cit., pp. 437-455.

Larrivée, L. and G. d'Amboise (1989), "Difficultés de recrutement dans les PME québécoises: quelques causes et solutions possibles", *Relations Industrielles*, Vol. 44, No. 3, pp. 487-506.

Lasher, H.J. and J.F. Grashof (1993), "Substance abuse in small business: Business owner perceptions and reactions", *Journal of Small Business Management*, Vol. 31, No. 1, pp. 63-72.

Latona, J.C. (1979), "Participative management in the small firm: a longitudinal study of an M.B.O. program", *American Journal of Small Business*, Vol. III, No. 4, pp. 15-22.

Le Louarn, J.Y. and R. Thériault (1984), *Politiques et pratiques en recrutement et sélection en personnel dans les organisations au Québec*, Association des professionnels en ressources humaines du Québec (APRHQ), HEC, Montreal, 79 p.

Lichtenstein, J. (1992), "Training small business employees: Matching needs and public training policy", *Journal of Labor Research*, XIII, 1, pp. 23-40.

Liouville, J. and M. Bayad (1995), "Stratégies de gestion des ressources humaines et performances dans les PME: résultats d'une recherche exploratoire", *Gestion 2000*, Vol. 11, No. 1, pp. 159-180.

Little, B.L. (1986), "The performance of personnel duties in small Louisiana firms: A research note", *Journal of Small Business Management*, Vol. 24, No. 4, pp. 66-69.

Mahé de Boislandelle, H. (1988), *Gestion des ressources humaines dans les PME*, Economica, Collection Techniques de Gestion, Paris, 322 p.

Mahé, H. et al. (1985), *La pratique de la gestion du personnel dans les PME*, Research report, CEGERH / FNEGE / IUT - Montpellier, 150 p.

Malaise, N. and V. De Keyser (1988), *Conditions de travail et petites et moyennes entreprises: Belgique*, Fondation européenne pour l'amélioration des conditions de vie et de travail, Loughlinstown House, Shankill, Co. Dublin, Ireland, 80 p.

Marlow, S. and D. Patton (1993), "Managing the employment relationship in the smaller firm: Possibilities for human resource management", Research Note, *International Small Business Journal*, Vol. 11, No. 4, pp. 57-64.

McEvoy, G.M. (1984), "Small business personnel practices", *Journal of Small Business Management*, Vol. 22, No. 4, pp. 1-8.

McGraw, P. and I. Palmer (1990), "Reluctant conscripts? Small business management attitudes to employee relations in travel agencies", *Journal of Industrial Relations*, Australia, Vol. 32, No. 4, pp. 513-522.

Mealiea, L.W. and D. Lee (1980), "Contemporary personnel practices in Canadian firms: An empirical evaluation", *Relations Industrielles*, Vol. 35, No. 3, pp. 410-421.

Morissette, R. (1993), "Canadian jobs and firm size: Do smaller firms pay less?", *Canadian Journal of Economics*, Vol. XXVI, No. 1, pp. 159-174.

Naro, G. (1990), "Les PME face à la gestion de leurs effectifs: comment adapter les ressources humaines aux impératifs stratégiques?", *Revue Internationale PME*, Vol. 3, No. 1, pp. 57-74.

Nebenhaus, D. (1990), "Les structures participatives d'influence du personnel sur les décisions: enquête auprès de PME", *Revue Internationale PME*, Vol. 3, No. 1, pp. 89-104.

Neiswander, D.K., B.J. Bird and P.L. Young (1990), "Embauche et gestion des premiers employés d'une petite entreprise", *Revue Internationale PME*, Vol. 3, No. 1, pp. 7-25.

Paradas, A. (1993), *Contribution à l'évaluation de la formation professionnelle en PME*, unpublished doctoral thesis (Management Science), F.D.S.É., I.S.E.M., Montpellier I et II, 620 p.

Paumier, A. and D. Gouadain (1984), "La gestion prévisionnelle des ressources humaines: une enquête auprès d'un échantillon d'entreprises régionales", *Direction et Gestion*, Vol. 6, pp. 53-68.

Peacock, R.W. (1994), "Training needs of small enterprise operators", *Small Enterprise Research*, Vol. 3, No. 1-2, pp. 95-x.

Poorsoltan, K. (1993), "OSHA's hazard communication standard and small business: A survey", *Journal of Small Business Management*, Vol. 31, No. 1, pp. 105-109.

Rainnie, A.F. and M.G. Scott (1986), "Industrial relations in the small firm", in J. Curran et al. (ed.), *The Survival of the Small Firm*, Vol. 2, Gower Publishing Co., Aldershot, pp. 42-60.

Ram, M. (1991), "The dynamics of workplace relations in small firms", *International Small Business Journal*, Vol. 10, No. 1, pp. 44-53.

Ram, M. and R. Holliday (1993), "Relative merits: Family culture and kinship in small firms", *Sociology: The Journal of the British Sociological Association*, Vol. 27, No. 4, November, pp. 629-648.

Roger, A. (1985), *Le suivi et l'appréciation du personnel dans les PME de services*, Research notes, I.A.E., Aix-en-Provence, CNRS 1984 Research Program "Activités de services et PME", No. 308, 84 p.

Rosanvallon, A. (1990), "Les politiques de formation dans les PME-PMI françaises: l'émergence de pratiques novatrices", *Revue Internationale PME*, Vol. 3, No. 1, pp. 75-87.

Rowden, R.W. (1995), "The role of human resource development in successful small and mid-sized manufacturing businesses: A comparative case study", *Human Resource Development Quarterly*, Vol. 6, No. 4, Winter, pp. 355-373.

Scherer, R.F., D.J. Kaufman and M.F. Ainina (1993), "Complaint resolution by OSHA in small and large manufacturing firms", *Journal of Small Business Management*, Vol. 31, No. 1, pp. 73-82.

Schuler, R.S. and D.L. Harris (1991), "Deeming quality improvement: Implications for human resource management as illustrated in a small company", *Human Resource Planning*, Vol. 14, pp. 191-207.

Scott, M.G., I. Roberts, G. Holroyd and D. Sawbridge (1990), *Management and industrial relations in small firms*, Research Paper, UK Department of Employment, London, No. 70.

Scott, P., B. Jones, A. Bramley and B. Bolton (1996), "Enhancing technology and skills in small- and medium-sized manufacturing firms: Problems and prospects", *International Small Business Journal*, Vol. 14, No. 3, April-June, pp. 85-99.

Shaw, K.N. and J.R. Lang (1985), "Executive compensation in emerging hi-tech industries", in J.E. Brothers (ed.), op. cit., pp. 389-393.

Smith, P. and F. Hoy (1992), "Job satisfaction and commitment of older workers in small businesses", *Journal of Small Business Management*, Vol. 30, No. 4, pp. 106-118.

Sutton, N.A. (1986), "A comparison of insurance and pension plans in large and small firms", *American Journal of Small Business*, Vol. 11, No. 2, pp. 15-22.

Thacker, J.W. and R.J. Cattaneo (1987), "The Canadian personnel function: Status and practices", in T.H. Stone and J.Y. Le Louarn (eds.), Report of the Annual Conference of the ASAC Annual Conference of the Personnel and Human Resource Group, Toronto, pp. 56-66.

Thériault, R. (1986), *Politiques et pratiques en matière de rémunération globale dans les entreprises au Québec*, Les Productions Infort inc., HEC, Montreal, 185 p.

Thériault, R. and J.Y. Le Louarn (1984), *Politiques et pratiques en évaluation de la performance du personnel dans les organisations au Québec*, APRHQ, Montreal, 87 p.

Wassermann, W. (1989), "Industrial relations in small and medium-sized enterprises in the Federal Republic of Germany", in Auer and Fehr-Duda, op. cit., pp. 143-174.

Chapter 12 - Conclusion

Amendola, M. and J.L. Gaffard (1988), *La dynamique économique de l'innovation*, Paris, Economica.

Baudrillard, J. (1972), *Pour une critique de l'économie du signe*, Paris, Gallimard.

Baumol, W.J. (1968), "Entrepreneurship and economic theory", *American Economic Review*, Papers and Proceedings, May.

Beccatini, G. (1987), *Mercato e forze locali: il distretto industriale*, Il Mulino, Bologna.

Beccatini, G. (1989), "Riflessioni sul distretto industriale marshalliano come concetto socio-economica", *Stato e Mercato*, 1.

Bernstein, L.J. (1995), *Des idées capitales*, Paris, Seuil.

Bourdieu, P. (1987), *Choses dites. Le sens commun*, Paris, les Éditions de Minuit.

Braudel, F. (1979), *Civilisation matérielle, économie et capitalisme, XVe et XVIIIe siècles*, Paris, Armand Colin, 3 volumes.

Braudel, F. (1985), *La dynamique du capitalisme*, Paris, Arthaud.

Camagni, R.P. (1991), "Local "milieu", incertainty and innovation networks: toward a new dynamic theory of economic space", in Camagni (ed.), *Innovation Networks. Spatial Perspective*, London, Belhaven.

Carrier, M. (1992), "Stucturation d'un système industriel de PME", Doctoral thesis, Université Laval.

Coleman, J. (1988), "Social capital and the creation of human capital", *American Journal of Sociology*, No. 94, pp. 95-120.

Cotta, A. (1980), *La société ludique*, Paris, Grasset.

Durand, T. (1989), "Management stratégique de la technologie", *Futuribles*, No. 137, Nov.

Figuier, L. (1867), *Vie des savants du moyen âge*, Paris, Librairie internationale.

Filion, J. (1989), "L'intrapreneur, un visionnant", *Revue PMO*, Vol. 5, No. 1.

Foray, D. (1990), "The secret of industry are in the air", Paper given at the HEC-Montreal conference entitled "The Innovators' Network", May 1-3.

Habermas, J. (1981), *Theorie des kommunikativen Handels, Frankfurt, Suhrkamp Verlag*.

Habermas, J. (1988), *Teoria dell'agire communicativo*, Bologne, Il Mulino, quoted by V. Vaggagini (1991).

Jacquemin, A. (1987), *La nouvelle organisation industrielle*, Paris, PUF.

Julien, P.A. (1989), "The entrepreneur and economic theory", *International Small Business Journal*, Vol. 7, No. 3, pp. 27-37.

Julien, P.A. (1991), "Le rôle des institutions locales et contrôle de l'information dans les districts industriels: deux cas québécois", *Revue d'économie régionale et urbaine*, No. 4.

Julien, P.A. and M. Marchesnay (1996), *L'entrepreneuriat*, Paris, Economica.

Kaldor, N. (1972), "The irrelevance of equilibrium economics", *Economic Journal*, Vol. 82, No. 3, pp. 1237-1256.

Kirzner, I.M. (1982), "The theory of entrepreneurship in economic of growth", in J.R. Kent, R.Sexton and R.Vesper (eds.), *Encyclopedia of Entrepreneurship*, Englewood Cliffs, Prentice Hall.

Laborit, H. (1974), *La nouvelle grille*, Paris, Laffond.

Lawrence, P.R. and J.W.Lorsch (1967), *Organization and Environment*, Massachussetts, Les Éditions d'Organisation.

Leibenstein, H. (1978), *General X-Efficiency Theory and Economic Development*, London, Oxford University Press.

Lorino, P. (1989), *L'économiste et le manager*, Paris, La découverte.

Machlup, F. (1967), "Theory of the firm: marginalist, behavioural, managerial", *American Economic Review*, Vol. 57, No. 1, pp. 1-33.

Marchesnay, M. and P.A. Julien (1990), "The small business: as a transaction space", *Entrepreneurship and Regional Development*, Vol. 2, June.

Morvan, Y. (1991), *Fondements de l'économie industrielle*, Paris, Economica, 2nd edition.

Norris, A. (1978), quoted by R.B. Robinson and J.A. Pearce II, "Research thrusts in small firm strategic planning", *Academy of Management Review*, Vol. 9, No. 1, pp. 129-137.

Ouchi, W. (1980), "Markets, bureaucracies and clans", *Administrative Science Quarterly*, No. 25, pp. 129-141.

Proulx, M.A. (1992), "Appartenance, utilités, fonctions. Le cas des milieux M.R.C. du Québec", *Canadian Journal of Regional Science*, Vol. 15, No. 2, pp. 307-326.

Raffa, M. and G. Zollo (1994), "The oscillating behavior of small innovative firms: a model", *Piccola Impresa*, No. 1, pp. 33-60.

Richardson, P. (1972), "The organization of industry", *Economic Journal*, Vol. 82.

Sabel (1992), "Studied trust: building new forms of co-operation in a volatile economy" in F. Pyke and W. Sengenberger, *Industrial Districts and Local Economic Regeneration*, Geneva, Institut Internationale d'Études Sociales.

Scitovsky, I. (1978), *The Joyless Economy*, Oxford University Press.

Simon, H.A. (1979), "Rational decision making in business organization", *American Economic Review*, Vol. 69, pp. 493-513.

Simon, H.A. (1980), *New Management. The Decision by Computers*, New York, MacMillan, 1980.

Smith, C. (1985), *La sémantique économique en question*, Paris, Calmann-Lévy.

Stigler, G. (1939), "Production and distribution in the short run", *The Journal of Political Economy*, Vol. 47, No. 3, pp. 305-327.

Taylor, N. (1965), "Entrepreneurship and traditional elites: the case of a dualistic society" in *Exploration in Entrepreneurial History/2nd series*, Spring/Summer.

Toulouse, J.M. (1979), *L'entrepreneurship*, Montreal, Fides.

Vérin, H. (1982), *Entrepreneurs. Entreprises. Histoire d'une idée*, Paris, Presses Universitaires de France.

Wallerstein, I. (1983), *Historical Capitalism*, London, McLelland.

Zurkovitch, E. (1985), "La dynamique du développement des technologies", *Revue économique*, Vol. 36, No. 5, pp. 897-915.